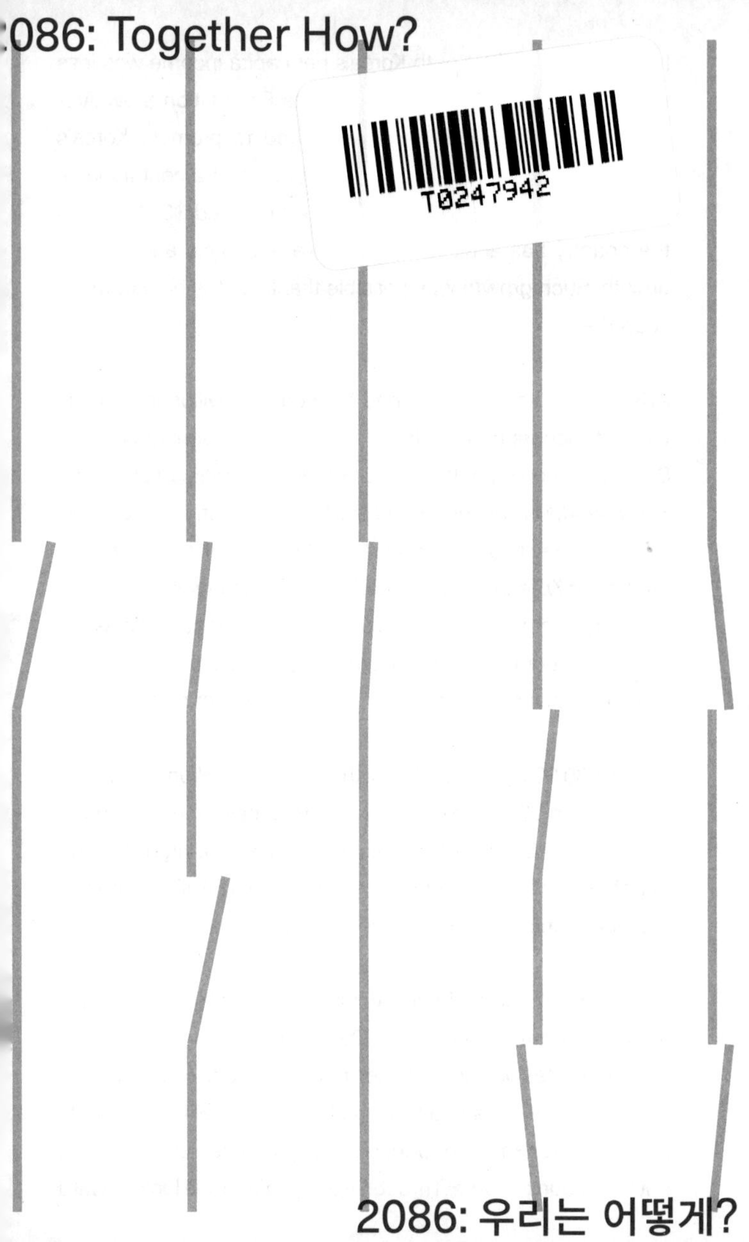
2086: Together How?
T0247942
2086: 우리는 어떻게?

In the 1970s, when South Korea's per capita income was less than $400, the Korea Culture and Arts Foundation (now Arts Council Korea (ARKO)) was established to promote Korea's arts and culture around the world. Today, half a century later, South Korea's per capita income has exceeded $35,000, and the country has achieved remarkable economic and cultural growth. Such growth was possible thanks to the help of many countries.

Arts Council Korea established the Korean Pavilion in 1995 as the last independent national pavilion in the Venice Giardini. Since the opening of the Korean Pavilion in 1995, artists Jheon Soo-cheon, Kang Ik-joong, and Lee Bul have been consecutively awarded special prizes in the Art Exhibition, taking the lead in promoting Korean art to the world. ARKO continues to hold fine exhibitions to promote Korean architecture abroad, such as the 2014 architecture exhibition *Crow's Eye View*, which won the Golden Lion, the highest honor at the Venice Biennale.

About 560,000 people visited the Korean Pavilion at the Art Exhibition in 2022, which was held amid the gradual easing of the two-year COVID-19 pandemic. This was the highest number of visitors since the opening of the Korean Pavilion, showing the world's interest in Korean culture and art.

At the 18th International Architecture Exhibition in 2023, through the exhibition titled *2086: Together How?*, the Korean Pavilion invites you to consider how we might overcome the environmental crisis and live together in 2086, when the world population is expected to reach its peak. These concerns will not be unique to Korea. Through this exhibition, we look forward to working together with you in solving the problem facing all of humankind, that is, how we will live in the future.

For the first time since the opening of the Korean Pavilion in 1995, the 2023 Korean Pavilion exhibition is hosted by two artistic directors. I would like to thank the two artistic directors, Soik Jung and Kyong Park, for their tireless work preparing the exhibition during the short time period of less than a year; the participating artists, for their efforts over an extended time producing works for the exhibition; and the exhibition promotion team, for all of their hard work behind the scenes. I would also like to express my extreme gratitude to the sponsors and partner organizations who supported this year's exhibition, including Woori Bank; ZAVA; LG Electronics; the Samsung Foundation of Culture; MCM; the University of California, San Diego Academic Senate; Gunsan-Si; Commonz Field Gunsan; the South Korean Ministry of the Interior and Safety; Graham Foundation for Advanced Studies in the Fine Arts, and among others.
Thank you.

Choung Byoung-Gug, Chair, ARKO

대한민국은 1인당 국민소득이 4백 불에도 미치지 못하던 1970년대에 한국의 문화예술 진흥을 위하여 한국문화예술진흥원 (現 한국문화예술위원회)을 설립하였습니다. 반세기가 지난 현재 대한민국의 1인당 국민소득은 3만 5천 불을 돌파하였으며 경제적으로도, 문화적으로도 놀라운 성장을 이루었습니다. 이러한 대한민국의 성장은 여러 국가의 도움이 있었기에 가능한 결과였습니다.

한국문화예술위원회는 1995년에 베니스 자르디니의 마지막 독립 국가관으로 한국관을 건립하였습니다. 한국관을 개관한 1995년부터 전수천, 강익중, 이불 작가가 연속으로 미술전에서 특별전을 수상하며 한국의 미술을 세계에 알리는 데 앞장섰습니다. 또한, 2014년에는 《한반도 오감도》라는 건축전으로 베니스 비엔날레 최고의 영예인 황금사자상을 수상하는 등, 우리 건축을 해외에 알리는 좋은 전시를 개최해 왔습니다.

2년여 간의 팬데믹이 조금씩 완화되는 상황에서 개최되었던 2022년 미술전에서는 약 56만 명의 관람객이 한국관을 방문하였습니다. 이는 한국관 개관 전시 이래 가장 높은 관람객 수를 기록한 것으로 한국의 문화예술에 대한 세계적 관심을 보여줍니다.

2023년 제18회 국제건축전에서 한국관은 《2086 : 우리는 어떻게?》라는 제목의 전시를 통해 세계 인구가 정점에 도달할 것이라고 예상되는 2086년에 우리가 환경 위기를 극복하고 함께 살아갈 수 있는 방법에 대한 고민을 함께 나눠보고자 합니다. 이러한 문제들은 비단 한국만의 문제는 아닐 것입니다. 이번 한국관 전시를 통해서 앞으로의 미래를 어떻게 살아갈 것인지, 온 인류가 당면한 문제를 풀어가는데 여러분과 함께하기를 기대합니다.

2023년 한국관 전시는 1995년 개관 이후 처음으로 두 명의 예술감독이 준비하였습니다. 1년이 채 되지 않는 짧은 기간 동안 전시 개최를 위해 애써주신 정소익, 박경 두 분의 예술감독과 전시작품 제작을 위해 오랜 기간 수고하신 참여 작가들, 그리고 보이지 않는 곳에서 고생하신 전시추진단에게 감사의 말씀 전합니다. 또한, 올해 전시에 힘을 실어 주신 우리은행, ZAVA,

LG전자, 삼성문화재단, MCM, 캘리포니아대학교 샌디에이고캠퍼스 평의원회, 군산시청, 군산소통협력센터, 행정안전부, 그라함재단 등 후원사와 협력기관에도 깊은 감사 인사를 드립니다.
감사합니다.

한국문화예술위원회 위원장, 정병국

Title	Page	Authors

Tomorrow's Myths

2086: Together How?

Tomorrow's Myths

Nick Axel — Hyewon Lee — Alice Bucknell — Yunjeong Han — Abdelhadi & O'Brien
Serang Chung — Federico Campagna

2086: Together How?

내일의 신화

니 아셀 — 이혜원 — 앨리스 버그넬 — 한윤정 — 이만 압델하디 & M. E. 오브라이언 — 정세랑 — 페데리코 캄파냐

2086: 우리는 어떻게?

Tomorrow's Myths

Nick Axel

10

닉 악셀

내일의 신화

Tomorrow's Myths

Nick Axel

Myths are relatively simple stories that, through the use of metaphor and other narrative devices, cut to the core of what it means to be human. Their messages are eternal, and through increasingly diverse storytelling practices, are often shared and passed down through the ages. By providing wider narratives that everyone can relate to, myths teach us about ourselves, about each other. They allow us to understand the bigger picture, and feel connected to greater significance and meaning. While new myths can emerge from the most quotidian practices and everyday habits of contemporary life, ancient ones are continually reinterpreted and contextualized within the present. Myths often operate on the foundations of non-normative, non-modern, non-scientific, non-rational epistemologies and cosmologies. Many myths teach us about death, disappointment, and destruction, while others teach us about love, about compassion, about harmony. Myths allow us to imagine another time, another way of being and living, and create bridges from the here and now to the there and then.

Today, we face an entangled world of political calamity, economic crisis, logistical breakdown, demographic revolution, and ecological collapse. With Tomorrow's Myths, a collaboration between e-flux Architecture and the curators of the 2023 Korean Pavilion at the Venice Architecture Biennale, we are interested in exploring the role, the significance, and the potential of myth within the daunting task of surviving these mounting challenges that threaten our existence. We have invited six architects, writers, artists, philosophers, and scientists to reflect on these questions and write new myths. What might the myths be that are created in 2086, after the biocultural revolution that is so desperately needed today? What myths might we create, or even be necessary to bring such about such transformations? How can we understand myth as an operative and creative force, one that is both intimately familiar and immediately accessible?

내일의 신화

닉 악셀

신화는 비교적 간단한 이야기로, 은유 및 여러 서사 장치를 사용하여 인간 존재의 의미를 핵심적으로 드러낸다. 신화의 메시지는 영원하며, 점점 다양해지는 이야기 전달 방식을 통해 여러 시대에 걸쳐 공유되고 전승된다. 모두가 공감할 수 있는 너른 서사를 제공함으로써, 신화는 우리 자신에 관해 또 서로에 관해 가르쳐준다. 신화는 전체적인 상을 이해하게 하고 더 큰 의의와 의미에 연결된 느낌을 갖게 해준다. 새로운 신화는 현대 생활의 평범한 관행과 일상적 습관에서 생겨날 수 있지만, 고대의 신화는 현재 속에서 계속해서 다시 해석되고 맥락을 얻는다. 신화는 종종 비규범적이고 비근대적이며 비과학적이고 비합리적인 인식론과 우주론의 토대 위에서 작동한다. 많은 신화가 우리에게 죽음과 낙담과 파괴를 가르치지만, 어떤 신화는 사랑과 연민과 조화에 관해 알려준다. 신화는 우리가 다른 시대 그리고 다른 존재와 삶의 방식을 상상하게 해주며, 지금 여기와 그때 저기를 잇는 가교를 만든다.

오늘 우리는 정치적 재앙, 경제 위기, 물류 붕괴, 인구 혁명, 생태 붕괴가 얽힌 세계와 마주하고 있다. e-flux Architecture와 2023 베니스비엔날레 국제건축전 한국관의 큐레이터들이 협업한 〈내일의 신화〉를 통해, 우리의 존재를 위협해 오는 난제들을 이겨낸다는 벅찬 과제 속에서 신화가 갖는 역할과 의미 그리고 가능성을 탐색해보려 한다. 우리는 여섯 팀의 건축가, 작가, 예술가, 철학자, 과학자를 초대해 이러한 문제를 숙고하여 새로운 신화를 쓰도록 요청했다. 오늘날 너무도 절실한 생물문화적 혁명이 일어난 이후 도래할 2086년에는 어떤 신화가 만들어질까? 그런 변화를 가져오려면 우리는 어떤 신화를 만들어야 할까? 신화가 필요하기는 할까? 우리에게 친숙하면서도 즉각적으로 활용할 수 있는 그런 영향력이자 창조력으로 신화를 이해하는 방법은 무엇일까?

The Declaration of Innocence

Hyewon Lee

14

이혜원

무죄선언

The Declaration of Innocence

Hyewon Lee

2020, ©Suyeon Yun

There is an abundance of data, predictions, and signs that the climate crisis is on the verge of catastrophe. However, I do not want to imagine a future without humans. Even in the very worst case, I don't want to give up hope that a small number of people, living close to the land in a small corner of the earth, will survive. The script for a play below, The Declaration of Innocence, *is the product of this frail hope. It borrows the form of Greek tragedy and summons dogs, pigs, and people who would have lived on a small island of the Solomon Islands in the South Pacific hundreds of years ago. Although the characters and animals appearing in the play are fictional, the story is based on archeological research on the extreme population control measures that the inhabitants of Tikopia chose for their common survival, and on news reports about how the islanders were able to survive without losing a single life when the entire island was devastated by a powerful cyclone at the turn of the twenty-first century.*

After people settled in Tikopia, which has a landmass of only 4.6 square kilometers, the population increased with the development of agriculture and livestock farming. This eventually led to the island becoming uninhabitable. But rather than abandoning the island, the people changed their farming methods to revive the natural environment. At the same time, in order to keep the population size down to a level that the island's ecosystem could support, parts of the population were forced to remain single, abortion was encouraged, and even newborn infants were killed. Or, in order to save the infant's life, one of the family members could choose to die, or be banished to the sea in a makeshift canoe loaded with some food. On top of this, around the year 1600, all the pigs on the island were slaughtered, and the islanders returned to a plant- and fish-based diet. This was not a temporary crisis-response, but a practice that has been ongoing for hundreds of years, continuing into the 1920s, when the New Zealand anthropologist Raymond Firth visited Tikopia.

Although the island's population control measures have changed over time, Tikopia still maintains a population size of about 1,200, as in the past. The islanders' extraordinary disaster response ability was once again brought to international attention in late 2002, shortly after the record-breaking cyclone Joe hit Tikopia. According to news reports at the time, they evacuated the children and elderly to the only small cave on the island, while the remaining residents, reading the direction in which the cyclone was moving, ran in the opposite direction for several days and nights. All the islanders survived.

2018, ©Suyeon Yun

Scene: *Much of the earth has been swept away by the devastation caused by the climate crisis, with only a small patch of nature and a small native village remaining. Just before dawn, in front of a low hut into which adults and even children must crawl, an old man is shrouding the corpse of a young man, laid out on a stretcher, with large leaves.*

Elderly Undertaker
Oh, indifferent gods and heartless humans! [1]
Why trim a hardy green leaf without pruning back old withered leaves?

Chorus of Elderly Bachelors (Left)
Tut-tut! This old man has lost his mind

Chorus of Elderly Bachelors (Right)
Humans accept the gust of fate when reduced to hunger

Chorus of Elderly Bachelors (Left)
A long long time ago, when I was a child,

a great big calamity was visited upon on this earth

Chorus of Elderly Bachelors (Right)

It was all because the mind had gone blind

Chorus of Elderly Bachelors (Left)

The heaven and ocean formed a union,
and ravaged everything on earth

Chorus of Elderly Bachelors (Right)

I cannot tell about its devastation,
for I hid in a dark cave and did not see

Chorus of Elderly Bachelors (Left)

When the sun again shone,
everything on earth floated like a buoy

Chorus of Elderly Bachelors (Right)

Even the dead were too afraid to rise up again

Chorus of Elderly Bachelors (Left)

Someone, a god stole us away,
helping us escape the destruction

Elderly Undertaker

What then was the intention if not to annihilate?
The screams of murdered infants echoed throughout the village

Chorus of Elderly Bachelors (Right)

You dastardly old man,
you dare say a father who dies in place of his child is not noble?

Chorus of Elderly Bachelors (Left)

You dare say a mother who does not give birth to a life to be killed is not virtuous?

Elderly Undertaker

Do you not hear the cry of screaming souls?

The soul of the young man,
slipping out of the corpse, begins to look around.

Man

Oh, nobly born child, where are you? Where are you?
Oh, my grieving family, where is my child?
Oh, my slumbering neighbors, have you not seen my child?

Soon after, the souls of the man's dog
and pig approach him.

Pig

Oh, dear master, I am not a foul pig.
I have not woken the infant.
I have not snatched away the infant's milk.

Dog

Oh, dear master, I am not a wicked dog.
I have not bitten the infant.
I have not snatched away the infant's food.

The man wandering through the wet fog at dawn
does not hear the appeals of the dog and the pig.

Man

Oh, nobly born child, where are you? Where are you?
Oh, my grieving family, where is my child?
Oh, my slumbering neighbors, have you not seen my child?

The dog and the pig follow the man, continuing their pleas. Just as Ani of Thebes at the court of the gods refuted one by one the forty-two sins the ancient Egyptians considered taboo, they proclaim their innocence.[2]

Dog

Oh, master, who swam with me the clear stream waters,
I have never fouled the water.
I have not obstructed the flow of water.
I have never taken water from the thirsty.

Pig

Oh, master, who made a bed for me to lie on with grass from golden fields,
I have never polluted the land.
I have not stolen the land.
I have never taken the bread of the poor.

Dog

Oh, master, who would lie with me on green fields listening to birdsongs,
I did not make the birds go silent.
I did not cut down the trees where the birds nested.
I did not deprive the birds of their food.

Pig

Oh, master, who always gave me hearty meals,
I have never envied the baby.
I have not envied the fat pigs.
I have never despised anyone.

Dog

Oh, master, who was tormented night after night by my sacrifice,
I have never wished for your suffering.
I have not terrorized you.
I have never despised you.

Dog and Pig

Oh, master, who could not look me in the eyes,
I did not wish for your suffering.
I did not terrorize you.
I did not despise you.

Gradually as dawn begins to break, people gather one by one in front of the hut and begin to sing.

Villagers

If~you~leave~now~when~will~you~return~If~you~leave~now ~when~will~you~return~
Tell~us~the~day~you~will~return~Tell~us~the~day~you~will~ return~
How~to~depart~how~to~depart~leaving~behind~your~precious ~child~
How~to~depart~how~to~depart~leaving~behind~your~precious ~family~
A~wealth~of~devoted~villagers~ but~ who~ will~ leave~ in~ your~

place~

Lifelong~friends~are~many~but~who~will~go~with~you~to~that~place~

The man finds the sleeping infant in the arms of a young woman and approaches them. Caressing the infant's face in his palms he kisses it. The woman does not feel the man's presence.

Man

Oh, child born of virtue, my precious child,
asleep in the arms of our friend without a care in the world.
You cannot see me but I am watching you.
Oh, child born without blame, my precious child,
the gift you gave me was your life.
The gift I gave you was my life.

A group of bachelors and spinsters appears amongst the crowd. Eight spinsters slowly lift the stretcher on which the corpse lay with matching footsteps, while four bachelors begin to wail.[3]

Wailing Bachelors

A-i-go~~A-i-go~~A-i-go~~A-i-go~~[4]

When the spinster holding the handbell leads with a slow tune, the spinsters carrying the funeral bier sing along, taking one step forward and one step back, repeatedly.

Handbell-Ringing Spinster

Leav~ing~home~Leav~ing~home~~~Our~friend~is~leav~ing~home~

Pallbearing Spinsters
Leav~ing~home~Leav~ing~home~~~Our~neigh~bor~is~leav ~ing~home~
Leav~ing~home~Leav~ing~home~~~Our~friend~is~leav~ing~ home ~
Leav~ing~home~Leav~ing~home~~~Our~neigh~bor~is~leav ~ing~home~

Wailing Bachelors
A-i-go~~A-i-go~~A-i-go~~A-i-go~~

The man follows the procession and approaches a crying woman.

Man
Oh, woman, who must live without guilt, do not weep.
Our child is sleeping In our friend's arms, our child sleeps.
Oh, woman, with whom I can no longer share a life, dry your tears.
Hold our child in your arms When the child awakes and cries for its mother, hold our child in your arms.

Wailing Bachelors
A-i-go~~A-i-go~~A-i-go~~A-i-go~~

The funeral procession begins to slowly circle the village, singing of memories of the deceased. Intermittently, an indecipherable refrain repeats.

Handbell-Ringing Spinster
De~part~ing~~De~part~ing~~Our~friend~is~de~part~ing~

Pallbearing Spinsters
De~part~ing~~De~part~ing~~Our~friend~is~de~part~ing~
Lo~lo-lo~lo-o-o-o~e-hwa-neom-cha~lo-o-hwa~
Lo~lo-lo~lo-o-o-o~e-hwa-neom-cha~lo-o-hwa~

Handbell-Ringing Spinster
De~part~ing~~De~part~ing~~Our~friend~is~de~part~ing~

Pallbearing Spinsters
De~part~ing~~De~part~ing~~Our~friend~is~de~part~ing~
Lo~lo-lo~lo-o-o-o~e-hwa-neom-cha~lo-o-hwa~
Lo~lo-lo~lo-o-o-o~e-hwa-neom-cha~lo-o-hwa~

Handbell-Ringing Spinster
Our friend with whom we hid in a cramped cave and with whom we cried together

Pallbearing Spinsters
Our neighbor with whom we ran together on that day of the savage winds
Lo~lo-lo~lo-o-o-o~e-hwa-neom-cha~lo-o-hwa~
Lo~lo-lo~lo-o-o-o~e-hwa-neom-cha~lo-o-hwa~

Handbell-Ringing Spinster
Three nights and four days without repose

Pallbearing Spinsters
We ran and ran
Lo~lo-lo~lo-o-o-o~e-hwa-neom-cha~lo-o-hwa~
Lo~lo-lo~lo-o-o-o~e-hwa-neom-cha~lo-o-hwa~

Handbell-Ringing Spinster
The whims of harsh winds

Pallbearing Spinsters
Running hither and thither
Lo~lo-lo~lo-o-o-o~e-hwa-neom-cha~lo-o-hwa~
Lo~lo-lo~lo-o-o-o~e-hwa-neom-cha~lo-o-hwa~

Handbell-Ringing Spinster
Running hither and thither

Pallbearing Spinsters
Running hither and thither
Lo~lo-lo~lo-o-o-o~e-hwa-neom-cha~lo-o-hwa~[5]
Lo~lo-lo~lo-o-o-o~e-hwa-neom-cha~lo-o-hwa~

Wailing Bachelors
A-i-go~~A-i-go~~A-i-go~~A-i-go~~

The crying woman sings behind the pallbearers.

Woman
A-i-go~~A-i-go~~ heartbreaking and lamentable
When spring comes next year will my husband return
How far is the road to heaven why is he leaving home

Pallbearing Spinsters
Lo~lo-lo~lo-o-o-o~e-hwa-neom-cha~lo-o-hwa~
Lo~lo-lo~lo-o-o-o~e-hwa-neom-cha~lo-o-hwa~

Wailing Bachelors

A-i-go~~A-i-go~~A-i-go~~A-i-go~~

The man approaches the woman and lovingly strokes her back.

Man

Oh, woman, who is to me like air to the birds, dry your tears.
There is not a single tree in this world that is unshaken by the wind.
Even if you live for a hundred years, if you take away all your worries, if you take away the days of sickness and slumber, you live no longer than forty years.
Whether too soon or too late, the time has come for me to go.

Wailing Bachelors

A-i-go~~A-i-go~~A-i-go~~A-i-go~~

The man's song bleeds into the song of the pallbearers.

Handbell-Ringing Spinster

Even with devoted villagers, who will leave in his place

Pallbearing Spinsters

Even with devoted friends, who will leave in his place
Lo~lo-lo~lo-o-o-o~e-hwa-neom-cha~lo-o-hwa
Lo~lo-lo~lo-o-o-o~e-hwa-neom-cha~lo-o-hwa

Handbell-Ringing Spinster

The road from which you cannot return, how is it you must travel it alone

Pallbearing Spinsters
Are you not afraid of the mountain, are you not afraid of the ocean
Lo~lo-lo~lo-o-o-o~e-hwa-neom-cha~lo-o-hwa
Lo~lo-lo~lo-o-o-o~e-hwa-neom-cha~lo-o-hwa

Wailing Bachelors
A-i-go~~A-i-go~~A-i-go~~A-i-go~~

As the pallbearers begin to ascend the steep hill, the handbell-ringing spinster raises her voice and sings in a fast-paced tune, boosting the pallbearers' strength. The shortened refrains are repeated in rapid succession.

Handbell-Ringing Spinster
My life without love my fate without children

Pallbearing Spinsters
E-hwa-neom-cha~lo-o-hwa~lo-o-hwa~~E-hwa-neom-cha~lo-o-hwa~lo-o-hwa~~

Handbell-Ringing Spinster
I will hold your child in my arms and pat your love on the back

Pallbearing Spinsters
E-hwa-neom-cha~lo-o-hwa~lo-o-hwa~~E-hwa-neom-cha~lo-o-hwa~lo-o-hwa~~

Handbell-Ringing Spinster
Do not worry about the savage winds I will hide your child in a cave

Pallbearing Spinsters

E-hwa-neom-cha~lo-o-hwa~lo-o-hwa~~E-hwa-neom-cha~lo-o-hwa~lo-o-hwa~~

Handbell-Ringing Spinster

Do not worry about your wife who no longer eats I will nourish and soothe her

Pallbearing Spinsters

E-hwa-neom-cha~lo-o-hwa~lo-o-hwa~~E-hwa-neom-cha~lo-o-hwa~lo-o-hwa~~

Wailing Bachelors

A-i-go~~A-i-go~~A-i-go~~A-i-go~~

The man sings to the procession.

Man

Oh my love who is like water to the fish rise up
Before the lake dries up again
Oh my friends who ran with me into the cave rise up
Before the savage winds strike again
My villagers with many words and many woes shake it off and rise up
Before the birds fall silent again

The dog and the pig sing as they approach the funeral procession.

Dog and Pig

Going going I am going to the place I used to live
Dear master dear villagers worry about me no more
In the beginning I came from the forest in the beginning I came from the mountain
Here and there I will be happy this and that I will eat
Even as chubby as I am I am still good at running
Your teeny tiny house not so comfortable it was
Yet you fed me and housed me so what else was I to do
Listen bad master of all the hardships I suffered I have forgotten
Listen good master a good lifetime I have lived
Worry about me no more and have a good life
Without disaster without misfortune have a good life
Going going I am going to the place I used to live

After returning from the water burial, the man's family,
friends, and neighbors adorn themselves
with flowers and leaves and gather in front of the hut.
The dog and the pig, wearing garlands, also join the crowd.
They all begin to sing and dance together.

All Together in Unison

Nice day pleasant day the day is so delightful
Kwae-ji-na~ching-ching-na-ne~~Kwae-ji-na~ching-ching-na-ne~~
Going going out to play I am going to the grassy fields I go to play
Kwae-ji-na~ching-ching-na-ne~~Kwae-ji-na~ching-ching-na-ne~~
Green grass clothes you are making and pretty birds befriending
Kwae-ji-na~ching-ching-na-ne~~Kwae-ji-na~ching-ching-na-ne~~
Going going across I am going across the stream I am crossing
Kwae-ji-na~ching-ching-na-ne~~Kwae-ji-na~ching-ching-na-ne~~
With clear stream water you are cooking and little fishes befriending

Kwae-ji-na~ching-ching-na-ne~~Kwae-ji-na~ching-ching-na-ne~~
Villagers old and young just let it go let it go let it all go
Kwae-ji-na~ching-ching-na-ne~~Kwae-ji-na~ching-ching-na-ne~~
Once you leave you cannot return so let it all go and do not squabble
Kwae-ji-na~ching-ching-na-ne~~Kwae-ji-na~ching-ching-na-ne~~

While everyone is dancing and singing together,
the man's soul reaches the entrance of the underworld.

Man
Oh, gods who I am meeting for the first time,
Why do you block the path of my soul, inquiring after my sins?
Is it a sin to toil in the fields dripping in sweat to feed your family?
Is it a sin to heat the house of elderly parents to keep them from the cold?
Is it a sin to feed the dog that trails my every step?
Thou shalt not commit adultery, so I have loved only one woman.
Wander alone like a rhinoceros, so I have traveled to the far distant road of the netherworld without a companion.

Oh, forgive me gods for not remembering each of your names.
Ask no more about the sins I have not committed, and release my soul.
Where to send it is your decision, so what dare I say on the matter.
Yet if you want to send me back to the world from which I came, let me return as a tree.
Flower or grass, bird or worm, dog or pig, what choice do I have on the matter.
They say that you have created human beings in the finest of molds .
Yet I dare say that you have made trees far superior to humans

1. Some part of the dialogue between the Elderly Undertaker and the Chorus of Elderly Bachelors was adapted from the lines of the chorus and characters that appear in the Greek tragedy *Agamemnon* by Aeschylus.

2. The song of the dog and the pig, in which it is repeatedly declared that they did not harm the land, water, or other living beings, is inspired by "The Declaration of Innocence" from *The Egyptian Book of the Dead*. That is, it is a declaration made by souls of the dead as they face the gods at the entrance of the underworld, enumerating the deeds that human beings should not commit while inhabiting the living world.

3. The funeral procession in the play is modeled after that of Yeondo, a small island on the southern tip of the Korean peninsula, where only women carry the funeral bier. For the way the speakers address others to alleviate the fear of leaving this world, I referenced the Korean translation of Bardo Thodol, a Tibetan scripture read by monks or acquaintances to the dead or dying. And for the lyrics of the songs sung by the characters in the play, I have appropriated phrases from the Bible, the Koran, the Sutta Nipāta, and the Bhagavad Gita, with particular focus on various Korean funerary songs, which I have modified to fit the context and flow of the play.

4. Translator's note: *Aigo* is a Korean expression that can be used similarly to the interjections "oh my!" "oh dear!" "dear me!" "good heavens!" as well as "ouch!" in English. It is a common yet versatile expression that is often used to express shock or surprise, but is also typically uttered by grieving family members, customarily women, at funerals and wakes.

5. Translator's note: This refrain is a Korean chorus-like refrain that typically accompanies folk dancing and music used to express joy and pleasure in various farming-village community celebrations.

무죄선언

이혜원

2020, ©윤수연

기후 위기가 파국으로 치닫고 있음을 말해주는 각종 데이터와 징후 예측들이 난무하지만, 나는 인간이 없는 미래를 상상하고 싶지 않다. 최악의 상황에도 지구 어느 한 모퉁이에서 자연과 친밀하게 살아가는 소수의 사람은 살아남을 것이라는 희망도 버리고 싶지 않다. 이 근거가 미약한 희망의 산물인 〈무죄선언〉은 그리스 비극의 형식을 빌려 수백 년 전, 남태평양 솔로몬 군도의 작은 섬에 살았을 개와 돼지와 사람들을 소환한다. 극에 등장하는 인물과 동물은 허구지만 이야기 자체는 티코피아에 살았던 사람들의 역사에 근거한 것이다. 그들이 공동의 생존을 위해 선택했던 극단적인 인구 조절 정책에 관한 고고학자들의 연구와 21세기가 시작된 직후 초강력 사이클론이 섬 전체를 초토화했을 때 이곳 사람들이 한 명도 목숨을 잃지 않고 살아남을 수 있었던 방법에 대한 언론보도를 참조하였다.

면적이 4.6km^2에 불과한 티코피아에 사람이 정착한 이후 농경과 축산이 발달하면서 인구가 증가했고, 섬 환경은 더 이상 사람이 살 수 없을 정도로 황폐해졌다. 이때 사람들은 섬을 버리고 떠나기보다는 자연을 되살리기 위해 농경 방식을 바꾸고, 인구를 섬 생태계가 부양할 수 있는 규모로 유지하

기로 했다. 이를 위해 일부 성인의 독신을 강요하고, 낙태를 권장하며, 피할 수 없는 경우, 갓 태어난 아기를 죽이거나 아기 대신 가족 중 한 명이 죽음을 선택하게 하였다. 약간의 음식과 함께 부실한 카누에 실린 채 바다로 추방되기도 했다. 그뿐만 아니라 1600년경에는 섬의 모든 돼지를 도살하고 식물과 물고기 중심의 식생활로 돌아갔다. 이러한 조치는 일시적인 위기 대응책이 아니라 수백 년 동안 이어진 관행이 되었고, 뉴질랜드의 인류학자 레이몬드 퍼스(Raymond Firth)가 티코피아를 방문했던 1920년대에도 계속되고 있었다.

시간이 지나면서 인구를 조절하는 방식은 달라졌지만, 티코피아는 과거와 마찬가지로 지금도 약 1,200명의 인구를 유지하고 있다. 이곳 사람들의 놀라운 재난 대처 능력은 2002년 말, 기록적인 강도의 사이클론 조가 티코피아를 강타한 직후 다시 한번 국제적인 주목을 받았다. 당시 기사들에 따르면 그들은 어린이와 노약자들을 섬에서 단 하나뿐인 작은 동굴로 대피시키고, 나머지는 며칠 동안 사이클론의 반대 방향으로 계속 달림으로써 전원 살아남았다.

2018, ©윤수연

배경: *기후 파국이 휩쓸고 지나간 후, 지구에는 약간의 자연과 작은 원주민 마을 하나가 남았다. 이른 새벽, 어른은 물론 아이들조차도 기어들어 가야 하는 낮은 오두막 앞에서 한 노인이 들것 위에 누운 젊은 남자의 시신을 커다란 나뭇잎으로 싸고 있다.*

늙은 염꾼

오, 신들은 무정하고 인간들은 비정하네 [1]

어찌하여 시든 잎사귀를 뜯지 않고 푸른 이파리를 잘라낸다는 말인가

늙은 독신자들(좌)

허어, 이 늙은이 정신 줄을 놓았구나

늙은 독신자들(우)

본디 인간은 굶주림에 시달릴 때 제 운명의 회오리를 받아들이는 법

늙은 독신자들(좌)

옛날 옛적 나 어릴 적 세상에 크나큰 재앙 있었네

늙은 독신자들(우)

모든 게 눈먼 마음 때문이었네

늙은 독신자들(좌)

하늘과 바다가 동맹을 맺고 땅 위의 모든 것을 유린했네

늙은 독신자들(우)

어떻게 유린했는지는 말하지 않으리 캄캄한 동굴 속에 숨어서 보지 못했으니

늙은 독신자들(좌)

태양이 다시 비추니 땅 위의 모든 것이 부표처럼 떠다녔네

늙은 독신자들(우)

죽은 자도 두려워서 다시 일어나려 하지 않네

늙은 독신자들(좌)

어떤 신께서 우리만 몰래 빼돌리셨는지 파멸을 면하도록 도와주셨네

늙은 염꾼

멸할 생각 없었으면 무엇하오
살해당한 어린 것들의 비명소리가 온 마을을 뒤덮었는데

늙은 독신자들(우)

자식 대신 죽는 아비가 고귀하지 않다는 말이오

늙은 독신자들(좌)

죽일 생명 낳지 않는 어미가 고귀하지 않다는 말이오

늙은 염꾼

오, 저 영혼들의 비명소리가 안 들린다는 말이오

염을 마친 시신에서 빠져나온 젊은 남자의 영혼이
주변을 두리번거리기 시작한다.

남자

오, 고귀하게 태어난 우리 아기, 어디 있니? 어디 있니?
울고 있는 가족들아, 우리 아기 어디 있소?
자고 있는 이웃들아, 우리 아기 못 보았소?

잠시 후, 개와 돼지의 영혼이 남자에게 다가온다.

돼지

오, 사랑하는 주인이여, 저는 나쁜 돼지가 아닙니다.
저는 아기를 깨우지 않았습니다.
아기의 우유를 빼앗지 않았습니다.

개

오, 사랑하는 주인이여, 저는 못된 개가 아닙니다.
저는 아기를 물지 않았습니다.
아기의 밥을 빼앗지 않았습니다.

새벽 운무 속을 서성이는 남자는 개와 돼지의 호소를 듣지 못한다.

남자

오, 고귀하게 태어난 우리 아기, 어디 있니? 어디 있니?
울고 있는 가족들아, 우리 아기 어디 있소?
자고 있는 이웃들아, 우리 아기 못 보았소?

개와 돼지가 남자를 따라다니며 읍소를 계속한다.
테베의 아니(Ani)가 신들의 법정에서 고대 이집트인들이 금기시했던
42가지 죄를 하나하나 부정하며 자신의 무죄를 주장하는 것처럼.[2]

개

오, 맑은 시냇물에서 함께 헤엄치던 주인이여, 저는 물을 더럽히지 않았습니다.
저는 흐르는 물을 막지 않았습니다.
저는 목마른 사람의 물을 빼앗지 않았습니다.

돼지

오, 황금빛 들판에서 거둔 풀로 누울 자리를 만들어주던 주인이여, 저는 땅을 오염시키지 않았습니다.
저는 다른 사람의 땅을 훔치지 않았습니다.
저는 가난한 사람들의 빵을 빼앗지 않았습니다.

개

오, 초록 들판에 누워 새소리를 함께 듣던 주인이여, 저는 새들을 침묵하게 만들지 않았습니다.
저는 새들이 둥지 튼 나무를 베지 않았습니다.
저는 새들의 먹이를 빼앗지 않았습니다.

돼지

오, 언제나 풍성한 식사를 내어주던 주인이여, 저는 아기를 질투하지 않았습니다.
저는 살진 돼지를 시기하지 않았습니다.

저는 아무도 미워하지 않았습니다.

개

오, 밤마다 저의 비명을 다시 듣는 주인이여, 저는 당신의 고통을 바라지 않았습니다.
저는 당신을 겁주지 않았습니다.
저는 당신을 미워하지 않았습니다.

개와 돼지

오, 차마 저의 눈을 마주 보지 못한 주인이여, 저는 당신의 고통을 바라지 않았습니다.
저는 당신을 겁주지 않았습니다.
저는 당신을 미워하지 않았습니다.

서서히 동이 트기 시작하고,
사람들이 하나둘 오두막 앞으로 모여들며 노래하기 시작한다.

합창

이제~가면~언제~~오나~이제~가면~언제~오나~~
오실~날이나~일러~주오~~오실~날이나~일러~주오~~
어찌~갈까~어찌~갈까~~금쪽~같은~자식~두고~~
어찌~갈까~어찌~갈까~~천금~같은~가족~두고~~
정든~이웃~많다~한들~누가~대신~떠나~줄까~~
친한~친구~있다~한들~누가~같이~떠나~줄까~~

남자가 젊은 여자에게 안겨 잠이 든 아기를 발견하고 다가간다. 양손으로 아기의 얼굴을 감싸면서 입을 맞추지만 여자는 남자의 존재를 느끼지 못한다.

남자

오, 고귀하게 태어난 우리 아기, 예쁜 아기.
우리 친구 품에 안겨 세상모르고 자는구나.
너는 나를 볼 수 없지만 나는 너를 보고 있다.

오, 고귀하게 태어난 우리 아기, 예쁜 아기.
네가 나에게 준 선물은 너의 생명이었다.
내가 너에게 준 선물은 나의 생명이었다.

한 무리의 젊은 독신자들이 군중 사이로 등장한다.
8명의 독신녀는 천천히 남자의 시신이 누워있는 들것을 들어 올리며
발을 맞추고, 4명의 독신남은 곡을 하기 시작한다.[3]

대곡꾼
아이고~~아이고~~아이고~~아이고~~

요령을 든 독신녀가 느린 가락으로 선창을 하자
상여꾼들이 따라 부르면서 한 걸음 앞으로 갔다가
한 걸음 뒤로 가기를 반복한다.

요령잡이
집~떠~난~다~~집~떠~난~다~~우~리~친~구~집~떠~난~다~~

상여꾼
집~떠~난~다~~집~떠~난~다~~우~리~이~웃~집~떠~난~다~~
집~떠~난~다~~집~떠~난~다~~우~리~친~구~집~떠~난~다~~
집~떠~난~다~~집~떠~난~다~우~리~이~웃~집~떠~난~다~~

대곡꾼
아이고~~아이고~~아이고~~아이고~~

남자가 상여 행렬 뒤에서 울고 있는 한 여자에게 다가간다.

남자
오, 고귀하게 살아있는 여인이여, 울음을 멈추구려.
우리 아기 자고 있소. 우리 친구 품에 안겨 우리 아기 자고 있소.

오, 더 이상 함께 할 수 없는 여인이여, 눈물을 거두구려.
우리 아기 안아 주오. 잠이 깨면 엄마 찾을 우리 아기 안아 주오.

대곡꾼
아이고~~아이고~~아이고~~아이고~~

상여꾼들이 망자와의 추억을 노래하며 천천히 마을을 한 바퀴 돈다.
중간중간 의미를 알 수 없는 후렴구가 삽입된다.

요령잡이
길~떠~난~다~~길~떠~난~다~~우~리~친~구~길~떠~난~다~~

상여꾼
길~떠~난~다~~길~떠~난~다~~우~리~친~구~길~떠~난~다~~
로~로로~로오오오~에화넘차~로오화
로~로로~로오오오~에화넘차~로오화~

요령잡이
길~떠~난~다~~길~떠~난~다~~우~리~친~구~길~떠~난~다~~

상여꾼
길~떠~난~다~~길~떠~난~다~~우~리~친~구~길~떠~난~다~~
로~로로~로오오오~에화넘차~로오화
로~로로~로오오오~에화넘차~로오화~

요령잡이
비좁은 동굴 속에 함께 숨어 함께 울던 우리 친구

상여꾼
모진 강풍 불던 날에 함께 뛰던 우리 이웃
로~로로~로오오오~에화넘차~로오화

로~로로~로오오오~에화넘차~로오화~

요령잡이

사흘 밤낮 쉬지 않고

상여꾼

달리고 또 달렸네

로~로로~로오오오~에화넘차~로오화

로~로로~로오오오~에화넘차~로오화~

요령잡이

모진 강풍 변덕 부려

상여꾼

이리 뛰고 저리 뛰고

로~로로~로오오오~에화넘차~로오화

로~로로~로오오오~에화넘차~로오화~

요령잡이

이리 뛰고 저리 뛰고

상여꾼

이리 뛰고 저리 뛰고

로~로로~로오오오~에화넘차~로오화

로~로로~로오오오~에화넘차~로오화~

대곡꾼

아이고~~아이고~~아이고~~아이고~~

울면서 상여꾼 뒤를 따라오던 여자가 노래를 부른다.

우는 여자
아이고~~아이고~~애닯고도 설운지고
다음 해에 봄이 온들 우리 남편 돌아올까
황천길이 몇만 린가 집 떠나서 어딜 가오

상여꾼
로~로로~로오오오~에화넘차~로오화
로~로로~로오오오~에화넘차~로오화~

대곡꾼
아이고~~아이고~~아이고~~아이고~~

남자가 우는 여자에게 다가와 등을 토닥인다.

남자
오, 새들에게 공기 같은 여인이여, 눈물을 거두구려.
이 세상 나무 중에 바람이 흔들지 않은 나무 한 그루도 없소이다.
인생 백 년 다 살아도 걱정 근심 다 제하고, 병든 날과 잠든 날 다 제하면
단 사십을 못 산다오. 앞서거나 뒤서거나 때가 되어 갈 뿐이오.

대곡꾼
아이고~~아이고~~아이고~~아이고~~

남자의 말이 상여꾼들의 노래에 묻힌다.

요령잡이
정든 이웃 있다 한들 누가 대신 떠나줄까

상여꾼
친한 친구 있다 한들 누가 같이 떠나줄까
로~로로~로오오오~에화넘차~로오화
로~로로~로오오오~에화넘차~로오화~

요령잡이
한번 가면 못 돌아올 길 어이하여 혼자 가나

상여꾼
저 산이 무서운가 저 바다가 무서운가
로~로로~로오오오~에화넘차~로오화
로~로로~로오오오~에화넘차~로오화~

대곡꾼
아이고~~아이고~~아이고~~아이고~~

상여 행렬이 언덕길을 오르기 시작하자 요령잡이가 목소리를 키워
빠른 가락으로 선창을 하며 상여꾼들의 힘을 북돋운다.
짧아진 후렴구가 더 자주 반복된다.

요령잡이
사랑 없는 내 신세야 자식 없는 내 팔자야

상여꾼
에화넘차~로오화~ 에화넘차~로오화~

요령잡이
너의 아이 품에 안고 너의 사랑 토닥인다

상여꾼
에화넘차~로오화~ 에화넘차~로오화~

요령잡이
모진 강풍 걱정 말게 금쪽같은 자네 아이 동굴 속에 숨겨 줄게

상여꾼

에화넘차~로오화~ 에화넘차~로오화~

요령잡이

곡기 끊은 자네 여인 걱정 말게 먹여 주고 달래 줄게

상여꾼

에화넘차~로오화~ 에화넘차~로오화~

대곡꾼

아이고~~아이고~~아이고~~아이고~~

남자가 모두를 향해 노래한다.

남자

오, 물고기의 물 같은 내 사랑아, 일어나오
호수가 다시 바닥을 드러내기 전에
오, 저 들판을 함께 달린 친구들아, 일어나게
모진 강풍이 다시 몰려오기 전에
말도 많고 탈도 많던 이웃들아, 툴툴 털고 일어나소
새들이 다시 침묵하기 전에

개와 돼지가 상여 행렬 옆으로 다가오며 노래한다.

개와 돼지

간다 간다 나는 간다 내 살던 곳으로 돌아간다
주인이여, 이웃이여, 내 걱정은 하지 마소
내가 원래 숲에서 왔소 내가 원래 산에서 왔소
여기저기 잘 다니고 이것저것 잘 먹는 건 나 따를 놈 없을 게요
내가 이리 통통해도 뜀박질 하나는 잘한다오
좁디좁은 당신 집이 편안치는 않았소만
먹여 주고 재워 주니 내가 어찌 마다할까

나쁜 주인 들어보소 나 고생한 것 다 잊었소
좋은 주인 들어보소 한세월을 잘 살았소
내 걱정은 접어두고 안녕히들 지내시오
재난 없고 우환 없이 안녕히들 지내시오
간다 간다 나는 간다 내 살던 곳으로 돌아간다

수장을 하고 돌아온 남자의 가족, 친구, 이웃들이 꽃과 나뭇잎으로 몸단장하고 오두막 앞에 다시 모였고, 목에 화환을 건 개와 돼지도 합류한다. 다 같이 춤추고 노래하기 시작한다.

합창

날씨 좋네 날씨 좋아 오늘 날씨 정말 좋네 쾌지나 칭칭나네 쾌지나 칭칭나네
간다 간다 놀러 간다 풀밭으로 놀러 간다 쾌지나 칭칭나네 쾌지나 칭칭나네
푸른 잔디 옷을 삼게 예쁜 새들 벗을 삼게 쾌지나 칭칭나네 쾌지나 칭칭나네
간다 간다 건너간다 실개천을 건너간다 쾌지나 칭칭나네 쾌지나 칭칭나네
맑은 냇물 밥을 삼게 작은 물고기 벗을 삼게 쾌지나 칭칭나네 쾌지나 칭칭나네
늙고 젊은 이웃들아 노소 노소 많이 노소 쾌지나 칭칭나네 쾌지나 칭칭나네
한번 가면 못 오나니 싸우지 말고 많이 노소 쾌지나 칭칭나네 쾌지나 칭칭나네

춤과 노래가 계속되는 동안 남자의 영혼이 저승 입구에 도착한다.

남자

오, 처음 뵙는 신들이시여,
어찌하여 제 영혼을 가로막고, 저의 죄를 물으시나이까?
땀 흘리며 밭을 일궈 식솔 먹여 살린 것이 죄입니까?
나이 든 우리 부모 추울까 봐 불 땐 것이 죄입니까?
허구한 날 저만 따른 강아지 밥 준 것이 죄입니까?
간음하지 말라 하여 한 여인만 사랑하였나이다.
무소의 뿔처럼 혼자서 가라 하여 멀고 먼 황천길을 동무 없이 왔나이다.

오, 일일이 성함을 기억하지 못해 송구스러운 신들이시여,

없는 죄는 그만 묻고, 제 영혼을 보내 주소서.
어디로 보낼지는 여러 신들 마음이니 제가 감히 무슨 말을 하오리까.
다만 제가 온 세상으로 다시 보내시려거든 부디 나무로 부탁드리옵니다.
꽃이든 풀이든, 새든 벌레든, 개든 돼지든 가릴 처지가 아니옵고,
틀 중에 가장 좋은 틀로 인간을 만드셨다는 것도 들었사오나
아무리 생각해도 신들께서는 인간보다 나무를 더 잘 만드시는 것 같나이다.

1. 늙은 염꾼과 독신자들의 대사는 많은 부분 그리스 비극 『아가멤논』에 등장하는 여러 인물의 대사를 차용 혹은 변형한 것이다.

2. 개와 돼지가 남자를 따라다니며 땅과 물과 다른 생명체들에 해를 끼치지 않았다고 주장하는 부분은 이집트 『사자의 서』 중에서 흔히 '부정형 고백' 혹은 '무죄선언'으로 불리는 대목에서 영감을 받았다. 이 대목에서 죽은 사람의 영혼은 신들 앞에서 세상에 사는 동안 짓지 말아야 할 죄목들을 하나하나 부정하며 무죄를 주장한다.

3. 극 중의 장례 의식은 여자들만 상여를 멜 수 있는 한반도 남쪽의 작은 섬 연도의 장례식을 모델로 했고, 화자들이 다른 사람을 호명하는 방식은 세상을 떠나는 것에 대한 두려움을 완화해주기 위해 승려나 지인들이 죽은 사람 혹은 죽어가는 사람 옆에서 읽어주는 티베트의 경전 『바르도 퇴돌』의 한국어 번역본을 참고했다. 그리고 극 중의 인물들이 부르는 노래의 가사는 한국의 다양한 상여 노래를 중심으로 성경, 코란, 숫타니파타, 바가바드기타 등에 나오는 문구들을 극의 흐름에 맞게 변형한 것이다.

Synthetic Loopholes

Alice Bucknell

앨리스 버크넬

합성 틈새

Synthetic Loopholes

Alice Bucknell

The game is conceived as a challenge of four parts, with its final level conjuring a breakdown of language through a multispecies AI.

A rock, a river, a building, a score. The Game, when it was still referred to as one, started out simply enough. It was a means of killing time in the third global pandemic in under a decade, when lockdown cycles seemed to merge into one infinitely long stretch of time spent indoors. This was time spent largely alone, loitering inside one's own personal biosphere: a climate-conditioned safe house removed from all the chaos Out There—raging wildfires, unsurvivable ozone levels, multispecies extinction. A bubble inside which to project the world's reinvention. A time spent dreaming up alternatives.

In hindsight, I realized the Game's instant success could be chalked up to the proximity it had to other tools and technological processes that became household staples in earlier pandemics. Ranging in complexity, these spanned from daily digital puzzles, language games, and text-to-image generators to virtual social spaces, AR filters, and motion capture devices for broadcasting one's physical activity. But above all, the Game bore the closest affinity to the wildly popular "Digital Earth" mindfulness apps, originally billed as self-guided psychodynamic therapy exercises. As satellite-based nature livestreams keyed on yet undamaged parts of the planet, they were designed to assist their cooped-up subscribers better process complex bouts of climate grief during extended periods of lockdown.

Many of the patients I interviewed when researching for the Game spoke of a kind of mind-body disassociation that arose from the sensory withdrawal of Inside Space. One woman emphasized a deep depression caused by the inability to feel the sun on her face in early spring, the crunch of leaves underfoot come autumn, and the cool whip of winter wind biting exposed skin. The body sought out what it could no longer sense, but the brain couldn't stomach that absence. It was as if the reduction of the senses also shut down the sense of self, negating one's existence in the world.

In designing the Game, I was asked to replicate some of these scenarios—with the unspoken subscript being to bring some of these feelings back to life. The commissioning body had read up on the basics of game mechanics; they understood the value of conflict and cooperation, a compelling theme and storyline, and the importance of aesthetics and rewards. In a sense, the look and feel of the Game wouldn't appear out of place in a line-up of popular Extended Play (EP) titles also released that year—virtual worlds made accessible through expensive multisensory body suits. But with the Game's intended social impact, the brief—and the world it represented—got a lot more complicated.

A recent social psychology paper receiving a great deal of attention at the time championed the idea of "synthetic sensing"—or the process of inducing real feelings through artificial environments. It didn't matter if the ecological context that stimulated these emotional states was completely fabricated, built inside a game engine and uploaded to the Game's cloud. In fact, this simulation was preferable; it was better to have little to no reminder of the state of the world Out There. But the pleasant feeling that overtakes the body while observing an 8K palm tree model wafting in gentle southern Californian golden hour light, or the sublime pin-prick feeling triggered by witnessing a pod of simulated whales erupting from a foggy, pixelated rendering of the Pacific Ocean—those emotions are completely genuine. What could these rich emotional states achieve beyond the context of their synthetic environments?

I was instructed to build a world that was oriented around the idea of a shared future. A remarkably outmoded social politics in this day and age, it felt equivalent to referencing the "common land" concept in medieval Europe. But by feeling more together, the Game's commissioners believed, a shared consensus mechanism, absent from the world in recent living memory, would soon follow. They thought that this abundance of feeling in gamespace could trigger what they called a synthetic loophole: a portal into a world of shared affect that had long since been abandoned in the world Out There. I was curious about this idea. I was also out of a job since the latest pandemic began, and had no counter-theory of my own. So I set to work.

History remembers the future; the future is always reinventing the past.

I started working on the Game the year that the world's population was supposed to climax. Despite the long-settled permacrisis, a state which had been forecasted by climate scientists and economists in the early 2020s, we had managed to clear that figure well ahead of schedule. But it seemed like the more humans that populated our planet, the less invested in its future they became. Perhaps this shouldn't come as a surprise, seeing as the burden of imagining the world differently was continually reassigned to the newest arrivals. As the more damning impacts of the climate crisis stretched out to a global omnipresence, people grew further apart, not closer together. Could it be any different in the artificial sensing space of the Game?

Set in a rendered landscape modeled on early computer desktop backgrounds, the Rock level integrates a full moon ritual with the coordination of player's decisions.

I designed the Rock level first. It was the perfect beginner experience—minimum user effort with maximum reward. Intended to coax even the least likely player into the magic circle of the Game and seed the desire to complete all four levels, the Rock level begins in a picturesque open field: verdant, grassy, green. It's a place that feels intimately familiar, yet nobody alive on Earth has ever experienced it firsthand. For design inspiration, I scraped the depths of the commissioner's digital media archives, uncovering a boon of naturalistic desktop backgrounds from computer operating systems dating back to the 1990s. Flattened, ambient, and hyperreal, I wanted to conjure the sense of a space that was forever just out of reach.

The player enters this world just as the sun sets. The first few pinpricks of stars flicker high up in the sky; bleeding backwards from orange, to grey, to midnight blue, it's hugged tight by the mountains and their thick underbelly of fog. A breeze kicks up in the mountains, rustling its way through the tall grass. If the player purchased the latest model of the Extended Play bodysuit, they will feel this motion as a pleasurable tingle, beginning at the top of their skull and fanning out through the base of their spine. A warm-up synthetic feeler.

Like the rest of the Game, the Rock level requires basic strategy, with an emphasis on the social dynamics of a shared goal. Players must cooperate as they fan out through the tall grass in search of special rocks—gnarled, glittering black chunks of compacted silicon. They don't know what they're supposed to be looking for; the task's instructions are kept intentionally vague, in order to heighten the players' emotional engagement within the Game. By copying the actions of other players or intuitively feeling out the situation, players will end up grabbing one of the silicon rocks and bringing it back to where they began—a shared clearing with concentric circles scrawled deep into the damp dirt. Ten rocks are placed inside ten rings. Then, they wait.

During the wait, Game time will accelerate; it's not unusual for ten days to pass in under an hour. When the full moon rises over the mountains on the horizon, the rocks will begin to hum. What begins as a faint tune eventually ramps up into a full-blown song that echoes across the field of scattered silicon. The player's view pans upwards and out toward the sky. Around them, the trampled grass—a living memory of their shared motions in search of the stones—gradually takes the shape of a crop circle. The pattern slowly loads into view through an upward-tracking camera, rigged to infinity. It hovers above them, propellers lightly buzzing, reminiscent of a hummingbird. Close your eyes. Can you see it?

> Long ago the river used to flood this place. Every five or six years, choked with rainwater barreling down from the mountains, it would break its banks, sweeping all traces of human civilization out to the sea. But the river was not flooding; it was returning. Against the linear march

The River level involves a synthetic Jump from a human to a nonhuman body, measured in multispecies memory and the aberrant flows of water.

of human progress, water is a shape-shifter; it remembers everything.

The River level is more complex. It requires what I call a synthetic Jump: a move from the player's physical body in the world into the simulated body of the river. This process is challenging, and can only happen organically through the player's own tactics; in the Game, there are no cheat codes.

To successfully complete the Jump, the player must undergo two state changes. The first—from physical body to virtual body—is second nature; we've all been doing it for years. The second is much harder: the player Jumps from the body of a human to that of a nonhuman, the River. To do this, they must understand that their character and the River are not two separate entities, but rather that they are the same body. When the Jump is completed, there's no obvious shift in the game mechanics or environment; it's the same old River. But the player will feel the change through their Extended Play suit: decentralized, it ripples through this shared body, unearthing new sensations at each watery mouth, elbow, and foot.

This ecosystemic body is more than the senses; it is an unraveling current of feeling. Its alluvial flows mark the rungs of nonlinear time we think of as experience. Like tracing one's fingers absentmindedly across the rings of a fallen tree, it is deep time rendered tactile in death. As you breathe in and out, life flows through the circuit board of your nervous system, replenishing the swimming pool of cells that unities your body with the ecological body of the Earth. The water returns, and the body remembers.

> Across the state changes of a weirded climate, people talk about revolutions as if the only thing to do with the past is to break up with it. A hard severance. This is, of course, impossible—and no less so in the simulated environment of the Game as in the world Out There. The trick is reorienting the map. Making people see differently what's already there.

Early on in my work as a game designer, well before building the Game, I learned about the importance of failure. Not in the sense of making a bad game that nobody played, but how failure functions in the game world; what other worlds it opens up. Historically, there were endless arcade games like Tetris or PacMan in which you can't win, so you just learn to lose more slowly. The inverse, of course, are classic RPGs, where even after all the quests have been completed and all the badges have been earned, you're left to roam that open-world environment which has shrunken from kingdom to container throughout the duration of gameplay. No closure, no satisfaction; a space where winning gradually starts to feel like its own special kind of losing.

As CPUs and graphics cards grew more advanced, glitches opened up another caveat that was failure-adjacent. I mean the edge-of-world gamespace you'd occasionally tumble into by accident—falling forever until you switched off the overheating console. What would a game that came to terms with its own failure look like? Would the gameplay experience feel like how a Borges story reads? An infinite library, where the universe is contained within the volume of a book; a perfectly impossible system that comes to life through the act of reading it?

By deconstructing a building in the third level,
players collaboratively uncover the productive potentials of failure and degrowth.

The Building level opens onto the edge of a lake. The sky is bruise purple, the landscape is ash red; a gigantic hollow sun, rendered in iridescent blue scales, rests half-sunken on the horizon, outlining the silhouette of a magnificent tower. And it's almost complete! You, the player, realize that it's up to you to top it out. But, there's a problem. Every other player in the game is told the opposite: the foundations are all wrong, the structure lacks integrity, the style is already outdated. It must be demolished and started anew.

When you place a brick, a dialog box pops up, informing you that a different brick in the structure has mysteriously disappeared. Every time you place another brick, twice as many bricks as the previous amount are instantly dislodged. 2, 4, 8, 16, 32, 64, 128... soon, the building starts to look like an ancient ruin, its Swiss cheese facade accumulating a steady permutation of losses. In the low score charts, your name flickers in bold lights before your eyes.

In game theory, outcomes are considered to be in Nash equilibrium when knowledge of the other players' strategies would not lead any player to change their own strategy. *You place a brick, and lose again.* But the mirror between gaming and reality can sometimes cloud over, becoming a vast, inscrutable void. *You remove a brick, and the two surrounding it instantly disappear. Peering through the hollow structure, you catch a shadow of movement on the other side*. In the real world, outside of gamespace's unique rule book, sociological studies show time and again that cooperation is commonly chosen in groups—even when the betrayal of others could lead to a better individual reward. *The hindering of progress suddenly feels like an open door, an invitation.* It's human nature to act together; it just takes the synthetic environment of a game world to act as a reminder. *You pull more bricks, and the faces of the other players begin to emerge.* The building shudders, distorted, and the tower and level go down—together.

The fourth level of the Game focuses on the creation of shared songs between players and nonhuman life on Earth.

Seen through the eyes of a machine trained on Anthropocentric belief systems, any vision of the future is a frankensteined regurgitation of the past. The world that players thought they were waking up to was a world that had already existed. Far from auguring any sense of prophetic culture, our technological advances lodged us in a recurring feedback loop. How can the cycle be broken? By getting away from our human-centric mythology and entering into an Earth-centric one.

When I made the Game, I wanted to get away from the totalizing authority of language. As I strapped myself into an EP suit to play a prototype of its first three levels, I realized the answer lied within the synthetic sensing brief. By shedding language and its neurotic impulse to make meaning, players could tap into a deeper understanding of the self and planet—somewhere beyond the Cartesian split of body-mind and the Anthropocentric divide of human and nonhuman. To my surprise, as I worked towards the completion of the Game, these two goals—my own and its commissioner's—became increasingly intertwined. Sound seemed like most collective sense, and music the most intentional form of listening. So it was obvious that the Game's final level should involve the collaborative creation of a score. Within the synthetic environment of the Game, this score could foster not just a deeper connection among players, but become a bridge between human and nonhuman worlds.

One day, a drought sees the mountains go up in flames; the next, a flood wipes out the last chunk of the old town. How to make sense of a world that makes a mockery of historical precedents and a *posteriori* knowledge systems? It was clear we needed new models. Out There, ecologists pioneered an AI-based data visualization approach known as State-Space Modelling (SSM) to map the increasingly aberrant trajectories of a weird new climate. As a type of model that yields to measurement errors across ecological time as it grapples with the messiness of live data, SSMs felt like an important metaphor for better understanding the conditions of the world we live in now, something that stretches beyond the paralyzing doomer mentality of climate forecasting.

In the stale recycled air of my own biosphere, I'd spend countless hours scrolling through online SSM collections, finding an odd sense of satisfaction in their wild, frenzied lines. The superimposition of sea lion migration patterns on the Pacific Coast on top of Colorado River water levels from the last two centuries; the movements of the two remaining Mountain Gorillas across high-altitude forests in Uganda transposed onto the growing surface area of synthetic banana plantations cropping up around the country's western plains; an Arctic Tern's flight pattern mapped onto the development of 3D-printed bamboo infrastructure in Hong Kong. There was a mysticism to this data interpolation, a suggestive interconnection that humans couldn't yet decipher. To me, they hinted at a kind of *lingua ignota*, an unknown language that stretched beyond the proxies of human imagination itself.

As a nerdy tribute to these beautiful, impenetrable diagrams and their hidden logic systems, I decided I'd run some of them through a sonification script to turn this ecological data into music, engineering my own multi-dimensional state-space model in the process. Players would, of course, be free to improvise in collaboratively creating their scores, but the musical backbone guiding the Game's final level would come from the Earth itself. Real time data, energy, and movement of the planet's nonhuman life were recorded from the world Out There, then communally synthesized into song.

Unlike music, humans once wielded language exclusively; they used the technology as a cognitive infrastructure, modeling the world around them and reinforcing their primacy over other lifeforms as they went. But through the rapid advances of AI-powered natural language processing models, language became sculpted more by machines than their human counterparts. Eventually, language

The Game's AI-powered engine enables players to create unique musical scores from live ecological data and sounds encoded from the world Out There.

became dislodged from the question of consciousness. The narrative of human exceptionalism that it towed around became a moot point; language was as synthetic as the artificial intelligence built to model it.

During this time, humans turned increasingly toward non-linguistic tools of communication, like music, gesture, and movement. They solicited the senses to reanimate what language closed down a hundred thousand years ago: altered states that transcend the vague approximations clawed at by words. In this era, the wordless transfer of complex emotional states and dreams through real-time gameplay became second nature. By listening to these climate songs composed by an interspecies AI, people became better communicators with the second body of the Earth. A shared ecological intelligence, co-authored by human, nonhuman, and machine, gave way to a new mythology for the planet.

Through the synthetic sensing environment of the Game, the breakdown of language leads to the collaborative creation of a new shared world.

Thanks to the multispecies musical apparatus of its fourth level, the Game really took off. A powerful feedback loop emerged between the songs generated in the Game and the score of nonhuman life on Earth; the interspecies modeling of gameplay slowly diffused into reality. Out There, nobody was sure who was doing the mapping and the modeling anymore—human or other—and it wasn't long before those distinctions started to break down, too. As the world Out There and the world of the Game morphed into mirror images of each other, the climactic conditions that separated human and nonhuman worlds lessened in their extremity. People began stepping out of their biospheres: tentatively at first, their exposure to the world limited by their EP suits, and then uninhibited, discovering a ready wayfinder in the sensory communication with rocks, rivers, wind patterns, and other ecological agents that they had built up in gameplay. The synthetic feedback loop of the Game gradually cultivated a new way of being and sensing with the world; Inside Space and Out There became one.

Shifting baseline syndrome describes a gradual change in how a system is evaluated, usually cross-checked against previous reference points. However, this slow gradation of change often registers as a non-event; short-term memory occludes the large-scale shifts made visible across deep time. A river, seemingly on course for survival, dries up over the years. A building, continuously redesigned to withstand a future threat, is never completed. A World, reduced to a word, gradually adopts processes of alternative meaning-making in order to transcend itself, language.

By tapping into the sound of the world, the Game's players unlocked an ecological consciousness that could be likened to deep time. The cause-and-effect model of recent history became obviously aberrant, something that an ecosystemic awareness could course correct towards a mutually survivable future. The artificial sensing space of the Game created a synthetic loophole between players and nonhumans, between a virtual environment and the Earth, auguring a new mythology in the process. I'd like to think of it as an answer, but in reality, this loophole opened up still more questions: meaning-making is always a two-way street, a dance between storytellers and their audiences, like movements in an improvised score. To what new shared worlds does this song lead? It's impossible to say, but easy to listen.

합성 틈새

앨리스 버크넬

The game is conceived as a challenge of four parts,
with its final level conjuring a breakdown of language through a multispecies AI.

암석, 강, 건물, 음악. 「더 게임」은 처음에 그저 그런 게임들 중 하나였다. 십 년이 안 되는 사이에 세 번째로 세계적 팬데믹이 닥쳤을 때, 이 게임은 시간 때우기에 좋은 수단이었다. 여러 번의 봉쇄가 이어지며 실내에서 지내는 시간이 결코 끝나지 않을 것만 같던 시절이었다. 맹렬한 산불, 생존 불가능한 오존 농도, 여러 생물종의 멸종 등 '저 바깥(Out There)'에서 벌어지는 온갖 혼돈에서 동떨어진 채 개인용 바이오스피어, 즉 기후가 조절되는 나만의 안전 가옥에서 대부분의 시간을 혼자 보냈다. 세계의 재발명을 투사하는 버블이었고, 대안을 꿈꾸는 시간이었다.

돌이켜보니, 「더 게임」은 이미 몇 차례의 팬데믹을 거치며 가정의 필수가 된 다른 도구 및 기술 프로세스들과 유사하기 때문에 즉각적인 성공을 거둘 수 있었던 것 같다. 이들 도구는 복잡성 면에서 수준이 다양해서, 디지털 퍼즐, 언어 게임, 텍스트-이미지 변환기에서부터 가상 소셜 공간, AR 필터, 사람의 신체 활동을 방송하는 모션 캡처 기기에까지 이르렀다. 하지만 그중에서도 「더 게임」은 대단한 인기를 누린 '디지털 지구' 류의 마음챙김 앱들과 가장 비슷했는데, 본래 자기안내식 심리역동 치료 훈련용이라고 홍보되던 것들이다. 이런 앱은 아직 파괴되지 않은 자연의 풍경을 포착하는 위성 기반의 실시간 방송으로, 갇혀 지내던 구독자들이 길어지는 봉쇄 기간에 한바탕씩 찾아오던 복합적인 기후 우울을 잘 다룰 수 있게 도와주도록 설계되었다.

「더 게임」의 사전 조사 차 인터뷰한 환자들 다수가 '내면 공간(Inner Space)'의 감각 위축으로 빚어진 일종의 심신 해리를 이야기했다. 어떤 여성은 초봄이면 얼굴에 내리쬐던 햇빛, 가을에 발밑에서 바스락대던 낙엽, 살을 에는 듯한 차가운 겨울바람을 더 이상 느낄 수 없다는 데에서 깊은 우울감을 느낀다고 강조했다. 신체는 더 이상 감각할 수 없는 것을 소구했지만, 뇌는 그런 부재를 감당해내지 못했다. 마치 감각의 축소가 자아 감각마저 차단하여, 내가 이 세계 안에 있다는 존재감을 부정하는 듯했다.

「더 게임」을 디자인하면서 나는 의뢰인으로부터 위와 같은 상황들을 재현해달라는 요청을 받았는데, 잃어버린 그런 느낌들을 되살려달라는 무언의 요구가 덧붙어 있었다. 의뢰인 측은 게임 메카닉스의 기초를 공부해두었기에 갈등과 협동의 가치, 설득력 있는 주제와 줄거리, 미학과 보상의 중요성 같은 문제를 이해하고 있었다. 어떤 의미에서 「더 게임」의 외양과 느낌은 같은 해 발매된 익스텐디드플레이(EP)용 인기 게임들—값비싼 다중감각 전신 슈트를 통해 접속할 수 있는 가상 세계—과 나란히 두어도 어색하지 않았을 것이다. 하지만 「더 게임」이 도모한 사회적 영향으로 인해 게임의 개요—그리고 게임이 재현하는 세계—는 더욱 복잡해졌다.

당시 큰 주목을 받았던 한 사회심리학 논문은 인공 환경을 통해 실제 감정을 유도하는 과정을 뜻하는 '합성 감지(synthetic sensing)' 개념을 지지했다. 이런 감정 상태를 자극하는 생태적 맥락이 완전한 가공의 산물로 게임 엔진 안에 구축되어 「더 게임」의 클라우드에 업로드된 것인지 여부는 중요하지 않았다. 사실 이런 식의 시뮬레이션이 더 바람직해서, '저 바깥' 세계의 상태를 연상시키는 것은 거의 넣지 않는 편이 나았다. 하지만 남부 캘리포니아의 부드러운 황금빛 햇살 속에 가볍게 흔들리는 8K 고해상도 야자나무 모델을 바라볼 때 기분 좋게 몸을 감싸오는 느낌이라던가, 안개 자욱한 태평양의 픽셀 렌더링에서 튀어나온 고래 무리의 시뮬레이션을 목격할 때 미세하게 느껴지는 숭고함은 완전히 진실된 감정이다. 이런 풍부한 감정 상태는 합성 환경이라는 맥락을 넘어 무엇을 성취할 수 있을까?

나는 공유된 미래라는 개념을 지향하는 세계를 구축하라는 지시를 받았다. 이제는 상당히 철 지난 사회정치 용어라, 중세 유럽의 '공유지' 개념이나 다름없이 느껴졌다. 하지만 의뢰인들은 더 많은 것을 함께 느끼면 근래 사람들의 기억에서 사라져버린 공동의 합의 메커니즘이 곧 뒤따를 것이라 생각했다. 그들은 게임 공간 속 감정의 풍요로움으로 일명 합성 틈새(synthetic loopholes), 즉 '저 바깥' 세계에서는 버려진 지 오래인 공유된 정동의 세계를 향한 관문을 열 수 있을 것이라 했다. 나는 이런 발상에 호기심이 동했다. 최근의 팬데믹으로 일자리도 잃은 데다, 특별한 이견이 있는 것도 아니었다. 그래서 작업에 착수했다.

역사는 미래를 기억하고, 미래는 늘 과거를 재발명하고 있다.

「더 게임」 작업을 시작한 것은 세계 인구가 정점에 달할 것이라던 해였다. 기후과학자들과 경제학자들이 2020년대 초에 예견했던 영속적 위기 상태가 오랜 기간 지속되어 왔음에도, 우리는 예측보다 일찍 그 정점에 도달했었다. 하지만 지구에 사는 인구가 늘어날수록, 지구의 미래에 대한 투자는 줄어드는 듯했다. 대안적 세계를 생각해 내는 일을 계속해서 다음 세대에게 미루어 왔던 것을 보면 그리 놀라운 이야기는 아닐 것이다. 더욱 파멸적인 기후위기의 여파가 세계 곳곳으로 확산될수록, 사람들은 서로 더 가까워지기보다 더욱 멀어지게 되었다. 「더 게임」의 인공 감지 공간에서라고 다를 것이 있었을까?

나는 우선 '암석' 단계를 디자인했다. 최소한의 노력으로 최대의 보상을 받을 수 있는, 완벽한 초심자용 경험이었다. 가장 의욕 없는 플레이어까지도 「더 게임」의 매직 서클로 끌어들여 네 단계를 모두 완료하고 싶게끔 유도하는 이 단계는 푸른 풀에 덮인 초록빛의 탁 트인 그림 같은 들판에서 시작된다. 그곳은 내적 친밀감이 느껴지지만, 지구상에 살아 있는 어느 누구도 직접 경험한 적이 없는 장소이다. 디자인의 영감을 찾기 위해 나는 의뢰인의 디지털 미디어 아카이브를 샅샅이 뒤졌고, 1990년대의 컴퓨터 운영체제에서 자연이 담긴 요긴한 배경화면들을 발견했다. 평평하고 잔잔하며 초현실적인, 나는 그렇게 영영 손에 닿지 않을 어떤 공간의 느낌을 불러내고 싶었다.

Set in a rendered landscape modeled on early computer desktop backgrounds, the Rock level integrates a full moon ritual with the coordination of player's decisions.

플레이어는 해 질 무렵 이 세계에 입장한다. 하늘 높이 샛별 몇 개가 반짝인다. 주황색에서 회색으로 또 검푸른색으로 물들어가는 하늘을 산허리의 안개와 산등성이가 단단히 껴안고 있다. 산에서 불어오는 바람이 키 높은 풀 사이를 바스락대며 지난다. 최신 EP 전신 슈트를 구입한 플레이어에게는 이런 움직임이 머리 꼭대기부터 등 아래로 퍼져가는 기분 좋은 찌릿함으로 느껴질 것이다. 합성 감각의 시동을 건다.

게임의 나머지 부분과 마찬가지로 '암석' 단계에도 기본 전략이 필요하다. 공공의 목표를 둘러싼 사회적 역학에 중점을 두는 전략이다. 플레이어들은 키 큰 풀숲에 흩어져 특별한 암석—울퉁불퉁하고 반짝이는 단단한 검은색 규소 덩어리—을 찾는 일에 힘을 모아야 한다. 그들은 무엇을 찾아야 하는지 모른다. 임무에 관한 내용은 모호하게 남겨진다. 이는 플레이어들의 감정적 참여도를 높이기 위한 의도적 설정이다. 다른 플레이어의 행동을 따라 하거나 직관적으로 상황을 파악해가며 플레이어들은 규소 덩어리 하나를 찾아들고 출발점으로 돌아온다. 축축한 흙 위로 동심원들이 깊게 그려진 공유 공터로 말이다. 10개의 암석이 10개의 원에 놓인다. 그런 다음, 기다린다.

기다리는 동안 「더 게임」의 시간은 점점 빠르게 흘러간다. 10일이 1시간 안에 흘러가는 일도 드물지 않다. 보름달이 지평선의 산 위로 떠오르면 암석들이 웅웅대기 시작한다. 처음에는 희미한 선율이었던 것이 커지며 본격적인 노래가 되어 규소 덩어리가 흩어진 들판에 메아리친다. 플레이어의 시점은 위로 당겨지며 하늘을 향한다. 그들의 주변으로 밟힌 풀—플레이어들이 돌을 찾아 함께 움직였음을 드러내는 살아 있는 기억—의 모양새가 점차 크롭 서클의 형태를 취한다. 무한대로 맞춰진 상향 트래킹 카메라가 천천히 그 패턴을 시야에 담는다. 벌새를 연상시키며 가볍게 프로펠러를 윙윙대는 카메라가 그들 위를 선회한다. 눈을 감아보라. 보이는가?

The River level involves a synthetic Jump from a human to a nonhuman body, measured in multispecies memory and the aberrant flows of water.

오래전 이곳엔 강이 범람하곤 했다. 5~6년마다 강은 산에서 쏟아지는 빗물로 가득 차 둑을 무너뜨리며 인류 문명의 모든 흔적을 바다로 쓸어내 버렸다. 하지만 강은 범람하던 것이 아니라 귀환하고 있었다. 일직선으로 행진하는 인간의 진보와는 대조적으로, 물은 형태변형자이며 모든 것을 기억한다.

‘강’ 단계는 좀 더 복잡하다. 이 단계를 위해선 내가 합성 ‘점프(Jump)’라 부르는 것, 즉 현실의 육신으로부터 강물의 가상 신체로의 이동을 해야한다 이 과정은 만만치 않은 데다, 오직 플레이어 본인이 요령껏 해야만 한다. 「더 게임」에 치트 코드란 없다.

성공적으로 ‘점프’를 마치려면 플레이어는 두 가지 상태 변화를 거쳐야 한다. 첫 번째는 물리적 신체에서 가상의 몸으로 이동하는 것으로, 우리 모두가 수년간 해온 일이라 이제는 너무 자연스러운 것이다. 두 번째는 훨씬 어렵다. 플레이어는 인간의 몸에서 비인간인 강의 몸으로 ‘점프’한다. 그러려면 플레이어는 자신의 캐릭터와 강이 두 개의 개체로 분리된 것이 아니라 같은 몸이라는 사실을 이해해야만 한다. ‘점프’가 완료될 때 게임의 메카닉스나 환경에 뚜렷한 변화는 없다. 그저 똑같은 ‘강’일 뿐이다. 하지만 플레이어는 EP 슈트를 통해 변화를 느끼게 될 것이다. 변화는 분산되며 잔물결처럼 공유된 몸을 타고 번져, 물로 이뤄진 입과 팔꿈치와 발에서 각각 새로운 감각을 찾아낸다.

이 생태계적 몸은 감각 이상의 것으로, 풀려나 흐르는 감정이다. 퇴적하며 흐르는 그것은 우리가 경험이라 생각하는 비선형적 시간의 층들을 표시한다. 쓰러진 나무를 무심코 어루만지는 손가락에 닿는 나이테처럼, 그것은 죽음 속에서 촉각적으로 형상화된 지질학적 시간이다. 숨을 들이쉬고 내쉬는 동안 생명은 신경계의 회로판을 통해 흐르며, 나의 몸과 지구의 생태적 몸을 하나로 만드는 세포들의 웅덩이를 채운다. 물은 돌아오고, 몸은 기억한다.

> 이상한 기후로 인한 상태 변화를 겪는 곳곳에서 사람들은 마치 과거로 할 수 있는 유일한 일이 과거와의 단절인 것처럼 혁명에 대해 이야기한다. 힘든 단절이다. 이는 물론 불가능하다. ‘저 바깥’ 세계에서만큼이나 「더 게임」의 시뮬레이션 환경에서도 불가능하다. 비결은 지도의 방향을 바꾸어 보는 데 있다. 사람들로 하여금 이미 있는 것을 달리 보게 하는 것이다.

나는 「더 게임」을 만들기 훨씬 전, 게임 디자이너 초창기 시절에 실패의 중요성을 배웠다. 아무도 거들떠보지 않을 형편 없는 게임을 만든다는 뜻에서가 아니라, 게임 세계에서 실패가 어떤 식으로 기능하는지, 그것이 어떤 다른 세계를 열어주는지에 관해서 말이다. 역사적으로 「테트리스」나 「팩맨」처럼 이기는 것이 불가능해서 그저 더 천천히 지는 법을 배우는 류의 아케이드 게임이 수도 없이 많았다. 그 반대는 물론 고전 RPG이다. 여기에서는 모든 퀘스트를 완료하고 배지를 다 얻은 후에도, 게임이 진행되는 동안 왕국에서 그릇 수준으로 축소되어 버린 오픈월드 환경에 남겨져 떠돌게 된다. 종결도 없고 만족도 없으니, 승리가 점차 특별한 종류의 패배로 느껴지기 시작하는 공간이다.

CPU와 그래픽카드가 점점 발전함에 따라, 버그들은 실패에 가까운 또 다른 위기들을 드러내었다. 그러니까 가끔씩 맞닥뜨리게 되는 세상의 끝과도 같은 게임 공간으로, 한 번 빠지면 콘솔 기기의 전원이 꺼질 때까지 멈추지 않고 추락하게 되는 그런 공간 말이다. 자신의 실패를 받아들인 게임이란 어떤 모습일까? 게임을 하는 것이 보르헤스의 이야기를 읽는 것처럼 느껴질까? 우주가 한 권의 책 속에 담겨 있는 무한한 도서관처럼, 읽힘으로써만 세상에 존재하게 되는 완벽하게 불가능한 시스템처럼 느껴질까?

By deconstructing a building in the third level,
players collaboratively uncover the productive potentials of failure and degrowth.

호수의 끝자락에서 '건물' 단계가 시작된다. 하늘은 멍든 듯한 보라색이고, 주변 풍경은 잿빛이 도는 붉은색이다. 보는 각도에 따라 계조를 달리하는 푸른색의 거대한 텅 빈 태양이 지평선에 반쯤 가라앉아 웅장한 탑의 실루엣을 드러낸다. 탑은 거의 완성되었다! 플레이어는 완공이 자신에게 달려 있음을 깨닫는다. 하지만 문제가 하나 있다. 게임에 참여한 다른 플레이어들은 모두 정반대로 알고 있다. 건물 기초는 모조리 잘못됐고, 구조 안정성이 결여된 데다, 진작에 철 지난 양식이라고 말이다. 탑을 철거하고 새롭게 시작해야 한다.

벽돌을 하나 놓으면, 대화창이 열리며 신기하게도 건물의 다른 벽돌 하나가 사라졌다고 알린다. 벽돌을 하나씩 놓을 때마다 그 전보다 두 배 많은 벽돌이 이내 사라진다. 2, 4, 8, 16, 32, 64, 128... 얼마 지나지 않아 건물은 고대의 유적처럼 보이기 시작한다. 손실의 교환이 꾸준히 축적되어 스위스 치즈 같은 모습이 된다. 하단의 점수표에는 굵직한 빛으로 쓰인 이름이 깜빡인다.

게임 이론에서는 상대방의 전략을 아는 것이 플레이어들의 자기 전략 수정으로 이어지지 않을 때, 결과가 내시의 균형 상태에 있다고 간주한다. *벽돌을 하나 놓으면, 다시 잃고 만다.* 하지만 게임과 현실 사이의 거울은 때때로 어둡게 흐려져 알 수 없는 거대한 공허가 된다. *벽돌을 하나 빼면, 주변의 벽돌 두 개가 곧바로 사라진다. 비어버린 구조물을 통해 반대편의 움직임이 희미하게 보인다.* 게임공간 특유의 규칙에서 벗어난 바깥의 실제 세계에서는, 다른 사람을 배신하는 것이 더 큰 개인적 보상으로 이어질 때도 집단에서 협력을 선택하는 경우가 많다는 사실이 사회학 연구를 통해 거듭 밝혀졌다. *진전을 방해하는 행위가 갑자기 열린 문으로의 초대처럼 느껴진다.* 함께 행동하는 것은 인간의 본성이다. 게임 세계의 합성 환경은 그저 이를 상기시킬 따름이다. *더 많은 벽돌을 허물면, 다른 플레이어들의 얼굴이 드러나기 시작한다.* 건물이 뒤틀리며 흔들리고, 탑과 함께 '건물' 단계가 무너져 내린다.

The fourth level of the Game focuses on the creation of shared songs between players and nonhuman life on Earth.

인류세 시대의 신념 체계를 학습한 기계의 눈으로 본다면, 미래에 대한 비전은 프랑케슈타인화된 과거의 역류일 뿐이다. 플레이어가 깨어났다고 생각한 세계는 이미 존재했던 세계였다. 기술의 발전은 예언적 문화의 전조를 보여주기는커녕, 우리를 반복되는 피드백 루프에 가두었다. 어떻게 해야 그 고리를 끊을 수 있을까? 인간 중심적 신화로부터 벗어나 지구 중심적 신화로 들어서면 된다.

「더 게임」을 만들면서, 나는 언어가 가진 총체화의 권위를 피하고 싶었다. 직접 EP 슈트를 입고 프로토타입의 첫 세 단계를 플레이하면서, 나는 그 해답이 합성 감지라는 개요에 있었음을 깨달았다. 언어 그리고 언어가 지닌 신경증적인 의미 생산의 충동을 떨쳐냄으로써, 플레이어는 데카르트적 신체와 정신의 분리, 또 인류세적 인간과 비인간의 분리를 넘어 자신과 지구에 대해 더 깊이 이해할 수 있다. 놀랍게도 「더 게임」의 완성에 가까워지면서 나의 목적과 의뢰인의 목적이 서로 점점 더 얽혀들었다. 소리는 가장 집단적인 감각이고, 음악은 가장 의식적인 듣기의 형식처럼 보였다. 그렇기에 공동의 음악 창작이 「더 게임」의 마지막 단계에 분명 포함되어야 했다. 「더 게임」의 합성 환경에서 그 음악은 플레이어 간의 심층적인 연결을 촉진할 뿐 아니라 인간 세계와 비인간 세계를 잇는 가교가 될 수 있다.

어느 날 가뭄으로 산이 화염에 휩싸이고, 다음에는 홍수가 일어나 남아 있던 옛 마을의 마지막 부분마저 쓸려나간다. 역사적 선례와 *후험적* 지식 체계를 조롱하는 세계는 어떻게 이해해야 할까? 우리에게는 분명 새로운 모델이 필요했다. '저 바깥'에서 생태학자들은 점점 비정상적인 궤적을 보이는 이상한 새 기후를 매핑하기 위해 상태-공간 모델링(SSM: State-Space Modelling)이라는 이름의 AI 기반 데이터 시각화 접근법을 개척했다. SSM은 실시간 데이터의 복잡성과 상호작용하며 생태적 시간에 편재하는 측정 오류를 수용하는 모델 유형으로서, 무기력한 패배주의적 기후 예측의 사고방식을 넘어서 현재 우리가 살고있는 세계의 상황을 더 잘 이해하기 위한 중요한 비유로 느껴졌다.

개인용 바이오스피어 속에서 재활용되는 탁한 공기를 마시며, 나는 온라인 SSM 결과들을 검색하는 데 긴긴 시간을 보냈고, 그 분방하고 정신없는 선들에서 묘한 만족감을 찾았다. 태평양 연안의 바다사자 이주 패턴을 지난 2세기간의 콜로라도강 수위 변화와 겹쳐보고, 마지막 남은 두 마리의 마운틴고릴라가 우간다의 고지대 숲을 건너는 움직임을 우간다의 서부 평원 주변에서 확장해가는 인공 바나나 농장의 표면 위로 옮겨보고, 북극제비갈매기의 비행 패턴을 홍콩의 대나무 3D 프린팅 인프라 개발에 매핑해보는 식으로 말이다. 이런 데이터 삽입에는 인간이 아직 해독할 수 없는 암시적인 상호연관성이라는 신비로움이 있었다. 그것들은 내게 일종의 *링구아 이그노타(lingua ignota)*, 즉 인간의 상상 능력을 넘어 뻗어가는 미지의 언어를 시사했다.

이처럼 아름다우면서 불가해한 다이어그램들과 그들의 숨겨진 논리 체계에 바치는 괴짜 같은 헌정으로, 나는 그중 일부를 음향화 스크립트에 돌려 생태적 데이터를 음악으로 바꾸기로 마음먹었다. 이를 위해 직접 다차원 상태-공간 모형을 설계했다. 물론 플레이어들이 자유롭게 즉흥으로 함께 음악을 만들 수 있지만, 「더 게임」의 마지막 단계를 이끄는 음악적 근간은 지구

자체에서 나온다. 지구의 비인간 생명체가 만드는 실시간 데이터, 에너지, 움직임이 '저 바깥' 세계에서 기록되고, 이후 공동으로 합성되어 노래가 된다.

The Game's AI-powered engine enables players to create unique musical scores from live ecological data and sounds encoded from the world Out There.

음악과 다르게, 인간은 한 때 독점적으로 언어를 휘둘렀다. 인간은 주변 세상을 모델링하고 다른 생명체에 대한 우위를 강화하는 인지적 기반구조로 언어라는 기술을 이용했다. 하지만 AI 기반 자연어 처리 모형이 급속히 발전하면서, 인간보다 기계가 언어를 더 많이 조형하게 되었다. 결국 언어는 의식이라는 문제에서 분리되었다. 언어가 이끌던 인간 예외주의의 서사는 이제 더 이상 당연하지 않았고, 언어는 언어를 모델링하기 위해 구축한 인공지능만큼이나 합성적이었다.

이 시기 인간은 음악, 몸짓, 움직임 같은 비언어적인 소통의 도구로 점차 방향을 돌렸다. 그러한 도구로 인해 감각은 언어가 수십만 년 전 폐쇄해버렸던 것, 즉 언어가 건져 올린 모호한 근삿값들을 능가하는 변화된 상태들을 소생시켰다. 이 시대에는 복잡한 감정의 상태와 꿈을 실시간 게임 속에서 비언어적으로 전달하는 것이 제2의 본성이 되었다. 종을 초월한 AI가 작곡한 이 기후의 노래를 들으며, 인간은 지구의 두 번째 몸과 더 나은 소통을 하게 되었다. 인간, 비인간, 기계가 공동으로 창조한 생태 지능은 지구를 위한 새로운 신화로 이어졌다.

네 번째 단계에 등장하는 다종적 음악 장치 덕분에, 「더 게임」은 정말로 큰 성공을 거두었다. 「더 게임」 안에서 생성된 노래와 지구에 사는 비인간 생명체의 선율 사이에 강력한 피드백 루프가 생성되었고, 종의 경계를 초월한 게임플레이의 모델링이 천천히 현실로 확산하였다. '저 바깥'에서 누가 매핑을 하

Through the synthetic sensing environment of the Game, the breakdown of language leads to the collaborative creation of a new shared world.

고 모델링을 하고 있는지—인간인지 다른 존재인지—를 누구도 확신할 수 없었다. 그리고 얼마 지나지 않아 그러한 구분도 무너지기 시작했다. '저 바깥' 세상과 「더 게임」의 세계가 서로의 거울처럼 변형되면서, 인간 세계와 비인간 세계를 가르던 극단적 기후 조건들도 완화되었다. 사람들은 각자의 개인용 바이오스피어 바깥으로 걸음을 내딛기 시작했다. 처음에는 시험 삼아 EP 슈트를 입고 제한적으로 접촉하였고, 나중에는 돌, 강, 바람 및 다른 생태적 요소들과 게임 속에서 감각적으로 소통하며 준비한 길잡이를 따라 거리낌 없이 나아갔다. 「더 게임」의 합성 피드백 루프는 점차 세상과 함께 존재하고 함께 지각하는 새로운 방식을 일구었고, '내면 공간'과 '저 바깥'은 하나가 되었다.

기준선 이동 증후군은 어느 체계의 평가 방식에 있어 나타나는 점진적 변화를 설명하는 용어로, 보통 이전의 기준점과 대조하는 교차확인을 거친다. 그러나 이처럼 느릿한 변화는 종종 비사건으로 기입되며, 단기 기억은 지질학적 시간에 걸쳐 가시화되는 대규모의 변화를 보이지 않게 만든다. 살아남을 것 같던 강은 세월이 지나며 말라붙는다. 미래의 위협을 이겨내기 위해 계속해서 재설계되는 건물은 결코 완성되지 못한다. 하나의 단어로 축소된 '세계'는 언어인 저 자신을 초월하기 위해 점차 대안적인 의미생산의 과정을 채택한다.

「더 게임」의 플레이어들은 세계의 소리를 활용하여 지질학적 시간에 비견할 수 있는 생태적 의식을 열었다. 근래 역사의 인과 모형은 명백하게 비정상적인 것이 되었다. 그리고 그 비정상이란 생태적 인식을 통해 상호 생존의 미래로 나아가도록 바로잡을 수 있는 것이다. 「더 게임」의 인공 감지 공간은 플레이어와 비인간 그리고 가상 환경과 지구 사이에 합성 틈새를 만들어내며 새로운 신화의 전조를 보였다. 나는 이를 하나의 답으로 생각하고 싶지만, 현실에서 이 틈새는 더 많은 질문을 낳는다. 의미생산은 언제나 양방향 도로이고, 이야기를 하는 사람과 듣는 사람이 함께 추는 춤, 즉흥적 선율에 맞춰 주고받는 몸짓이다. 이 노래는 어떤 새로운 공동의 세계로 이끌어줄까? 말로 하긴 어렵지만, 듣는 것은 어렵지 않다.

Ecological Communities

Yunjeong Han

한윤정

생태계를 닮은 생태적 공동체들을 만들자

Ecological Communities

Yunjeong Han

Ecological Civilization

If there is any civilization remaining on earth in the year 2086, it will be an ecological civilization. An anti-ecological industrial civilization that exceeds the earth's capacity will likely still exist on a much smaller scale than today, but we will no longer call it "civilization." People in regions that fail to adapt to the rapidly changing conditions on earth or fail to build an ecological civilization will live lives like scenes from disaster movies, constantly pressed for survival.

Civilization is a paradigm found in human history, and refers to the foundations of cosmology and nature, the production and use of energy and matter, forms of power that enable governance and integration, and values, ethics, and educational systems that reproduce all of the above. However, there has never been a perfect civilization, and each and every civilization has embarked on a path of extinction, as the strengths on which each civilization was built eventually became weaknesses, leading to its decline. Modern material and mechanical thinking promoted science and technology and the development of productive forces, but also brought about a troubling situation in which industrial civilization stands in opposition to nature.

An ecological civilization is one that is built according to the principles of the ecosystem in which it is situated. According to Jeremy Lent, "insights into how ecologies self-organize offer a model for how we could organize human society in ways that could permit sustainable abundance. Organisms prosper when they develop multiple symbiotic relationships, wherein each party to a relationship both takes and gives reciprocally." Up until now, civilization has been thought as antagonistic to nature, and has meant conquering it to satisfying human needs. However, we now know that the highest form of civilization is one that is in harmony with nature.[1]

The "Gaia 2.0" declaration insists on changing the structure of society according to the three scientifically proven operating principles of Gaia.[2] 1) A materially closed earth ecosystem: instead of using fossil fuels, which are unsustainable inventions that block material circulation, we need to use solar energy and transition to a circular economy. 2) A microbial network that gives rise to the earth's biogeochemical cycles: for a successful circular economy, it is necessary to support a network of human actors capable of the horizontal transfer of information, rich functional diversity, and dispersed control. 3) The self-regulation of Gaia: as it is currently difficult to maintain equilibrium in a natural state, human self-awareness is important, and can be obtained through the establishment of sensory (scientific) institutions and infrastructures that shows the gap between reality and illusion in addition to the politics of transition.

While thinking about the global, we must reorganize the local. In the midst of pursuing a common idea of ecological civilization, numerous forms of ecological civilizations must be built to enable self-reliance and coexistence at the local level. The philosopher Alfred North Whitehead left us a lesson about the required civilizational transition. "[Humans] can persuade or be persuaded by the disclosure of alternatives, the better and the worse. Civilization is the maintenance of social order, by its own inherent persuasiveness as embodying the nobler alternative... Thus in a live civilization there is always an element of unrest. For sensitiveness to ideas means curiosity, adventure, change."[3] Civilization should refuse to decline by settling for the present. Instead, it should insist on continued development, anxiously but hopefully pursuing ideas that challenge systemic inertia. What we need now is an adventure towards ecological civilization.

Ecotopia Emerging

Ernest Callenbach's futuristic novel *Ecotopia* (1975) depicts the civilization that humankind must build in order to survive.[4] The northern part of California, Oregon, and Washington has become independent from the federal union of the United States and established as an independent "stable-state" called Ecotopia. Rumors abound about Ecotopia, which has closed its borders for an orderly transition. Twenty years after independence, Will Weston, a newspaper reporter from New York receives permission to cover it for the first time and makes a visit. Life in Ecotopia, which appears strange to the eyes of the average American, is an exemplary roadmap towards sustainability.

Energy comes from the sun and wind. Bicycles and public transportation such as trains have replaced cars. Residents worship trees and use them to build houses and most household items. No chemicals are used except for plastic that decomposes. With a completely circular economy, a stable state without waste is maintained. They have even transformed the concepts of wealth and work. Content with a frugal life, they do not overwork to earn unnecessary money. Enterprises are owned and operated by cooperatives. Living in diverse communities beyond the family, they advocate free love that is faithful to sexual desire. Political discussions using interactive cable television are frequent. All this may have initially appeared unrealistic, but today, fifty years after the book was first published, some aspects are becoming a reality in many parts of the world seeking transition.

Politics was key to building Ecotopia. The ecological transition required the rearrangement of the means of production, dismantling corporate giants dependent on fossil fuels and nuclear power, and reallocating government subsidies. It had to also break away from global trade and the global division of labor. Change was impossible within the established forms of politics, which was so deeply in collusion with interest groups. Separation, therefore, became the main driving force. Following separation from the Union, the Survivalist Party that built Ecotopia and their leader, the female president Vera Allwen, adopted a long-term isolation policy. This is reminiscent of the American Revolutionary War, which fought against British colonial rule, as well as the "Socialism in one country" policy adopted in the former Soviet Union.

However, unlike the former Soviet Union, which promoted rapid economic growth in the same way as capitalism to justify distribution, Ecotopia's values and means of production remained distinct from the outside world. The prequel to *Ecotopia, Ecotopia Emerging* (1981) depicts the situation at the time of independence.[5] Despite approaching ecological catastrophes such as rising energy prices, economic crises, and the advent of cancer caused by chemicals, resistance to change by the government and industry, who sought to protect their interests, remained strong. The Survivalist Party, which had been gaining power in the three progressive western states after an accident and leak at a nuclear power plant, pushes for secession from Washington DC through a referendum.

There are two key elements that contributed to the emergence of this new civilization. First was the development of a new energy source. Lou Swift, a young female scientist, broke through the obstruction of corporations and universities and their pursuit of a technological monopoly, and invented a solar cell that anyone can easily make. Today, in the real world, the unit cost of renewable energy is rapidly declining to the point that it can replace fossil fuels or nuclear power.[6] The second key element that brought about Ecotopia was the emergence of a political community and mobilization of people who support the sustainability revolution.[7] The Survivalist Party played this role in the novel, but major countries around the world today, including South Korea, are experiencing democratic crises. National representative democracy is unable to cope with climate and ecological crises. Thus, it has become the most important task of the twenty-first century to gather citizens who will create a wave of revolutionary change and transform politics.

A Community of Communities

Openness and cooperation is more important than separation and isolation because the world today is fatally interconnected. Ecological catastrophes that used to occur in certain regions have turned into a global climate crisis. The Chernobyl nuclear power plant accident in 1986 was caused by a mistake of power plant engineers and decimated people and nature within a 500-kilometer radius. However, the cataclysmic flood that struck Pakistan in 2022 was affected by climate change as a result of carbon dioxide emitted by developed countries and caused devastating destruction over an area of 75,000 square kilometers. Ecotopia in the age of climate crisis cannot be established by constructing liberated zones in isolated areas or exporting specific models to other areas after experimentation. The organizing principle of civilization itself must change to an ecological model, and the small community will become its building block.

Local economy activist Helena Norberg-Hodge has called the community an "ancient future". [8] If past communities were based on kinship, regionalism, and traditional culture, the community of the future is based on shared beliefs and mutual trust. A local community is ideal, but an electronic community that connects distant members would also work. In a reality where centrally controlled social movements do not work as in the past, communities are advantageous for bringing people together and keeping people engaged. According to Carlo Petrini, a community has two values.[9] First, community presents the need to transition from a competitive society to a cooperative society. Leaving behind the competitive discourse of professional success, personal achievement, and social recognition, it recognizes the value of everyone. Second, community becomes the ground on which "emotional intelligence" and "austere anarchy" are applied and practiced. This oxymoron points to the condition in which individual freedom and group order coexist.

By belonging to a community, individuals can live by enjoying relational goods that exist and circulate outside a monetary economy. Relational goods are transacted based on need, and can be enjoyed by all community members. They are common, and not owned by individuals. But they also cannot be monopolized, because they only exist within an active relationship and when participating in a community. They cannot be bought or sold, only cultivated and protected. In the same way that families often share necessary goods free of charge, extended communities share relational goods. To borrow the words of the former president of Uruguay José Mujica, who was born a farmer: "Being poor doesn't mean you don't have anything, it means being outside of your community".[10] An ecological civilization takes the concrete form of communities. While a community is autonomous and independent as an individual unit, it pursues symbiosis by exchanging and cooperating with other communities.

An ecological civilization community of the twenty-first century must meet at least five conditions. 1) A community from below: it is not organized from above according to an imposed ideology, but democratically constituted according to the local situation and the needs of its members. 2) A global community: it must connect with groups that pursue similar ideas around the world beyond regions and nations. A series of global social movements, such as the Arab Spring, Occupy Wall Street, Black Lives Matter, and #MeToo, have had an impact beyond borders. This is also the case with universal basic income, the economics of happiness, degrowth, and the ecological civilization movement. 3) A community of objects: ecological democracy must be realized with the acceptance of non-human animals and nature as citizens alongside human beings inclusive of nationality, race, class, and gender. 4) A community that includes science and technology: the use of science and technology necessary for the ecological transition is important to prevent retreating to a pseudo-archaic community. We need to dismantle the science and technology monopoly of the state and expert groups and create a governance structure that combines science and technology with politics. 5) A community that pursues degrowth: the most important goal is the transition to degrowth, which changes the purpose of life from growth to happiness while living within the limits of the earth's capacity. For this to happen, a community must become a commons.

The politics of such a community can be called "plant democracy." This means that we should suspend animalistic (centralized) operations that rigidly coordinate all activities of the organism, and instead mimic the autonomous and decentralized model of the plant, in which all parts of the organism generate, regenerate, and contribute to the welfare of the whole while not being dependent on a center. When individuals have a sense of belonging to a community and attempt to develop thought through dialogue—the most useful political tool, able to break through deadlocks—a genuine politics of participation and dedication to the common good is possible. Pointing to this form of politics, eco-theologian John Boswell Cobb Jr. has stated: "Every community should be part of a community of communities".[11]

Lessons from Evolutionary Biology

Décroissance ("degrowth") is a concept first used by French philosopher André Gorz in 1972. In that year, the first United Nations Conference on the Human Environment was held in Stockholm, and *Limits to Growth* was published by the Club of Rome. At the time, Gorz posed the following question: "Is the earth's balance, for which no-growth—or even degrowth—of material production is a necessary condition, compatible with the survival of the capitalist system?" A few years later, in 1980, he also claimed that "Today a lack of realism no longer consists in advocating greater well-being through degrowth and the subversion of the prevailing way of life. Lack of realism consists in imagining that economic growth can still bring about increased human welfare, and indeed that it is still physically possible".[12] Even today, fifty years later, this "unrealistic" view still remains mainstream. However, the concept of degrowth has also grown steadily to become a keyword that brings together progressives around the world in the face of climate and ecological crises and inequality.[13] Degrowth is not a matter of forcing painful austerity or asceticism onto the world, as pro-growth advocates claim, but to pursue care and symbiosis by changing life's values and orientation.

For degrowth, it is important to expand the commons, both tangible and intangible resources owned not by the state nor by individuals but by the public. The history of the commons dates back to the Charter of the Forest, which was originally signed by King John of England in 1215 as part of the Magna Carta. This charter guaranteed the economic rights of freemen to common land (the forests) that had been customarily used without legal right.[14] This shows that the political and juridical rights of citizens were only possible when rights to the common land—the foundation of economic self-sufficiency—were guaranteed. The spirit of the enclosure movement, which began with the start of the industrial revolution and established private property rights over public lands, prevailed for over two hundred and fifty years. But today, it is now coming to an end, and the commons are coming back.

The commons is not simply a matter of sharing resources and goods among its members. We need to change our ownership-oriented thinking, pursue use value rather than exchange value, and restore our relationships with nature, non-human animals, and fellow humans. The commons asks us to see all living beings not as independent entities but as potentialities created within relationships. Moving beyond modern thought that looked upon the state of nature from the perspective of competition and conflict, the struggle of all against all, and the survival of the fittest, we need to think complexly about the duality of competition and cooperation in an ecosystem. We must learn from evolutionary biology, which has moved beyond the principle of the "survival of the fittest", and proven instead the fact of the "survival of the friendliest".[15]

The fact that altruistic behavior or cooperation is advantageous to survival for humans as well as animals is becoming more established. The difference between chimpanzees and bonobos is affection. It is because of kindness that the small and clever Homo sapiens survived, and not the Neanderthal with its good physique. The skill of kindness, matching one's heart with other members of society, is advantageous for cooperative work and makes a larger-scale society and the cultivation of more intricate skills possible. The recognition that the principle of life is cooperation, not competition, has already been widely influential across various fields of research, such as in social epidemiology, neuroscience, behavioral economics, relational capital, and happiness research.

However, there has also been no shortage of critique linking evolutionary biology with the social sciences. For example, on the question of natural selection, mainstream evolutionary theory emphasizes genetic and individual selection, but a small number of evolutionary biologists have begun considering that group selection played an important role in the process of evolving sociality, such as altruism and empathy, which are the foundations of human cooperation. Namely, group selection makes people altruistic despite personal harm. The debate between Edward Osborne Wilson, who supports this view, and Richard Dawkins, who is an advocate of individual selection, is well known.

The evolutionary biologist David Sloan Wilson also supports the theory of group selection. According to him, because altruistic behavior in general is easily exploited by those who only take help from others and do not give back, it is difficult to explain human altruism with the theory of individual selection alone. However, it can be explained by the theory of group selection: if our ancestors belonged to one of several small groups, and each group had a different ratio of altruistic people to exploiters, the group with more altruistic people would survive more successfully. Wilson argues that these differences in success rates between groups have made humans more cooperative today. Wilson also brings in Elinor Ostrom's theory of the commons to demonstrate the validity of group selection. In opposition to Garrett Hardin's "tragedy of the commons," which puts forth the claim that human selfishness led to the destruction of common resources, Ostrom identifies eight principles from historical case studies for effectively maintaining the commons.[16] These principles provide evidence that altruism at the group level can be exercised, given the right conditions, and can be applied to human activities in various fields and at different scales to transform the deep structure of civilization.

Human selfishness and altruism cannot be approached as a dichotomy and differ depending on the conditions. The tragedy of the commons did in fact occur, but there are ways to avoid it. If the community of the future is to be based on the commons, we must learn from the successes of past commons in bringing about collective altruism. As a result of globalization, the scope of the commons has gradually expanded from land, forests, and rivers for collective production to the atmosphere and oceans. The smaller the size of the community, the more easily the rules of the commons can be maintained. However, climate and ecological crises, pandemics, inequality, and other global issues require more thought and wisdom as to how these principles of cooperation can be applied on a greater scale.

1. Jeremy Lent, "We Need an Ecological Civilization Before It's Too Late," Open Democracy, October 21, 2018, accessed January 31, 2023, www.opendemocracy.net/en/transformation/we-need-ecological-civilization-before-it-s-too-late/.

2. Timothy M. Lenton and Bruno Latour, "Gaia 2.0 Could Humans Add Some Level of Self-Awareness to Earth's Self-Regulation?" *Science* 361, no. 6407, September 2018, 1066-1068.

3. Alfred North Whitehead, *Adventures of Ideas* (New York: The Free Press, 1967), p. 83.

4. Ernest Callenbach, *Ecotopia* (New York: Bantam, Reissue edition, 1990).

5. Ernest Callenbach, *Ecotopia Emerging* (Berkeley: Banyan Tree Books, 1981).

6. www.industrynews.co.kr/news/articleView.html?idxno=42998

7. In the supplementary chapter "What is to be Done" in the thirtieth anniversary edition of *Limits to Growth*, Donella Meadows says there have been three revolutions in human history in response to population growth and environmental destruction. The first was the Agricultural Revolution, the second was the Industrial Revolution, and the remaining one being the Sustainability Revolution.

8. localfutures.org/publications/ancient-futures-book-helena-norberg-hodge/

9. Carlo Petrini, *Terrafutura: Dialoghi con Papa Francesco sull'ecologia integrale* (in Italian), (Giunti, 2020).

10. Carlo Petrini, *Terrafutura: Dialoghi con Papa Francesco sull'ecologia integrale* (in Italian), (Giunti, 2020).

11. www.openhorizons.org/ten-ideas-for-saving-the-planet.html

12. André Gorz quoted in Giacomo D'Alisa, Federico Demaria, and Giorgos Kallis, eds., *Degrowth: A Vocabulary for a New Era* (Routledge, 2014), 1.

13. Beginning in Paris in 2008, conferences by international research communities on the subject of degrowth have been held in Barcelona (2010), Montreal (2011), Venice (2012), Leipzig (2014), and Budapest (2016), and in the last one to two years, and even in South Korea major academic journals have been taking up degrowth in the last one to two years.

14. www.nationalarchives.gov.uk/education/resources/magna-carta/charter-forest-1225-westminster/

15. Brian Hare and Vanessa Woods, *Survival of the Friendliest: Understanding Our Origins and Rediscovering Our Common Humanity* (Random House, 2020).

16. Elinor Ostrom's 8 rules for managing the commons are: 1. Define clear group boundaries. 2. Match rules governing use of common goods to local needs and conditions. 3. Ensure that those affected by the rules can participate in modifying the rules. 4. Make sure the rule-making rights of community members are respected by outside authorities. 5. Develop a system, carried out by community members, for monitoring members' behavior. 6. Use graduated sanctions for rule violators. 7. Provide accessible, low-cost means for dispute resolution. 8. Build responsibility for governing the common resource in nested tiers from the lowest level up to the entire interconnected system. See Elinor Ostrom, *Governing the Commons: The Evolution of Institutions for Collective Action* (Cambridge, UK: Cambridge University Press, 1990).

생태계를 닮은 생태적 공동체들을 만들자

한윤정

생태문명 Ecological Civilization

2086년 지구상에 문명이 남아있다면 그것은 생태문명일 것이다. 여전히 지구 용량을 초과하는 반생태적인 산업문명이 지금보다 훨씬 작은 규모로 존재하겠지만, 우리는 그것을 더 이상 '문명'이라 부르지 않을 것이다. 급변하는 지구의 조건에 적응하지 못하거나 생태문명을 건설하는 데 실패한 지역의 사람들은 재난영화의 장면들처럼 생존에 급급한 채 문명의 기준에 못 미치는 삶을 살아갈 것이다. 그렇다면 문명이란 무엇이고 생태문명이란 무엇일까.

문명은 인류의 역사에서 발견되는 패러다임으로 우주론과 자연관, 에너지와 물질의 생산과 사용, 통치와 통합을 가능하게 하는 권력의 형식, 가치관과 윤리관 및 그것을 재생산하는 교육제도 등의 토대 일체를 말한다. 그러나 완전한 문명은 없었으며 하나의 문명을 일으킨 장점이 종국에는 쇠퇴를 야기하는 단점이 되곤 하였기에 각각의 문명은 소멸의 길로 접어들었다. 근대의 물질적·기계적 사고는 과학기술과 생산력의 발전을 촉진했지만, 바로 그러한 사고가 산업문명을 자연과 대립하는 곤혹스러운 상태로 이끌었다.

생태문명은 생태계의 원리에 따라 문명을 건설할 것을 권유한다. 제레미 렌트(Jeremy Lent)에 따르면, "생태계가 스스로 조직하는 방식을 통찰함으로써 지속가능한 풍요가 가능한 인간 사회의 모델을 찾을 수 있다. 유기체는 각자가 호혜적으로 주고받으며 다수의 공생 관계를 발전시킬 때 번창한다." 지금까지의 문명은 자연을 정복하면서 인간의 필요를 충족시키는 가운데 자연과 문명을 대립적으로 생각해왔다. 그러나 인간의 지식이 최고 수준에 이른 지금, 우리는 자연과 조화를 이루는 문명이 최고의 문명임을 알게 됐다.[1]

'가이아 2.0' 선언은 과학적 사실로 입증된 가이아의 세 가지 작동원리에 따라 사회의 구조를 바꾸자고 주장한다.[2] ①물질적으로 닫혀 있는 지구 생태계: 물질순환을 가로막는 지속 불가능한 발명품인 화석연료 대신 태양에너지를 활용하고 순환적인 경제로 전환해야 한다. ②지구의 생물지화학 순환을 만들어낸 미생물의 네트워크: 성공적인 순환경제를 위해서는 정보의 수평적 교환, 풍부한 기능적 다양성, 분산적 제어가 가능한 인간 행위자들의 네트워크를 지원해야 한다. ③가이아의 자기규제: 자연 상태로 평형을 유지하기 어려운 현재 상황에서는 인간의 자기인식이 중요하며, 이를 위해서는 실재와 현상의 격차를 보여주는 감각 기관(과학 제도) 인프라 구축과 함께 전환의 정치가 중요하다.

우리는 지구를 생각하면서 지역을 재조직해야 한다. 생태문명이라는 공동의 관념을 추구하는 가운데 지역 단위의 자립과 공생이 가능하도록 수많은 형태의 생태문명'들'을 건설해야 한다. 철학자 알프레드 노스 화이트헤드(Alfred North Whitehead)는 우리에게 요구되는 문명의 전환에 대한 교훈을 남겼다. "인간은 선악의 선택지를 보여줌으로써 설득할 수도, 설득될 수도 있다. 문명이란 보다 고상한 선택지를 구현하는 것으로, 그 자체에 내재하는 설득력에 의해 사회질서를 유지하는 것이다. (...) 그렇기 때문에 활기찬 문명에는 항상 불안의 요소가 있기 마련이다. 관념에 대한 감수성은 호기심이나 모험이나 변화를 의미하는 것이기 때문이다."[3] 현재에 안주함으로써 쇠퇴해가는 것을 거부하고 지속적인 번영을 추구하는 문명은 체제의 관성에 도전하는 관념을 추구하며, 그를 향해 불안하지만 희망적인 모험을 시도한다. 지금 우리에게 필요한 것은 생태문명을 향한 모험이다.

에코토피아의 출현 Ecotopia Emerging

어니스트 칼렌바크(Ernest Callenbach)의 미래 소설『에코토피아(Ecotopia)』(1975)는 인류가 살아남기 위해 건설해야 하는 문명의 모습을 그린다.[4] 미국 캘리포니아주 북부, 오리건주, 워싱턴주는 연방으로부터 독립해 에코토피아라는 독립국을 세운다. 질서 있는 전환을 위해 국경을 폐쇄한 에코토피아에 관해서는 무성한 소문만이 난무한다. 독립 이후 20년이 지난 시점에서 뉴욕의 신문기자인 윌 웨스턴이 처음 취재 허락을 받고 그곳을 방문한다. 평균적인 미국인의 눈에는 기이하게 보이는 에코토피아의 삶은 지속가능성을 향한 모범적인 로드맵이다.

그들은 태양과 바람으로부터 에너지를 얻는다. 자가용을 자전거와 철도 등 대중교통으로 대체했다. 나무를 숭배하며 집을 짓거나 대부분의 생활용품을 만드는 데 목재를 활용한다. 썩는 플라스틱을 제외하고는 화학물질을 사용하지 않는다. 순환경제 체제가 완성돼 쓰레기가 없는 안정된 상태를 유지한다. 그들은 부와 일에 대한 개념도 바꾸었다. 검소한 생활에 만족하기 때문에 불필요한 돈을 벌기 위해 과로하지 않는다. 기업은 협동조합이 소유하고 운영한다. 가족을 넘어 다양한 공동체를 이뤄 살아가며 성적 욕망에 충실한 자유연애를 옹호한다. 쌍방향 케이블 텔레비전을 이용한 정치토론이 수시로 벌어진다. 이런 모습은 비현실적으로 보이지만 50여 년이 지난 지금, 그중 일부는 전환을 추구하는 세계 여러 지역에서 실현되고 있다.

에코토피아 건설의 핵심은 정치이다. 생태적 전환을 위해서는 화석연료와 원자력에 의존하는 거대기업을 해체하고 정부 보조금을 재배정함으로써 생산수단을 재배치해야 한다. 또한 세계적인 무역 및 분업체제로부터 이탈해야 한다. 이익집단과 결탁한 기성 정치로는 변화가 불가능하다. 따라서 분리는 소설을 끌어가는 주요 동력이 된다. 에코토피아를 건설한 생존자당과 그들의 지도자인 여성 대통령 베라 올웬은 연방으로부터의 분리에 이어 오랜 기간 고립정책을 선택했다. 이는 영국 식민지 통치에 맞서 싸웠던 미국의 독립전쟁과 함께, 구소련에서 채택한 '일국 사회주의'를 연상시킨다.

그러나 구소련이 분배를 명분으로 자본주의와 같은 방식의 급속한 경제성장을 추진했던 것과 달리, 에코토피아는 외부 세계와 뚜렷이 구분되는 가치관과 생산수단을 가졌다.『에코토피아』의 프리퀄인『에코토피아 비긴즈(Ecotopia Emerging)』(1981)[5]는 독립 당시의 상황을 그린다. 에너지 가격 상승과 경제 위기, 화학물질로 인한 암 발병 등 생태재앙이 다가오고 있음에도 자신들의 이익을 지키려는 정부와 산업계의 저항은 거세기만 하다. 진보적 정치 성향의 서부 3개 주에서 권력을 장악해가던 생존자당은 원자력 발전소에서 방사능 유출 사고가 터지자 주민투표를 통해 워싱턴 D. C.로부터의 분리를 추진한다.

새로운 문명의 등장에는 두 가지 요소가 있다. 첫째, 새로운 에너지원의 개발이다. 소설 속 젊은 여성 과학자 루 스위프트는 기술 독점을 추구하는 기업과 대학의 방해를 뚫고 누구나 쉽게 만들 수 있는 태양전지를 발명한다. 오늘날 신재생 에너지의 발전단가는 화석연료나 원자력을 대체할 정도로 급속히 낮아지고 있다.[6] 둘째, 지속가능성 혁명[7]을 지지하는 사람들의 출현과 연결이다. 소설에서는 생존자당이 이런 역할을 충분히 해냈지만, 오늘날 한국을 비롯한 세계 주요 국가들은 생태 위기와 민주주의 위기를 동시에 겪고 있다. 국가 단위의 대의민주주의 제도는 기후생태위기에 제대로 대처하지 못한다. 따라서 혁명적 변화의 물결을 일으킬 시민들을 모으고 정치를 바꿔내는 일이 21세기의 가장 중요한 과제가 됐다.

공동체들의 공동체 community of communities

분리와 고립보다 개방과 협력이 더 중요한 이유는 지금의 세계가 치명적으로 연결돼 있기 때문이다. 특정 지역에서 발생하던 생태재앙은 전 지구적인 기후위기로 바뀌었다. 1986년 체르노빌 원전 사고는 원전 기술자들의 실수로 발생했고 반경 500킬로미터 안의 사람과 자연을 살상했다. 그러나 2022년 파키스탄을 덮친 대홍수는 선진국들이 배출한 이산화탄소로 인한 기후변화의 영향으로 75,000제곱킬로미터에 걸쳐 엄청난 피해를 입혔다. 기후위기 시대의 에코토피아는 고립된 지역에 해방구를 건설하거나 특정한 모델을 실험한 뒤 다른 지역으로 수출하는 근대적 방식으로는 성립할 수 없다. 문명의 조직원리 자체가 생태적 모델로 바뀌어야 하며 그 단위는 작은 공동체가 될 것이다.

지역경제운동가 헬레나 노르베리 호지(Helena Norberg-Hodge)는 공동체를 '오래된 미래'라고 불렀다.[8] 과거의 공동체가 혈연과 지연, 전통과 문화에 기반을 두었다면 미래의 공동체는 신념의 공유와 상호 신뢰에 기반한다. 지역공동체라면 더할 나위 없이 좋겠지만 멀리 떨어진 구성원을 이어주는 전자공동체도 가능하다. 공동체는 과거처럼 중앙에서 통제하는 사회운동이 작동하지 않는 현실에서 사람들을 모으고 지속적인 참여를 유도하는 데 유리하다. 카를로 페트리니(Carlo Petrini)에 따르면,[9] 공동체는 두 가지 가치를 갖는다. 첫째, 공동체는 경쟁사회에서 협력사회로 전환할 필요성을 나타낸다. 직업적 성공과 개인적 성취, 사회적 인정이라는 경쟁력 담론을 벗어나 모든 이들의 가치를 인정한다. 둘째, 공동체는 '정서적 지성'과 '엄격한 무정부 상태'가 적용되고 실행되는 배경이 된다. 이런 모순어법은 개인의 자유와 집단의 질서가 공존하는 상태를 가리킨다.

개인은 공동체에 속함으로써 화폐경제의 바깥에서 관계재를 누리며 살아갈 수 있다. 관계재는 공동의 재화이며, 개인의 소유가 아니라 모든 구성원이 누려야 하는 것이다. 이것은 관계가 수행되고 공동체에 참여할 때만 존재하기에 독점하지 못한다. 사고팔 수 없으며 가꾸고 보호하는 것만 가능하다. 가족끼리 필요한 재화를 아무 대가 없이 나누는 것과 마찬가지로 확장된 공동체는 관계재를 공유한다. 농민 출신인 우루과이의 전 대통령 호세 무히카(José Mujica)의 말을 빌자면 "가난하다는 것은 가진 게 없다는 의미가 아니라 공동체 밖에 있다는 것"이다.[10] 우리가 전 지구에서 수많은 생태문명들을 건설하고자 할 때 그 구체적인 모습은 생태문명을 지향하는 공동체들이다. 그것은 개별 단위로서 자율적이고 독립적인 한편, 다른 공동체와 교류하고 협력하면서 공생을 추구한다.

21세기의 생태문명 공동체는 적어도 다섯 가지 조건을 갖춰야 한다. ①아래로부터의 공동체: 주어진 이념에 따라 위로부터 조직되는 게 아니라 지역의 상황과 구성원들의 필요에 따라 민주적으로 구성되어야 한다. ②지구적 공동체: 지역, 국가를 넘어 전 세계에서 비슷한 이상을 추구하는 집단과 연결돼야 한다. 아랍의 봄, 월가 점거, 블랙 라이브스 매터(Black Lives Matter), 미투 등 일련의 전 지구적 사회운동은 국경을 넘어 영향을 미치며 새로운 흐름을 형성해왔다. 기본소득, 행복의 경제학, 탈성장, 생태문명 운동도 마찬가지이다. ③사물들의 공동체: 국적, 인종, 계급, 젠더를 망라한 인간과 함께 비인간 동물, 자연까지 구성원으로 받아들여 생태민주주의를 실현해야 한다. ④과학기술을 포함한 공동체: 의고적인 공동체로의 후퇴를 막기 위해 생태적 전환에 필요한 과학기술의 활용이 중요하다. 국가와 전문가 집단의 과학기술 독점을 해체하고 과학기술과 정치를 결합한 거버넌스를 만들어야 한다. ⑤탈성장을 추구하는 공동체: 가장 중요한 목표는 지구 용량의 한계 안에서 살아가며 삶의 목적을 성장에서 행복으로 바꾸는 탈성장으로의 이행이다. 이를 위해 공동체는 커먼즈(commons)가 되어야 한다.

이런 공동체의 정치는 '식물민주주의'라 부를 수 있다. 뇌에서 유기체의 모든 활동을 엄격하게 조정하는 동물식(중앙집권적) 운영을 중단하고, 조직의 모든 부분이 생성하고 재생하면서 중심에 의존하지 않고 전체의 복지에 기여하는 식물의 자치적·분산적 모델을 모방하자는 뜻이다. 개인이 공동체에 소속감을 갖고 가장 유용한 정치적 도구인 대화를 통해 사고의 발전을 꾀하여 교착 상태를 극복할 수 있을 때, 공동체를 위한 진정한 참여와 헌신이라는 의미를 실현하는 정치가 가능하다. 이런 정치의 모습을 가리켜 생태신학자 존 B. 캅 주니어(John Boswell Cobb, Jr.)는 "모든 공동체는 공동체들의 공동체의 부분이어야 한다."[11]고 표현했다.

진화생물학의 교훈 The Lessons from Evolutionary Biology

탈성장(décroissance)은 프랑스 철학자 앙드레 고르(André Gorz)가 1972년 처음 사용한 개념이다. 그해에는 스톡홀름에서 첫 유엔환경회의가 열리고 로마클럽의 위임으로 『성장의 한계』가 출간되기도 했다. 당시 고르는 이렇게 질문했다. "지구의 균형을 이루기 위해서는 탈성장이 필요조건이다. 그렇다면 지구의 균형은 성장과 이윤을 추구하는 자본주의 체제와 양립할 수 있는가?" 그는 또한 "오늘날(1980년대) 비현실적인 주장은 탈성장이 아니라 경제성장이 여전히 인간 복지를 증진하고 물리적으로 경제성장이 가능하다고 상상하는 것"이라고 했다.[12] 50년이 지난 지금까지도 고르가 지적했던 '비현실적' 주장이 여전히 주류를 이루지만, 탈성장이라는 개념 역시 꾸준히 성장해 기후생태위기와 불평등에 맞서는 전 세계 진보 진영을 묶어주는 열쇳말이 됐다.[13] 탈성장은 성장주의자들의 논리처럼 고통스러운 내핍이나 금욕주의적 세계를 강요하는 게 아니라 삶의 가치와 방향을 바꾸어 돌봄과 공생공락을 추구하자는 것이다.

탈성장을 위해서는 국가도 개인도 아닌 공공이 소유한 유·무형의 자원인 커먼즈를 확대하는 일이 중요하다. 커먼즈의 역사는 1215년 영국의 존 왕이 자유민의 정치적·사법적 권리를 보장한 '마그나카르타(Magna Carta)'와 함께 서명한 '삼림헌장(Charter of the Forest)'으로 거슬러 올라간다. 관습적으로 내려오던 공유지(숲)에 대한 자유민의 경제적 권리를 보장한 이 헌장은 마그나카르타와 더불어 '영국의 자유 대헌장들(The Great Charters of Liberties of England)'이라 불린다.[14] 이는 시민들의 정치적·사법적 권리는 자급의 토대인 공유지의 공유권을 보장받을 때 가능했다는 점을 보여준다. 산업혁명이 시작되면서 공유지를 막아 사유재산권을 확정한 인클로저 운동의 정신이 지배해온 250여 년의 산업문명 시대가 저물어가는 지금, 커먼즈가 다시 돌아오고 있다.

커먼즈는 단순히 구성원들끼리 자원과 재화를 공유하는 일이 아니다. 소유 위주의 사고를 바꾸고 교환가치보다 사용가치를 추구하며 자연과 비인간 동물, 동료 인간들과의 관계를 회복해야 한다. 모든 존재를 독립된 실체가 아니라 관계에서 생성되는 잠재태로 바라볼 것을 요구한다. 자연 상태를 경쟁과 갈등, 만인 대 만인의 투쟁, 적자생존의 시각으로 바라보던 근대의 사고를 넘어 현대 물리학과 생물학이 제시하는 증거들을 따라 생태계의 경쟁과 협력이라는 이중성을 복합적으로 사고해야 한다. 인간성을 재해석하기 위해 적자생존(Survival of the Fittest)의 원리를 벗어나 '다정한 것이 살아남는다(Survival of the Friendliest)'[15]는 사실을 증명한 진화생물학으로부터 배워야 한다.

동물뿐만 아니라 인간에게도 이타적 행동이나 협동이 생존에 유리하다는 사실은 갈수록 확고해지고 있다. 침팬지와 보노보의 차이는 다정함이다. 체격조건이 좋은 네안데르탈인이 아니라 작고 영리한 호모사피엔스가 살아남은 것도 다정함 때문이다. 다른 사회구성원들과 마음을 맞춰가는 다정함의 기술은 협동 작업에 유리하며 더 큰 규모의 사회와 더 까다로운 기술개발을 가능하게 한다. 이미 생명의 원리가 경쟁이 아닌 협력이라는 인식은 다양한 연구 분야에 폭넓은 영향력을 미치고 있다. 건강과 병에 미치는 사회적 요인을 연구하는 사회역학, 타자의 아픔을 자신의 아픔으로 인식하는 미러 뉴런 연구 등의 뇌과학, 경제학과 심리학을 연결한 행동경제학, 사람 사이의 신뢰와 공동체 혹은 관계의 질에 관한 관계자본 연구, 인간의 행복감과 경제 발전 등 행복의 구성 요소에 관한 연구 등이 이어졌다.

그러나 진화생물학을 사회과학과 연결하는 데 대한 비판도 적지 않았다. 대표적인 논쟁은 자연선택에서 개체선택과 집단선택의 문제이다. 주류 진화이론은 개인의 유전자 차원에서 작용하는 개체선택을 받아들이는데 비해 소수의 진화생물학자만이 집단 차원에서도 자연선택이 중요한 역할을 했을 것이라 여겨왔다. 이들은 인간 협력의 기반이 되는 이타주의와 공감 능력 등 사회성이 진화하는 과정에서 집단선택이 작용했을 것으로 본다. 즉, 집단선택이 개인의 손해에도 불구하고 이타적 인간을 만든다는 것이다. 이를 지지하는 에드워드 오스본 윌슨(Edward Osborne Wilson)과 개체선택의 옹호자로 『이기적 유전자』를 쓴 리처드 도킨스(Richard Dawkins)의 논쟁은 유명하다.

데이비드 슬론 윌슨(David Sloan Wilson) 역시 집단선택 이론을 지지하는 진화생물학자이다. 그의 설명은 이렇다. 일반적으로 이타적 행동은 다른 이의 도움만을 취하고 다시 돌려주지 않는 사기꾼에 의해 쉽게 악용되기 때문에(뒤에 나오는 '공유지의 비극'에 해당한다.) 개체선택 이론만으로는 인간의 이타성을 설명하기 어렵다. 하지만 집단선택설은 이를 설명할 수 있다. 우리 조상들이 여러 작은 집단에 속해 있고 각 집단마다 이타적 인간과 사기

꾼의 비율이 달랐다면, 이타적 인간이 더 많은 집단이 더 성공적으로 살아남을 것이다. 윌슨은 이런 집단 간의 성공률 차이가 오늘날 인간을 협력적으로 만들었다고 주장한다. 윌슨은 집단선택의 타당성을 입증하기 위해 커먼즈 연구자인 엘리너 오스트롬(Elinor Ostrom)의 이론을 가져온다. 인간의 이기심이 공유자원을 파괴했다는 결과를 내놓은 개럿 하딘(Garrett Hardin)의 '공유지의 비극'에 맞서 오스트롬은 역사상 존재했던 커먼즈의 성공사례를 연구함으로써 공유지의 비극을 피하고 상호협력에 기초해 커먼즈를 효과적으로 유지하는 여덟 가지 원칙을 발견했다.[16] 이 원칙들은 적당한 조건이 주어지면 개인의 이기심보다는 집단 차원의 이타성이 발휘된다는 증거가 된다. 이 원칙들을 다양한 영역과 규모의 인간 활동에 적용함으로써 지금 우리에게 필요한 공동체를 설계하고 심층구조를 전환하는 원리로 활용할 수 있다.

인간의 이기성과 이타성은 어느 쪽이 맞다는 식의 이분법으로 접근할 수 없으며 조건에 따라 달라진다. 공유지의 비극은 실제로 존재했지만, 그것을 피할 수 있는 방법도 있다. 미래의 공동체가 커먼즈에 기반을 두어야 한다면 집단적 이타성을 유도하는 과거 커먼즈의 성공사례로부터 배워야 한다. 커먼즈의 범위는 공동생산을 위한 토지, 숲, 강으로부터 점점 확대되었으며, 경제의 세계화에 따라 대기와 대양까지 아우른다. 공동체의 규모가 작을수록 커먼즈의 규칙이 잘 유지되는 데 유리하다. 그러나 기후생태위기, 팬데믹, 불평등과 같은 전 지구적인 문제들은 이런 협동의 원리를 어떻게 더 큰 규모에서 적용할 수 있을지에 대한 더 많은 고민과 지혜를 요구한다.

1. Jeremy Lent, "We Need an Ecological Civilization before It's Too Late," openDemocracy, October 21, 2018, www.opendemocracy.net/en/transformation/we-need-ecological-civilization-before-it-s-too-late/.

2. 티모시 M. 렌턴, 브뤼노 라투르, "가이아 2.0-인간은 지구의 자기규제에 자기인식을 더할 수 있을까", 우지수 역, *에피* 9호 (2021):202-212.

3. 알프레드 노스 화이트헤드, *관념의 모험*, 오영환 역, (파주: 한길사, 1997).

4. 어니스트 칼렌바크, *에코토피아*, 김석희 역, (서울: 정신세계사, 1991).

5. 어니스트 칼렌바크, *에코토피아 비긴즈*, 이재경 역, (서울: 도솔, 2009).

6. 정한교, "2020년 글로벌 재생에너지 LCOE 하락… 태양광, 전년 대비 7%↓", *인더스트리뉴스*, 2021년 7월 17일, www.industrynews.co.kr/news/articleView.html?idxno=42998.

7. 도넬라 메도즈는 『성장의 한계』 30주년 기념판에 추가된 '무엇을 할 것인가' 라는 장에서 인류 역사에서 인구 증가와 환경 파괴에 대응하는 세 번의 혁명이 있었는데 첫 번째가 농업혁명, 두 번째가 산업혁명이며 남은 것은 지속가능성 혁명이라고 했다.

8. "Ancient Futures," Local Futures, accessed April 6, 2023, www.localfutures.org/publications/ancient-futures-book-helena-norberg-hodge/.

9. 카를로 페트리니, 지구의 미래, 김희정 역, (서울: 성안당, 2022).

10. 카를로 페트리니, 같은 책.

11. 존 B. 캅 주니어, *지구를 구하는 열 가지 생각*, 한윤정 편역, (서울: 지구와사람, 2018).

12. 자코모 달리사, 페데리코 데마리아, 요르고스 칼리스, *탈성장 개념어 사전*, 강이현 역, (홍성: 그물코, 2018).

13. 탈성장을 주제로 삼는 국제 연구공동체들의 연합회의가 파리(2008)를 시작으로 바르셀로나(2010), 몬트리올(2011), 베니스(2012), 라이프치히(2014), 부다페스트(2016)에서 개최되었으며, 한국에서도 최근 1~2년 사이 주요한 학술 잡지들이 탈성장을 다루고 있다.

14. "Charter of the Forest, 1225," The National Archives, accessed March 16, 2023, www.nationalarchives.gov.uk/education/resources/magna-carta/charter-forest-1225-westminster/.

15. 브라이언 헤어, 버네사 우즈, *다정한 것이 살아남는다*, 이민아 역, (파주: 디플롯, 2021).

16. 오스트롬이 제시한 여덟 가지 원칙은 다음과 같다.
①누가 무엇에 접근하고 어떤 이익을 얻을 수 있을지 명확하게 정의해야 한다.
②규칙은 주민의 상황과 지역의 생태적 필요에 따라 결정되어야 한다. ③사람들이 규칙을 작성하는 데 참여하면 규칙을 따를 가능성이 더 커진다. 의사 결정에는 가능한 한 많은 사람을 참여시켜야 한다.
④규칙이 설정되면 사람들이 규칙을 지키는지 확인하는 방법이 필요하다.
⑤규칙을 어긴 사람을 무조건 배제하는 대신 다양한 제재의 등급을 마련해야 한다.
⑥갈등이 생기면 비공식적이고 효율적으로 해결해야 한다. ⑦커먼즈의 규칙은 상위의 정부로부터 합법적인 것으로 인정돼야 한다. ⑧커먼즈는 더 큰 네트워크 안에 자리 잡을 때 가장 잘 작동한다. 관개 네트워크라면 그 강의 상류를 사용하는 다른 사람들과 함께 협력해야 한다.

Sharaner Maash, or a haunting from the time before

Eman Abdelhadi & M. E. O'Brien

이만 압델하디 & M. E. 오브라이언

샤라너 마시, 혹은 이전 시대의 유령

Sharaner Maash, or a haunting from the time before

Eman Abdelhadi & M. E. O'Brien

My friend Latif,

I'm on Fire Island, and I met a ghost. I had to tell you, and apparently the only way to do so is a handwritten letter! They cut off our phones and AUGS. This is such a bizarre format, but here we are.

I think I told you that I had decided to go to that memory thing Belquees invited me to. She called it a *Sharaner Maash*. So, two days ago, I arrived here on the ferry. I love the beach, and the island isn't flooded this time of year. Horribly hot, but the marsh has shade and we can swim in the ocean.

We are sleeping in a campground that is set up in the marsh about a ten-minute walk from Cherry Grove. Belquees's friend Nourah was assigned a tent near mine—do you know her? Short, curly hair? Chicago-based? That first night we were both clueless and both looking for Belquees, so we stuck together and explored the grounds.

Belquees stayed vague when I asked about this all, so the ghosts came as a surprise. The first night they walked out of the marsh suddenly while we were milling around waiting for things to start. Nourah called out, pointing as the first ghost came walking up towards us. Others trailed behind them. I had seen the holo projectors mounted on trees, but it still came as a shock. In a few minutes we were surrounded.

It was chaotic. The ghosts started talking to us. They seemed to have no idea where they were, what they were doing here. I realized that based on their dress and accents, they were most likely holos of pre-rev people. That filled me with dread. I have never really understood people from the time before. I hate to say it, but I think they disgust me a bit. I never got into the popular historical dramas set in the twenties. I love early century horror films, but slasher movies don't help me make sense of their sad lives.

One ghost came up to me. She was a brown woman dressed in a weird monochrome outfit. She was so agitated, she kept asking me if I could help her get to "Elmhurst Hospital." I asked if she was injured, she said she worked as a Nurse's Assistant. She kept saying, "I won't get in before curfew unless I leave now." I have no idea what a curfew is. I kept thinking about her afterwards though.

Belquees and the other organizers clearly put a lot into historical authenticity, because the people felt real. The holo projectors were spread through the whole campsite, so the ghosts could appear and go anywhere. You can see through them, but it still feels like a presence. It's creepy, in ways both exciting and unpleasant. I dread the idea of having to spend a month having much of anything to do with that past, but I like the horror genre elements of it all.

Do you want more letters? My hand hurts writing this, but I'd do it if you will actually read them. I need to figure out how this letter sending thing works too. Let me know you got this.

—Kayla D. H. Puan

Friday, 2 Aug. 2086, Cherry Grove, Fire Island, Mid-Atlantic

Sun, August 4

Kayla—

I got your letter girl. Yes! Please write more. I am actually really excited to hear about your experience. It connects up to my current project.

Remember how I got into hospice work a few years back? When Matt overdosed, it hit me hard. I realized I had to think a lot more about death. I've spent my life doing gestational support, and it felt like the next step. Long story, but eventually I got involved in building a memorial at Hart Island in the Bronx. I've moved into the City Island Commune to work on it. I think what you are doing is a variation on a project from Rio called *mêses de memória*. I heard Belquees took a clipper trip to Rio last year to research them. The memorial park at Hart is a similar model. I am worried I might be giving too much away if I tell you details about the project, as you seem like you actually have the chance to discover it by actually experiencing it. So cool.

We are still in an early design phase of the park, so I'd love to hear more about how things are structured there. Like are you with the "ghosts" the whole time? Are you mostly with one or are you meeting lots of different people? I love that you are calling them ghosts, that really resonates. Do you think they know they are dead?

—Latif Timbers

City Island Commune, Long Island Sound

LT—

Oh, that is wild. I knew you were involved with something about Hart since you moved up to the Bronx, but I had no idea it was about this memory stuff. Tell me more about Hart Island. It's a graveyard, right? Where does the name Hart come from? If you are doing holos of dead people, what do you base them on?

The ghosts come and go. I keep running into the woman I mentioned. I try to avoid her gaze to be honest. She makes me so uncomfortable, just radiating anxiety. She keeps asking me about the hospital. I finally had to make up some story about how she was in an accident and was here to recoup. She seems confused, about the decade, the being a dead holo thing, and a lot else.

Because our phones don't work here, I had to find a bot to explain what a curfew is. Apparently, the armies or police from the time before would ban people from walking around the street at a particular time. And you could die or be locked up if you "broke curfew." Can you imagine living like that? How did these people put up with that? It's pathetic.

No one has claimed the second bunk in my tent, should I offer it to Nourah? Her tent-mate didn't show either.

—KDHP, 6 August 2086 (Tuesday), Fire Island

(Next day!)

Latif—

It is totally a ghost story, I was right. I haven't sent you yesterday's letter yet. Last night when I got to my tent, there were two surprises.

The first was a note, signed by Belquees. I should have realized with the Bangla name that this whole thing was her deal. She wrote:

> By now, you've met your partners on this journey. Each of them died an unmarked death. They were not buried properly, mourned properly. It is your job to shepherd them out of this life with a kindness they could not have in the time before. In so doing, you will learn about their time and, we hope, come to better appreciate your own.

The dead who haven't been grieved right, that is definitionally a haunting. I've always been into ghosts in my photography and film work, and I loved watching old ghost stories. I am not sure I want to be in one though.

It all got more intense when that anxious woman wandered into my tent and sat on the other bunk. She has been assigned to me! Apparently, many of the ghosts drifted off through the afternoon, and those left moved into tents.

I finally asked the woman about her life. I have been replaying it in my head ever since. Here's what I remember.

> My name is Feroza. I was born and raised in a slum on the outskirts of Dhaka. My dad drove a rickshaw, my mom cooked and cleaned and took care of us. My brothers and sisters and I would help her out when we could. I was good at school. When I got good marks, my parents told me to focus on studying. My siblings all stopped going after grammar school, but I kept going. Everyone worked except me, I felt bad about that. I begged my mom to let me work with my sister; our aunt

had gotten her a job cleaning rich people's houses in the city. But my job was to study. I studied and studied and studied. I even got all the way to university. Our whole neighborhood celebrated when I graduated from high school. Everyone bought food and sweets. I wore my mother's best sharee and felt like a bride that day.

I met my husband at university. Osman and I were both from poor areas and everyone knew it. We studied together and talked about our dreams. I wanted a life outside the slums, but his dreams were even further away. He wanted to take us to America. He finished his degree before me and made his way over to New York. The only work he could find was driving a taxi, nothing in engineering. He got tired, and finally sent for me. I knew I would need to work. A woman in my building, another Bangladeshi lady who became like a sister to me, introduced me to a rich family in Manhattan that needed a housekeeper. I ended up cleaning houses with my sister after all. I started studying for my nursing assistant license nights after work. Then we had Belquees.

That was when it all kind of crashed down inside me.

"Belquees? Belquees Chowdhury?" I asked.

All these things about Belquees' family started whirling in my head. I remembered suddenly where I had heard the hospital name. Oh Latif, my chest hurt, and I almost started crying. I excused myself and ran outside. I felt overwhelmed.

I sat by the fire for a long time thinking of Belquees. Of her father, still in love with Feroza after all these years, still mourning her. I had forgotten Feroza's name; in my memory she was just Belquees' mother.

You must remember what happened to Elmhurst, to Belquees' mother?

I am crying now as I write this. Fuck history, I hate it. I have always told myself that people from before were weak, that I would have fought back harder, I wouldn't have just suffered like they did. I hate them. I don't like it here. I want to go back to Newark, to be home.

I'll send these both in the morning with the ferry mail.

—Kayla/7 Aug./Wed.

Friday, August 9, 2086
K—

I'm anxious to hear what happened. Yes, mourning those that haven't been grieved adequately, that is part of the whole idea of memorial parks and the *mêses de memória*. Please write again.

You asked about Hart Island. It was used for a century as a burial ground for the extremely poor and many imprisoned people of New York City. Over a million people are buried there. It has mass graves from three pandemics—AIDS in the twentieth century, COVID in the twenties, and LARS from the forties. No one knows the origin of the name Hart. There hasn't been any connection established to the early settler family with that name. It is land of the Siwanoy, but we don't think they had a name for it.

We are designing these holos to be run by AIs. Everything is based on historical people buried on the island. We construct their personality drivers through social media, bureaucratic records, and recorded video calls. We imagine the holos will be sitting or standing near where the person they are based on is buried. They'll have conversations with people who come by, recounting to visitors the stories of their lives. But there is a lot we haven't worked out.

Much of our current memorial design is trying to explain to park visitors the basic concepts of poverty and houselessness. But I don't want the holos to just be pedagogical tools for kids. I want to—to hold the dead. I feel like if anyone would have given some thought to taking seriously the import of honoring the past, it would be Belquees.

I recommend, as a friend, sticking with the whole thing. I trust Belquees and know you do too. I hear you that it is painful.

—Latif Timbers, City Island, Bronx

Latif—

It has been an intense week since I last wrote to you. The night I figured out who Feroza was, I couldn't sleep at all. I crashed the next day, sleeping until sundown. I didn't want to tell her what happened to Elmhurst, I didn't want to face any of it. I know it is not my trauma, but meeting her brought up so much. I went through a phase when I was young, around my sojourn, of learning to grieve my father. I went to where he was killed fighting fascists in Colorado and did a whole ceremony for him. But mostly I'm not someone who spends time in the past.

When Feroza was assigned to my tent, I already felt pretty... frayed. Like worn thin and vulnerable and more open than I'd like. I have heard from my parents and my crèche and the movies about how people lived. But talking with the ghosts those first few days it felt—closer. Like they were all so stressed about food, money, housing, health. Everything was about money and scarcity and desperation. "They all look so tired," that was Nourah's comment.

The day after Feroza came to my tent, when I finally dragged myself out of bed towards dusk, we started talking. I avoided the heavier topics. Strangely, Feroza and I actually really hit it off. We are about the same age, but kind of pretended like we were adolescent girls at camp. Since then, we have spent a lot of time together. We went ocean kayaking (me lugging around a portable holo projector!), we went to calisthenics, we did a pottery project together. She used holographic clay. It was a little silly. We got along really well. We could make each other laugh, it was sweet and kind and really fun. The silliness helped us talk.

She decided I was an older friend of Belquees; at one point she said I was probably one of her daughter's school teachers. I asked her to tell me stories about Belquees as a small child, and Feroza had some really good ones. Apparently, one time, Belquees got mad at a guard at a military checkpoint and her parents had to carry her off before she started hitting him. She kept yelling—in Bangla or English, I'm not sure—"You show respect to my daddy!" Another time, she was beaten up trying to defend a kid who was being bullied in her grade.

Feroza also asked me about my life. I told her about my many parents, my photography teaching, about having a child with my five-set, and the life of the commune at Ironbound. I tried to be careful not to reveal too much about the discrepancies between our timelines. I think at some point she just decided to roll with the incongruities and strangeness of her being here and it all not matching up.

I found myself really caring about her, and I pushed myself to not just tune it out when she said stuff I didn't understand. There was so much I didn't understand, still don't. The desperation, the exhaustion, the fear she carries every day. I couldn't fathom how hard she worked. Eight hours! Twelve hours! So incredibly long. Over and over and over and over. She didn't seem to notice how terrible that all was. I wanted her to hate it, I wanted her to get angry. I would push her, but she always said, "We make do."

I know you read a lot of history. Some of these words are probably more familiar to you than they have been to me. Sometimes I make a mental list of words to look up next time I find a bot. But "make do"! Make do I still cannot understand. I will not understand. It is everything weak and sad and terrible in the world before.

Feroza told me about her neighbor whose cancer treatments used up their families' "savings." The neighbor died anyway, when the hospital shut down right after they had paid a deposit on her surgery. I barely understand what money was, but their whole lives—their literal lives—were ruled by it! No other hospital would take her as LARS-47 had already taken off, and no one could afford another deposit anyway. Then at the end of the story, again she shook her head and said, "We make do."

I was worked up, so I asked her "What does that mean, when you say you 'make do'?"

"It means we try our best with what we have."

I lost it.

"You try your best? That was your best?! I've read about your time! They were living in mansions! They had personal yards as big as this island! There were people with their own private orbitals, their own private armies. There were people drinking flecks of gold on cappuccinos! You let them run all over you and your people. What was wrong with you? We'd never let that happen now. I don't understand, I will never understand what you people were doing." I stomped off, already regretting my outburst.

I fucked it up, the whole experiment. I am supposed to be caring for this broken person, but instead I shamed her over her friend's death. I hate them for not fighting harder. Like they just lived with their souls crushed out of them. I told you once that I felt like human history began with the communes, with the revolution, and I wasn't entirely joking. Living under the rule of money was already death; they were never alive in the first place.

It's been a few hours since all this happened. I'm still very worked up. I'll write to you again when I calm down.

Love,

Kayla DH Puan, 14 August 2086 (Wednesday afternoon)

---

14 August (Wed. night, same day)

I avoided Feroza through a lot of the afternoon. When I finally went back to the tent, she really laid into me. She was so mad. Here is what I remember.

You think you are better than me. You are from the future, I can tell. You won't tell me, but I have heard other people talking, I get it. I don't understand how it is possible, but it doesn't make you better than me. Do you know how we fought? We fought every day to stay alive. We fought over and over for something better, even when we failed. They tried to close our hospital last month. We wouldn't let them. We're running it for the people. We took it over. We were not going to let them shut another hospital down. We're not taking any money; we are giving healthcare to everyone who needs it. We took over the supplies, we're our own bosses now. We're working for us, for each other, for our sick friends and neighbors and family members. We're feeding ourselves, but it's hard, it is so hard. We're not the first ones you know. To try. Others before us have done it for generations. After storms and fires, during protests and occupations and disasters, in the midst of battles. We took care of each other.

But we fail, again and again. I know we fail, but that doesn't mean we were weak. We were always up against so much. We are up against it now. The curfews are getting more strict. The army is closing in. I know I will die in that hospital. I feel it in my bones. And when I do, others will come in and try again. Because it's that, that's what makes us human. I don't know which generation will win. But I know every generation will try. You are from that time, aren't you, after it all? After someone wins. I am not stupid. I see what you are. Your contempt, your confidence, your ease. You don't understand me at all.

We were quiet. I told her that she does die in that hospital. She asked the year she died—2049—and it was the present for her. She asked how. I finally told her the longer version that Belquees told us after our oral histories were published. I told her how the hospital occupation was a huge inspiration for communization throughout New York City. About how it went on for months and became successful as a vision of healthcare for need, beyond the money economy. About the US army bombing the building, killing everyone inside, including her. About how her family couldn't find her body, despite days of searching, because no one was identifiable. And how this was a pivot in the struggle in New York, about the communes and assemblies and driving the army and police out and that we did win, we did finally win. I told her what they did at the hospital was key in it all.

She asked about me knowing Belquees. "Yes, your daughter is my friend. Belquees. She goes on to do great things, talks about you all the time. Osman-Uncle too. They keep you alive, in memory."

She asked why she was here. I said, for her *janazah*.

She is sleeping now in the cot. I will be going to sleep soon. I feel pretty sure she won't be here when I wake up. I get it now, what we are doing here.

—Kayla DH Puan

Aug. 16
Kayla—

Holding you close, my friend. I know you aren't into religion, but keeping both you and Feroza in my prayers today.

—Latif, City Island Commune

My beloved friend, Latif—

We just finished the *ghusl*. After Feroza disappeared, I spent the next two days building a sculpture in her likeness. They had all the materials to do it here. Then another two days glued to a bot, learning everything I could about the proper way to wash a Muslim body, to prepare it for burial, to send it to the next life.

The day of her ghusl, Belquees and her father Osman joined me.

"I knew I could trust you with this," she said. We washed Feroza from head to toe in warm water, gently massaging her hair, her hands, her feet. We wrapped her gently in a sheet of cotton and carried her to her grave. We lowered her into the earth, and Belquees cried and recited Quran.

The other campers gathered, and I told Feroza's story. I had not really known the past. I thought they all had their spirits ripped from their bodies, and were all just empty shells of defeat. I thought they weren't like us, just the false consciousness they warned us about in crèche. The commune, I thought, was the beginning of humanity, when we went from pathetic broken things to full creative beings in charge of our destinies. But Feroza was human. Feroza was human all along. Feroza was gloriously and beautifully human even in defeat. She missed the commune by three years, but helped birth it. She did not wait for it to give her life, she was life.

I come home soon. I have a couple of other memorials to help with before I do. I'd like to see you, to spend some time together.

I'd like to help you with the memorial park. I can tell you one meaning of the word "Hart," because it is one of my middle names. A hart is an old word for a deer, often an adult red deer. There aren't any more red deer now. They were fast, usually furtive, and so beautiful. My parents saw one when they were on a group hiking trip in Vermont. That day they decided my old name, and included Hart in its honor. When I took my new name, that was the one I kept. That was one of the last times anyone anywhere reported seeing a red deer. I imagine that maybe the deer had already gone extinct, and my parents saw a ghost. Maybe I'll design a holo of a red deer to roam the island. There is so much to grieve.

Thank you for the letters. I love you so much Latif.

Your comrade and friend,
—K
Kayla Dorothy Hart Puan
Sunday, 22 August 2086
Cherry Grove, Fire Island, Mid-Atlantic Seaboard,
North America

This story is a continuation of the authors' speculative novel, *Everything for Everyone: An Oral History of the New York Commune, 2052–2072* (Common Notions, 2022).

샤라너 마시, 혹은 이전 시대의 유령

이만 압델하디 & M. E. 오브라이언

내 친구 라티프에게,

나는 지금 파이어섬에 있고, 유령을 만났어. 네게 얘기하고 싶었는데, 그럴 유일한 방법이 손편지뿐이야! 전화도 증강현실 기기도 다 끊겼거든. 편지라니 참 이상한 방식이지만, 이렇게 됐네.

벨키스가 초대했던 추모 관련 일에 가기로 했다고 얘기했던 것 같은데. 벨키스는 그걸 *샤라너 마시(Sharaner Maash)*라고 불렀어. 그래서 이틀 전 연락선을 타고 이곳에 왔지. 해변이 참 좋고, 또 이 시기엔 섬이 물에 잠기지 않아. 끔찍하게 덥지만 습지에 그늘이 있고 바다에서 수영도 할 수 있어.

우린 체리글로브에서 걸어서 10분 거리의 습지에 세워진 캠프장에서 묵어. 벨키스의 친구 누라가 내 근처에 텐트를 배정받았는데, 누라 알아? 키 작고 곱슬머리에 시카고 사는? 첫날 밤에는 우리 둘 다 아무것도 모르는 상태로 벨키스를 찾고 있었어. 그렇게 둘이 뭉치게 돼서 같이 주변을 돌아다녔어.

내가 이 모든 것에 대해 물었을 때 벨키스는 계속 애매하게 굴었거든. 그래서 유령은 깜짝 놀랄 일이었어. 첫날 밤 뭔가 시작되길 기다리며 서성이는데 갑자기 유령들이 습지에서 걸어 나왔어. 누라는 첫 번째 유령이 우리 쪽으로 걸어오는 것을 가리키며 소리를 질렀지. 다른 유령들이 느릿느릿 그 뒤를 따라왔어. 나무 위에 설치된 홀로그램 영사기를 진작에 보았음에도 여전히 충격이었어. 몇 분 뒤 우리는 유령들에게 둘러싸였지.

혼란스러웠어. 유령들이 우리에게 말을 걸기 시작했어. 자기들이 어디에 있는지, 여기서 뭘 하는지 전혀 모르는 눈치더라. 옷차림이랑 억양을 보니 분명 전혁명시대 사람들의 홀로그램이었어. 그래서 두려움이 일었어. 이전 시대 사람들을 정말로 이해해 본 적은 없거든. 이런 말 하기는 싫지만, 그 시절 사람들한테 좀 혐오감을 느끼는 것 같아. 난 2020년대 배경의 인기 사극에 빠져 본 적이 없어. 21세기 초에 나온 공포 영화들은 좋아하지만, 그렇다고 슬래셔 영화가 그 시절 사람들의 서글픈 삶을 헤아리는 데 도움이 되지는 않잖아.

유령 하나가 내게 다가왔어. 이상한 단색 옷을 입은 갈색 피부의 여인이었지. 여자는 매우 흥분해서는 '엘름허스트 병원'까지 가게 도와줄 수 있냐고 자꾸 물었어. 어디 다치셨냐고 물었더니, 자기는 간호조무사로 일한다고 했어. "지금 출발하지 않으면 통금 시간 전에 들어갈 수가 없어요." 여자는 계속 그렇게 말했어. 통금이라니 무슨 말인지 도통 모르겠다. 그렇지만 그 뒤로 계속 그녀가 생각나.

벨키스랑 다른 기획자들이 역사적 사실성에 꽤나 노력을 기울인 게 분명해. 그 사람들이 진짜처럼 느껴졌거든. 홀로그램 영사기가 캠프장 전역에 설치되어 있어서 유령들은 어디든 출몰할 수 있어. 유령은 투명하지만, 여전히 존재감이 느껴지는 듯 해. 기이해, 흥미진진한 동시에 한편으론 불쾌하고. 그 시절과 관련된 일을 경험하면서 한 달을 보내야 한다는 생각에 걱정이지만, 그래도 공포 영화 같은 점들은 마음에 들어.

편지 계속 보낼까? 쓰느라 손이 아프지만, 네가 정말 읽는다면 쓸게. 편지들이 어떻게 배달되는 건지도 알아봐야겠다. 받으면 알려줘.

—케일라 D. H. 푸안
2086년 8월 2일 금요일, 중대서양주 파이어섬 체리글로브에서

8월 4일 일요일
케일라—

편지 받았어, 얘. 좋지! 더 보내줘. 네 경험에 대해 듣게 돼서 정말로 신나. 내가 지금 하는 프로젝트하고도 관련 있고.

몇 년 전 내가 어떻게 호스피스 일을 시작하게 됐는지 기억나? 맷이 약물을 과다복용했을 때, 정말로 충격이었지. 죽음에 관해 더 많이 생각해야 함을 깨달았어. 평생 임신 지원 일을 하면서 살았는데, 다음 단계가 왔다는 느낌이었지. 얘기가 길지만, 결국에 브롱크스에 있는 하트섬에 추모관을 건설하는 데 참여하게 됐어. 그 일을 하려고 시티섬 코뮌으로 이사도 했지. 지금 너는 리우에서 '기억의 달(mêses de memória)'이라 불리는 프로젝트의 한 버전에 참가한 것 같아. 벨키스가 작년에 연구차 리우에 다녀왔다고 들었어. 하트의 추모 공원도 비슷한 모델이야. 프로젝트에 대해서는 자세히 이야기하지

않을게, 미리 너무 많이 알아버리면 안 되잖아. 모처럼 직접 경험할 기회가 생긴 거니까 말이야. 정말 멋지다.

여기는 아직 공원 설계의 초기 단계여서 그쪽은 일이 어떤 구조로 되어 있나 더 듣고 싶다. '유령들'이랑 내내 같이 있는 식인가? 주로 한 명이랑 지내, 아니면 여러 다른 사람들을 만나? 네가 그들을 유령이라고 부르는 게 좋다. 정말 울림이 있는 말이야. 네가 보기엔 그 사람들이 자기들이 죽은 걸 아는 것 같아?

—라티프 팀버스
롱아일랜드해협 시티섬 코뮌에서

LT—

와, 대단하다. 네가 브롱크스로 이사하고 나서 하트섬 일에 참여한다는 건 알았지만, 그게 이 추모 관련 일인지는 전혀 몰랐어. 하트섬 얘기 더 들려줘. 묘지 맞지? 하트라는 이름은 어디에서 온 거야? 혹시 네가 죽은 사람들의 홀로그램 작업을 하고 있다면, 그건 뭐를 근거로 만드는 거야?

유령들은 나타났다 사라졌다 해. 저번에 말한 그 여인과 계속 마주쳐. 솔직히 그녀의 눈길을 피하려고 해. 불안을 뿜어내면서 나를 너무 불편하게 하거든. 그녀는 자꾸 병원에 관해 물어. 결국에는 그녀가 어떤 사고를 당한 후 이곳에 회복하러 왔다는 얘기를 지어내야만 했어. 그녀는 혼란스러워 보여. 그 10년, 죽은 홀로그램이 된 것, 또 다른 여러 일에 관해서 말이야.

여기서는 전화기가 되질 않아서 통금이라는 게 뭔지 설명해줄 봇을 찾아야 했어. 보아하니, 이전 시대에는 군인이나 경찰이 특정 시간대에 사람들이 거리를 다니는 걸 금지했나 봐. 게다가 '통금을 어기면' 죽거나 감금될 수도 있었고. 그렇게 산다는 게 상상이 가? 이 사람들은 어떻게 견뎠을까? 불쌍해.

아무도 내 텐트의 빈자리에 들어오지 않는데, 누라한테 와서 쓰라고 얘기해볼까? 누라의 텐트 파트너도 나타나지 않았어.

—KDHP, 2086년 8월 6일(화요일), 파이어섬에서

(다음 날!)
라티프—

내 말이 맞았어. 완전 유령 이야기야. 어제 쓴 편지는 아직 못 부쳤네. 어젯밤 텐트로 돌아왔더니 두 가지 놀라운 일이 있었어.

먼저 벨키스가 서명한 쪽지가 하나 있었어. '샤라너 마시'라는 그 벵골어 이름에서 이 모든 게 벨키스의 계획이었다는 걸 알아차렸어야 했는데. 쪽지의 내용은 이랬어.

> 지금쯤이면 이번 여정에서 너의 파트너가 될 사람을 만났겠지. 그 사람들은 표식도 없는 죽음을 겪었어. 제대로 매장되지도, 애도 받지도 못했지. 네가 할 일은 그들이 이전 시대에는 받지 못했던 친절을 베풀어 이생으로부터 벗어나도록 인도하는 거야. 그 과정에서 너도 그들이 살던 시대에 관해, 또 바라건대 네가 사는 시대에 관해서도 더 잘 이해하게 될 테고.

제대로 애도 받지 못한 죽은 자, 정의에 따르면 그게 유령이야. 사진과 영화 작업을 하면서 언제나 유령에 관심 있었고, 또 오래된 유령 이야기들을 보는 것도 좋아했어. 내가 그 이야기 속에 들어가고 싶은지는 모르겠지만.

이 불안한 여인이 내 텐트로 들어와서 남은 침상에 앉았을 때 상황은 훨씬 더 심각해졌어. 그녀가 나의 파트너로 배정되어 있었던 거야! 그러고 보니 오후 동안 많은 유령이 차츰 사라졌는데, 사라진 유령들은 텐트로 들어간 거였어.

마침내 그 여인에게 인생 이야기를 물어봤어. 그때부터 머릿속에서 계속 그녀의 대답을 되뇌고 있어. 기억나는 내용은 이래.

> 내 이름은 페로자예요. 다카 외곽의 빈민가에서 태어나 자랐죠. 아버지는 인력거를 몰았고 어머니는 요리하고 청소하며 우리들을 돌보셨어요. 형제자매들과 나는 틈이 나는 대로 어머니를 돕곤 했죠. 나는 공부를 잘했어요. 좋은 성적을 받아오면 부모님은 공부에 집중하

라고 하셨죠. 남매들은 중학교까지만 다녔지만, 나는 계속 공부했어요. 나만 빼고 모두 일을 해서 마음이 안 좋았죠. 어머니에게 나도 언니랑 같이 일하게 해달라고 사정했어요. 고모가 언니한테 시내 부잣집 청소 일을 잡아줬거든요. 하지만 내가 할 일은 공부였어요. 공부하고 또 공부했죠. 심지어 대학까지 갔어요. 내가 고등학교를 졸업했을 땐 마을 사람들이 전부 모여 축하해줬어요. 모두가 음식이랑 과자를 가지고 왔죠. 나는 엄마의 제일 좋은 사리를 입었고 그날은 새신부가 된 기분이었어요.

대학에서 남편을 만났어요. 오스만과 난 가난한 지역 출신이고, 그건 모두가 아는 사실이었어요. 우린 함께 공부하며 미래를 이야기했죠. 나는 빈민가에서 벗어난 삶을 원했지만, 오스만의 꿈은 그보다도 훨씬 멀리 나아갔어요. 그이는 우리를 미국으로 데려가고 싶어 했지요. 오스만은 나보다 먼저 학업을 마치고 뉴욕으로 떠났어요. 그이가 거기서 구할 수 있던 유일한 일은 택시 운전이었고, 공학 쪽 직장은 없었어요. 그러다 지친 그는 결국 나를 불렀죠. 일을 해야 한다는 걸 알았어요. 같은 건물에 방글라데시인 여자가 또 한 명 살았는데, 나한테 친언니 같은 분이었죠. 그 언니가 날 맨해튼의 한 부잣집에 소개해줘서 가정부로 일하게 됐어요. 그러니까 결국엔 언니랑 같이 청소부로 일하게 된 셈이죠. 퇴근 후 밤에는 간호조무사 자격증 공부를 하기 시작했어요. 그때 우리에게 벨키스가 생겼고요.

바로 거기서 내 안의 모든 게 무너져 내린 거야.

"벨키스요? 벨키스 초드리?" 나는 물었어.

벨키스의 가족에 관한 모든 것들이 머릿속에서 빙글빙글 돌기 시작했어. 그 병원 이름을 어디서 들었는지 그제야 생각났지. 아 라티프, 가슴이 아팠고, 울음이 터질 것 같았어. 양해를 구하고는 밖으로 뛰쳐나왔지. 감정이 북받쳤어. 난 한참 동안 불 가에 앉아 벨키스 생각을 했어. 벨키스의 아버지 생각도. 이 모든 세월이 지나고도 여전히 페로자를 사랑하고, 아직도 그녀를 애도하는 그분을. 나는 페로자라는 이름을 잊어버렸던 거야. 내 기억 속에서 그분은 그저 벨키스의 엄마였으니까.

엘름허스트 병원에, 또 벨키스의 어머니에게 무슨 일이 있었는지 너도 분명 기억하지?

이 편지를 쓰면서도 울고 있다. 망할 놈의 역사. 정말 싫어. 이전 시대 사람들은 나약하다고, 나라면 더 세게 저항했을 거라고, 그들처럼 그저 당하고 있지만은 않았을 거라고, 나 자신에게 항상 그렇게 말해왔었어. 그 사람들이 미워. 여기 있는 것도 싫어. 뉴어크로, 집으로 돌아가고 싶어.

이 편지들은 아침 연락선 편에 부칠게.

—케일라/ 8월 7일/ 수요일

2086년 8월 9일 금요일
K—

무슨 일이 있었는지 듣고 나니 걱정이 된다. 그래, 적절하게 애도되지 못한 사람들을 애도하는 것. 그게 추모 공원과 기억의 달이라는 발상의 일부야. 부디 다시 편지 보내줘.

하트섬에 관해 물어봤었지. 여긴 백 년 동안 뉴욕시의 극빈자와 수감자 다수를 위한 매장지로 쓰였어. 백만 명 넘는 사람들이 그 섬에 묻혀 있어. 섬에는 세 번의 팬데믹, 그러니까 20세기의 AIDS, 2020년대의 COVID, 2040년대의 LARS 때 만들어진 거대한 공동묘지들이 있어. 아무도 하트라는 이름의 유래는 몰라. 그 이름을 가진 초창기 정착민 가족하고도 아무 연관이 없었고. 섬은 시와노이 부족의 땅인데, 그들이 섬에 이름을 붙인 건 아닌 것 같아.

우리는 이 홀로그램들이 AI로 작동되도록 설계하고 있어. 모든 게 다 이 섬에 묻힌 과거의 인물들을 기반으로 해. 소셜 미디어, 행정 기록, 영상 통화 녹화물을 통해 그들의 인격 드라이버를 구축하지. 우리는 그 홀로그램들을 그들이 기반한 실존 인물들이 묻힌 묘지 근처에 앉거나 서 있게 하려 해. 그들은 찾아온 사람들과 대화를 나누면서, 방문객에게 자기 삶을 이야기할 거야. 하지만 아직 우리에겐 해결 못 한 부분이 많아.

현재 추모 공원의 설계는 공원 방문객에게 빈곤과 노숙의 개념을 설명하는데 상당 부분 초점을 맞추고 있어. 그래도 홀로그램이 아이들을 위한 교육 도구에 머물지는 않으면 좋겠어. 나는 죽은 이들을 머물게 하고 싶어 싶어. 과거를 기리는 의미를 진지하게 생각해 본 사람이 있다면, 아마 벨키스일 거야.

친구로서 네가 포기하지 않고 끝까지 계속해나가길 권해본다. 나는 벨키스를 믿어. 너도 그렇단 걸 알아. 고통스럽다는 네 심정 이해해.

—라티프 팀버스, 브롱크스 시티섬에서

라티프—

지난번 편지 이후로 강렬한 한 주를 보냈어. 페로자가 누구인지 알게 된 날 밤, 잠을 잘 수가 없었어. 다음 날에야 잠이 들어서 해가 떨어질 때까지 잤어. 엘름허스트 병원에 무슨 일이 벌어졌는지 그분에게 얘기하고 싶지 않았고, 그 일을 마주하기도 싫었어. 그게 내 트라우마가 아니란 건 알지만, 페로자와의 만남으로 인해 너무 많은 것들이 떠올랐어. 내가 어렸을 적, 성년 맞이 여행 즈음해서 아버지를 애도하는 방법을 배우는 시기를 거쳤어. 콜로라도에서 파시스트들과 싸우다 돌아가신 장소도 가봤고, 온전한 의식도 올렸지. 하지만 대체로 나는 과거에 머무는 사람이 아니야.

페로자가 내 텐트에 배정됐을 때 나는 벌써부터 꽤나……신경이 곤두선 느낌이었어. 소진되어 부서질 것만 같았어. 너무 가까워지는 것 같았고. 이전 사람들이 어떻게 살았었는지는 부모님께, 보육원에서, 영화에서 들었지. 하지만 처음 며칠 유령들과 얘기를 나눴더니 더 가깝게 느껴졌어. 있잖아, 그들은 모두 음식, 돈, 집, 건강 문제로 스트레스를 받았어. 모든 게 다 돈, 물자 부족, 절망의 문제였어. “그 사람들 전부 너무 피곤해 보여.” 누라가 내린 평이야.

페로자가 내 텐트에 온 다음 날, 나는 해 질 녘이 되어서야 겨우 침대에서 몸을 이끌고 나와서 페로자와 이야기를 시작했어. 무거운 주제는 피했어. 이상하게도 페로자와 나는 실제로 죽이 잘 맞았어. 서로 나이가 비슷한데, 꼭 캠프에 온 사춘기 여자애들처럼 굴었지. 이후로 같이 많은 시간을 보냈어.

바다에 나가서 카약도 타고(내가 휴대용 홀로그램 영사기를 지고 다니면서!), 체조도 하고, 도예도 같이 했어. 페로자는 홀로그램 점토를 썼어. 조금 우스웠지. 우린 아주 잘 지냈어. 서로를 웃게 했어. 다정하고 친절하고 정말 즐거웠어. 철없이 구는 게 대화에 도움이 됐어.

페로자는 내가 벨키스의 나이 많은 친구라고 결론을 내렸어. 한번은 내가 벨키스의 학교 선생님인가 하더라. 그분에게 벨키스의 어릴 적 얘기를 들려달라고 했는데, 정말 재밌는 얘기들이 있었지. 한 번은 군 검문소에서 화가 난 벨키스가 보초에게 달려들기 전에 부모님이 떼어놔야 했었대. 벵골어인가 영어인가로 벨키스는 계속 소리 질렀대. "우리 아빠한테 예의를 갖춰!"라고. 또 한 번은 동급생들에게 괴롭힘당하는 친구를 지키려다가 얻어맞았고.

페로자는 나에 대해서도 물었어. 나한테는 여러 명의 부모님이 있고, 사진을 가르치고, 5인조로 함께 아이를 하나 키우고 있다고, 또 아이언바운드의 코뮌 생활이 어떤지도 얘기했어. 우리 둘이 사는 시간대가 서로 다르다는 걸 들키지 않으려 조심했지. 내 생각에 페로자는 어느 순간에 자신이 여기 있다는 사실로 빚어진 불일치와 이상한 점들 모두를 그냥 받아들이고 적응하기로 한 것 같아.

내가 그녀를 정말로 아끼게 되었다는 걸 깨달았고, 나로서는 이해하지 못하는 얘기를 들을 때도 그냥 넘기지 않으려고 노력했어. 이해가 안 되는 게 너무 많았고, 지금도 그래. 그녀가 매일 짊어진 그 절박함, 피로, 두려움 말이야. 그분이 얼마나 열심히 일했는지 짐작도 할 수 없었어. 8시간을! 12시간을! 너무 길잖아. 일하고, 일하고, 일하고 또 일하다니. 그 모든 게 얼마나 끔찍한지 그녀는 짐작도 못 하는 것 같았어. 그녀가 진저리 치길 바랐어. 화를 내길 바랐어. 그렇게 몰아가면, 대답은 항상 이랬어. "살아 내는 거죠."

너 역사 많이 읽잖아. 어떤 이야기들은 나보다 네게 더 친숙하겠지. 때때로 나는 다음에 봇을 만나면 찾아볼 단어 목록을 머릿속에 작성해. 하지만 '살아 내다'니! 살아 낸다는 말이 아직도 이해가 안 돼. 나는 이해하지 않을 거야. 이전 세계에서는 모든 게 나약하고 슬프고 끔찍해.

페로자가 암 치료를 받느라 가족 '저금'을 다 쓴 이웃 이야기를 해줬어. 그분은 결국에 돌아가셨대. 가족이 수술 보증금을 내자마자 병원이 문을 닫았을 때 말이야. 돈이라는 게 뭔지 전혀 이해가 안 가지만 그 사람들 인생 전체가, 말 그대로 목숨이 돈에 지배됐었어! LARS-47이 이미 유행하기 시작해서 다른 어떤 병원도 이웃분을 받아주지 않았고, 어쨌거나 보증금을 다시 마련한다는건 누구도 상상할 수 없는 일이었대. 얘기를 마치면서 페로자는 또다시 머리를 절레절레하며 말했어. "살아 내는 거죠."

나는 흥분해서 물었어. " '살아 낸다'니, 그게 무슨 뜻이에요?"

"지금 있는 걸로 최선을 다한다는 뜻이에요."

나는 무너졌어.

"최선을 다해요? 그게 최선이었어요? 당신이 살던 시대에 관해 읽었어요. 그 인간들은 대저택에 살고 있었다고요! 이 섬만큼이나 큰 개인 정원을 가졌어요! 개인 우주 궤도를 가진 사람들도, 자기 군대를 가진 사람들도 있었어요. 금가루 뿌린 카푸치노를 마시던 사람들도 있었고요! 당신은 그 인간들이 당신들을 깔아뭉개고 다니게 내버려 뒀어요. 도대체 뭐가 잘못돼서 그랬죠? 우리라면 절대 그런 일이 일어나게 두지 않아요. 이해가 안 돼요. 당신네 사람들이 뭘 했는지 영영 이해 못 할 거예요." 나는 쿵쿵대며 나와버렸어. 화를 터뜨린 걸 벌써 후회하면서.

내가 실험 전체를 망쳤어. 상처 입은 이 사람을 돌봐줘야 하는데, 대신에 친구분의 죽음을 두고 그녀를 모욕했어. 더 거세게 맞서 싸우지 않은 그들이 싫어. 그 사람들은 영혼이 짓밟힌 채 그냥 살아갔던 거야. 인류의 역사는 코뮌과 함께 시작됐다고, 혁명과 함께 시작된 거라고 네게 말한 적 있지. 그거 완전히 농담만은 아니었어. 돈의 지배 아래 사는 삶은 이미 죽음이니까, 애초부터 그들은 살아있지를 않았어.

이 모든 일이 벌어지고 두 시간쯤 지났네. 아직도 많이 속상해. 진정되면 또 편지 쓸게.

사랑을 담아,

케일라 DH 푸안, 2086년 8월 14일 (수요일 오후)

8월 14일(수요일. 같은 날 밤)

오후 내 페로자를 피했어. 결국에 다시 텐트로 돌아갔더니, 페로자가 나에게 쏟아붓더라. 진짜 화가 나 있었어. 기억나는 내용은 이래.

> 너는 네가 나보다 잘났다고 생각하지. 네가 미래에서 왔다는 건 알겠네. 너는 나한테 알려주지 않으려고 하지만, 다른 사람들이 하는 얘기를 들어서 알아. 어떻게 그게 가능한지는 이해가 안 되지만, 그렇다고 해서 네가 나보다 나은 건 아니야. 우리가 어떻게 투쟁했는지 알기나 해? 매일 살아남으려고 싸웠어. 조금이나마 더 나아지기 위해 싸우고 또 싸웠어. 심지어 실패를 한 때에도 말이야. 그 인간들이 지난 달 우리 병원을 폐쇄하려 했지. 그렇게 하게 두지 않았어. 우린 사람들을 위해 병원을 운영하고 있어. 우리가 접수했지. 그들이 다른 병원을 닫게 두지도 않을 거야. 우리는 돈을 받지도 않고, 필요한 모든 사람에게 의료 서비스를 제공해. 물품도 우리가 차지했고, 이제 우린 그들을 위해 일하지 않아. 우린 우리를 위해, 서로를 위해, 아픈 친구와 이웃과 가족을 위해 일하고 있어. 자력으로 꾸려가고는 있지만 힘들어, 정말 힘들어. 우리가 처음인 것도 아니잖아, 맞서 보는 것 말이야. 우리보다 앞선 시대의 사람들도 수 세대에 걸쳐 해왔던 일이지. 폭풍과 화재 후에도, 시위와 점거와 재난 중에도, 전쟁의 와중에서도 말이야. 우리는 서로를 돌봤어.
>
> 그래도 우리는 실패해, 실패하고 또 실패해. 나도 알아 우리가 실패한 거. 하지만 그렇다고 우리가 약했다는 뜻은 아니야. 우린 언제나 수많은 일에 맞섰어. 지금도 저항하고 있고. 통금이 점점 엄격해져. 군대가 점점 다가와. 나도 내가 저 병원에서 죽을 거란 걸 알아. 그게 뼛속 깊이 느껴져. 내가 죽으면 다른 사람들이 내 자리에서 또다시 노력하겠지. 왜냐면 그거야말로 우리를 인간으로 만드는 거니까. 어느 세대에 이르러 승리하게 될지는 모르지. 하지만 모든 세대가 노력할 거라는 건 알아. 너는 그 모든 게 다 지나간 다음 시대의 사람이지? 누군가가 이긴 다음 말이야. 나도 바보가 아냐. 네가 어

떤 사람인지 다 보여. 네가 드러내는 경멸, 자신감, 편안함. 너는 나를 전혀 이해 못 해.

우리는 말이 없었어. 나는 그녀가 정말 그 병원에서 생을 마친다고 말해드렸지. 그녀는 자기가 몇 년도에 죽었는지—2049년—를 물었어. 그게 그녀의 현재였어. 그녀는 어떻게 됐느냐고 물었어. 결국에 우리 구술사가 출간된 다음에 벨키스에게 들은 더 긴 버전의 이야기를 들려드렸어. 병원 점거가 뉴욕 전역에 걸쳐 일어난 코뮌화에 얼마나 큰 영감이 되었는지. 어떻게 코뮌화가 몇 달 동안 이어져 화폐 경제를 넘어선, 필요를 위한 의료의 비전으로서 성공을 거두게 되었는지. 미군의 병원 건물 폭격으로 그녀를 포함한 안에 있던 모든 사람들이 죽었다는 것도. 며칠에 걸친 수색에도, 시신들의 신원을 확인할 수 없어 가족들이 그녀의 시신을 찾지 못했다는 사실도. 이 일이 어떻게 뉴욕 투쟁의 구심점이 되었는지에 대해. 코뮌과 집회, 군과 경찰을 몰아낸 일에 대해. 그리고 우리가 승리했다고, 마침내 승리를 거두었다고 말이야. 그때 병원에서 당신들이 한 일이 그 모두의 핵심이었다고 말씀드렸어.

그녀는 나에게 벨키스를 아느냐고 물었어. "네, 따님이 제 친구예요. 벨키스. 줄곧 대단한 일을 해 왔고, 항상 당신에 관해 이야기해요. 오스만 아저씨도요. 당신은 두 사람 기억 속에 살아 있어요."

그녀는 왜 자신이 여기 있느냐고 물었어. 그녀의 *장례(janazah)*를 위해서라고 했지.

지금 그녀는 간이 침상에서 자고 있어. 나도 곧 잘 거야. 일어나보면 그녀가 여기 없을 거라는 확신이 들어. 이제 알겠어. 우리가 여기에서 무얼 하고 있는지를.

—케일라 DH 푸안

8월 16일

케일라—

내 친구, 널 꼭 안아줄게. 네가 종교를 믿지 않는다는 건 알지만, 오늘 너와 페로자 두 사람 모두를 위해 기도할게.

—라티프, 시티섬 코뮌에서

사랑하는 내 친구, 라티프—

우린 이제 막 *구슬(ghusl)*을 마쳤어. 페로자가 사라진 후, 이틀을 그녀를 닮은 조각상을 만들며 보냈지. 여기에 모든 재료가 마련돼 있었어. 그리고 다음 이틀은 봇과 붙어 지내면서 시신을 씻어 장례 준비를 하고 다음 생으로 보내드리는 무슬림 의식의 절차에 대해 가능한 모든 걸 배웠지.

그녀의 구슬이 있던 날, 벨키스와 벨키스의 아버지 오스만도 함께 자리했어.

"너를 믿고 이 일을 맡길 수 있을 줄 알았어." 벨키스가 말했어. 우리는 페로자를 머리부터 발끝까지 따뜻한 물에 씻기고, 머리카락과 손발을 부드럽게 마사지했어. 그녀를 면으로 된 천에 부드럽게 감싸 무덤으로 옮겼지. 그녀를 땅속으로 내려놓았고, 벨키스는 울며 쿠란을 낭송했어.

다른 캠프 참가자들도 모였기에 페로자의 이야기를 들려주었어. 나는 과거를 정말로 알지는 못했지. 그들은 몸에서 영혼이 찢겨나간 사람들이고, 패배의 빈 껍데기에 불과하다고 생각했었어. 그들은 우리와는 다르다고, 보육원에서 우리에게 경고했던 대로 그냥 허위의식이라고 생각했어. 코뮌으로부터 인류가 시작되었다고, 그제야 비로소 한심하게 망가진 상태로부터 벗어나 스스로의 운명을 책임지는 온전한 창조적 존재가 되었다고 생각했어. 하지만 페로자는 인간이었어. 처음부터 내내 그랬어. 패배의 와중에도 영광스럽고 아름답게 인간이었어. 그녀는 3년 차이로 코뮌을 놓쳤지만, 코뮌이 태어나게 도왔지. 그녀는 코뮌이 삶을 주길 기다리지 않았어. 그녀가 곧 삶이었어.

곧 집으로 돌아가. 그러기 전에 다른 추모식 두어 개가 더 있어. 네가 보고 싶고, 같이 시간을 보내고 싶어.

네 추모 공원 일을 돕고 싶다. 내가 '하트'라는 단어의 한 가지 뜻은 말해줄 수 있어. 왜냐면 그게 내 가운데 이름이거든. 하트는 사슴을, 대개 다 자란 붉은 사슴을 뜻하는 옛말이야. 이제는 더 이상 붉은 사슴을 볼 수 없지. 그 사슴들은 빨랐고, 보통 눈에 잘 안 띄었고, 아주 아름다웠어. 부모님이 버몬트에 하이킹하러 갔을 때 한 마리를 보셨어. 그날 부모님이 내 예전 이름을 지었고, 붉은 사슴을 기리는 의미로 이름에 하트를 넣었어. 내가 새로 이름을 지었을 때도 바로 그 이름만은 간직했어. 그 이후에는 누구도, 어디에서든 붉은 사슴을 목격했다는 이야기를 들어본 적 없어. 어쩌면 그 사슴은 진작에 멸종했고, 부모님은 그 유령을 본 게 아닐까 상상해. 어쩌면 섬을 돌아다니는 붉은 사슴 홀로그램을 디자인하게 될지도 모르겠다. 애도해야 할 것이 너무 많아.

편지 고마워. 많이 사랑해 라티프.

너의 동지이자 친구,

—K

케일라 도로시 하트 푸안

2086년 8월 22일 일요일

북아메리카 중대서양주 파이어섬 체리그로브에서

이 이야기는 작가들의 사변 소설『모두를 위한 모든 것: 뉴욕 코뮌 구술사 2052-2072』(커먼 노션스, 2022)의 후속이다.

A Story of Eight Cities

Serang Chung

정세랑

여덟 도시 이야기

A Story of Eight Cities

Serang Chung

In 2086, without precedent, a great, discretionary power was granted to the organization for the Decarbonization Initiative. People from all walks of life united by a shared vision temporarily put aside their main professions and sat down at the roundtable. In order to extract society from that self-destructive addiction called mass production and mass consumption that had been underway for nearly 200 years, the meeting that would last until the very end went on. Finally, it was Ara Choi, considered by many to be the genius architect of the time, who came up with a plausible idea.

"Ultimately, isn't it a sense of belonging that gives you as much pleasure as consumption? What if you could pick a lifestyle and live within it all the time, like the way you follow an idol or a sports team? If every group standardizes an architectural form, clothing style, and food materials, wouldn't it be possible to manage resource production without waste?"

"What would you call such a group?"

"A clan, if you have to put a name on it. When you combine a city and a clan..."

Ara Choi inadvertently fingered the edges of Italo Calvino's *Invisible Cities*, the book she was holding in her hands.

"Would that be possible? Won't people get tired of it? What if you want to change in the middle?"

"It's possible you would want to change, but think of a baseball team, have you ever changed the team you've been rooting for?"

Ara Choi looked around at the people at the meeting.

They were all shaking their heads.

"I haven't changed my favorite team once since I chose them when I was ten. They haven't won a championship in thirty years, and it still makes my blood boil."

"The sense of belonging... is something you hold onto even if you think it's wrong in the middle of it."

"It has to be beautiful. It should be beautiful and enjoyable. If both of those criteria aren't met, it would be unsustainable."

It was not surprising that an architect came up with such an idea. It is not uncommon for a city or a village to have various restrictions and regulations to maintain its unique style. It was the marketer who then realized the idea of the architect. As is often the case with successful marketing, over time it took on the appearance of myth.

The First City

They chose the crow as a symbol. Crows love shiny metals. They love many types of metals, but mostly aluminum. This recyclable metal became a modular home, a beautiful dome, and feather-like cladding. Building materials, once produced, remained in a closed loop for near eternity.

The people enjoy wearing black clothes, and since it is calculated that no part is discarded from the initial cut cloth, the clothes, falling in straight lines, are comfortable to wear. The fabrics, produced in limited quantities each year, have subtle differences, even if they are all in the same color. Because the production quantity is determined through astute data analysis, there is no instance of wastage or lack. And even in the case an exception arises, it can be resolved.

People in this modern city are perennially busy, and

hence prefer personalized nutrition cubes that are easy to store and consume.

The Second City

The mushroom is their icon. They lay claim to anything that can be decomposed. The houses are built with wood and mushroom mycelium as the main materials. Every year, they like to challenge themselves to see how high a wooden structure can be built. They revived traditional architectural techniques and devised new methods for designing columns, beams, and rafters that interlocked perfectly.

They wear off-white plant-based clothing. Probably because it goes well with the houses. Each year, they dye fabric in various mushroom patterns in limited editions. The clothes are beautiful when worn, and when buried in the ground, decompose in a matter of weeks.

The mushroom burgers are famous. It is often somewhat forced upon their visitors.

The Third City

The inhabitants wanted a dolphin as their mascot. But they were referred to as spiders from outside, so it ended up being a spider. Re-weaving ocean debris, fishing nets in particular, the whole city resembles a labyrinth of hammocks. Naturally, the nets are secured with steel cables used on ships.

There are well-equipped floor panels for rolling anything on wheels of any kind, but gloves made of rubber and split-toed shoes are commonly worn, as there are inhabitants who occasionally want to get off the road and explore the nets. Since the city has the color of green fishing nets, striped T-shirts in purple shades are worn to easily distinguish people. Each year, clothing with stripes of different thickness and spacing is produced, rousing collectors.

They take pride in products made from seaweed.

The Fourth City

Opinions were initially divided as to whether the city should be called a city. It started with a group of campers and the units gradually grew larger. Quickly distributing fresh groceries has always used up a lot of energy, but turning this problem on its head, these inhabitants chose to move the city to sites of seasonal production. They move around all year, mapping winding roads and taking care of distribution between cities while working as short-term laborers during the harvest season.

"You know those old-time campers, they would say they loved being in nature, but then they changed tents every year and used a ton of disposables. What a disaster!"

"Of course, we can say this because we're past the days of burning firewood for ambience."

New camping gear is rarely produced. Items from the past are more than enough. Old tents are combined to make grand public structures. The representative color naturally took on a shade between beige and khaki. People from other cities refer to them as plovers.

They share seasonal food recipes every year.

The Fifth City

Amidst the climate crisis, good-natured knitters unraveled old sweaters. Strands of yarn circulated endlessly. When people learned that sheep, alpacas, and goats that had been liberated in the process had nowhere to go, they decided to take them in. Each inhabitant would adopt one animal as a pet, and carefully shear the animal in the spring to produce new yarn. Sheep that were genetically modified early on couldn't live without being sheared. Thus, the inhabitants took charge of the responsibility. Pet-sheep grooming became as wide-ranging as dog grooming. The helmet cut, the heart-shaped cut, etc., long- and short-term trends abounded.

Several ruined cities have been knitted over. Broken pillars and gaping roofs, everything that was cracked or run down.

It had nothing to do with the animals, but for some reason, the city's plant-based cheese is regarded as the finest.

The Sixth City

The city was built through 3D printing using polymers made of sugarcane and straw. It was designed like an anthill, at first unintentionally, and later with purpose. The air circulation structure modeled on an anthill suited the city well. They chose a light pink, especially beautiful in the setting sun, for the city color.

Since the structure did not let in much sunlight, people wear light-colored clothing and prefer luminous fabrics. In order to extend the life of luminescent fibers, they invented several waterless laundering methods.

Predictably, their sugary deserts are famous.

The Seventh City

More than any other city, this city believes in permanence. Going beyond hundred-year-old buildings, they dream of thousand-year-old buildings. The region was selected with earthquakes, typhoons, and floods in mind, and the buildings were constructed with a structure eight times stronger than ordinary buildings. Pillars are positioned on the exterior of the structure so that the interior can be flexibly modified. One never knows what peoples' tastes might be like in the future.

Color experts were mobilized to create the most timeless color scheme. An exquisite ice gray that suits anyone serves as the primary color, to which five accent colors were added. Much of their effort goes into developing abrasion resistant fabric.

Passionate about planting oak trees with great carbon storage capacity, they are famous for a variety of acorn dishes.

The Eighth City

They insist that bamboo should be the material of the future. In particular, why bamboo is a superior material than sugarcane. The panda is their mascot, but it is somewhat incongruous for this tenacious group of people. It would appear as if they decided to resolve all matters of food, clothing, and shelter with bamboo. Occasionally, they also use rattan, and make good application of patterns from Asian paintings.

Their representative menu consists of bamboo shoots and bamboo rice.

***

A few other city models were attempted, but none were realized. The inhabitants of the cities that were established loved the cities to which they belonged. Most of them did not leave the city of their birth. Similar to inheriting the political stripes of one's caregivers, they lived their whole lives with the sense of belonging that they felt at a young age, and only a few left in search for a different way of life. People who sought to explore other cities infused vitality between them. Cities one wasn't born into were always attractive travel destinations, and because of their many aspects that cannot be known through travel alone, there were many exchange programs for each turning point in their lives. If you wanted to, you could try living in every city, but rather than those who went so far as to try, the majority tended to explore two or three cities in depth.

"The idea that everyone can experience everything is a lie that has passed its expiration date."

"It's a lie that corporations used to tell. To try to sell you something. We know that when you try to experience everything, you just end up drifting about until the end."

The next to be deployed for the continuity of cities were storytellers. Over time, the members of the Decarbonization Initiative have changed, but new members inherited their orientation. They came to the agreement that it was time to overlay the narrative. Nothing survives longer or more persistently than a story, so they decided to attach them to cities like a bonding or reinforcing agent. Most of the storytellers came on board with nondisclosure agreements. Some stories were produced and disseminated through official channels, while others were created and spread in more subtle ways.

***

A ghost story first enveloped the Eighth City. It told of something living in the bamboo forest. Even in the age of reason, bamboo groves at night struck people's hearts with a particular darkness. The fear that something might be lurking out of sight was ever-present. At first it was said to be a wild animal that might bite people, then it was said to be an escaped convict, but it was mostly rumored to be the spirit of a dead person.

"Wait a minute. Is this a rumor we made up?"

The people in charge of the project were perplexed.

"No, but don't you think we should use it?"

So, the people in charge created the "answering being." It was a simple device made up of a microphone, speaker, and natural language processing AI, but the results were effective. People with questions shouted them deep into the bamboo grove, and sometimes an answer came back. The answers were ambiguous yet appropriate, and at times extremely sharp.

"The key is that it has to be 'sometimes.' It's no fun if it answers every time you ask a question."

It was effective to adjust it to the most random setting possible. There were times when answers came back to many people in the middle of the day, or when it came back to a single person at the break of dawn. There were times when it answered in succession, and there were times when there were no answers for over a month. The storytellers carefully selected books from which sentences would form the basis of its answers. As one would expect, copyright holders signed confidentially agreements and received royalties.

"The sentences that came out of the book the other day were inappropriate. Nonetheless, language that is too dated would be disengaging to contemporary folks. Let's set the period to about fifty years ago and choose books from that time frame."

The AI's answers, derived from adding and melting books-on-books, even touched the project managers' hearts to an astonishing degree. People, of course, noticed that the ghost stories, regardless of how they began, were developing into slick contrivances, but delighted in them anyway.

A musical with a runtime of six hours was produced for the people of the Seventh City. It was a musical based on the life of Shin Minhee, an anthropoid scholar who discovered a new antibiotic. Act One presents the story of Shin Minhee's birth and childhood in the Seventh City. It is elaborately composed of anecdotes of the loss of her sister to an epidemic, her tragic breakup with her first love, and how she waged a campaign on behalf of urban ecosystems with her friends. Act Two, which started again after the break, had a completely different feel. The depiction of the story leading up to her research with gibbons and the episode with the poachers was both dramatic and grand. Utilizing even the space above the audience's heads, the gibbons with their spectacular movements, masterpieces of Peninsula Robotics, appeared as if they were actually alive. The combat scene with the poachers that formed the climax of Act Two was favorably received. Even the pacifists had no qualms about wanting to see the death of the poachers. Act Three sings movingly about Shin Minhee's discovery and how it went on to save countless lives. While observing a black-handed gibbon, Shin watches the gibbon bring a never-before-seen plant to its wound, which she then relays to the botanists and microbiologists. The three scholars engaged in a secretive love triangle was an overreach. It was a choice taken for the masses, but those who belonged to the same research center at the time couldn't help but grumble.

"Can you believe how they just made all that up? It wasn't love, it was just collegiality!"

"Why can't dry stories just be dry?"

The musical was staged every year on the anniversary of the city's founding. The performance hall was designed more perfectly than in any other city, so people from other cities came to visit the Seventh City to see the musical.

The Sixth City was the hub of the idol industry. It was the fans that were the first to raise questions about the wasteful aspects of the idol industry. The culture of throwing away albums without even opening them, or just clicking without listening to increase the streaming count has completely changed. Deliberations on and attempts to bring about more gratifying experiences, while consuming less, pressed on. While wrestling with the problem of how to replace the sense of accomplishment people used to feel through sales rankings, a planner from the Decarbonization Initiative came up with the AR quest. The gently winding roads and dim interiors of the Sixth City were well suited for AR content. An exciting competition began over which idols' fans could complete the most quests. Music and dance still held center stage, but there were additions that exceeded expectations. At the end of the year, the results of the quest were announced alongside a string of award ceremonies. The quests consisted of a good mix of electronic gaming and public service activities. This was not surprising as it had been idol fans that originally created the largest expanse of forest area.

A children's book author born and raised in the Fifth City wrote a children's book with a baby sheep as the main character. Danbom, the baby sheep, was experiencing hair loss.[1] No matter what she tried, her hair wouldn't grow.

"If I am a sheep but not fluffy, then what am I?"

When the first volume of Danbom's struggles to find the meaning of life and existence was greatly loved, the Decarbonization Initiative immediately made the author into a full-time writer so she could focus solely on the Danbom series. As the books piled up, the baby sheep worked through the relationship between herself and the world in a healthy way. The image of Danbom growing into an adult sheep with neither excessive self-hatred nor excessive self-love but with confidence touched a part of people's hearts that other stories had been unable to reach. The Decarbonization Initiative made enterprising use of the Danbom series in the form of animation and educational content. Not just children in the Fifth City, but children in every city grew up reading the Danbom sheep series. Travelers arriving in the Fifth City, when they came across a baby sheep, would cry out "Danbom!" on the verge of tears. Baby sheeps pet-owners found such travelers ridiculous, all the while inwardly taking pleasure in the thought: "My sheep must look like Danbom!"

The people of the Fourth City wanted to open a circus from the beginning.

"It just makes sense, if we move around in big tents like these, why would we do something other than hold a circus? I mean, wouldn't that be strange?"

When the artistic direction of the circus was taking off, the added rock climbing elements were quite refreshing, given that the people of the Fourth City were basically mountaineers. Bouldering holds were wedged all over the stage both visible and hidden, and the performers, who appeared to have overcome gravity, used the space three-dimensionally. Many storylines were drawn up, but the story that was most loved was the story of the people of the Fourth City setting out to find a young teenager, who upon arriving from another city for an exchange program fell into distress. With every performance, the originating city of the youth was changed. Taking into account the teenager's personage, who was lovable but careless and unprepared, it was a good idea to do so. The protagonist's mishaps, the crisscrossing paths of the search party, and the mythical beings issuing from natural objects that the protagonist encounters in delirium, were all portrayed through pantomime. The people of the Fourth City found the people of other cities excessively talkative, and were satisfied with their choice to use pantomime. Without even a single word, the circus viewers could leave the stage tent with a good tip or two on how to survive when thrown into the wilderness.

If the people of the Fourth City were mountain climbers, the people of the Third City were divers. For this group of people, who obtain diving licenses like a driver's license, a legend about undersea treasures was prepared.

"They say that the slush fund was hidden on an island that was submerged by the rise in sea level."

"Whose slush fund? What form was it in?"

At first, it was naturally assumed to be in gold, but others began to appear with different ideas, such as stolen art or ancient artifacts, technical information that had been forgotten but people wanted to restore, or a riddle that would unlock the inheritance of a celebrity if solved. There were people who would dive once or twice and then forget about it. But there were also those who persistently devoted all of their leisure time to it. Once every few years, an intriguing element worth calling a clue was discovered, but the definitive treasure has yet to be found.

"Every time we dive, we come out with trash. Do you think they're using this to clean up the trash?"

"Those Decarbonization folks, they must be at it again."

The people who hid the treasure smiled nonchalantly. If one were found, then they would hide another. The list of candidates has been around for hundreds of years. No one knew until the list was made that there were so many types of treasures that could withstand water as well as time.

The people of the Second City created an action game with a large assortment of anthropomorphized mushroom characters. If you were determined to figure out why the mushrooms had to fight each other, the reasoning was bizarre, but no one really pushed it because the mushroom characters were shockingly cool. The wood pinkgill mushroom threw off its satgat like a martial arts master,[2] and the skirt train of the veiled lady mushroom was mesmerizing. The lobster mushrooms attacked in clusters and the magic mushrooms assaulted the mind. Players loved the staghorn mushroom's handsomely raised horns and the cinnamon cap mushroom's bobbed hair. When edible and poisonous mushrooms resembled each other, it was accompanied by a background story about siblings or rivals with hidden secrets around their birth and lineage. The game controls were simple but the storylines lavish. All of those stories were not merely used to deliver knowledge about poisonous mushrooms. Instead, it came closer to capturing the sense of wonder about objects of a different kind. It was a game that seemed to say all along that while some peculiar organisms may be good or bad for people, their complex and elusive existence arouses wonder, and it is when people wonder that they are most human. The game has been loved for a very long time. The winners are always elementary school students.

The people of the First City realized one day that a story was hidden like a code in their favorite spelling game. Since when, and who was it, that started hiding the story? Everyone suspected the storytellers of the Decarbonization Initiative, but surprisingly they didn't have a hand in it. Rather, the Initiative was also startled and in the process of monitoring it.

They observed with astonishment those who were discovering, adding to, and developing stories that no one appeared to have made up.

"What if the story gets too dark? Shouldn't we intervene then?"

"A story that ends in despair won't be written. Some may push it that way out of malice, but it won't end like that."

An unprecedented collaborative production ensued. A story soon diverged into several directions. The stories became similar and then dissimilar. They were either completely disconnected or mutually influencing one other. They were either focused on amplifying emotions or concentrated on conveying a message. The side that sought to impose order and the side that reveled in the chaos clashed vigorously.

***

Cities will be built and destroyed. Even if the city were to perish, those who believe that stories will leave behind the outlines of the city have taken over the warp and weft of the loom. And eventually, whether they exist inside or outside of the story has become uncertain. That is up to you to decide.

Translator's note

1. The sheep's name, Danbom, means "sweet spring" in Korean.
2. The *satgat* is a conical shaped hat often made of bamboo originating in East, South, and Southeast Asia.

여덟 도시 이야기

정세랑

2086년에, 탈탄소 체제를 위한 이니셔티브 조직에 유례없이 막강한 재량권이 부여되었다. 같은 뜻을 가진 각계의 인물들이 잠시 본업을 내려두고 원탁에 둘러앉았다. 대량 생산과 대량 소비라는 200년 가까이 된 자기 파괴적인 중독으로부터 스스로를 건져내기 위해, 끝날 때까지 끝나지 않을 회의가 이어졌다. 마침내 그럴듯한 의견을 낸 것은 당대의 천재 건축가로 불리는 최아라였다.

"소비만큼의 쾌감을 주는 건 역시, 소속감 아닌가요? 아이돌을 좋아하거나 스포츠팀을 좋아하는 것처럼 하나의 라이프 스타일을 골라 그 안에서 쭉 살아갈 수 있다면요? 집단마다 건축양식, 의류 스타일, 식자재를 통일하면 자원 생산도 낭비 없이 관리할 수 있지 않을까요?"

"그런 집단을 뭐라고 불러야 하죠?"

"굳이 부르자면 부족(clan)? 도시와 부족을 결합시킨다면……."

최아라는 무심히 들고 있던 이탈로 칼비노의 책, 『보이지 않는 도시들』의 모서리를 만지작거렸다.

"그게 될까? 사람들이 질려하지 않을까? 중간에 바꾸고 싶어 하면 어떡해요?"

"바꾸고 싶어 할 수도 있지만, 야구팀을 생각해봐요, 응원하던 팀을 바꾼 적 있나?"

최아라가 회의에 참석한 다른 사람들을 돌아보았다. 모두 고개를 저었다.

"열 살 때 정한 이후로 한 번도 바꾸지 않았습니다. 우승을 30년째 못 하고 있지만 여전히 피가 끓어올라요."

"소속감은…… 설령 중간에 틀렸다는 생각이 들어도 계속하게 하죠."

"아름다워야 해. 아름답고 즐거워야 해. 그 두 가지가 다 충족되지 않으면 지속성을 잃을 거예요."

건축가가 그런 아이디어를 낸 것은 의외의 일은 아니었다. 도시나 마을이 고유의 색을 유지하기 위해 여러 제약과 규약들을 두었던 경우는 흔하니까. 건축가의 아이디어를 실현화시킨 것은 마케터였다. 성공적인 마케팅이 종종 그렇듯, 시간이 흐르자 신화의 모습을 띠게 되었다.

첫 번째 도시

상징으로 까마귀를 택했다. 까마귀들은 빛나는 금속들을 사랑한다. 여러 금속을 사랑하지만 주로 알루미늄을 사랑했다. 이 재활용이 용이한 금속은 모듈 주택이 되고 아름다운 돔이 되고 깃털 같은 외장재가 되었다. 한 번 생산된 건축재는 폐쇄된 루프에 영원에 가깝게 머물렀다.

시민들은 검은 옷을 즐겨 입었고 재단부터 버려지는 부분이 없도록 계산했으므로, 직선으로 툭 떨어지는 옷들은 편안했다. 매년 한정 생산되는 원단들은 같은 색이라도 미묘하게 달랐다. 치열한 데이터 분석으로 생산량을 정했기 때문에 남는 일도 부족한 일도 거의 없었다. 예외가 생겨도 해결할 수 있었다.

이 현대적인 도시의 사람들은 여전히 바빠서, 보관과 섭취가 편한 개인 맞춤 영양 큐브를 선호한다.

두 번째 도시

버섯을 아이콘으로 삼았다. 분해되는 것들이라면 뭐든 자신들의 것이라고 규정했다. 목재와 버섯 균사체를 주재료로 집을 지었다. 목재 건물을 얼마나 높이 지을 수 있는지 매년 새로운 도전을 하는 걸 좋아했다. 전통 건축의 기술을 되살리고 또 없던 기술을 고안해 완벽하게 맞물리는 기둥과 보, 서까래를 설계했다.

미색의 식물성 소재 옷들을 입었다. 아무래도 그게 집과 어울리니까. 매해 한정판으로 각종 버섯들의 패턴을 염색했다. 옷들은 입을 때는 아름다웠고 땅에 묻으면 몇 주 만에 썩어 없어졌다.

버섯으로 만든 버거가 유명하다. 방문자들에게 다소 강권되곤 한다.

세 번째 도시

본인들은 돌고래를 마스코트로 선택하고 싶어 했지만, 바깥에서 거미라고 불렀기 때문에 결국 거미가 되었다. 해양 쓰레기, 특히 어망을 재직조해서 도시 전체가 해먹으로 된 미로나 다름없었다. 역시 선박에서 쓰였던 강철 케이블로 그물을 고정시켰다.

어떤 종류의 바퀴든 구를 수 있도록 잘 갖추어진 바닥 패널이 존재했지만, 가끔 길을 벗어나 그물 위를 탐험하고 싶어 하는 시민들이 있어 고무로 된 장갑과 발가락이 갈라진 신발이 보편적으로 이용되었다. 어망의 초록색이 도시의 색깔이 되었으므로 사람들을 잘 분간하기 위해 보라 계통의 줄무늬 티셔츠를 입는다. 해마다 다른 굵기와 간격의 줄무늬 옷들이 생산되어서 수집가들을 자극했다.

해조류를 가공한 식품에 자부심이 있다.

네 번째 도시

이들의 도시를 도시라 불러야 할지 초기에는 의견이 갈렸다. 한 무리의 캠퍼들에서 시작해 점점 단위가 커졌다. 식료품을 신선하고 신속하게 유통시키는 것에는 언제나 큰 에너지가 들었는데, 이들은 발상을 뒤집어 제철식품 생산지로 도시가 움직이는 방향을 택했다. 1년 내내 이동하며 꼬불꼬불한 경로를 그렸고, 수확 시기의 단기 노동자인 동시에 도시 간 유통을 맡기도 했다.

"옛날 캠퍼들 말야, 자연 속에 있는 순간을 사랑한다고 말해놓고, 매년 텐트를 바꿨고 일회용품을 잔뜩 썼어. 엉망이었지?"

"낭만을 위해 장작을 태우던 시절에서 벗어났으니까 하는 말이지."

새로운 캠핑용품은 거의 생산되지 않았다. 과거의 물건들로도 충분했다. 공용 건물을 위해 오래된 텐트들을 합쳐 거대하게 만들기도 했다. 대표 색깔은 자연스레 베이지와 카키 사이가 되었다. 다른 도시 사람들은 이들을 물떼새라고 불렀다.

제철식품 레시피를 매년 공유한다.

다섯 번째 도시

기후 위기 속에서 다정한 뜨개질 애호가들은 오래된 스웨터들을 풀어헤쳤다. 실들은 끝없이 순환했다. 그러다가 해방된 양들, 알파카들, 염소들이 갈 곳이 없다는 걸 알게 된 사람들이 동물들과 함께 살기로 마음먹었다. 한 사람당 한 마리씩을 반려로 삼아, 봄이면 털을 조심스럽게 깎아 새 실을 생산하기로 했다. 일찍이 개량된 양들은 사람이 털을 깎아주지 않으면 살 수 없게 되어버렸으니 책임을 지는 일이었다. 반려견 미용만큼이나 반려양 미용이 다양해졌다. 헬멧컷, 하트컷 등 길고 짧은 유행이 돌았다.

폐허가 된 도시 몇 개를 뜨개질로 덮어갔다. 깨진 기둥들과 뚫린 지붕들을, 금가고 누추해진 모든 것들을.

동물들과는 별 상관이 없지만, 어째선지 이 도시의 식물성 치즈가 가장 고급품 취급을 받는다.

여섯 번째 도시

사탕수수와 짚을 기반으로 한 폴리머를 3D 프린팅해 도시를 지어갔다. 처음에는 의도 없이, 나중에는 의도를 갖춰 개미집처럼 디자인했다. 개미집을 모사한 공기 순환 구조는 도시에 적합했다. 석양 속에서 특히 아름다운 연한 핑크색을 도시의 색으로 골랐다.

채광에는 약한 구조였으므로, 밝은색 옷을 기본으로 하고 발광 섬유를 선호했다. 발광 섬유를 오래 쓰기 위해 물을 사용하지 않는 세탁법들을 여럿 발명했다.

예측 가능하다시피, 설탕 디저트가 유명하다.

일곱 번째 도시

어느 도시보다 영원을 믿었다. 백년 건물을 넘어서, 천년 건물을 꿈꿨다. 지진, 태풍, 홍수를 감안하여 지역을 골라 보통 건물보다 여덟 배는 강력한 구조로 건축을 했다. 기둥이 건물 바깥쪽에 있어서 내부는 유연하게 고칠 수 있도록 했다. 훗날 올 사람들의 취향은 알 수 없으니까.

색상 전문가들을 동원해 가장 질리지 않는 색상 팔레트를 구성했다. 누구에게나 어울릴 만큼 절묘한 아이스 그레이를 바탕으로 다섯 가지 포인트 색상을 더했다. 항마모 섬유 개발에 전력을 다하고 있다.

탄소 저장 능력이 큰 참나무를 심는 데 열정적이라, 각종 도토리 요리가 유명하다.

여덟 번째 도시

미래의 재료는 대나무여야 한다고 집요하게 주장하곤 한다. 특히 사탕수수보다 대나무가 왜 더 나은 재료인지에 대해서. 마스코트는 판다지만 이 집요한 사람들에게 다소 어울리지 않는 경향이 있다. 의식주를 모두 대나무로 해결하고자 마음먹은 것처럼 보일 정도다. 가끔 등나무도 사용하기는 하며, 동양화의 패턴을 잘 활용한다.

죽순 요리와 대나무 통밥이 대표 메뉴다.

***

몇 개의 도시 모델이 더 시도되었지만 자리 잡지 못했다. 자리 잡은 도시의 시민들은 자신이 속한 도시를 사랑했다. 대개는 태어난 도시를 떠나지 않았다. 양육자의 정치색을 물려받는 것과 비슷해서, 어린 나이에 느낀 소속감으로 평생을 살았고 일부만이 다른 삶의 양식을 찾아 떠났다. 다른 도시를 탐색하고자 하는 사람들이 도시들 사이의 활기를 만들어냈다. 태어나지 않은 도시는 언제나 매력적인 여행지였고, 여행만으로는 알 수 없는 부분이 컸으므로 삶의 전환기마다 교환 프로그램이 많았다. 원한다면 모든 도시에서 살아볼 수 있지만 그렇게까지 시도하는 사람들보다는 두세 도시를 깊이 탐색하는 이들이 다수였다.

"모두가 모든 것을 경험할 수 있다는 건 유효기간이 끝난 거짓말이야."

"회사들이 하던 거짓말이지. 뭔가를 팔아먹으려고. 전부를 경험하려 하다간 부유(浮游)하다 끝난다는 걸 우린 알아."

도시들의 영속성을 위해 그다음으로 투입된 것은 스토리텔러들이었다. 시간이 흘러 탈탄소 이니셔티브의 구성원들은 바뀌었지만 방향성은 이어받았다. 이제 이야기를 입힐 차례라는 동의에 이르렀다. 이야기보다 오래 끈질기게 살아남는 것은 없으니 접착제처럼, 보강재처럼 도시에 덧대어보자고. 다수의 스토리텔러들이 비밀유지합의서와 함께 합류했다. 어떤 이야기들은 공식적인 경로로 또 어떤 이야기들은 보다 은근한 방식으로 창작되어 퍼져나갔다.

***

여덟 번째 도시를 처음 감싼 것은 괴담이었다. 대나무 숲에 무언가 살고 있다고 했다. 과학의 시대에도 밤의 대나무 숲은 사람들 마음속에 깃든 어둠을 일으키곤 했다. 시야의 바깥에 무언가 도사리고 있을지도 모른다는 두려움은 여전히 존재했다. 처음에 그것은 사람을 물지도 모를 야생동물이라고 했고, 그다음은 탈주한 범죄자라고 했고, 죽은 이의 영혼이라는 소문이 가장 많았다.

"어, 잠깐. 이거 우리가 만든 소문인가?"

프로젝트의 담당자들은 당황했다.

"아뇨, 하지만 이용하기 좋겠는데요?"

그래서 담당자들은 '대답하는 존재'를 만들었다. 마이크와 스피커, 자연어 AI라는 간단한 장치였지만 효과는 좋았다. 질문이 있는 사람들이 대나무 숲 깊숙이 그 질문을 외치면 가끔 대답이 돌아왔다. 그 대답들은 모호하면서도 적절했고 때로 아주 날카로울 때도 있었다.

"핵심은 '가끔'이어야 한단 거예요. 물을 때마다 대답하면 그건 재미가 없지."

설정을 최대한 랜덤으로 맞춘 것이 유효했다. 대낮의 여러 사람들에게 대답이 돌아올 때도 있었고, 새벽의 한 사람에게 돌아올 때도 있었다. 연달아 대답할 때도 있었고 한 달 넘게 대답이 없을 때도 있었다. 대답이 될 문장들은 스토리텔러들이 고심하여 고른 책들을 바탕으로 한 것이었다. 저작권자들 역시 비밀유지합의서에 사인하고 저작권료를 지급받았다.

"엊그제 나온 책의 문장들은 안 돼. 그렇다고 너무 오래된 말들도 지금 사람들과는 유리될 거야. 50년쯤으로 기간을 잡고 책을 고르자."

책과 책을 더하고 녹여 AI가 하는 대답들은 프로젝트 담당자들도 놀랄 만큼 마음을 파고들었다. 사람들은 물론 괴담이, 출발이야 어쨌든 매끈한 장치로 발전하고 있다는 걸 알아챘지만 알아챈 채로도 즐겼다.

일곱 번째 도시 사람들을 위해서는 러닝 타임 여섯 시간짜리 뮤지컬이 제작되었다. 새로운 항생물질을 발견한 유인원 학자 신민희의 실제 삶을 토대로 한 뮤지컬이었다. 1부는 신민희가 일곱 번째 도시에서 태어나 보낸 어린 시절에 대한 내용이었다. 전염병에 손아래 자매를 잃고, 첫사랑과 안타깝게 헤어지고, 친구들과 함께 도시생태계 관련 캠페인을 벌였던 일화들로 오밀조밀 구성되었다. 휴식 시간 후 다시 시작되는 2부는 분위기가 완전히 달랐다. 긴팔원숭이를 연구하게 되기까지의 사연과 밀렵꾼들과의 에피소드가 극적이고 웅장하게 그려졌다. 관객들 머리 위의 공간까지 활용하여 화려한 움직임을 보이는 긴팔원숭이들은 페닌슐라 로보틱스의 역작으로, 정말 살아 있는 것처럼 보였다. 2부 클라이맥스의 밀렵꾼들과의 전쟁 신이 큰 호평을 받았는데, 평화주의자들도 밀렵꾼들의 죽음만큼은 거리낌 없이 보고 싶어 했기 때문이었다. 3부는 신민희가 검은손긴팔원숭이를 관찰하다가 한 번도 본 적 없는 식물을 상처에 가져다 대는 모습을 식물학자와 미생물학자에게 알린 일이 어떻게 수많은 사람들의 목숨을 구하게 되었는지 감동적으로 노래했다. 3부의 무리수는 세 학자를 은근한 삼각관계 구도로 그린 것이었다. 대중적인 선택이긴 했지만 당시 같은 연구 센터에 속했던 사람들이 투덜거릴 수밖에 없었다.

"막 지어내는 것 좀 봐, 완전 동료애였다고!"

"건조한 이야기는 그냥 건조하게 하면 안 돼?"

뮤지컬은 매년 도시의 기념일에 상연되었다. 어느 도시보다 완벽하게 설계된 공연장을 갖고 있었기에, 다른 도시 사람들도 뮤지컬을 보기 위해 일곱 번째 도시를 방문하곤 했다.

여섯 번째 도시는 아이돌 산업의 중심지였다. 아이돌 산업의 낭비를 조장하는 면에 대해 먼저 문제를 제기한 것은 아이돌 팬들이었다. 음반을 뜯지도 않고 버리던, 듣지 않고 스트리밍 수를 올리기 위해 클릭만 하던 문화가 완전히 변했다. 덜 소비하되 더 충만한 경험이 가능하도록 고민과 시도들이 이어졌다. 판매 순위에서 느꼈던 성취감을 무엇으로 대체하면 좋을지 골머리를 앓다, 탈탄소 이니셔티브의 한 기획자가 AR 퀘스트를 떠올렸다. 여섯 번째 도시의 부드럽게 굽어 있는 길들과 약간 어두운 실내는 AR 콘텐츠에 적합했다. 어떤 아이돌의 팬들이 가장 많은 퀘스트를 완료하는지를 두고 즐거운 경쟁이 시작되었다. 음악과 춤이 여전히 핵심이었지만 기대를 뛰어넘는 확산들이 있었다. 연말이면 퀘스트 결과들이 발표되었고 시상식들도 즐비했다. 퀘스트들에는 오락 활동과 공익 활동이 적절하게 배합되어 있었는데 원래도 가장 많은 면적의 숲을 조성했던 건 아이돌 팬들이었기에 새로운 이야기는 아니었다.

다섯 번째 도시에서 나고 자란 동화 작가는 아기 양이 주인공인 동화책을 썼다. 아기 양 단봄에게는 탈모 증상이 있었다. 아무리 애를 써도 털이 자라지 않았다.

"양인데 복슬복슬하지 않다면, 그럼 난 뭐지?"

단봄이 삶의 의미를, 존재의 의미를 찾아 고민하는 내용의 첫 권이 크게 사랑받자, 탈탄소 이니셔티브는 당장 작가를 전업 작가로 만들었다. 오로지 단봄 시리즈에 집중할 수 있도록. 아기 양은 책이 쌓여갈수록 자신과 세계 사이의 관계를 건강히 조율해갔다. 지나친 자기혐오도 자기애도 하지 않으면서 자기 확신은 있는 어른 양이 되어가는 모습은 사람들의 마음속 다른 이야기들이 미처 가닿지 못했던 부분을 건드렸다. 탈탄소 이니셔티브는 단봄 시리즈를 애니메이션으로, 학습 콘텐츠로 힘껏 활용했다. 다섯 번째 도시뿐 아니라 모든 도시의 어린이들이 아기 양 단봄 시리즈를 읽으며 자라났다. 그래서 여행객들은 다섯 번째 도시에 도착해 아무 아기 양이나 보고 울먹이며 "단봄아!"를 외치곤 했다. 아기 양의 반려인은 그런 여행객들을 우스꽝스럽게 여기면서도 "내 양이 단봄이를 닮았나 보군."하고 내심 좋아하곤 했다.

네 번째 도시 사람들은 처음부터 서커스를 하고 싶어 했다.

"그렇잖아, 이렇게 대형 텐트로 옮겨 다니는데 서커스가 아니라 다른 걸 하면? 그건 이상하잖아?"

서커스의 예술성은 도약을 거듭하는 중이었는데, 네 번째 도시 사람들이 기본적으로 산악인이었기 때문에 암벽등반의 여러 요소들이 추가되자 또 신선했다. 무대 곳곳에 볼더링 홀더들이 보이게, 보이지 않게 박혀 있었고 중력을 이겨낸 것처럼 보이는 연기자들이 공간을 입체적으로 사용했다. 여러 이야기들이 창작되었지만 가장 사랑받았던 이야기는 다른 도시에서 교환 생활을 하러 온 청소년이 조난을 당하자, 네 번째 도시 사람들이 그 청소년을 찾아 나서는 이야기였다. 공연이 재상연될 때마다 주인공 청소년의 출신 도시가 바뀌었는데, 사랑스럽지만 준비가 부족하고 부주의한 이 인물의 성격을 고려할 때 매번 바뀌는 쪽이 나았다. 주인공의 실수들과 주인공을 찾아 나선 사람들의 어긋남, 주인공이 착란 속에서 만나는 자연물에서 비롯된 신화적 존재들이 무언극으로 표현되었다. 네 번째 도시 사람들은 다른 도시 사람들이 지나치게 말이 많다고 여겼고, 무언극을 택한 것에 만족감을 느꼈다. 한마디 말 없이도, 서커스를 본 사람들은 야생에 내던져졌을 때 어떻게 하면 살아남을 수 있을지 한두 가지 괜찮은 팁을 얻은 채 공연 텐트를 나설 수 있었다.

네 번째 도시 사람들이 산악인이라면, 세 번째 도시 사람들은 다이버였다. 운전면허를 따듯 잠수 면허를 따는 이들을 위해 해저 보물에 대한 전설이 준비되었다.

"해수면 상승으로 수몰된 섬에, 사실 비자금이 숨겨져 있었대."

"누구의 비자금이? 어떤 형태로?"

처음에는 뻔하게 금으로 추정되었지만 도난된 예술품이나 오래된 유물, 잊혔지만 모두 복원하고 싶어 하는 기술 정보, 풀면 유명인의 상속권을 얻게 되는 수수께끼 등 변형된 추측을 하는 이들이 나타났다. 한두 번 잠수해 보고 잊는 사람이 있는 반면, 끈질기게 여가시간을 다 바치는 축들도 있었다.

몇 년에 한 번씩 단서라 부를 만한 흥미로운 요소들이 발견되었지만 결정적인 보물은 아직 발견되지 않았다.

"우리, 잠수할 때마다 쓰레기를 가지고 나오잖아. 쓰레기 치우려고 이용하는 거 아냐?"

"탈탄소 이니셔티브 녀석들, 또 장난친 거겠지."

보물을 숨겨둔 사람들은 느긋한 미소를 지을 뿐이었다. 하나가 발견되면 다른 것을 또 숨길 셈이었다. 후보 목록이 몇백 년 치는 되었다. 물에도 시간에도 상하지 않을 보물의 종류가 그렇게 많을 줄, 목록을 쓰기 전에는 알지 못했다.

두 번째 도시 사람들은 버섯을 의인화한 캐릭터들이 잔뜩 등장하는 액션 게임을 만들었다. 왜 버섯들이 치고받고 싸워야 하는지 따지고 들면 기이했지만, 캐릭터화가 충격적으로 근사하게 되는 바람에 아무도 따지고 들지 않았다. 삿갓버섯은 무술의 고수처럼 삿갓을 벗어던졌고, 망사버섯의 옷자락은 황홀하게 표현되었다. 점버섯들은 집단 공격을 했고 환각버섯은 정신 공격을 했다. 플레이어들은 사슴뿔버섯의 멋지게 솟아오른 뿔과 개암버섯의 단발머리를 사랑했다. 식용버섯과 독버섯이 닮았을 때, 출생의 비밀이 있는 형제자매나 라이벌로 배경 스토리가 그려졌다. 조작은 단순하지만 스토리는 풍성한 게임이었다. 그 모든 이야기들이 그저 독버섯을 구분할 지식을 제공하기 위해서만 쓰이지는 않았다. 그보다는 이질적인 대상들에 대한 경이감을 담아내기 위한 것에 가까웠다. 어떤 독특한 생물들이 사람들에게 이로울 수도 해로울 수도 있지만 그 복잡하고 이해하기 어려운 존재 자체로 감탄을 불러일으킨다고, 사람들이 가장 사람다울 때는 감탄할 때라고, 내내 말하는 게임이었다. 게임은 아주 오랫동안 사랑받았다. 챔피언은 언제나 초등학생들이었다.

첫 번째 도시 사람들은, 어느 날 자신들이 즐겨하던 철자 게임에 암호처럼 이야기가 숨겨져 있다는 것을 깨달았다. 언제부터, 누가 이야기를 숨기기 시작했을까? 모두 탈탄소 이니셔티브의 스토리텔러들을 의심했지만, 의외로 그들은 개입하지 않았다. 오히려 깜짝 놀라 모니터링하는 중이었다. 아무도 만들지 않은 이야기를 발견하고 덧붙이고 만들어가는 이들을 신기해하면서.

"이야기가 너무 어두워지면 어떡하지? 그땐 개입해야 하지 않을까?"

"절망으로 끝나는 이야기는 쓰이지 않을 거야. 몇몇이 악의를 가지고 그렇게 몰아갈지도 모르지만, 끝내는 그렇게 되지 않을 거야."

유례없는 공동 창작이 이어졌다. 하나의 이야기가 이내 갈래갈래 갈라졌다. 이야기들은 닮았다가 닮지 않아졌다. 완전히 분리되거나 서로 영향을 주고받았다. 감정을 증폭시키는 데 집중하거나 메시지를 전하는 데 치중했다. 질서를 부여하려는 축과 혼란에 매혹을 느끼는 축이 팽팽하게 부딪혔다.

***

도시들은 세워졌다 스러질 것이었다. 도시가 스러진다 해도, 이야기가 도시의 윤곽선을 남기리라고 믿는 이들이 베틀의 북과 바디를 넘겨받았다. 그들이 이야기의 안에 존재하는지 밖에 존재하는지는 모호해지고 말았다. 그 점은 당신이 정해야 한다.

The Perfection of Mythology

Federico Campagna

페데리코 캄파냐

신화의 완성

The Perfection of Mythology

Federico Campagna

Andalusia, the southernmost strip of Spain. For centuries, the vanguard of the Islamic world in Europe and the intellectual garden of the Mediterranean. Issuing from a melting pot of Muslims, Jews, and Christians, Andalusian mystics like Ibn Arabi, poets like Ibn Hazm, and philosophers like Ibn Rashid and Maimonides, inaugurated currents of thought that went on to change the world far beyond their place of origin. Among their ranks, there was also a lesser known, but not less interesting, writer. His name was Ibn Tufail, and he was well respected in his time as a proficient astronomer, theologian, and physician. Today, he is known mainly as the visionary author of one of the earliest philosophical science fictions. His novel, translated into Latin as "The Self-Taught Philosopher," described the life of a child growing up alone on a desert island. Raised by a gazelle, the boy spent his childhood exploring the laws of nature, of divinity, and of his own thought. Through a combination of empirical observation and abstract speculation, he eventually grew to become the greatest philosopher of his imaginary age.

Thus, Ibn Tufail claimed, all true philosophers are born: by looking around and inside themselves, and then translating their observations into practical abstractions that can guide their lives.

Despite its originality, and unbeknownst to its author, the method proposed by Tufail could boast illustrious ancestors. Its genealogy, however, had to wait until the twentieth century to be fully revealed. In their 1969 book *Hamlet's Mill*, scholars Giorgio de Santillana and Hertha von Dechend identified the same approach at the heart of another form of wisdom, chronologically anterior but in no way lesser than philosophy: mythology. Having carefully examined the first known myths, as found in the earliest extant written records from the fourth millennium BC, Santillana and Dechend discovered that what appeared initially as a collection of fantasy tales, contained in fact very precise references to the astronomical movements that were visible in the sky at the time of their composition. Gods and heroes could be read as the narrative clothing of the celestial bodies, while their deeds and adventures offered a mythological translation of the regular movement of the night-sky. It was thus, according to Santillana and Dechen, that the scientific minds of different archaic civilizations came up with similar mythological narratives to describe the same celestial events. Mythological language, then, should be understood as an authentic form of knowledge, deriving from empirical observation and calculation.

The sequence of this process, here as in Tufail's story, is important. First comes empirical observation, together with its mathematical recording. Second comes the mythical or philosophical translation of these observations. First came astronomy, then astrology. Or in other words, at the most primitive level of thought we find the so-called "exact" sciences, while at a further level of intellectual refinement, we have what is today most commonly discarded as the fantastic inventions of myth, or the impractical ruminations of philosophy.

To those archaic minds, to whom we owe the foundation of our contemporary edifice of knowledge, the value judgement between scientific "objectivity" and mythological narrative was the opposite of ours today. Science appeared as the mere representation of visible reality, while mythology was deemed as its abstraction and practical perfection.

This inversion might sound surprising. But there is an advantage of expressing narratively what could otherwise be communicated through the clear language of facts. To understand this, however, let us expand our exploration of mythology to include not only astronomical observations, but the empirical observation—and when possible, calculation—of all the things and events that populate a lifetime.

For each of us, life begins in darkness. We have no recollection of the moment we were born. We remember nothing at all of what happened to us before our birth. We come into the world completely unaware, unprepared, and baffled. What are we doing here? What is "here"? And who are we? Through the years of our education, we are taught, not how to resolve these existential questions, but a series of techniques with which we can cope with their insolubility. These techniques, going under the general name of "knowledge" (scientific, technical, psychological, political, etc.), consist in a series of powerful narratives through which we might be able to suspend our disbelief towards our absurd existential condition: being "alive", within a "body" and a "personality," inside a "world," at a "time" and a "space," all of whose actual material referents remain obscure.

By focusing our attention on these collective narratives, we can finally release ourselves from the metaphysical and existential doubts that torment each of us in private. We become able to identify ourselves with our own identity, and to reduce the world around us to the linguistic labels that have been assigned to each of its parts.

But at times, as in our contemporary age, these narratives prove so effective, that our suspension of disbelief begins to slide into actual belief in their absolute validity. They cease being perceived as narratives, becoming instead "facts." This ideological turn, which appears to endow us with a firm grasp on the true "nature" of the world, affords a great deal of tranquility. We cease questioning the unsettling mystery in which we are steeped, and we cease tormenting ourselves about the limits of our understanding. But this tranquility comes at a cost. It requires that we accept being imprisoned within the narratives with which we have wrapped reality. Tranquility in exchange for freedom: the eternal dilemma.

Mythology approaches this situation from a different angle. It has a gentle approach, which doesn't question the legitimacy of the other discourses with which we attempt to bridle the wild horse of reality. Indeed, as Santillana and Dechend claim, it maintains a close connection with scientific knowledge. But, at the same time, it entertains a close relationship with that unsettling abyss which other collective narratives attempt to relegate at an unbridgeable distance.

Mythology is aware of being a form of narrative, rather than a set of factual truths, and it is not ashamed of presenting itself as such—with all the flaws and contradictions that befall fictions. Thus, in Ancient Egypt, it was possible to swap names and attributes among the different divinities, including the Creator, with the unproblematic ease of a modern writer dealing with the characters of their literary novel: Amun became Atum, who became Ra, who became Ptah, while always remaining fundamentally the same god. Names are only names, after all, while the true reality of existence (the secret name of each thing) far exceeds the grasp of language. What counts is not the precision of a definition, but its effect.

Mythology is not a sealed system of knowledge. It is replete with contradictions, and is constantly traversed by a movement between high and low, the cosmic and the mundane, tragedy and comic relief. It mirrors the experience of life itself, with its absurd combinations of eternity and time, knowledge and ignorance, impotence and freedom. It does not dismiss the plight of living beings and their request for a system of sense that might rescue them from the abyss of Chaos. Rather, it coats the raw kernel of reality with names, characters, stories, all apparently endowed with a literal meaning. But it refrains from catering to this need by neutralizing the mystery of reality, and thus imprisoning the world into a rigid catalogue of definitions that present themselves as absolutely true, factual, and actual. Mythology remains equidistant between the conceptual bridles with which we attempt to tame the Chaos of reality, and the unsettling wildness that always teems beneath any inhabitable Cosmos (a universe that is, etymologically, the space of "order" and "beauty").

It is in this way that the soft, self-conscious narrative of mythology can be seen as an abstraction and practical perfection of hard and "factual" forms of knowledge. Precisely in being fantastical—at a mid-point between natural realism and supernatural silence—mythology offers a unique method to cope with our deepest existential bafflement. Myths transform our existential doubts into *skepsis*: a double enquiry into the senseless darkness which engulfs us and the imaginary light which we need to shed around ourselves. It is a form of existential wisdom combined with abstract knowledge. Mythology, in this sense, is the nurturing parent of philosophy, and the legitimate offspring of science.

The Renaissance Garden is a concrete metaphor that can deepen our consideration of the relationship between mythology, philosophy, and science. Despite the variety of its actual instances, the essential structure of Renaissance Garden is typically composed of three sections: the *hortus*, a productive area with fruit trees and vegetables; another area dedicated to geometric shapes (both architectural and natural, as with topiaries); and the *bosco*, an area where trees and plants grow wild, and where most statues and statuesque fountains can be found. Like many traditional gardens of antiquity, starting with the Persian *paridaiza*, and like most ancient urban spaces to which the Renaissance looked back for inspiration, from the temple-structure of the standard Roman city to the circular perfection of the new-town of Baghdad, the Renaissance Garden represents a microscopic double of the structure of the universe.

If taken on their own, the productive *hortus*, reminiscent of contemporary science, and the abstract perfection of the geometric section, like a neatly arranged philosophical system, fail to provide the essence of a Renaissance Garden. Indeed, the universe is not only made of productive and abstract dimensions. It also contains unfathomable silences and intermediate spaces, the *ta metaxy* discussed by Plato that connect the different dimensions of existence. Yet the language through which these intermediate spaces reveal the dimensions of reality to one another remains always partly obscure to each other, and foreign to all: they speak a mythological language.

Like mythology, the *bosco* is this intermediate station between opposites: Cosmos and Chaos, art and nature, language and ineffability, presence and destruction, time and eternity. The presence of statues in the *bosco* should be interpreted not merely as an aesthetic pleasantry, but a tool of cognitive enhancement. For the very nakedness of nature (that is, the nakedness of reality before and beyond language) evoked and embodied by the *bosco*'s wild growth, is incomprehensible and paradoxically veiled to human understanding. It is only the symbolic presence of the work of art, functioning like a distorting mirror, that might be able to point the viewer towards that ineffable dimension of reality.

More than just offer a visual representation of the conceptual structure of mythology, the Renaissance *bosco* sheds a light on the relevance of mythological form for the contemporary problem of understanding a new relationship between the so-called "natural" environment and the realm of anthropic activities. Unlike the *hortus*, where nature is enslaved to production, or the geometrical area of the garden, where it is reduced to conceptual cataloguing, the *bosco* suggest that it is possible to envisage a cognitive collaboration between anthropic and non-anthropic forces. Through mythologization, it is possible to imagine the cohabitation of different forms of existence as a kind of suspended equilibrium, where just as in the *bosco*, the statue reveals the meaning of the ivy at the same moment as the ivy eats into its stone. It is a space where death and life, eternity and time, reside intertwined, and no one dares to pronounce their preference for one or the other.

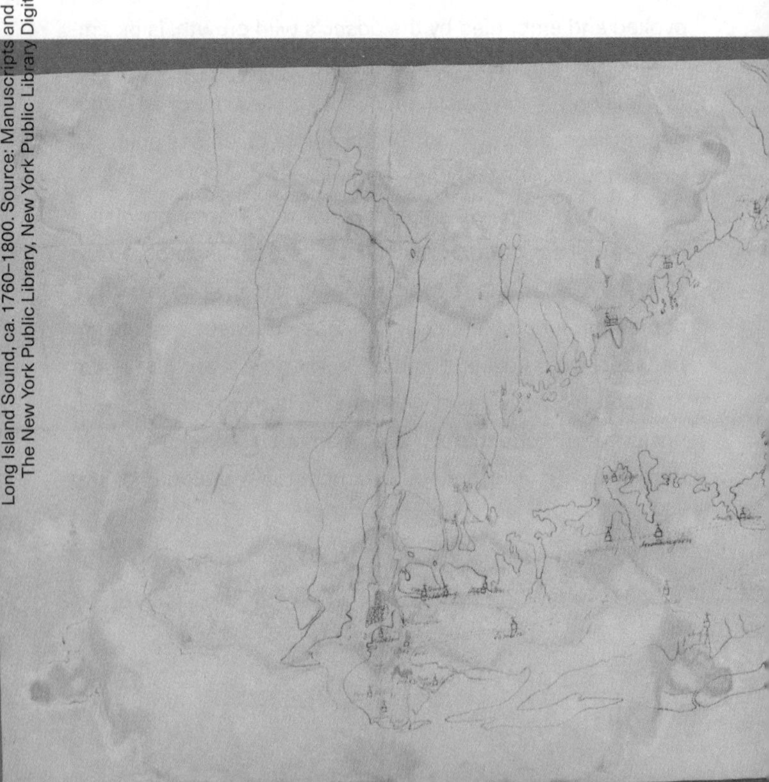

Long Island Sound, ca. 1760–1800. Source: Manuscripts and Archives Division, The New York Public Library, New York Public Library Digital Collections.

신화의 완성

페데리코 캄파냐

스페인의 최남단, 안달루시아. 수 세기 동안 그곳은 유럽 내 이슬람 세계의 전초지였고 지중해 연안 지성의 정원이었다. 무슬림, 유대인, 기독교인이 어우러진 용광로에서는 이븐 아라비(Ibn Arabi)와 같은 안달루시아 신비론자들, 이븐 하즘(Ibn Hazm)과 같은 시인들, 그리고 이븐 라시드(Ibn Rashid)나 마이모니데스(Maimonides)와 같은 철학자들이 탄생하여 그들 출신지뿐만 아니라 그 너머의 세상을 변화시켜 온 사상의 흐름을 창시하였다. 그중에는 덜 알려졌지만 그렇다고 흥미로움이 덜하지 않은 작가도 한

롱 아일랜드 사운드, 1760-1800 경. 출처: 필사본 및 문서기록 부서, 뉴욕공립도서관, 뉴욕 공립도서관 디지털 컬렉션.

사람 있었다. 그의 이름은 이븐 투파일(Ibn Tufail)이며, 당대 뛰어난 천문학자, 신학자, 의사로서 존경받았다. 오늘날 그는 주로 최초의 철학적 공상과학 소설 중 하나를 쓴 선구적 작가로 알려져 있다. 라틴어로 '스스로 깨우친 철학자'라고 번역된 그의 소설은 무인도에서 홀로 자란 아이의 삶을 서술하였다. 가젤의 돌봄으로 큰 소년은 자연과 신성, 그리고 자기 생각의 법칙을 탐구하며 유년 시절을 보냈다. 경험적 관찰과 추상적 사유의 결합을 통해, 소년은 결국 그가 살던 상상적 시대의 가장 위대한 철학자로 자랐다.

따라서, 이븐 투파일은 모든 진정한 철학자는 주변을 살펴보고 자신을 들여다본 후, 관찰한 바로부터 삶을 인도할 수 있는 현실적 추상을 이끌어 냄으로써 태어난다고 주장한다.

독창적인 주장임에도 불구하고, 또 투파일 본인은 알지 못했어도, 그가 제안한 방법론에는 저명한 원형이 있었던 듯하다. 하지만 그 계보는 20세기에 이를 때까지 완전히 드러나지 않았다. 철학자 조르조 데 산틸라나(Giorgio de Santillana)와 헤르타 폰 데센트(Hertha von Dechend)는 그들의 1969년 저서 『햄릿의 맷돌』에서 철학보다 연대적으로 앞서지만 결코 그에 못지않은 또 다른 지혜의 형식, 신화의 접근법이 그와 동일함을 발견하였다. 현존하는 가장 오래된 문서로 전해지는 기원전 4천 년의 기록에서 최초의 알려진 신화들을 꼼꼼히 살펴본 결과, 산틸라나와 데센트는 처음에는 환상담 모음으로 보였던 이야기들이 사실 지어진 당시 하늘에 나타난 천체 운동을 매우 정확히 언급하고 있다는 사실을 발견했다. 신과 영웅은 천체에 입혀진 일종의 서사적 의상이라 할 수 있고, 그들의 행동과 모험은 밤하늘의 주기적 운동에 대한 신화적 해석을 제공했다. 산틸라나와 데센트에 따르자면, 여러 고대 문명의 과학 지성들이 동일한 천체 사건을 설명하기 위해 비슷한 신화적 서사를 만들어낸 것은 이러한 연유에서였다. 그러므로 신화적 언어는 경험적 관찰 및 계산에서 비롯하는 지식의 사실적 형식으로 이해해야 한다.

여기 투파일의 이야기에서 보다시피, 이 과정의 순서가 중요하다. 먼저 경험적 관찰과 함께 그에 대한 수학적 기록이 등장한다. 두 번째로 관찰에 대한 신화적 혹은 철학적 해석이 온다. 먼저 천문학이 있었고, 그다음 점성술이었다. 달리 말해 가장 초기 단계의 사유 층위에서 소위 '정확한' 과학이 발견되고, 지적 정제가 이뤄지는 더 발전된 층위에 오늘날 흔히 공상적인 신화적 산물이라거나 쓸모없는 철학적 반추라며 버려지는 것이 있다.

오늘날 우리가 누리고 있는 지적 체계의 토대를 마련해준 저 고대의 지성가들은 과학적 '객관성'과 신화적 서사에 대해 우리와는 반대되는 가치판단을 내렸다. 과학은 시각적 현실의 단순한 재현으로 간주되었고, 신화는 그것의 추상이자 현실적 완성으로 여겨졌다.

이런 전도가 놀랍게 들릴지 모르겠다. 그러나 사실의 명료한 언어로 전달하는 대신 서사적으로 표현하는 데에는 분명 장점이 있다. 이제 이 점을 이해하기 위해 신화에 대한 탐구를 천체 관측뿐만 아니라 일생에 벌어지는 모든 일과 사건에 대한 경험적 관찰 그리고 가능하다면 계산으로까지 확장해 보도록 하자.

우리의 삶은 어둠에서 시작된다. 우리에게는 태어나던 순간에 대한 기억이 없다. 태어나기 전에 무슨 일이 있었는지 아무것도 기억하지 못한다. 우리는 전혀 모르는 상태로 아무런 준비 없이 당황한 채 이 세상에 태어난다. 우리는 여기서 무얼 하고 있는가? '여기'는 무엇인가? 그리고 우리는 누구인가? 수년에 걸친 교육을 통해 우리는 이런 실존적 문제를 해결할 방법이 아니라 그것을 해결할 수 없다는 사실에 대처할 일련의 기법을 배운다. '지식'(과학적, 기술적, 심리적, 정치적 등등)이라는 총칭으로 통하는 이런 기법은 어떤 '지식'과 '공간'의 '세계'에서 '신체'와 '인격' 안에 '살아 있다'는 부조리한 실존적 조건을 향한 불신을 유예해줄지 모를 일련의 강력한 서사로 구성된다.

이러한 집단적 서사에 관심을 맞춤으로써, 은밀히 우리를 괴롭히던 형이상학적이고 실존적인 의심에서 마침내 해방될 수 있다. 우리는 자신을 자신의 정체성과 동일시하고, 주변 세상을 각 부분에 할당된 언어적 라벨로 축소할 수 있게 된다.

그러나 때로는 이러한 서사들이 너무도 효과적인 나머지, 오늘날의 우리가 그러하듯 불신을 보류하는 것을 넘어 서사들이 절대적으로 타당하다고 실제로 믿는 지경에 빠지기 시작한다. 서사는 더 이상 서사로 여겨지지 않고 '사실'이 되어버린다. 세계의 진정한 '본성'을 파악할 능력을 부여해주는 듯한 이런 이데올로기적 전환으로부터 우리는 상당한 평온을 얻는다. 우리를 불안하게 하는 수수께끼에 관해 질문하기를 멈추고, 우리의 오성에는 한계가 있다는 사실에 더 이상 괴로워하지 않는다. 하지만 이러한 평온에는 대가가 따른다. 이를 위해 우리는 현실을 은폐하고자 우리가 만들어낸 서사 속에 갇히는 처지를 받아들여야 한다. 자유와 맞바꾼 평온이자, 영원한 딜레마이다.

신화는 이러한 상황에 다른 각도로 접근한다. 신화의 접근법은 부드러운데, 우리가 현실이라는 야생마에 고삐를 채우려고 쓰는 다른 담론들의 정당성을 문제 삼지 않는다. 산틸라나와 데센트가 주장한대로, 신화는 분명 과학적 지식과 긴밀한 관계를 유지한다. 하지만 동시에 다른 집단적 서사들이라면 닿을 수 없을 만큼 멀리 밀어 놓으려 하는 불안한 심연과도 밀접한 관계를 유지한다.

신화는 자신이 사실에 기반한 진실의 집합이라기보다 서사의 한 형식임을 의식하고 있다. 또한 허구에 따르는 모든 흠결과 모순을 가진 그 자체로서의 자신을 드러내기를 부끄러워하지 않는다. 그래서 고대 이집트에서는 창조주를 포함하는 신들의 이름과 속성을 마치 현대의 소설가가 작품 속 인물들을 다루듯 쉬이 교체할 수 있었다. 아문은 아툼이, 아툼은 라가, 라는 프타가 되면서도, 근본적으로는 언제나 같은 신으로 남아 있었다. 결국에 이름은 이름일 뿐이고, 존재의 진정한 현실(모든 것들의 숨겨진 이름)은 언어의 범위를 훌쩍 넘어선다. 중요한 것은 정의의 정밀함이 아니라 그 효과이다.

신화는 봉인된 지식 체계가 아니다. 그것은 모순으로 가득하며, 높음과 낮음, 우주적인 것과 현세적인 것, 비극과 막간 사이를 오가는 움직임들이 끊임없이 그것을 관통한다. 신화는 영원과 시간, 지식과 무지, 무기력과 자유가 불합리하게 조합된 삶 자체의 경험을 거울처럼 비춘다. 신화는 생명체들이 처한 곤경을, 혼돈의 심연으로부터 구해줄 분별의 체계를 바라는 그들의 요구를 내치지 않는다. 오히려 가공되지 않은 현실의 알맹이에 이름, 인물, 이야기 등 문자 그대로의 의미를 명백하게 부여받은 것들을 덧씌운다. 하지만 현실의 신비를 무력화함으로써, 그리하여 진실이고 사실이며 실제인 것으로 제시되는 엄격한 정의들의 목록 속에 세계를 가둠으로써 생명체들의 요구에 영합하는 일은 삼간다. 신화는 현실의 혼돈(Chaos)을 길들이려 동원하는 개념적 고삐들과 거주 가능한 모든 우주(Cosmos, 어원적으로 '질서'와 '미'의 공간으로서의 세계)의 이면에 언제나 가득한 불안한 야생성 사이에서 등거리를 유지한다.

이러한 면에서 신화의 부드럽고 자의식적인 서사를 견고하고 '사실에 입각한' 지식 형식의 추상이자 현실적 완성으로 볼 수 있다. 정확히 공상적—자연적 리얼리즘과 초자연적 침묵 사이의 중간점—이라는 점에서 신화는 가장 깊은 실존적 당혹감에 대처할 독특한 방법을 제공한다. 신화는 우리의 실존적 의혹을 *철학적 회의(skepsis)*로, 즉 우리를 사로잡는 의미 너머의 어둠과 우리 자신에게 드리워야 할 상상적 빛에 대한 이중의 질문으로 변모시킨다. 그것은 추상적 지식과 결합한 실존적 지혜의 형식이다. 이런 점에서 신화는 철학의 부모이고 과학의 적자이다.

신화, 철학, 과학의 관계에 대한 고찰에 깊이를 더해줄 구체적 은유로 르네상스 정원이 있다. 실제 사례가 무척 다양하지만, 르네상스 정원의 본질적 구조는 세 개의 구역으로 이뤄진다. 과실수와 채소가 있는 생산 영역인 *호르투스(hortus)*, 기하학적 형상(토피어리(topiary, 장식적 전정법)처럼 건축적인 동시에 자연적인)에 집중한 또 다른 구역, 그리고 나무와 식물이 자생하면서 또 대부분의 조각상과 우아한 분수를 찾을 수 있는 *보스코(bosco)*이다. 페르시아의 *파리다이자(paridaiza)*를 위시한 많은 고대 정원처럼, 또 표준적인 고대 로마 도시의 신전 구조부터 바그다드 신도시의 원형적 완벽성까지 르네상스가 영감을 찾아 되돌아보았던 대부분의 고대 도시 공간처럼, 르네상스 정원은 우주 구조의 미시적 사본을 재현한다.

단독으로 놓고 보면, 현대 과학을 연상시키는 생산적인 *호르투스*와 깔끔하게 정리된 철학 체계처럼 추상적 완벽성을 지닌 기하학적 구역은 르네상스 정원의 본질을 제공하지 못한다. 실로, 우주는 생산적 차원과 추상적 차원으로만 이뤄지지 않는다. 우주에는 헤아릴 수 없는 침묵과 사이의 공간들, 존재의 여러 차원을 잇는 플라톤의 *타 메탁시(ta metaxy)*도 포함된다. 하지만 이런 사이 공간들이 서로에게 현실의 차원을 드러내는 언어는 언제나 서로에게 부분적으로 모호하고 또 모두에게 이질적이다. 즉 그들은 신화적 언어를 말한다.

*보스코*는 신화처럼 코스모스와 카오스, 예술과 자연, 언어와 형언불가능성, 현존과 파괴, 시간과 영원 등 양극단 사이에 존재하는 정류장이다. *보스코*에 자리한 조각상들은 그저 미적 치레가 아닌, 인식 강화의 도구로서 이해해야 한다. *보스코*의 야생적 생장이 일깨우고 구현하는 자연의 벌거벗음(즉 언어에 앞서고 언어를 뛰어넘는 그 자체로서의 현실)은 불가해하고 역설적으로 인간의 오성에 가려져 있기 때문이다. 왜곡된 거울처럼 기능하는 예술 작품의 상징적 존재만이 보는 이에게 그 형언할 수 없는 차원의 현실을 알려줄 수 있는지도 모른다.

신화의 개념적 구조를 그저 시각적으로 재현하는 것 이상으로, 르네상스 정원의 *보스코*는 소위 '자연' 환경과 인류 활동 영역의 새로운 관계에 대한 이해라는 동시대의 문제에 있어 신화적 형식이 지닌 타당성을 조명한다. 자연을 생산의 노예로 삼는 *호르투스*나, 자연을 개념적 목록화로 축소하는 기하학적 정원 구역과는 다르게, *보스코*는 인간적인 힘과 비인간적인 힘 사이의 인지적 협업을 상상할 수 있음을 시사한다. 신화화를 통하여, 일종의 유예된 평형 상태로서 존재의 여러 형식이 공존하는 모습을 상상할 수 있는데, 그러한 균형 속에서는 마치 *보스코*에서처럼 조각이 담쟁이덩굴의 의미를 드러내는 바로 그 순간 담쟁이덩굴이 조각상의 돌을 부식시킨다. 그곳은 죽음과 삶, 영원과 시간이 서로 얽혀 살아가는 곳으로, 누구도 감히 어느 한쪽이 다른 한쪽보다 더 좋다고 표명하지 못하는 공간이다.

2086: Together How?

Kyong Park — Soik Jung — Yehre Suh — Yerin Kang + Lee Chi-hoon

Nahyun Hwang + David Eugin Moon — Wolsik Kim — Jaekyung Jung

2086: Together How?

2086: 우리는 어떻게?

박경 — 정소익 — 서예례 — 강예린 + 이치훈 — 황나현 + 데이빋 유진 문 — 김월식 — 정재경

2086: 우리는 어떻게?

Why 2086? Because of 1492

Kyong Park

박경

2086년, 1492년으로부터

Why 2086? Because of 1492

Kyong Park

Why are we so "isolated" when we are supposed to be so "connected" through globalized information, finance, commodities, and even culture? Why are we so insecure about our future when so many of us are living at unprecedented levels of wealth, consumption, and freedom? Why is the great advancement in our civilization is taking us closer to extinction than to our perfection? How did this great divergence of human fate begin?

Allow me to speculate that it could have been 1492, when Columbus "discovered" America at the terminal year of eight centuries of Reconquista that expelled Islamic culture and states completely from the Iberian Peninsula. These two very closely related events unfurled a series of shifts in the global paradigm that, in my view, has brought us to our "climatic endgame." It was the beginning of the rise of Western Europe, later the West, which has come to define and dominate the way of life for most of us on this planet, including other life forms.

Recovering Europe

After centuries in the dark, Europe was beginning to recover and flourish again. The Black Death (1346–1353) that killed nearly half of its people ironically brought higher labor costs, which may have induced higher birth rates. A growing population and proliferation of towns put an enormous strain on an already devastated landscape and abandoned farmland.

With only 10% of England and Scotland still wooded around 1550, "more than half of Britain's fuel energy came from coal" already.[1] Similar resource depletion and environmental devastation occurred in the Iberian Peninsula and crept into the continental core. Europe needed resources and supplies for its demographic and economic recovery during the late medieval period of the 15th century. The use of fossil fuel energy began in Western Europe.

Exhausting its resources and desperate for trade with Asia, Europe needed to go around the de facto blockade by Islamic states more than ever. Reconquista had turned the Iberian Peninsula from the bridge to Africa into the bottleneck for the movement of people and goods from Europe. They had no other place to go except into the deep ocean, and they did. Naturally, they plunged from the terminal shores of the European peninsula, which they had just liberated. Compared with Zheng He's seven expeditions with 28,000 crewmen on a fleet of 317 ships across the Indian Ocean into East Africa (1405–1433),[2 3] Columbus, with his 3 ships and 90 men, was a rogue expedition from embryonic states. But they changed the world in turn, not with ideals, but with the ambition to profit, the character that came to imprint the climatic endgame of today.

---

1. Ian Morris, *Why the West Rules—For Now* (New York: Farrar, Strauss and Giroux, 2010).
2. Edward L. Dryer, *Zheng He: China and the Oceans in the Early Ming, 1405–1433*, Library of World Biography (New York: Pearson Longman, 2007).
3. Zheng Ming, "The Archaeological Researches into Zheng He's Treasure Ships," The Beijing Association for the Studies of Zheng He's Voyage, updated November 2, 2004, https://web.archive.org/web/20080827195453/http://www.travel-silkroad.com/english/marine/ZhengHe.htm.

Brutal and Desperate Europe?

But how could few brute men on such pitiful ships lead to "the command of all the oceans of the world within half a century and subjugated some of the most highly developed regions of the Americas within a single generation"?[4] According to William H. McNeill, it was "(1) a deep-rooted pugnacity and recklessness operating by means of (2) a complex military technology, most notably in naval matters; and (3) a population inured to a variety of diseases."[5]

In blurring courage and brutality, the recklessness of Cortez and Pizarro in the Americas and Almeida and Albuquerque in the Indian Ocean threatened the distinction of good and evil. Since the arrival of Columbus, the genocide of the natives in West Indies, known as the "Black Legend," included such horrors as the feeding of young babies to Spanish war dogs. This and other barbaric crimes, too numerous to list here, were well documented by the Dominican friar Bartolomé de las Casas (1484–1566)and later illustrated by Theodor de Bry (1528–1598).[6] Such irresponsibility, without any remorse, is the kind of relation that we have increasingly applied to our nature. It is probable that we learned our eco-genocide by first practicing on our own species, just as the current nativized masters in many Latin American territories have learned from their own European slave masters.

Did the relentless religious wars and other conflicts between countless states during the Wars of the Reformation (1522–1712) breed such brutalism? Deaths from massacres, genocide, diseases, and famines ranged from 7 million to 17.7 million people, about 9 to 22% of Europe's population in 1600.[7] The Thirty Years' War (1618–48) alone killed one-third of the population in current Germany. The residue would have been the escalation of military, diseases, and brutality, the three ingredients that played key role in colonial imperialism.

Is the West's violent history responsible for its later deeds—to kill 85 million to 107 million people in the two World Wars in just ten years, or drop 1,665 tons of bombs, including napalm, on Tokyo to kill some 100,000 people on one single night, 9–10 March 1945? Was the dropping of atomic bombs on Hiroshima and Nagasaki guided by an implicit racism to prevent further death of Western soldiers, who were more valued than Japanese citizens who became the live subjects for atomic testing, relegated to the status of animals?

Beyond McNeill's diagnosis of "a deep-rooted pugnacity and recklessness operating by means of a complex military technology," could our violence to other humans be furthered into the destruction of the earth? Or was it just a few exceptional men who were intoxicated by the sense of adventure, and enormous profit to be made, to become the original venture capitalists in the Renaissance? Is this why Darwinian ideas and "the survival of fittest" readily sprouted in Europe? Was the beginning of Anthropocene in 1492, when the culture that would define it

---

4 William H. McNeill, *The Rise of the West: A History of the Human Community* (Chicago: University of Chicago Press, 1991).

5 McNeill, *The Rise of the West.*

6 David E. Stannard, *American Holocaust: The Conquest of the New World* (Oxford: Oxford University Press, 1992).

7 *Encyclopaedia Britannica Online*, s.v. "history of Europe," by Jacques Barzun, Donald Weinstein, and Geoffrey Russell Richards Treasure, accessed February 22, 2023, https://www.britannica.com/topic/history-of-Europe/Demographics.

8 McNeill, *The Rise of The West.*

9 Morris, *Why the West Rules—For Now.*

crossed the Atlantic, when the Christian world took "a small step for a man, one a giant leap for mankind" and began to dominate the world and its nature?

The most brutal atrocities of the colonizers of the Americas were conducted not by them but by what they carried—smallpox, measles, typhus, and other diseases. So powerful was this biological warfare that Cortes's path alone reduced the population of central Mexico from 11 million (1519) to 1.5 million (1650).[8] The genocides of Tahina people after Columbus landed in Hispaniola (Dominican Republic and Haiti) bore a similar death toll. The death trails in Central and South America were laid by de Léon in Puerto Rico, Velázquez in Cuba, and Balboa along the Pacific Ocean. They did not come from some laboratory in Wuhan.

Colonizing the World

The windfall from the triangle trade across the Atlantic is greatly under credited by those who claim that the West, which includes Australia, New Zealand, Canada, and the United States, rose purely by its own effort and ingenuity. We are grateful to the theories of comparative advantages by David Ricardo (1772–1823) and free markets by Adam Smith (1723–1790), while the contribution of labor and resources from the colonial lands are forgotten. Regardless, the *Economist* enthused in 1851, "the period of the last fifty years... has witnessed a more rapid and astonishing progress than all the centuries which have preceded it. In several vital points the difference between the 18th and the 19th century, is greater than between the first and the 18th, as far as civilized Europe is concerned."[9]

Western colonial imperialism was an insatiable extractor of nature, setting off the globalizing chain of production, consumption, and waste. We became the slayer of the earth, not its caretaker. This is when our road to the climate endgame began, in 1492.

Greed from the West

Why trouble with the old colonial history? Is this when greed and wealth took on a whole new purpose and level? Were the conquistadors "like a man in desperation, crazy, mad, out of their minds with greed for gold and silver?" A testament of this, Francisco Pizarro kidnapped and ransomed Inca king Atahualpa and forced him to fill a room twenty-two feet long, seventeen feet across, and eight feet high twice with silver and once with gold. After doing so in just two months, he was beheaded and dismembered (1513).[10] This marked the beginning of the extraction of 150,000 tons of silver and gold from the mountains of Peru and Mexico, a third of which was used to pay for a trade deficit with China.[11]

The privateer and slave trader Sir Francis Drake (c. 1540–

---

10 Morris, *Why the West Rules—For Now*.

11 Morris.

12 Hermann Kreutzmann, "Afghanistan and the Opium World Market: Poppy Production and Trade," *Iranian Studies* 40, no. 5 (December 2007): 605–621.

13 William Travis Hanes and Frank Sanello, *The Opium Wars: The Addiction of One Empire and the Corruption of Another* (United States: Sourcebooks, 2004), 21, 24, 25.

14 Karl E. Meyer, "The Opium War's Secret History," *New York Times*, June 28, 1997, https://www.nytimes.com/1997/06/28/opinion/the-opium-war-s-secret-history.html.

15 Morris, *Why the West Rules—For Now*.

1596) brought a 4,700% return to his investors. One of them, Queen Elizabeth I of the House of Tudor (r. 1558–1603), used three-quarters of her profit to clear England's entire foreign debt. In gratitude, she bestowed Drake the title of "Sir." Here, piracy and royalty become indistinct, as in how the East India Companies of Britain, France, and the Netherlands operated.

Precious cargo did not just include gold and silver from the Americas. The British East India Company also began to grow opium in the Bihar and Benares regions along the Ganges River and export it to China in the late 17th century.[12] Production reached 260 tons per annum in 1796[13] and soared to 1950 tons in 1833 when American merchants, including the grandfather of future President Franklin D. Roosevelt, joined.[14] Just as before, the opium trade helped to pay for the British trade deficit with China, this time under Queen Victoria (r. 1837–1901).[15] Greed reached a new pinnacle, the crown.

But allow me to shift to the 2022 flooding of Pakistan, which submerged 10–12% of the entire nation while destroying nearly 1 million houses and damaging about 1.4 million others. More than a million livestock were killed, and 8,149 miles of roads and 4,389 bridges were destroyed and damaged. But this flood was the deadliest in Pakistan only since the South Asian floods in 2020. In reaction, activists there were beginning to advocate "climate reparation." Huma Yusuf, a columnist for the Pakistani newspaper *Dawn*, describes it this way:

> "There's growing recognition that countries like Pakistan, which contribute to less than 1% of greenhouse gas emissions, are now bearing the brunt of the greenhouse-gas-emitting activities of industrialized nations that have been happening not just in recent decades, but basically since the Industrial Revolution - and that if

you see that, the cumulative contribution to the greenhouse gases comes from the G20. It's not coming from countries like Pakistan or Bangladesh, but that is where the effect is being felt. The industrialized nations that have profited from it are the ones that we now believe should be helping with this big bill."[16]

The environmental crisis is not only about recent or upcoming despoilments; it has a significant history already. To apply an equal level of ecological responsibility to newly and historically polluting nations is asking the former to forget centuries of industrial, agricultural, and technological pollutions by their colonial masters. This is nothing less than extending the privilege of the colonial era into the environmental era, akin to how so many industrial and energy companies left their pollution behind to local communities after relocating or closing. The future of climate remediation is absolutely tied to past climate destruction.

Indeed, it is tied not just to the history of pollution but to the legacy of colonialism. It is as if the British Raj donated its environmental destruction to the people of South Asia as the parting gift for their independence. Huma Yusuf is not asking the British empire to restore Pakistan to its precolonial condi-

16 Huma Yusuf, "Advocates Call on U.S. to Help Flooded Pakistan in the Name of Climate Justice," *Morning Edition*, interview by Steve Inskeep, *Morning Edition*, NPR, September 23, 2022.
17 Shashi Tharoor, "Viewpoint: Britain Must Pay Reparations to India," *BBC News*, July 22, 2015, https://www.bbc.com/news/world-asia-india-33618621.
18 Jason Hicket, "How Britain Stole $45 Trillion from India," *Al-Jazeera*, December 19, 2018, https://www.aljazeera.com/opinions/2018/12/19/how-britain-stole-45-trillion-from-india.

tion, nor to compensate for the environmental problems that they left behind. Rather, she is simply making the case for the wealthy nations to share green technologies and financial burden with the poorer nations that are on the front lines of the climate crisis.

We should think that "environmental reparation" should goes beyond financial aid and green technologies. What about forced seizures or undercompensated purchase of land and labor during the colonial period, including slavery and indentured labor, not to mention the extraction of vast "natural resources" from the New World and beyond? What about the destruction of the South Asian textile industry by the British Empire, which plummeted India's share of the world economy from 23% in the 18th century to down to 4% when the Brits left it in poverty?[17] This is what gave the birth of Industrial Revolution to England, transferring to it the command of world history that enabled the rise of the West. Economist Utsa Patnaik calculated that Britain extracted about $45 trillion from India from 1765 to 1938, more than 17 times the annual GDP of the United Kingdom today[18]—to say nothing of the tens of millions, even hundreds of millions, of South Asians who worked unpaid or underpaid to make the British people more prosperous. What about the 4.25 million South Asians who served in the British India Army to defend Britain in both World Wars? Were they compensated equally to the English soldiers?

There is no doubt that all the above costs of colonialism are inextricably tied with today's environmental crisis. You might consider that they were the capital investments and operational costs associated with the future climate endgame. The logic of paying dividends owed to the original investors—the slaves, serfs, prisoners, and other colonial subjects—

would be applicable in all colonial territories. But will the profiteers of colonial and environmental legacy, the consumers at the Empires of Progress, pay back what they owe? They are hardly aware of their legacy of environmental destruction in distant lands and times; they are hardly aware of it in their own land and time.

Among other artifacts of colonial privilege are the borders in Africa and North Americas that are straight as arrows. They are marks of the "scramble of Africa" and "Manifest Destiny," the visualization of world by "advanced civilizations" who willfully wrote their rights over the territories of the "barbarians." Besides disregard for the morphologies of terrains and cultures, this Cartesian expression of Western liberalism dissected complexities of native ecosystems into simple maps that made their gaze legal. Even the butchering of livestock into different choice meats gives more respect to biomorphic nature than was given to Africa. Why did this become so natural?

"Finders keepers, losers weepers," a children's rhyme that became popular in Britain in the 1800s and in America soon afterwards, could explain it all. Its origin lies with "res nullius" in the ancient Roman law, which meant "things without a master" or "nobody's things," legal objects that could be taken by anyone as property, including undomesticated animals, lost slaves, or abandoned buildings. Later, under the name of "terra nullius," it was used as the doctrine for Domingo de Soto (1535) and many other explorers, who would claim ownership of the land where they came ashore, declaring that it was "discovered" by them and previously unclaimed or unoccupied. For these conquistadores, not only the land they saw or on which

---

19 Ellen Meiksins Wood, *The Origin of Capitalism* (London: Verso, 2002).

they stood but lands unseen or even purely imagined became their possessions once they entered their consciousness. The mind became the most powerful conqueror, as whatever it thought became its.

Such magnanimous power of imperial thoughts may be best explained by the Treaty of Tordesillas in 1494, in how the emerging empires of Portugal and Spain agreed to divide the entire Christian world between them. Running north and south between the respective islands of their "discovery"—the Cape Verde Islands, claimed by Dom Prince Henry the Navigator (1444), and Hispaniola, claimed by Columbus (1492)—virtually everything, known or unknown, to the east belong exclusively to the Portuguese, and everything to the west for the Spanish. Once greed achieved infinity, the ideology of expansion became a political and religious doctrine for the global anthropocentrification of nature. It was the most essential fodder for the vociferous capitalism that demanded to expand to profit wherever and forever. But like the Mongols, who could not conquer beyond Legnica, Poland, or the Pannonian valley in the Balkans—beyond limit of the western steppes that could feed their horses—Progress has an Achilles's heel in running out of the nutrition of capitalism, the planet's ecosystem, and its consuming population.

For expansion to profit, it needed enclosure, or even better, exclusion. Perhaps the most important moment in the evolution of this took place by the settlement of the "Glorious Revolution" (1688) after the English Civil War (1642–1651). As a compromise, monarchical state gave increasingly profitable large farming landlords the rights to enclose common lands, or the open fields that community shared, and turn them into private properties known as parliamentary enclosures.[19] In claiming that individual property is a God-given natural right, John Locke declared that the right to own was established by a man who mixed his labor into the land to make it productive and profitable. Imbued with the ideology of imperialism, his labor theory of property was the foundation in how private property made our quest for liberty, freedom, and justice conceivable.[20] This meant that nature had to be privatized and converted into a resource and land monetized from its natural state to a "natural resource."

This idea of remaking nature into artificial systems is ancient. As hunters and gatherers, we could move from one place that ran out of food and water to another place that had them. However, from the moment we began agriculture we gave up our mobility. Once fixed to a place for a lifetime or generations, we began to build irrigation canals and dams to make sure we always had water.

According to the *Guanzi,* a seventh century BCE ancient Chinese political and philosophical text, a debate took place how the Duke of Huan (r. 685–643 BC) of the state of Qi should stabilize the river floods that were threatening his people's livelihood and his political authority. Those whom we might now call naturalists suggested moving the embankments further way from the city to make a basin to accept the flood. Instead, the Duke built a more powerful levee to control and enforce the river into submission.[21] We began to go against the will of nature, alter it to our needs and visions. We started to "own" nature.

---

20 John Locke, *Two Treatises of Government* (London, 1669).
21 Guilio Boccaletti, *Water: A Biography* (New York: Pantheon Books, 2021).
22 Boccaletti, *Water*.
23 Raymond Williams, *Culture and Materialism* (London: Verso, 1980).

It seems that the advice that the Duke of Huan took has been well taken everywhere else since. As indisputable proof that humanity did not "go with the flow of nature," there are forty-five thousand dams around the world today.[22] According to Raymond Williams, "we grew in confidence in our desire and in our capacity to intervene" in nature.[23] From then on, water had to come to us. "There it is. Take it," are the famed words of William Mulholland at the 1913 opening ceremony of the Los Angeles Aqueduct, which he had built to bring water from Owens Lake to the people of Los Angeles, 375 km away.

If agriculture is the foremost anthropogenic act in our Leviathan love for changing the world, then Land Ordinances by the United States government from 1784 and onwards went far beyond just taking a bite in the Garden in Eden. This doctrinal practice rationalized systematic expansion toward the west, through trails of broken treaties with indigenous Americans, and deforested and plowed nature into ranches and farms. It would be sacrilegious to compare this with the destruction of Amazon rainforest, as it was the privilege of Western colonial empires to declare Manifest Destiny as heroic and divine. Subdivided and sold over three-quarters of the continental United States, the Land Ordinances' Cartesian mosaics, in one- or six -square mile parcels, were imprinted with county lines, townships, and farmlands, a history violently engraved onto the ground of colonial implementation. Through this unquestionable "redrawing" of nature into its own image, the United States continued to pierce the soul of the First Nations people, who were massacred, deported, and interned across a vast land that was colonized to be Westernized. Often associated with the Jeffersonian ideal of democracy, bringing up the question of "who writes history," Manifest Destiny is where democracy lied.

Europeanization of Nature

Even more stunning was the awesome success of European agriculture in the New World. Europeans exported their grass, plants, and crops, which flourished with their cattle, horses, and goats. Spreading like wildfire, they decimated native flora and even advanced ahead of colonists. By 1600, Mexico's flora was mostly Eurasian, dominated by Mediterranean plants.[24] The geographer Al Crosby writes, "[they] advanced with forces of 'suprahuman,' as manifestations of forces impinging on human affairs that are more powerful, undeviating, and pervasive than human will."

From Argentina to Texas, cattle, pigs, and sheep ran wild and bred herds millions strong, creating what Crosby calls "Neo-Europes"—transplanted versions of colonists' homelands, complete with familiar crops, weeds, and animals, far beyond Chinatowns. The Europeanization of the Americas is an ecological version of Karl Polanyi's Great Transformation, one might say. In an act described as "white plague" by the historian Niall Ferguson, the European colonists clear cut 168 million acres of American virgin forest between 1850 and 1900, more than ten times Britain's farmable area.[25]

---

24 Alfred W. Crosby, *Ecological Imperialism: The Biological Expansion of Europe, 900–1900*, Canto Classics (Cambridge: Cambridge University Press, 2015).

25 Morris, *Why the West Rules—For Now*.

26 Carolyn Merchant, *The Death of Nature: Women, Ecology, and the Scientific Revolution* (San Francisco: Harper Row, 1980).

27 "World Population to Reach 8 Billion on 15 November 2022," United Nations Department of Economic and Social Affairs, accessed February 22, 2023, https://www.un.org/en/desa/world-population-reach-8-billion-15-november-2022.

The great power of their ecological imperialism gave the Europeans a sense of Providence, where their destiny was chosen by their god. Carolyn Merchant wrote that for "Protestants such as John Locke, John Calvin, and the New England Puritans, God had authorized human dominion over the earth."[26] Since there appear no obstacle to their God-given will, and since the technological power of the European Christian man seemed infinite, the idea of remaking the world into the Garden of Eden 2.0, in which they could eat as many apples as they wished, was not totally unthinkable.

Did the outgrowth of unlimited power and infinite greed that took root in imperial colonialism flower into the ideology of Progress and eternal growth? What is the statute of limitations on bringing past ecological devastation as a crime against humanity, and for being held responsible for the consequences felt now and in the future? Again, we return to Huma Yusuf, because her request is directed to the imbalance of power and the importance of history in environmental reparation.

Mechanization of Nature

On November 15, 2022, we reached a population of eight billion, well beyond the two billion,[27] that some experts think is the ideal human population for the planet's energy. Of course, there is not just the question of how many people Earth can feed but whether its products are available equally to all of us, including to nature. But still, we have gone far beyond the 0.89 billion marks, when Malthus theorized that the population explosion from abundance would lead us to famines and diseases. How?

The Columbian Exchange also brought new crops from the New World to the Old World. There "they grew where nothing else would, survived wretched weather, and fattened farmers and their animals wonderfully," and "millions of acres of them were planted, from Ireland to the Yellow River" in the sixteenth century.[28] This may have contributed to the doubling of Europe's population between 1500 and 1750.[29] "The population has grown so much that it is entirely without parallel in history," one Chinese scholar recorded in 1608. French observers agreed that people were breeding "like mice in a barn."[30] Maybe this growth brought Malthus to publish "An Essay on the Principle of Population" in 1798.

The current population was reached despite various Malthusian human behaviors, such as countless famines and massacres in the USSR, the People's Republic of China, and elsewhere; millions of deaths during the mass migrations in the division of post-British South Asia and the fall of the Ottoman Empire; the colonial epidemics in the New World already mentioned; and the 110–125 million killed in the two great World Wars, including the Holocaust. So why did the Malthusian catastrophe never come?

Of course, there was the mechanization of agriculture and the great advancements in transportation that enlarged

---

28 Morris, *Why the West Rules—For Now.*

29 David Levine, "The Population of Europe: Early Modern Demographic Patterns," *Encyclopedia of European Social History, Encyclopedia.com*, updated March 20, 2023, https://www.encyclopedia.com/international/encyclopedias-almanacs-transcripts-and-maps/population-europe-early-modern-demographic-patterns.

30 Morris, *Why the West Rules—For Now.*

31 Garret Hardin, *The Ostrich Factor: Our Population Myopia* (Oxford: Oxford University Press, 1999).

the markets. But besides improved health and longer life, perhaps the biggest source of the population explosion may be the invention of the Haber–Bosch process (1894–1911). The era of chemical fertilizers had arrived, and the world, mostly in the West, was able to produce more food per hectare than ever before, with the New World providing almost unlimited land and enslaved labor. While it took us millennia to reach a population of one billion by 1804 (estimated), we have prodigiously added one billion more every 12–14 years since 1960. Sure, population increases can become exponential even from small rises each year, like interest rates from your savings.[31] But why so high?

The Green Revolution in agriculture came to quadruple global food production between 1950 and 2000, so the world's population quadrupled in the twentieth century too. For that, the father of this revolution, Norman Borlaug, was honored with the Nobel Peace Prize (1970), and Malthus became a distant memory. But it is also important to remember that Fritz Haber, the "father of fertilizer," is also known as the "father of chemical warfare" for his pioneering work in developing poison gases for the first World War. Are our life and death, then, just two sides of the same coin, with "progress" rolling it down to either our nirvana or our extinction?

Idea of Progress

Starting from Columbus's voyage in search of resources for Europe, the rewards from these foreign acquisitions were far beyond the acquirers' wildest wishes. Was this all due to the sheer exceptionalism of Europe, suddenly awoken from its deep slumber in the Dark Ages with the knowledge of ancient Greece? Or, like a plant that flourishes from its surrounding nutrition, did the mixture of the conquered, enslaved, and expropriated give them the alchemical magic to launch a string of phenomena, from the Age of Discovery to the Enlightenment, to the Scientific and Industrial Revolutions, to liberalism, democracy, socialism, communism, and more? Every one of these was a phenomenal idea that thoroughly transformed the world, bringing a parallel set of practices of urbanization, modernization, Westernization, and globalization of our world life. Like their diseases and flora, these ideas of the Europeans spread far and wide along the routes of imperial colonization and were then marketized. What was the underlying force that generated such magisterial movements, one after another?

The chain that holds the jewels of Western advancements is the "idea of progress," where everything must change and replaced by something newer. It is about breaking out from the contained and static world, alas, the Garden of Eden. It is about being unilateral, directional, and dynamic, while constantly advancing forward. There was nothing useful about the past. The West is never to return to Ancient Greece, where it was believed that change would lead to demise, or ancient China, where balance was sought over disturbance. So, the idea the West brought to the world is Progress, the most spectacular concept of power. But is it sustainable? Does it have an end?

---

32 Joseph Schumpeter, *Capitalism, Socialism, and Democracy* (New York: Harper and Brothers, 1950).

33 "Global Trade Hits Record High of $28.5 Trillion in 2021, but Likely to Be Subdued in 2022," UNCTAD, updated February 17, 2022, https://unctad.org/news/global-trade-hits-record-high-285-trillion-2021-likely-be-subdued-2022.

Growth Forever

Higher population, higher production, and higher consumption are the "triad of progress." Everything must be more and upward in the "growth forever" economy. In "creative destruction,"[32] a much happier feedback machine between human and nature than the mortality-inferring Malthusian catastrophe. It is then nature that must be sacrificed so that our good life can continue. We do not have to model after the European swift, a bird who feeds her eggs to her offspring during food shortage.

With exponential advancements in industry, transportation, and communication, we have almost completed the total absorption of local markets into the ever-expanding world market, which is designed for ever greater production and consumption. From the medieval market towns in Europe, which had the commercial range of one day's travel (10 km), we have reached the historical record of $28.5 trillion in trade in 2021 thanks to the container shipping system, international banking, and financial capitalism.[33] The fact that this was achieved during the COVID-19 pandemic shows that the infinity of our greed was more infectious than the virus. Could it then be that the power of creative destruction of the world has become so prodigious and mutable that even if we tried to, we could no longer stop it? Is the surplus from our production a virus that depletes the earth, and the profit from our consumption a disease that ravages our humanity?

It is hard to fathom the scale of our growth, like picturing a trillion dollars in your head. The closest that I came to visualizing it was a nest of thirty jumbo shrimps cradled on a single plate. It was on a window display at a once-popular chain restaurant in the United States called Shrimp Shack. That's whole lot of shrimp for one person, I thought. Then I imagined millions of plates of shrimps across America and wondered how many shrimps the world must produce every day. Apologies for sharing my nightmares with shrimps.

Then I thought, does each person really need to eat 30 shrimps in one meal, and why? The answer is in the sermons of Edward Louis Bernays, the first prophet for the Church of Capitalism, better known in the secular world as "the father of public relations." The American promoter of the work of Sigmund Freud, Bernays may have industrialized the libidinal desires of his uncle's theory into mass consumption. He revolutionized the public mind from the "capitalism of necessity" to "capitalism of desires," perhaps making all of us into Pavlov's dog.
Thus, our Freudian desires are swept away from the therapist's couch into town-sized shopping malls where we can unleash our stratospheric, never-satisfied "desires" in the windowless suburban Eden.

We all must have consumed these capitalistic-psychiatric pills, which instantly make our depression over here and stress over there go away in a dazzling spectacle of unlimited

---

34 Adam Curtis, dir., *The Century of the Self*, episode 1, "The Happiness Machines," aired April 29, 2002, on BBC, video, June 20, 2016, https://youtu.be/DnPmg0R1M04.

choices. Western capitalism is a democracy that flows into a mind-bending ambient music that sooth us to submit our hard-earned money to the investors and board member whom we will never know or meet but are following our every transaction until our death, may be even after. The globalized cult of unlimited production and consumption and its propaganda of unprecedented prosperity amid the uneven developments of exploitation and colonialism are brilliantly documented and narrated in *The Century of The Self* by Adam Curtis.[34] In the series, Bernays explains his infamous feminist "Torches of Freedom," which started the movement to get women to smoke—you guessed right—paid for by the tobacco companies.[35] Democracy, too, can be purchased in a world where almost everything is up for sale. Yes, we are told to recycle and reduce pollution and so on, but few are mindful to stand up against the freedom of consumer's choice and say that our houses and cars should be made smaller so that they consume less materials and energy to make. Try to tell people that we should buy less or simply make less things. You will be accused of being unpatriotic, or even worse, identified as a commie.

Afterall, GDP is the most widely believed religion today. We freak out if we get into recession, or if the population is shrinking and aging, or the birth rate is cliffing off. But tell me why these things are bad for the environment rather than the economy. Has anyone yet discovered that growth and progress are the genome of the Anthropocene? If not, then it is at least of the national interest. On the eve of the 9/11 attack, President George W. Bush told his "fellow Americans" to take their families to Disney World and "enjoy life the way we want it to be enjoyed." He made it clear that Americans' duty was to protect capitalism from terrorists and show their patriotism to the automobile, retail, and entertainment industries.[36] Buy and buy. Waste and waste.

We find all kinds of ways to validate ourselves by diligently recycling or working to reduce our environmental footprints while our industries pass carbon credits around the globe. But we continue to make and consume more than ever. George Monbiot aptly describes the pathetic environmental collectivism when we congratulate ourselves for fighting back against throwaway coffee cups and plastic straws, but then go buy reusable cotton bags that are as environmentally destructive as 20,000 plastic ones.[37] What about diligent recyclers who might have a second or third home and fly more than 100,000 km on business class per year to earn those houses? The best sustainable buildings are not the ones that gets high environmental certifications or awards, but the ones that never get built at all. The lifespan of most commodities is increasingly shortening to bring obsolescence and disposable ever closer. There is now a new lifestyle emerging in South Korea where people buy something to drive or wear just for one day. The lifespan of commodity as culture is shorter than that of com-

---

35 Curtis, "The Happiness Machines," video, 10:35–21:00.

36 Emily Stewart, "How 9/11 Convinced Americans to Buy, Buy, Buy: Consumer Patriotism Is the American Way," *Vox*, September 9, 2021, https://www.vox.com/the-goods/22662889/september-11-anniversary-bush-spend-economy.

37 George Monbiot, "Capitalism Is Killing the Planet – It's Time to Stop Buying Into Our Own Destruction," *Guardian* (UK edition), October 30, 2021.

38 J. B. Bury, *The Idea of Progress* (n.p.: Aeterna Classics, 2018), Apple Books.

39 Bury, *The Idea of Progress*.

40 General Report on the Census of India, 1891, C. (2d series) 7181.

41 *Encyclopaedia Britannica Online*, s.v. "British raj," accessed March 15, 2023, https://www.britannica.com/event/British-raj.

42 Hannah Arendt, *The Origins of Totalitarianism* (New York: Harcourt, Brace and Company, 1951).

modity as material.

In the first complete statement about the idea of Progress, Turgot wrote that the "human race [is] advancing as an immense whole steadily" along "geography and climate."[38] He proclaimed that this would take us to a time "in which all the inhabitants of the planet would enjoy a perfectly happy existence."[39] But will his "Universal History" be for everyone, or just for his European friends?

Such "con-sumptuous" happiness cannot be for everyone, because we are not all equal in the wonderful world of capitalism. The colonial British empire demonstrated this beyond any doubt by ruling its Raj of 470 million square kilometers and 300 million people (1891)[40] with only 20,000 government workers (1882)[41] and 65,000 British soldiers (1867). This clearly indicates that one British was worth more than 3,000 South Asians, a sense of superiority that would support Hannah Arendt's supposition that racism was born in the colonial states.[42] A reversal of the conquistadores who carried diseases of the body, racism is a disease in the mind of empires, brought home by their returning colonists.

Democracy Lies

Once in Europe, Universal History took on a scientific cloak in the eugenics of Sir Francis Galton, a half cousin of Charles Darwin. Later coined as "the survival of the fittest" by Herbert Spencer, the two together promulgated the idea that human race can improve only through the elimination of "unfits." Turgot's Universal History was bathed under racial lights; his economic liberalism was to empower the fits over unfits. Opposed to the Muslim "invasion" into the heart of Europe, Renaud Camus's "Great Replacement" theory has inspired contemporary white nationalism, an eerie reversal of the Reconquista of the Iberian Peninsula in 1492. Donald Trump's stinging accent when pronouncing "China" echoes theory of inferiority in Asian culture as the "despotic states" during the era of Great Divergence, an explanation most used to answer why the industrial revolution began in Western Europe and not in the Far East.

When Galton's social Darwinism was fused with Malthus' population theory, an idea of Anglo-Saxon superiority on American soil combusted in "Manifest Destiny" by John Fiske (1885). So popular was his idea that he was invited to speak on it to President Hayes, Chief Justice Waite, General Sherman, and the Cabinet members of the American government.[43] Embedded in "Teutonic" democracy, his vision of America was 700 million Anglo-Saxons, probably best illustrated John Gast painting of "American Progress" (1872). There, Columbia, the allegorical personification of the United States with "The Star of the Empire" on her head, is pulling a telegraph wire and a schoolbook, leading stagecoaches of settlers chasing the fleeing indigenous people. The glorious expansion of Europe in

---

43 Richard Hofstadter, *Social Darwinism in American Thought* (Boston: Beacon Press, 1992).

44 "2022 Year in Review: 100 Million Displaced, 'A Record That Should Never Have Been Set,'" UN News, updated December 26, 2022, https://news.un.org/en/story/2022/12/1131957.

45 Jeanne Batalova, "Top Statistics on Global Migration and Migrants," Migration Information Source, *Migration Policy Institute*, July 21, 2022, https://www.migrationpolicy.org/article/top-statistics-global-migration-migrants.

46 Institute for Economics and Peace, "Over One Billion People at Threat of Being Displaced by 2050 Due to Environmental Change, Conflict and Civil Unrest," September 9, 2020.

North America was echoed in the essay "Lebensraum" by Friedrich Ratzel (1901), which eventually required the deportation and extermination of Slavs, Jews, and others in the Holocaust. This not only replayed the extermination and internment of the First Nations people in America but predicated the expansion of the "Lebensraum" of Jews over Palestinian in Israel. History may repeat, but in another place, with different people swapping their roles.

Why am I connecting Holocausts with environmentalism? Almost certainly, the climate's changes will continue to favor the dominant race, economy, and even geography. Many nations in the global south, along with other underdeveloped and developing nations elsewhere, are already being conscripted to the front line of the unleashing environmental crisis. From these early signs, I wonder how racism and colonialism, which were deeply sown into our nature by the will of Progress, would react to the condition of retrogression when scarcity, not plenty, becomes the rule of our nature in the future.

Mobility will be the key to survival in climate change. We need to regain the mobility that we lost to agriculture. Already there are 100 million displaced people (2022)[44] and 281 million international migrants (2020)[45], and the sum of these numbers could rise to 1.2 billion by 2050.[46] Economic migration and climate migration will be increasingly inseparable, eventually becoming one. Some think that the rising forces of mass migration will inevitably destroy the national border. This will happen when the people from the privileged states join climate migrants from the less privileged states, because they too will have to move. The center of our global population is already moving from the current 27th to the ideal 45th northern parallel.[47] Will this set off a domino-like global migration, where people from the south move into cities and homes left behind by those who moved further north? If so, the question is who will govern the future mobility? Climate Airbnb? Hopefully not.

Self-Assured Destruction (SAD)?

After we survived the mutually assured destruction (MAD) of the Cold War, we are now on a race against time to keep Celsius, meters, NRR, TFR, PPM, PPT, MWh, and most of all, % in check. We have become insanely obsessed with these numbers, as if our destiny in the climate endgame hangs on them.[48 49] They have become our magical numbers of the future.

But this numbers game is a scapegoat. By constantly measuring and presenting them through media, labs, institutes, and corporations, we are creating a grand fantasy that the problems are all floating and flickering "out there" and away from us. They seem to encapsulate the crisis in some abstracted cosmic bubbles, floating harmlessly in media and cultural spaces, where we cannot see and touch their material reality. They seem so far away from us, offering the illusion of safety.

The problems are not "out there," but all "inside of us,"

---

47 Gaia Vince, *Nomad Century: How Climate Migration Will Reshape Our World* (New York: Flatiron Books, 2022).

48 Luke Kemp et al., "Climate Endgame: Exploring Catastrophic Climate Change Scenarios," *Proceedings of the National Academy of Sciences* 119, no. 34 (2022).

49 Peter Schwartz and Doug Randal, "An Abrupt Climate Change Scenario and Its Implications for United States National Security," California Institute of Technology Jet Propulsion Lab, 2003.

50 Kemp et al., "Climate Endgame."

51 Schwartz and Randal, "An Abrupt Climate Change Scenario."

who are producing those numbers. Instead of being mesmerized by them, like in some New Age rituals, we need have a very hard and direct assessment of our culture and history. We need to fix our broken selves as a civilization, and only then can we reconcile with our environment.

But are we capable of such self-correction? Did the idea of Progress, in making us look only forward, atrophy our ability to be reflective critically? Is the era of controlling the future, not only that of nature but our own, coming to an end? If so, then who will control our future in the future?

It will be history, but not ours. History, which we always thought was about us and written by us, now wants to liberate itself from us. Like nature, it fears its own extinction, along with everything else that encounters us, the most invasive and destructive form of life in the world. History now wants to come back life and no longer be the necropolis for our "great deeds." The real Universal History, not Turgot's, wants to put our history on trial for crimes against nature. It wants to know how we designed the climate endgame.[50][51]

2086: Together How? aims to interrogate our Faustian ideology of progress and how we have sought unlimited material pleasure through industrialization, colonization, and globalization. The exhibition asserts that not only will the environmental crisis force us to invent a better ecocultural paradigm, but it will also be our best and last chance to become a better humanity. "Together how?" is the question until the year when our population is supposed to peak.

2086년, 1492년으로부터

박경

세계화된 정보, 금융, 상품, 그리고 문화를 통해 '연결'되어 있어야 마땅할 텐데 우리는 왜 그렇게 '고립'되어 있을까? 그 많은 사람이 전례 없는 수준의 부와 소비와 자유를 누리는데도 우리는 왜 그렇게 미래에 대해 불안해할까? 어째서 문명의 위대한 진보는 우리를 완전함보다 멸종에 더 가까이 데려가고 있을까? 이러한 인류 운명의 큰 괴리는 언제 또 어디에서 시작된 것일까?

이베리아반도에서 이슬람 문화와 국가를 몰아낸 800년간의 재정복 운동(Reconquista)이 막을 내렸던, 그리고 콜럼버스가 미국을 '발견'하였던 1492년이라고 감히 추측해 본다. 긴밀하게 연결된 이 두 사건이 세계적 패러다임에 일련의 변화를 일으키며 우리를 '기후 엔드게임'에 이르게 했다는 것이 나의 견해이다. 이때 부상하기 시작한 서유럽, 훗날의 서구는 생명체를 포함한 지구상의 모든 것들이 살아가는 방식을 정의하고 지배하기에 이른다.

유럽의 재기

수 세기의 암흑기를 지나 유럽은 다시 회복하여 번영기에 들어섰다. 인구의 거의 절반을 앗아간 흑사병(1346~1353)은 역설적이게도 임금 상승으로 이어졌으며, 이것이 출생률의 상승을 견인했을 것이다. 인구 증가와 도시 확산은 이미 황폐해진 지세와 방치된 농지에 엄청난 부담을 가하고 있었다.

잉글랜드와 스코틀랜드 면적의 10%만이 아직 삼림지이던 1550년 무렵, 이미 "영국 연료 에너지의 절반 이상이 석탄에서 나왔다."[1] 이베리아 반도에서도 비슷하게 자원 고갈과 환경 파괴가 일어나 대륙의 중심으로 파고들었다. 중세 말엽, 15세기의 유럽에서는 인구와 경제의 회복을 위한 자원 및 물자의 수요가 늘어나게 되었다. 그리하여 서유럽에서 화석 연료 에너지가 사용되기 시작했다.

자원이 고갈되고 아시아와의 교역이 절실했던 유럽에는 그 어느 때보다도 이슬람 국가들에 의한 사실상의 봉쇄 상태를 우회할 필요가 있었다.

유럽과 아프리카를 잇던 이베리아반도는 재정복운동 이후, 유럽의 사람과 물자 이동이 정체하는 병목이 되었다. 그들에게는 저 깊은 대양 외에 달리 갈 곳이 없었고, 그래서 그렇게 하였다. 그리고 당연하게도 그들은 갓 해방시킨 유럽의 그 반도 끝 해안에서 바다로 뛰어들었다. 정화가 28,000명의 선원이 탄 317척의 선단을 이끌고 인도양을 건너 동아프리카를 향해 떠난 일곱 번의 원정(1405-1433)[2 3] 과 비교하면, 3척의 배에 90명의 선원과 나선 콜럼버스의 원정은 미숙한 꾸러기 원정대나 다름없었다. 하지만 결국에 그들이 세상을 바꾸었다. 그들이 품은 것은 이상이 아니라 이윤에 대한 야망이었으니, 오늘날의 기후 엔드게임에 각인된 특징이다.

잔혹하고 악에 받친 유럽?

그런데 초라한 배를 탄 소수의 잔인한 사람들이 어떻게 "반세기 만에 세상의 바다를 모두 장악하고 한 세대 만에 아메리카 대륙에서 가장 발전한 지역들을 정복"할 수 있었던 것일까?[4] 윌리엄 H. 맥닐(William H. McNeill)에 따르면, "(1) 뿌리 깊은 호전성과 무모함 (2) 특히 해군에서 두드러진 복합적 군사 기술 (3) 다양한 질병에 내성을 지닌 인구"[5] 때문이었다.

코르테스와 피사로는 아메리카 대륙에서, 알메이다와 알부케르크는 인도양에서 용기와 잔인함의 차이를 흐리며 무모하게 날뛰었고 그들의 행위는 선악의 구별을 위협했다. 콜럼버스가 상륙한 이래 서인도제도에서는 '검은 전설(Black Legend)'로 알려진 원주민 집단학살이 자행되었는데, 그중

---

1 Ian Morris, *Why the West Rules—For Now* (New York: Farrar, Strauss and Giroux, 2010).

2 Edward L. Dryer, *Zheng He: China and the Oceans in the Early Ming, 1405–1433*, Library of World Biography (New York: Pearson Longman, 2007).

3 Zheng Ming, "The Archaeological Researches into Zheng He's Treasure Ships," The Beijing Association for the Studies of Zheng He's Voyage, updated November 2, 2004, https://web.archive.org/web/20080827195453/http://www.travel-silkroad.com/english/marine/ZhengHe.htm.

4 William H. McNeill, *The Rise of the West: A History of the Human Community* (Chicago: University of Chicago Press, 1991).

5 McNeill, T*he Rise of the West*.

에는 어린 아기들을 스페인 군견의 먹이로 준 것과 같은 끔찍한 만행도 있었다. 너무 많아서 다 나열할 수도 없는 야만적인 범죄를 도미니크회 수도사이자 개혁주의자였던 바르톨로메 데 라스 카사스(Bartolomé de las Casas, 1484~1566)가 기록으로 남겼고, 이후 테오도르 드 브리(Theodor de Bry, 1528~1598)가 삽화로 담아냈다.[6] 아무런 가책 없는 그런 무책임을 우리는 점차 자연과의 관계에 적용하였다. 라틴아메리카 여러 지역에 토착한 현대의 노예주들이 자신들을 부리던 유럽인에게서 행태를 배웠듯, 우리도 처음에는 같은 인간에게 생태학살을 행하며 배웠을 것이다.

종교개혁 전쟁(Wars of the Reformation, 1522~1712) 기간 수많은 국가 사이에 벌어진 무자비한 종교 전쟁과 분쟁이 이런 잔인함을 낳았을까? 대학살, 민족말살, 질병, 기근으로 죽은 사망자 수는 700만 명에서 1,770만 명으로, 1600년 당시 유럽 인구의 9%에서 22%에 달한다.[7] 30년 전쟁(The Thirty Years' War, 1618~1648)만으로도 현재 독일 인구의 3분에 1에 달하는 사람들이 목숨을 잃었다. 이는 식민 제국주의의 세 가지 핵심 요소인 군대, 질병, 잔학성의 부상(浮上)이라는 잔재를 남겼을 것이다.

불과 10년 만에 두 차례의 세계 전쟁으로 8,500만에서 1억 700만 명의 사망자를 내고, 1945년 3월 9일에서 10일로 넘어가던 하룻밤 사이 도쿄에 네이팜탄을 포함하는 1,665톤의 폭탄을 투하해 10만 명을 살해하는 등 서구의 이후 행적은 그동안의 폭력적인 역사에 기인한 것일까? 히로시마와 나가사키에 투하된 원자폭탄을 유도한 것은 동물의 지위로 격하되어 핵무기의 산 실험 대상이 된 일본 시민보다 더욱 소중한 서구 병사의 추가적인 죽음을 막으려던 암묵의 인종주의가 아니었을까?

"복합적인 군사 기술을 수단으로 작동하는 뿌리 깊은 호전성과 무모함"이라는 맥닐의 진단을 넘어, 다른 인간에 대한 인간의 폭력이 지구의 파괴로까지 나아갈 수 있었던 것일까? 아니면 그저 모험의 감각과 막대한 이윤에 취해 르네상스 시대의 원조 벤처 자본가가 된 소수의 이례적인 사람들 때문이었을까? 그리하여 다윈주의와 '적자생존'의 사상이 유럽에서 쉽게 싹틀 수 있었던 것일까? 인류세의 시작은 그것을 정의하게 될 문화가 대서양을 건너왔으며 기독교 세계가 "한 사람에게는 작은 발걸음이지만 인류에게는 거대한 도약"을 내딛고 세계와 자연을 지배하기 시작하였던 1492년이었다고 할 수 있을까?

아메리카 대륙의 식민지 개척자들이 저지른 제일 잔혹한 만행은 그들 자신이 아니라 그들이 옮긴 천연두, 홍역, 티푸스 및 기타 질병에 의해 행해졌다. 이 생물학적 전쟁은 너무도 위력적이었다. 코르테스의 침입만으로도 중앙멕시코 지역의 인구가 1,100만 명(1519)에서 150만 명(1650)으로 줄어들었고[8], 콜럼버스가 히스파니올라섬(현 도미니카공화국 및 아이티)에 상륙한 뒤 벌어진 타이노족 집단학살도 비슷한 수의 사망자를 냈다. 푸에르토리코에서는 데 레온이, 쿠바에서는 쿠에야르가, 태평양을 따라서는 발보아가 중남미에 죽음의 길을 닦았다. 그것들은 우한의 어느 실험실에서 나온 것이 아니었다.

세계의 식민화

호주, 뉴질랜드, 미국을 포함한 서구의 부상이 순전히 그들의 노력과 창의성 때문이었다고 주장하는 이들은 대서양을 가로지른 삼각무역이 낳은 횡재를 대단히 과소평가한다. 우리는 데이비드 리카도(David Ricardo, 1772~1823)의 비교우위론과 애덤 스미스(Adam Smith, 1723~1790)의 자유시장론에 감사하면서도, 식민지 노동력과 자원의 기여에 관해서는 잊어버린다. 어찌 됐든, 1851년 『이코노미스트』는 이렇게 격찬했다. "지난 50년간... 이전의 모든 세기보다 더 빠르고 눈부신 진보가 일어났다. 문명화된 유럽에 관한 한, 몇 가지 주요 지점에서 18세기와 19세기의 차이는 1세기와 18세기의 차이보다 크다."[9]

서구의 식민 제국주의는 만족을 모르고 자연을 쥐어짜며 생산과 소비와 폐기의 세계적 연쇄를 만들어냈다. 우리는 지구를 돌보는 자가 아닌 도살하는 자가 되었다. 1492년, '기후 엔드게임'으로 향하는 우리의 여정이 시작되었다.

---

6 David E. Stannard, *American Holocaust: The Conquest of the New World* (Oxford: Oxford University Press, 1992).

7 Encyclopaedia Britannica Online, s.v. "history of Europe," by Jacques Barzun, Donald Weinstein, and Geoffrey Russell Richards Treasure, accessed February 22, 2023, https://www.britannica.com/topic/history-of-Europe/Demographics.

8 McNeill, *The Rise of The West*.

9 Morris, *Why the West Rules—For Now*.

서구의 탐욕

무슨 이유로 오래된 식민 역사를 문제 삼을까? 탐욕과 부가 완전히 새로운 목적을 갖고 새로운 수준에 이르게 된 것이 이때였을까? 정복자들은 "금과 은에 대한 탐욕에 미쳐 정신이 나가 발악하는 인간"이나 다름없었나? 프란시스코 피사로(Francisco Pizarro)라는 인물이 이를 증명한다. 그는 잉카의 왕 아타후알파를 납치해 몸값을 요구하며, 길이 22피트 너비 17피트 높이 8피트의 방을 은으로 두 번 금으로 한 번 채울 것을 강요했다. 불과 두 달 만에 요구 조건을 채웠지만, 아타후알파는 목이 잘리고 사지가 절단되고 말았다(1513).[10] 이를 시작으로 페루와 멕시코의 산맥에서 15만 톤의 금과 은이 채굴되었고, 그중 3분의 1이 중국과의 무역적자를 메우는 데 쓰였다.[11]

사략선의 선장이자 노예 상인이던 프랜시스 드레이크 경(Sir Francis Drake, 1540~1596?)은 투자자들에게 4,700%의 수익을 안겨주었다. 그중 한 사람이 튜더가의 엘리자베스 1세 여왕(1558~1603 재위)으로, 여왕은 투자 수익의 4분의 3을 들여 잉글랜드가 진 외채 전액을 청산했다. 사의의 표시로 여왕은 드레이크에게 '경'이라는 칭호를 하사하였다. 영국, 프랑스, 네덜란드 동인도회사들의 운영 방식에서도 그러했듯, 여기에서 해적과 왕실의 구분이 흐려진다.

귀중한 화물에 아메리카 대륙에서 나온 금과 은만 포함된 것은 아니었다. 영국 동인도회사도 17세기 후반 갠지스강 유역의 비하르와 베나레스 지역에서 아편을 재배해 중국 수출에 나섰다.[12] 1796년의 연간 생산량은 260톤에 달했고,[13] 훗날 미국 대통령이 된 프랭클린 D. 루스벨트의 조부를 비롯해 미국의 상인들이 합류한 1833년에는 1,950톤까지 치솟았다.[14] 이전과 마찬가지로 아편 무역은 영국의 대중국 무역 적자를 메꾸는 데 도움이 되었는데, 이번에는 빅토리아 여왕(1837~1901 재위) 치하였다.[15] 탐욕은 새로운 정점인 왕위에 도달하였다.

이야기를 2022년 파키스탄의 홍수로 돌려보겠다. 이때 전 국토의 10~12%가 물에 잠겼고, 100만 채의 가옥이 파괴되었으며 140만 채의 가옥이 파손되었다. 가축 100만 마리 이상이 죽었고, 도합 8,149마일 길이의 도로와 4,389개의 교량이 파괴 또는 파손되었다. 불과 얼마 전인 2020년에 있었던 남아시아 홍수 사태 이후 파키스탄에서 발생한 가장 치명적인 재해였다. 이에 대응하여 파키스탄의 활동가들은 “기후 배상”을 주장하기 시작했다. 파키스탄의 일간지 『던』의 칼럼니스트 후마 유수프(Huma Yusuf)는 이렇게 설명한다.

> “온실가스 배출량이 채 1%도 되지 않는 파키스탄 같은 나라들이 최근 몇십 년 수준이 아니라 기본적으로 산업혁명 이래 줄곧 산업국이 배출해 온 온실가스의 직격탄을 맞고 있다는 인식이 확산되고 있다. 살펴보면 온실가스 배출 누적량이 G20 국가에서 비롯되었음을 알 수 있다. 파키스탄이나 방글라데시 같은 나라는 원인을 제공하지 않았지만 결과를 체감하는 곳이다. 이제 우리는 그로부터 이익을 본 산업국이야말로 이 막대한 청구서 지불을 도와야 한다고 믿는다.”[16]

환경 위기는 가까운 과거나 머지않은 미래의 약탈에 국한된 문제가 아니다. 이미 상당한 역사를 지니고 있다. 새로이 오염을 일으키는 나라와 역사적으로 오염을 일으켜온 나라에 동일한 수준의 생태적 책임을 적용한다는 것은 전자에게 그들의 식민 지배자가 수 세기 동안 일으킨 산업적, 농업적, 기술적 오염을 잊으라 요구하는 것과 같다. 이는 식민 시대의 특권을 환경 시대로 연장하는 것과 다르지 않으며, 수많은 산업 및 에너지 기업이 공장을 이전하거나 폐쇄한 다음 지역 공동체에 오염을 남기고 떠나는 방식과 유사하다. 기후 복원의 미래는 기후 파괴의 과거와 절대적으로 결부된다.

실제로 그것은 오염의 역사뿐만 아니라 식민주의가 남긴 유산과도

---

10 Morris, Why the West Rules-For Now.

11 Morris.

12 Hermann Kreutzmann, “Afghanistan and the Opium World Market: Poppy Production and Trade,” *Iranian Studies* 40, no. 5 (December 2007): 605–621.

13 William Travis Hanes and Frank Sanello, *The Opium Wars: The Addiction of One Empire and the Corruption of Another* (United States: Sourcebooks, 2004), 21, 24, 25.

14 Karl E. Meyer, “The Opium War's Secret History,” *New York Times*, June 28, 1997, https://www.nytimes.com/1997/06/28/opinion/the-opium-war-s-secret-history.html.

15 Morris, *Why the West Rules—For Now.*

16 Huma Yusuf, “Advocates Call on U.S. to Help Flooded Pakistan in the Name of Climate Justice,” *Morning Edition*, interview by Steve Inskeep, *Morning Edition*, NPR, September 23, 2022.

연결되어 있다. 이는 마치 영국령 인도제국이 남아시아 사람들에게 독립을 축하한다며 작별 선물로 환경 파괴를 쾌척한 것과 같다. 후마 유수프가 대영제국에 요구한 바는 파키스탄을 식민 이전 상태로 복구하라는 것도 그들이 남기고 떠난 환경 문제를 보상하라는 것도 아니다. 그저 부유한 나라에 기후 위기의 최전선에 선 가난한 나라들과 친환경 기술을 공유하고 재정 부담을 나누자고 주장할 뿐이다.

우리는 '환경 배상'을 재정 지원이나 친환경 기술을 넘어서야 하는 무엇으로 보아야 한다. 신대륙과 그 너머에서 이뤄진 막대한 '천연 자원' 채취는 말할 것도 없고, 노예제와 계약 노동을 포함해 식민지 시대에 토지와 노동력을 강제로 압류하거나 헐값에 사들인 일은 어떻게 보아야 하는가? 18세기 세계 경제 점유율 23%를 차지하던 인도를 빈곤에 빠뜨려 점유율을 4%로 곤두박질치게 한 대영제국의 남아시아 섬유산업 파괴는 또 어떤가?[17] 이로써 영국에 산업혁명이 탄생하였고, 영국에 서구의 부상을 가능케 한 세계사의 지배력을 안겼다. 경제학자 웃사 파트나이크는(Utsa Patnaik)는 1765년부터 1938년까지 영국이 인도에서 수탈한 금액이 약 45조 달러라고 추산했는데, 이는 지금 영국의 연간 GDP의 17배가 넘는 금액이다.[18] 하물며 이는 영국 국민의 번영을 위해 무급이나 저임금으로 일한 수천만 심지어 수억 명의 남아시아인은 논외로 한 계산이다. 영국령 인도군에 복무하며 두 차례의 세계 대전에서 영국을 지킨 425만 명의 남아시아인은 또 어떤가? 그 사람들도 영국 군인과 동등한 보상을 받았나?

앞서 언급한 식민주의의 모든 비용은 분명 오늘날의 환경 위기와 밀접하게 결부된다. 이를 미래 기후 엔드게임과 연관된 자본 투자 및 운영 비용으로 볼 수도 있다. 노예, 농노, 포로, 기타 식민지적 주체 등 오래전의 투자자에게 빚진 배당금을 지급한다는 논리는 모든 식민지 영토에 적용할 수 있을 것이다. 하지만 식민지 및 환경 유산의 수익자인 저 진보의 제국(Empires of Progress)의 소비자들이 자기가 진 빚을 갚으려 할까? 그들은 멀리 떨어진 땅과 시대에 일어난 환경 파괴가 남긴 유산을 거의 알지 못한다. 그들은 자기가 사는 땅과 시대에 일어난 파괴조차도 거의 자각하지 못한다.

식민지배의 특권이 남긴 또 다른 유물에는 아프리카와 북아메리카의 화살처럼 곧게 뻗은 국경선들이 있다. 그것들은 '아프리카 분할(scramble of Africa)'과 '명백한 운명(Manifest Destiny)'이 남긴 표식으로, '야만인'의 영토에 제멋대로 자신의 권리를 기입한 '진보 문명'이 세계를 시각화한 결과물이다. 이렇게 데카르트적 좌표로 표현된 서구 자유주의는 지형과 문화의 형태를 무시할뿐더러, 복잡한 토착 생태계를 잘게 절단하여 자기 시선을 합법화하는 단순한 지도로 만들어버렸다. 아프리카에는 가축을 도축해 여러 부위의 고기로 가공할 때 생물형태의 본연에 보이는 만큼의 존중도 표해지지 않은 듯하다. 이런 일이 왜 그토록 자연스러워졌을까?

1800년대 영국과 미국에서 잇달아 유행한 동요 「주운 사람 임자, 잃은 사람 바보」로 이 모두를 설명할 수 있을지도 모른다. 그 기원은 '무주물(res nullius)'이라는 고대 로마법에 있는데, '주인 없는 물건' 내지 '누구의 것도 아닌 물건'을 뜻하는 말로, 길들여지지 않은 동물, 잃어버린 노예나 버려진 건물 등 누구라도 소유로 삼을 수 있는 법적 대상을 말한다. 이후에는 '무주지(terra nullius)'라는 이름으로, 도밍고 데 소토(Domingo de Soto, 1535)를 비롯한 많은 탐험가들이 자신들이 상륙해 '발견'한 땅에 대해 이전에 누구도 소유하거나 점유한 적이 없다고 선언하며 그 소유권을 주장할 때 드는 교리로 쓰였다. 정복자들에게는 눈으로 보고 발을 디딘 땅뿐만 아니라 눈에 보이지 않고 순전히 상상만 한 땅일지라도 일단 의식에 들어오면 그들의 소유가 되었다. 생각한 것은 무엇이든 자기 것이 되었기에, 정신이야말로 가장 강력한 정복자가 되었다.

제국주의적 사고가 지닌 그토록 거대한 힘은 두 신흥 제국 포르투갈과 스페인이 1494년 기독교 세계 전체를 나누어 갖기로 합의한 토르데시야스 조약으로 가장 잘 설명할 수 있다. 두 나라가 각자 '발견'한 섬들—항해왕자 엔리케가 발견한 카보 베르데 군도(1444)와 콜럼버스가 발견한 히스파니올라섬(1492)—사이를 남북으로 가로질러, 그 동쪽의 사실상 모든 기지와 미지의 땅은 포르투갈이 서쪽은 스페인이 독점하였다. 탐욕이 무한

---

17 Shashi Tharoor, "Viewpoint: Britain Must Pay Reparations to India," *BBC News*, July 22, 2015, https://www.bbc.com/news/world-asia-india-33618621.

18 Jason Hicket, "How Britain Stole $45 Trillion from India," *Al-Jazeera*, December 19, 2018, https://www.aljazeera.com/opinions/2018/12/19/how-britain-stole-45-trillion-from-india.

에 이르자, 확장의 이데올로기는 전 지구적으로 자연을 인간중심화하는 정치적, 종교적 교리가 되었다. 언제 어디서나 이윤을 향한 확장을 외쳤던 목청 큰 자본주의에 있어 그것은 꼭 필요한 먹이였다. 하지만 몽골인들이 말을 먹일 수 있는 서부 초원의 한계선인 폴란드의 레그니차나 발칸산맥의 판노니아 계곡 너머를 정복할 수 없었던 것처럼, 진보는 자본주의의 영양분인 지구 생태계와 소비 인구의 고갈이라는 아킬레스건을 갖고 있었다.

이익을 향한 확장을 위해서는 인클로저가, 아니 더 나아가 배제가 필요했다. 이러한 전개에서 가장 중요했던 순간은 영국 내전(1642~1651) 이후 '명예혁명(Glorious Revolution, 1688)'의 조치가 시행되며 등장했다. 영국은 군주정을 유지하기 위한 타협책으로 점점 더 많은 수익을 내던 대농장주에게 공유지나 지역 주민이 함께 쓰던 노지에 울타리를 둘러 사유지로 전환할 수 있는 권리, 일명 의회 인클로저를 수여하였다.[19] 존 로크(John Locke)는 개인의 재산은 천부의 자연권이라 주장하며, 소유권은 토지에 노동을 투입하여 생산성과 수익성을 만든 자에 의해 성립한다고 선언했다. 제국주의 이데올로기에 물들어 있던 로크의 재산에 대한 노동 이론은 사유재산에 의한 해방과 자유와 정의의 추구를 가능케 한 토대였다.[20] 이는 자연을 사유화하여 자원으로 전환하고 토지를 자연 상태에서 '천연 자원'으로 만들어 수익화해야 한다는 뜻이었다.

자연을 인공의 체계로 개조한다는 발상은 오래전부터 있었다. 사냥하고 채집하던 인간은 지내던 곳에서 음식과 물이 떨어지면 다른 곳으로 이동할 수 있었다. 하지만 농경을 시작한 순간 인간은 이동성을 포기하였다. 일생을 아니면 수 세대를 한곳에 붙박여 살게 되면서, 인간은 물을 항상 확보할 수 있게 관개 수로와 댐을 짓기 시작했다.

기원전 7세기 고대 중국의 정치 및 철학서 『관자』에 따르면, 제나라의 환공(BC 685~643 재위)이 어떻게 해야 백성의 생활과 그의 정치적 권위를 위협하던 홍수를 안정시킬 것인가를 두고 토론이 있었다. 지금이라면 자연주의자라 불릴 이들은 제방을 도시에서 더 멀리 옮겨 범람하는 물을 수용할 유역을 만들자고 제안했다. 하지만 제환공은 그 대신 더 강력한 제방을 지어 강을 통제하여 강제로 복종시켰다.[21] 우리는 자연의 의지를 거슬러 우리의 필요와 비전에 맞게 자연을 바꾸기 시작했다. 자연을 '소유'하기 시작했다.

이후 어디에서나 제환공이 택한 조언을 받아들인 듯하다. 오늘날 전 세계에 45,000개의 댐이 있다는 사실은 인류가 '자연의 흐름에 따르지' 않았음을 증명한다.[22] 레이먼드 윌리엄스(Raymond Williams)에 따르면, 자연에 "개입할 욕망과 능력에 인간이 점점 더 자신감을 갖게 되었다."[23] 그때부터 물은 우리에게 찾아와야만 했다. "저기 있으니 가져가십시오." 1913년 윌리엄 멀홀랜드(William Mulholland)가 오언스 호수에서 375km 떨어진 로스엔젤레스의 시민들에게 물을 공급하기 위해 지은 로스앤젤레스 대수로의 개통식에서 했던 유명한 말이다.

세계의 개조를 향한 인간의 리바이어던적 사랑에서 제일 먼저 등장한 인위적 행위가 농경이라면, 1784년 미국 정부가 도입한 공유지 조례(Land Ordinances)는 에덴동산에서 한입 베어 무는 수준을 훌쩍 뛰어넘은 것이었다. 미국 정부는 이러한 방침의 실행으로 아메리카 원주민과의 조약을 파기하면서 숲을 베고 땅을 갈아 목장과 농장을 지으며 서부로 나아가는 체계적 확장 과정을 합리화했다. 이를 아마존 우림 파괴와 비교한다면 불경스러운 일이 될 텐데, 명백한 운명을 영웅적이고 신성하다고 선언하는 행위는 서구 식민 제국의 특권이었기 때문이다. 미국 본토의 4분의 3 이상을 분할하여 판매한 공유지 조례로 그려진 1제곱마일 내지 6제곱마일의 데카르트 모자이크에는 군·구 이하 행정구역과 농지의 경계선 등 식민주의 시행의 지반 위에 폭력적으로 각인된 역사가 새겨져 있다. 이처럼 자연을 여지 없이 자신의 이미지로 '다시 그리는' 작업을 통해, 미국은 식민지배를 받으며 서구화되어 버린 이 광대한 땅에서 학살, 추방, 억류를 겪은 원주민들의 영혼을 계속 뚫고 나아갔다. 종종 제퍼슨식 민주주의의 이상과 결부되며 "누가 역사를 서술하는가"라는 질문을 제기하는 명백한 운명은 민주주의가 거짓을 말한 지점이다.

---

19 Ellen Meiksins Wood, *The Origin of Capitalism* (London: Verso, 2002).
20 John Locke, *Two Treatises of Government* (London, 1669).
21 Guilio Boccaletti, *Water: A Biography* (New York: Pantheon Books, 2021).
22 Boccaletti, *Water*.
23 Raymond Williams, *Culture and Materialism* (London: Verso, 1980).

자연의 유럽화

신대륙에서 유럽식 농업이 거둔 대단한 성공은 훨씬 놀라웠다. 유럽에서 넘어간 목초, 식물, 작물은 소, 말, 염소들과 함께 무성히 자랐다. 식물들은 산불처럼 번져 신대륙의 토착 식생을 몰아냈는데, 심지어 식민지 개척자들보다도 빠르게 앞서 나아갔다. 1600년 무렵에는 멕시코의 식생 대부분이 유라시아 종으로, 지중해 지역 식물이 주를 이루었다.[24] 지도제작자 알 크로스비(Al Crosby)는 이렇게 말했다. “[식물은] 인간의 의지보다 더욱 강력하고 꾸준하게 널리 퍼지며 인간사에 영향을 미치는 힘의 발현으로서 ‘초인적인’ 힘으로 나아갔다.”

아르헨티나에서 텍사스까지 소와 돼지와 양들이 방목되어 수백만 마리의 무리를 이루었고, 크로스비가 말한 “신-유럽”—식민지 개척자들의 고국을 이식해 놓은 듯 친숙한 작물과 잡초와 동물을 모두 갖추어 차이나타운 수준을 넘어선—이 만들어졌다. 아메리카 대륙의 유럽화는 칼 폴라니(Karl Polanyi)가 말한 거대한 전환(Great Transformation)의 생태 버전이라고도 말할 수 있다. 역사학자 나이얼 퍼거슨(Niall Ferguson)이 “백사병”이라 묘사했던 행위로, 유럽인 식민지 개척자들은 1850년부터 1900년 사이 영국 내 경작 가능 면적의 10배가 넘는 1억 6천8백만 에이커의 아메리카 원시림을 깨끗이 베어냈다.[25]

생태 제국주의의 거대한 힘은 유럽인에게 자신의 운명이 신에 의해 선택된 것이라는 섭리 의식을 심어주었다. 캐롤린 머천트(Carolyn Merchant)는 “존 로크, 존 캘빈, 뉴잉글랜드 청교도 같은 신교도에게 인간의 지구 지배는 신이 승인한 것이었다”라고 말했다.[26] 신의 뜻을 가로막을 것이 없어 보였고 유럽 기독교인의 기술력도 무한해 보였기에, 원하는 만큼 사과를 양껏 먹을 수 있는 에덴동산 2.0으로 세계를 개조한다는 발상이 전혀 터무니없는 것은 아니었다.

제국적 식민주의에 뿌리를 둔 무한한 힘과 끝없는 탐욕의 결과 진보와 영원한 성장이라는 이데올로기가 꽃피운 것일까? 과거의 생태 파괴를 반인류 범죄로 소환하여 현재와 미래의 결과에 대해 책임을 물을 공소시효는 언제까지일까? 다시 한번 우리는 후마 유수프에게로 돌아간다. 그녀의 요구가 환경 배상에 있어 권력의 불균형과 역사의 중요성을 향하고 있기 때문이다.

자연의 기계화

2022년 11월 15일 인구는 80억 명에 도달했다.[27] 일부 전문가들이 지구 자원을 고려한 이상적인 인구라고 보는 20억 명을 훨씬 넘는 숫자이다. 물론 지구가 얼마나 많은 사람을 먹여 살릴 수 있는가의 문제 외에도 지구의 산물이 자연을 포함하는 우리 모두에게 공평하게 돌아갈 것인가의 문제도 있다. 하지만 맬서스가 풍요로 인한 인구 폭발이 기아와 질병을 야기할 것이라면서 거론했던 8억 9천만 명이라는 숫자를 우리는 한참 넘어서고 말았다. 어떻게 된 일일까?

콜럼버스의 교환(Columbian Exchange)으로 신대륙에서 구대륙으로도 새로운 작물이 들어왔다. 구대륙에서 "그것들은 다른 어떤 작물도 자라지 않는 곳에서도 자라났고 혹독한 날씨를 이겨냈으며 농부와 가축을 훌륭히 살찌웠고", 16세기에는 "아일랜드에서 황하까지 수백만 에이커의 땅에 재배되었다."[28] 1500년부터 1750년 사이 유럽의 인구가 두 배로 늘어난 것도 그 덕분일 수 있다.[29] 1608년 한 중국 학자는 "인구가 역사상 아예 유례가 없을 만큼 너무도 많이 증가했다"고 기록했다. 프랑스의 연구자들은 사람들이 "헛간의 생쥐처럼" 번식하고 있다는 데 동의했다.[30] 이런 성장으로 인해 맬서스가 1798년 「인구 원리에 관한 소고」를 발표할 수 있었는지도 모른다.

---

24 Alfred W. Crosby, *Ecological Imperialism: The Biological Expansion of Europe, 900–1900*, Canto Classics (Cambridge: Cambridge University Press, 2015).

25 Morris, *Why the West Rules—For Now.*

26 Carolyn Merchant, *The Death of Nature: Women, Ecology, and the Scientific Revolution* (San Francisco: Harper Row, 1980).

27 "World Population to Reach 8 Billion on 15 November 2022," United Nations Department of Economic and Social Affairs, accessed February 22, 2023, https://www.un.org/en/desa/world-population-reach-8-billion-15-november-2022.

28 Morris, *Why the West Rules—For Now.*

29 David Levine, "The Population of Europe: Early Modern Demographic Patterns," *Encyclopedia of European Social History, Encyclopedia.com*, updated March 20, 2023, https://www.encyclopedia.com/international/encyclopedias-almanacs-transcripts-and-maps/population-europe-early-modern-demographic-patterns.

30 Morris, *Why the West Rules—For Now.*

소비에트 연방과 중화인민공화국 및 기타 지역에서의 수많은 기근과 학살, 영국 식민지배 이후의 남아시아 영토 분할과 오스만제국의 몰락이 낳은 대규모 이주 과정에서 발생한 수백만의 사망자, 앞서 언급한 신대륙 식민지의 전염병, 홀로코스트를 포함해 두 차례의 세계 대전에서 발생한 도합 1억 1천만 명에서 1억 2천5백만 명에 이르는 사망자 등, 인류가 벌인 다양한 맬서스적 행위에도 불구하고 인구는 지금의 숫자에 도달했다. 그렇다면 어째서 맬서스적 대재앙은 오지 않은 것일까?

물론 농업의 기계화가 있었고 시장을 키운 운송 분야의 거대한 발전도 있었다. 하지만 건강 개선과 수명 연장 외 인구 폭발의 가장 큰 원인은 하버-보슈법(1894~1911)의 발명일지 모른다. 화학 비료의 시대가 도래했고, 주로 서구를 중심으로 세계는 신대륙에서 제공하는 무한에 가까운 토지와 노예 노동으로 헥타르당 식량 생산량을 그 어느 때보다 끌어올릴 수 있었다. 1804년 인구 10억 명(추산)에 도달하기까지 1천 년이 걸린 반면, 1960년 이후로는 12~14년마다 10억 명씩 인구수가 막대하게 더해졌다. 물론 인구는 예금 이율처럼 매년 조금씩 오르는 것만으로도 기하급수적으로 늘어날 수 있다.[31] 하지만 왜 그렇게나 높아진 것일까?

농업 분야의 녹색 혁명으로 1950년부터 2000년 사이 세계 식량 생산량이 네 배로 늘었고, 그에 따라 세계 인구도 20세기에 네 배로 뛰었다. 녹색 혁명의 아버지 노먼 볼로그(Norman Borlaug)는 그 공로로 노벨 평화상을 수상했고(1970), 맬서스는 아득한 옛이야기가 되고 말았다. 하지만 '비료의 아버지' 프리츠 하버(Fritz Haber)가 1차 세계대전에 쓰인 독가스를 선구적으로 개발한 '화학전의 아버지'이기도 하다는 사실을 기억하는 것 역시 중요하다. 그렇다면 인간의 삶과 죽음이란 '진보'가 굴리는 동전의, 열반과 멸종이라는 양면에 불과한 것일까?

진보라는 사상

유럽을 위한 자원을 찾아 콜럼버스가 항해에 나선 이래, 이렇게 해외 취득물로 얻은 보상은 취득자들의 기대를 훨씬 뛰어넘었다. 이 모두가 순전히 중세 시대의 깊은 잠에 빠져 있다가 고대 그리스 지식의 힘으로 불현듯 깨어난 유럽이 이루었다는 예외주의 때문이었을까? 아니면 식물이 주변의 양분으로 자라나듯, 정복당하고 노예가 되고 수탈을 당한 사람들이 유럽인에게 연금술의 마법을 선사했기에 발견의 시대(Age of Discovery)부터 계몽주의, 과학 및 산업 혁명, 자유주의, 민주주의, 사회주의, 공산주의에 이르는 일련의 현상이 일어날 수 있었던 것일까? 그 하나하나가 다 세상을 완전히 탈바꿈시킨 경이로운 사상으로, 세계의 생활을 도시화하고 근대화하고 서구화하고 세계화하는 평행한 실천들을 불러왔다. 유럽인의 질병과 식물상이 그러했듯, 유럽인의 사상도 제국주의적 식민화의 경로를 따라 멀리 또 널리 퍼져나갔고 이후 시장화되었다. 그토록 권위 있는 움직임을 연이어 발생시킨 기저의 힘은 무엇이었을까?

서구 발전의 보석들을 꿰는 실은 모든 것을 더 새로운 것으로 바꾸고 대체해야 한다는 '진보 사상'이다. 진보란 애석하지만 에덴동산, 그 닫혀 있고 정적인 세계에서 탈주하는 사상이다. 진보는 일방성, 방향성, 역동성을 지니는 동시에 끊임없이 앞으로 나아가는 사상이다. 과거에는 유용한 것이 없다. 변화가 멸망으로 이어질 수 있다고 믿었던 고대 그리스나 동요보다 균형을 추구했던 고대 중국으로 서구가 돌아가는 일은 절대 없을 것이다. 서구가 세계에 가져온 사상은 힘의 가장 스펙타클한 개념인 진보이다. 하지만 그것은 지속가능한가? 끝은 있을까?

영원한 성장

더 많은 인구와 생산과 소비는 '진보의 삼위'이다. '영원한 성장'의 경제에서 모든 것은 늘어나고 상승해야 한다. "창조적 파괴"[32]에서는 사망률을 추론하는 맬서스적 재앙보다 훨씬 행복한 피드백 기계가 사람과 자연 사이에서 작동한다. 그렇다면 우리의 풍족한 생활이 계속될 수 있게 희생되어야 하

---

31 Garret Hardin, *The Ostrich Factor: Our Population Myopia* (Oxford: Oxford University Press, 1999).

32 Joseph Schumpeter, *Capitalism, Socialism, and Democracy* (New York: Harper and Brothers, 1950).

는 쪽은 자연이다. 먹이가 부족한 시기가 오면 알을 낳아 새끼에게 먹이는 유럽칼새를 모범으로 삼을 필요는 없다.

산업, 운송, 통신 분야의 기하급수적 발전으로, 더 많은 생산과 소비를 위해 설계된 확장일로의 세계 시장에 지역의 시장들이 완전히 흡수되는 과정이 거의 마무리되었다. 하루 이동 거리(10km)가 상업의 범위였던 중세 유럽의 시장 마을에서, 이제는 컨테이너 운송 시스템과 국제적인 은행 및 금융 자본주의 덕분에 2021년 무역 규모 28조 5천억 달러라는 역사적 기록에 도달했다.[33] 코로나19 팬데믹 기간에 이런 기록을 달성했다는 사실은 인간의 무한한 탐욕이 바이러스보다 더 전염성이 높다는 사실을 보여준다. 그렇다면 세계를 창조적으로 파괴하는 힘이 너무도 거대하고 변덕스러워서 아무리 노력한대도 막을 수 없게 된 것일까? 생산에서 나온 잉여는 지구를 고갈시키는 바이러스이고, 소비에서 나온 이윤은 인류를 파괴하는 질병일까?

더욱 많은 소비

성장의 규모를 가늠하기란 머릿속으로 1조 달러를 그려보는 것만큼 어렵다. 내가 상상한 가장 가까운 모습은 한 장의 접시에 놓인 점보 새우 서른 마리였다. 미국에서 한때 인기 있었던 식당 체인점인 슈림프 쉑 쇼윈도에 그렇게 진열되어 있었다. 한 사람이 먹기에 참으로 많은 새우라는 생각이 들었다. 그러고는 미국 전역에 있을 수백만 접시의 새우를 상상하였고, 도대체 전 세계에서 매일 새우가 얼마나 많이 나와야 하는 건가 생각했다. 개인적인 새우 악몽을 이야기한 점에 대해 양해를 구한다.

그러고는 생각했다. 정말로 한 사람이 한 끼에 새우 서른 마리를 먹어야 하는 이유가 있나? 자본주의라는 교회의 첫 선지자로 속세에서는 '홍보의 아버지'라고 알려진 에드워드 루이스 버네이스(Edward Louis Bernays)의 설교에 그 답이 있다. 지그문트 프로이트(Sigmund Freud)의 작업을 미국에 알린 버네이스는 외삼촌인 프로이트의 리비도적 욕망 이론을 대량소비 영역으로 옮겨 산업화하였는지도 모른다. 버네이스는 '필수품의 자본주의'에서 '욕망의 자본주의'로 대중의 정신을 획기적으로 바꿔놓았고, 어쩌면 우리 모두를 파블로프의 개로 만들었다. 그리하여 우리의 프로이트적 욕망은 상담가의 소파에서 도시 규모의 대형 쇼핑몰로 휩쓸려 갔고, 우리는 그 창문 없는 교외의 에덴동산에서 만족을 모르는 하늘 높은 '욕망'을 마음껏 풀어놓을 수 있게 되었다.

분명 우리 모두가 무한한 선택의 눈부신 장관 속에서 여기의 우울과 저기의 스트레스를 곧바로 없애주는 이런 자본주의-정신의학의 약물을 삼켜왔다. 서구 자본주의는 잔잔하면서도 환각적인 음악 속으로 흘러드는 민주주의로, 그 음악은 우리의 마음을 달래어 우리가 알 일도 만날 일도 없지만 죽을 때까지 아니, 죽은 다음에도 우리의 거래 내역을 하나하나 추적하는 투자자와 이사회 임원들에게 힘들게 번 돈을 가져다 바치게 만든다. 애덤 커티스(Adam Curtis)의 〈자아의 세기〉는 무한한 생산과 소비에 대한 세계적 숭배, 그리고 착취와 식민주의가 낳은 불균등한 발전 속에서 나타난 유례 없는 번영에 대한 선전을 탁월하게 기록하고 들려주었다.[34] 이 다큐멘터리 시리즈에서 버네이스는 담배 회사의 돈을 받아 여성의 흡연을 유도하는 운동을 시작하는데 페미니즘을 이용했던 저 악명 높은 '자유의 횃불'에 관해 설명한다.[35] 모든 것이 판매 대상인 세계에서는 민주주의도 구입이 가능하다. 재활용을 하고 공해를 줄이라고는 하지만, 집도 차도 더 작게 만들어 재료와 에너지 소비를 줄여야 한다고 말하며 소비자 선택의 자유에 맞서는 사람은 찾아보기 힘들다. 사람들에게 적게 사거나 그냥 적게 만들자고 해보라. 애국심이 없다고 비난받든가 심하게는 빨갱이로 몰릴 것이다.

결국에 GDP는 오늘날 가장 널리 믿어지는 종교이다. 우리는 경기 침체에 들어선다거나 인구가 감소하고 노령화한다든가 출생률이 절벽 아래로 추락한다고 하면 기겁을 한다. 하지만 이런 것이 경제가 아니라 환경에 안 좋은 이유가 있다면 말해 주길 바란다. 성장과 진보가 인류세의 게놈이라는 사실이 진작에 밝혀지지 않았던가? 그게 아니라도 최소 국익의 게놈이다.

---

33 "Global Trade Hits Record High of $28.5 Trillion in 2021, but Likely to Be Subdued in 2022," UNCTAD, updated February 17, 2022, https://unctad.org/news/global-trade-hits-record-high-285-trillion-2021-likely-be-subdued-2022.

34 Adam Curtis, dir., *The Century of the Self*, episode 1, "The Happiness Machines," aired April 29, 2002, on BBC, video, June 20, 2016, https://youtu.be/DnPmg0R1M04.

35 Curtis, "The Happiness Machines," video, 10:35–21:00.

9/11 테러가 일어나기 전날, 조지 W. 부시 대통령은 "동료 미국 시민 여러분"에게 가족을 데리고 디즈니월드에 가서 "원하는 방식으로 삶을 즐기시라"고 했다. 그는 테러리스트로부터 자본주의를 보호하며, 자동차 산업과 소매업과 엔터테인먼트 산업에 애국심을 발휘하는 것이 미국인의 의무임을 분명히 하였다.[36] 사고 또 사라. 낭비하고 또 낭비하라.

산업체들이 전 세계로 탄소배출권을 거래하는 동안, 우리는 부지런히 재활용하고 환경발자국을 줄이고자 노력하며 스스로를 정당화할 온갖 방법을 찾는다. 하지만 우리는 어느 때보다 많은 생산과 소비를 이어가고 있다. 일회용 커피컵과 플라스틱 빨대에 맞서 싸움을 자축하고는 비닐봉지 2만 장만큼 환경을 파괴하는 다회용 면 소재 가방을 사러 간다며, 조지 몬비오(George Monbiot)는 우리의 한심한 친환경 집단주의를 적절하게 묘사한다.[37] 집을 두 세 채 소유하며, 그런 집을 마련하기 위해 비즈니스 클래스로 매년 10만 마일 이상 비행하는 부지런한 재활용 실천가는 어떤가? 가장 지속가능한 건물이란 우수 환경 인증이나 상을 받은 건물이 아니라 아예 지어지지 않은 건물이다. 대부분의 상품 수명은 점점 더 줄어 노후화와 폐기를 더욱 앞당긴다. 지금 한국에서는 사람들이 딱 하루 몰 차나 하루 입을 옷을 사는 새로운 라이프스타일이 출현하고 있다. 문화로서의 상품은 물질로서의 상품보다 수명이 짧다.

진보라는 사상에 관한 최초의 완전한 서술에서 튀르고는 "지리와 기후"를 따라 "인류는 거대한 전체로서 천천히 앞으로 나아가고 있다"고 썼다.[38] 그는 이것이 우리를 "지구상의 모든 거주자가 완벽히 행복한 생활을 누릴" 시대로 이끌 것이라 공언했다.[39] 하지만 그가 말하는 "보편사"가 모두를 위한 것일까 아니면 유럽의 친우들만을 위한 것일까?

그렇게 "함께-호사"하는 행복은 모두에게 돌아갈 수가 없다. 자본주의라는 멋진 세계에서 우리 모두가 평등한 것은 아니기 때문이다. 영국의 식민지였던 인도제국은 이 사실을 4억 7천만 평방킬로미터의 땅과 3억 명의 인구(1891)[40]를 단 2만 명의 공무원과 6만 5천 명의 군대(1867)[41]로 통치하며 여지 없이 증명했다. 이는 한 명의 영국인이 3천 명의 남아시아인보다 가치 있음을, 인종주의가 식민 국가에서 배태되었다는 한나 아렌트의 가정을 뒷받침하는 우월 의식이 존재했음을 분명하게 보여준다.[42] 정복자들이 몸의 질병을 식민지에 옮겼다면, 귀환하는 식민주의자들은 인종주의라는 정신의 질병을 제국에 옮겼다.

한때 유럽에서 보편사는 찰스 다윈(Charles Darwin)의 반사촌인 프랜시스 갤턴 경(Sir Francis Galton)의 우생학으로 과학의 외피를 둘렀다. 허버트 스펜서(Herbert Spencer)가 훗날 '적자생존'이라 명명한 개념으로 갤턴과 스펜서는 '부적자'를 제거해야만 인류가 향상될 수 있다는 생각을 퍼뜨렸다. 튀르고의 보편사에는 인종주의의 시각이 물씬했고, 그가 말하는 경제적 자유주의는 부적자보다 적자에게 힘을 실어주는 것이었다. 유럽의 중심부를 향한 무슬림의 '침공'에 반대하는 르노 카뮈(Renaud Camus)의 '백인 대체론(Great Replacement)'은 1492년 이베리아반도 재정복운동의 으스스한 역전인 현대의 백인민족주의를 고무하였다. 도널드 트럼프가 "차이나"를 발음할 때의 쏘는 듯한 억양에는 아시아 문화 열등론이 반향되어 있다. 대분기 시대(Great Divergence)에 '전제 국가'에 머물렀기에 아시아 문화가 뒤떨어진 것이라 주장하는 이 이론은 산업혁명이 왜 극동 아시아에서가 아니라 서유럽에서 시작되었나를 설명할 때 가장 많이 동원된다.

갤턴의 사회적 다윈주의가 맬서스의 인구론과 융합하자, 미국 땅에서 앵글로색슨이 우월성을 가진다는 발상이 존 피스크(John Fiske)의 '명백한 운명(1885)'에서 불타올랐다. 헤이스 대통령, 웨이트 대법원장, 셔먼 장군 및 미국 정부 관료에게 초청 강연을 할 정도로 피스크의 생각은 인기가 높았다.[43] '튜턴족식' 민주주의에 뿌리를 둔 그는 앵글로색슨 7억 인의 나라로 미국

---

36 Emily Stewart, "How 9/11 Convinced Americans to Buy, Buy, Buy: Consumer Patriotism Is the American Way," *Vox*, September 9, 2021, https://www.vox.com/the-goods/22662889/september-11-anniversary-bush-spend-economy.

37 George Monbiot, "Capitalism Is Killing the Planet – It's Time to Stop Buying Into Our Own Destruction," *Guardian* (UK edition), October 30, 2021.

38 J. B. Bury, *The Idea of Progress* (n.p.: Aeterna Classics, 2018), Apple Books.

39 Bury, *The Idea of Progress*.

40 General Report on the Census of India, 1891, C. (2d series) 7181.

41 *Encyclopaedia Britannica Online*, s.v. "British raj," accessed March 15, 2023, https://www.britannica.com/event/British-raj.

42 Hannah Arendt, *The Origins of Totalitarianism* (New York: Harcourt, Brace and Company, 1951).

43 Richard Hofstadter, *Social Darwinism in American Thought* (Boston: Beacon Press, 1992).

의 비전을 그렸는데, 아마도 존 개스트(John Gast)의 회화 〈미국의 진보〉(1872)가 이를 가장 잘 보여줄 것이다. 그림에서 머리에 단 '제국의 별'로 미국을 상징적으로 의인화한 컬럼비아는 교과서를 들고 전신선을 끌며, 도망가는 원주민을 쫓는 정착민의 역마차를 이끌고 있다. 유럽이 북아메리카에서 펼친 영광스러운 확장은 프리드리히 라첼(Friedrich Ratzel)의 에세이 「레벤스라움」(1901)에서 되풀이되었고, 결국에 홀로코스트로 슬라브인, 유대인 및 기타 민족을 추방하고 말살할 것을 요구하기에 이르렀다. 이는 미국에서 벌어진 구대륙인 말살과 억류를 재연하였을 뿐 아니라, 이스라엘에서 유대인이 팔레스타인 사람에게 벌인 '레벤스라움'의 확대를 예언하였다. 역사는 반복될 수 있다. 다만 다른 곳에서, 역할을 바꾼 다른 사람들에 의해 일어날 것이다.

나는 왜 홀로코스트를 환경주의에 연결 짓는가? 의심의 여지 없이 기후변화는 우세한 인종과 경제, 심지어 지리에 계속해서 유리하게 작용할 것이다. 남반구의 여러 국가를 비롯해 다른 지역의 저개발국과 개발도상국들이 이미 환경 위기의 최전선에 소집되고 있다. 이런 초기 징후들로 보아, 앞으로 풍요가 아닌 부족이 인간 본성의 규칙이 될 때, 진보의 의지가 우리 본성에 깊이 심어 놓은 인종주의와 식민주의가 그런 퇴행 상황에 어떻게 대응할지 궁금하다.

이동성은 기후 변화에 있어 생존의 열쇠가 될 것이다. 농경으로 인해 잃어버린 이동성을 되찾아야 한다. 이미 1억 명의 실향민과(2022)[44] 2억 8천 1백만 명의 국제 이주민(2020)이 발생하였는데,[45] 2050년이면 그 숫자가 12억 명까지 오를 수 있다.[46] 경제 이주와 기후 이주는 점점 불가분해져 결국 하나가 될 것이다. 어떤 이들은 대규모 이주의 증가가 필연적으로 국경을 붕괴하리라 생각한다. 이런 사태는 특권 국가의 사람들이 저특권 국가의 기후 이주자들과 합류할 때 벌어질 것이다. 그들 역시 이주해야만 할 것이기 때문이다. 세계 인구의 중심은 이미 현재의 북위 27도에서 최적의 북위 45도로 이동 중이다.[47] 이로 인해 더 북쪽으로 이주한 사람들이 남기고 간 집과 도시로 남쪽 사람들이 이동해 들어가는 글로벌 이주 도미노 현상이 시작될까? 그렇다면 문제는 미래의 이동성을 누가 다스리느냐가 아닐까? 기후 에어비엔비? 아니기를 빈다.

자가확증파괴?

냉전 시대의 상호확증파괴에서 살아남은 우리는 이제 섭씨, 미터, NRR, TFR, PPM, PPT, MWh 그리고 무엇보다 %를 억제하기 위해 시간과의 경쟁을 벌이고 있다. '기후 엔드게임'에서의 인간 운명이 전적으로 달린 것처럼, 우리는 그런 숫자에 비정상적으로 집착하게 되었다.[48 49] 숫자들은 우리 미래의 매직 넘버가 되고 말았다.

하지만 이런 숫자 게임은 희생양이다. 미디어, 실험실, 연구소, 기업을 통해 끊임없이 숫자를 측정하고 발표함으로써, 우리는 문제들이 멀리 '저 바깥'에서 떠다니며 흔들리고 있다는 거대한 환상을 만들고 있다. 숫자들은 우리가 볼 수도 만질 수도 없는 미디어와 문화의 공간 속을 무해하게 떠다니는 어떤 추상화된 우주적 거품 속에 위기를 집어넣고 감싸버린 듯하다. 그것들은 우리에게서 너무 멀어 보여, 안전하다는 환상을 불러일으킨다.

문제들은 '저 바깥'이 아니라 그런 숫자를 만들어내는 '우리 안'에 있다. 뉴에이지 의식에 빠진 듯 숫자들에 넋을 잃을 것이 아니라, 우리의 문화와 역사를 아주 냉정하고 단도직입적으로 평가해야 한다. 우리는 망가져버린 문명으로서의 자아를 고쳐야 하며, 그래야만 환경과 화해할 수 있다.

---

44 "2022 Year in Review: 100 Million Displaced, 'A Record That Should Never Have Been Set,'" UN News, updated December 26, 2022, https://news.un.org/en/story/2022/12/1131957.

45 Jeanne Batalova, "Top Statistics on Global Migration and Migrants," Migration Information Source, *Migration Policy Institute*, July 21, 2022, https://www.migrationpolicy.org/article/top-statistics-global-migration-migrants.

46 Institute for Economics and Peace, "Over One Billion People at Threat of Being Displaced by 2050 Due to Environmental Change, Conflict and Civil Unrest," September 9, 2020.

47 Gaia Vince, *Nomad Century: How Climate Migration Will Reshape Our World* (New York: Flatiron Books, 2022).

48 Luke Kemp et al., "Climate Endgame: Exploring Catastrophic Climate Change Scenarios," *Proceedings of the National Academy of Sciences* 119, no. 34 (2022).

49 Peter Schwartz and Doug Randal, "An Abrupt Climate Change Scenario and Its Implications for United States National Security," California Institute of Technology Jet Propulsion Lab, 2003.

하지만 우리에게 그런 자가교정의 능력이 있나? 오로지 앞만 바라보게 한 진보 사상이 비판적 성찰 능력을 위축시키지는 않았나? 자연의 미래는 물론 우리 자신의 미래까지도 통제하는 시대가 저물고 있나? 그렇다면 앞으로 우리의 미래는 누가 통제할까?

그 답은 역사이겠지만, 우리의 역사는 아닐 것이다. 우리는 항상 역사를 우리에 관해 우리가 쓴 것이라 생각해왔지만, 그런 역사는 이제 우리에게서 해방되고 싶어 한다. 자연처럼 역사도 자신의 멸종을 두려워한다. 세상에서 가장 침략적이고 파괴적인 생명체인 인간과 마주친 다른 모든 것들과 마찬가지로 말이다. 역사는 이제 생명을 되찾고 더 이상 인간의 '위업'을 위한 묘지에 머물지 않으려 한다. 튀르고가 말한 대로가 아닌, 진정한 의미의 보편사는 우리 역사를 자연에 대한 범죄의 심판대에 올리고 싶어 한다. 우리가 어떻게 '기후 엔드게임'을 설계했는지를 알고 싶어 한다.[50][51]

《2086: 우리는 어떻게?》는 우리의 파우스트적 진보 이데올로기에 관해 또 우리가 어떻게 산업화, 식민화, 세계화로 무한한 물질적 쾌락을 추구해왔는가를 묻고자 한다. 환경 위기로 우리는 더 나은 생태문화의 패러다임을 창안할 수밖에 없을 뿐 아니라, 그것이 더 나은 인류가 될 최선이자 최후의 기회가 되리라고 전시는 역설한다. "우리는 어떻게?"는 인구가 정점에 달할 것으로 추산되는 그 해까지 계속될 질문이다.

---

50 Kemp et al., "Climate Endgame."

51 Schwartz and Randal, "An Abrupt Climate Change Scenario."

Our Choices Are...

Soik Jung

정소익

우리의 선택은

Our Choices Are...

Soik Jung

Despite the fact that we are more "connected" than ever before thanks to the globalization of information, culture, finance, production, and distribution, why is each of us "isolated?" We enjoy unprecedented levels of wealth, technology, consumption, and convenience of mobility, so why do we continue to live with scarcity and insecurity? And why have we come face to face with environmental collapse and population extinction scenarios? What do these contradictions mean? How should we confront this?

The exhibition 2086: Together How? *tells us that the answer to these questions lies in our choices, that everything we enjoy and all the crises we face are the result of the choices humankind has made until now. It suggests, therefore, that only when we reevaluate the choices we have made thus far and their consequences, that is, only when we choose to reform the ways we live and think to a biocultural approach, can we find answers to these questions and get through the present crises. The exhibition aims to provide an opportunity for people to think and act independently in this regard. We hope it will become an opportunity to escape from the condition of "cheerful robots"* [1] *and, going further still, to take the initiative in change, that is, in sharing in the process of reaching the top of "the ladder of citizen participation."* [2]

---

1 This concept presented, by C. Wright Mills in his book The *Sociological Imagination* (Oxford: Oxford University Press, 1959), refers to human beings who lack free will and ideas and become passive tools within a massive, segmented, and mechanized society, that is, human beings who lose their freedom by internalizing everything as an individual problem without recognizing the problems in their social structure. Mills emphasized that we should always think, doubt, and imagine sociologically in order not to fall into these errors.

The moment-to-moment choices in our lives operate as variables that determine the future of the Earth and humankind. Because individuals appear insignificant in the grand flow of history, it is easy to look upon broad trends and changes passively. It is also easy to rationalize this kind of passive attitude. However, the current situation has been created through the push and pull of the flow of history and the choices of each individual. Each individual's desire to be a little more comfortable, to have a little more, and to show a little more have become the wishes and desires of the community as a whole, laying the foundation for selfishness and the primacy of quantitative growth in our society. They have fostered capitalism, which threatens the solidarity and survival of the community. Politics and policy are simply the expression of these processes. The way each person views the community, the thoughts they have about globalization and capitalism, the values they pursue, and their habitual, inertial behavior are the flapping wings of the butterfly that led to the huge typhoon that we face.

The exhibition *2086: Together How?* invites visitors to take the opportunity to think about this, pose questions, and make choices. It also urges visitors to clearly recognize their

---

2 Sherry Arnstein, "A Ladder of Citizen Participation," *Journal of the American Planning Association* 35 no. 4 (1969): 216–224. Arnstein's type of civic participation is presented with the metaphor of a "ladder" with the following rungs: Stage 1, Manipulation; Stage 2, Therapy; Stage 3, Informing; Stage 4, Consultation; Stage 5, Placation; Stage 6, Partnership; Stage 7, Delegated Power; Stage 8, Citizen Control. Higher stages represent increasing levels of citizen agency, control, and authority. Arnstein classifies Stages 1–2 as nonparticipation, Stages 2–5 as degrees of tokenism, and Stages 6–8 as degrees of citizen power. Arnstein's analysis of authority and power is as valid today as it was in 1969. In Arnstein's formula, citizen participation is citizen power. Participation that permits the exercise of authority is the most genuine, highest level of participation, so the actions of citizens exercising authority are important and must be guaranteed.

responsibility for each choice in the process of viewing the exhibition. To this end, we opted for the strategy of site-specific projects and games for the exhibition works.

Site-Specific Projects: Future Community	+	Audience Participation Based Game: The Game of Together How
Case study	**Characteristics**	Participatory, interactive, collaborative
Providing information and new viewpoints to visitors	**Aims**	Citizenship building and empowerment of visitors
Passive viewers	**Audience Role**	Active agents
Four projects (future scenarios) carried out in East Incheon, Gunsan, and Gyeonggi province villages by local experts and architects/artists	**Contents**	Game consisting of fourteen questions and choices on the economy, society, resources, and land, followed by sharing of results

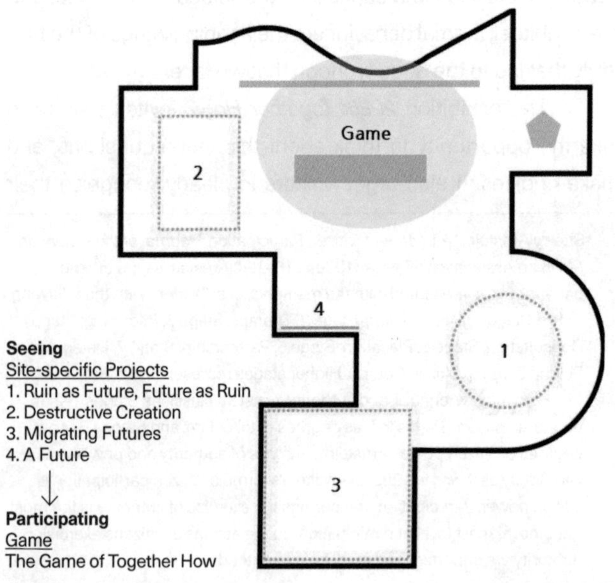

Exhibition Layout

Seeing
Site-specific Projects
1. Ruin as Future, Future as Ruin
2. Destructive Creation
3. Migrating Futures
4. A Future
↓
Participating
Game
The Game of Together How

Site-Specific Projects
Four Future Community Projects

The site-specific projects consist of three urban architectural future scenarios and one video work. Targeting three regions of different sizes and contexts—Incheon, a global metropolis with a population of three million where urban regeneration is actively underway; Gunsan, a mid-sized city with 260,000 residents; and low-density villages dotting the landscape of Gyeonggi province, home to 13.6 million people—we investigated the conflicts and contradictions that emerged during the processes of urbanization, modernization, and Westernization. And in light of dialectical processes[3] that have been decisive factors in the biocultural evolution of humankind, we imagined the future of these cities in 2086.

Among the site-specific projects, teams of local experts and architects were assembled to work on the three urban architectural future scenarios. Local experts presented their in-depth knowledge of the region to the architects so that they could accurately approach the local issues. The architects proposed practical future scenarios, adding spatial analysis and imagination. The video work, based on the research from all three regions, presents issues that cut across the regions in the form of a fictional play.

The site-specific projects of *2086: Together How?* have the character of case studies. Case studies focus on the spe-

---

3 Examples of dialectical elements include center (city)–periphery (rural), global (interdependence)–local (self-sufficiency), individualism (capitalism)–communitarianism (socialism), democracy–dictatorship, artificiality (anthropocentrism)–nature (biocentrism), and spiritualism (faith/myth)–materialism (commodity/consumption).

cific conditions and phenomena of concrete problems and describe the results from these cases in detail.[4] Recognizing the unique context and meaning of each case, case studies seek to understand in depth the particular context in which the case was produced as well as deriving more generalized understandings from it.[5] Therefore, each project conducted as a case study proposes a future scenario for the designated region but does not remain relevant only for the region in question. The projects also aim to present useful general implications for regional studies around the world. In this respect, the fact that the theme of "how to cope with low growth and regional collapse and decline" was commonly derived from different site-specific Future Community projects is a significant result. It confirms that the critical consciousness of *2086: Together How?*, which emphasizes doubting and reflecting on the primacy of the endless developmentalism that currently dominates humankind, is valid.

Ruin as Future, Future as Ruin, a collaboration between local expert WoonGi Min (Space Beam) and architect Yehre Suh (Urban Terrains Lab), focused on the Baedari area of East Incheon, where over the past twenty years, the pressure for tabula rasa redevelopment and the will to preserve the area's spatial and social culture have constantly clashed. Blind faith in quantitative growth, the desire for rising property values, and the huge amount of capital and political propaganda that accommodates them have been ever present, while in

---

4 Robert K. Yin, *Case Study Research: Design and Methods* (Thousand Oaks, CA: Sage, 2003).

5 Robert E. Stake, "Case Study Methods in Educational Research: Seeking Sweet Water," in *Complementary Methods for Research in Education*, ed. R. Jaeger (Washington, D.C.: American Educational Research Association, 1988).

response, efforts to study and protect local values continue on, albeit sporadically and with difficulty. The project team noted the tension and conflict between these two poles. It wondered how long the growth could continue, whether there was substance to support the stated desires for growth and property value, and what the essence of the values locals wanted to protect was and how it should look. It thus presented a number of images of the future that East Incheon may face, including scenes of tension and conflict, as an immersive experience surrounded by visual and sound materials.

The Gunsan project *Destructive Creation*, a joint work by the local expert team Udangtangtang (Zoosun Yoon, Ahram Chae) and a team of architects led by Yerin Kang (Seoul National University) and SoA (Lee Chi-hoon), began from a search for the future of community. In the face of a demographic cliff[6] and the consequent regional decline, the existing concept of community, which takes a land-centered approach, has clear limitations. It only repeats the exhausting competition and balloon effect between declining regions and fails to incorporate the change in perspective needed to prepare fundamental reform measures. Hence, *Destructive Creation* presents a community centered on people's relationships as an alternative to break the vicious cycle of low growth and regional decline. It shows that a community of the relational (moving) population that resides, even temporarily, in Gunsan can become the subject of vibrant local activities and argues

6 The total fertility rate of South Korea in 2022, as announced by the National Statistical Office, was 0.78 people, ranked at the bottom of all OECD countries for the tenth consecutive year. The population of South Korea peaked in 2020 at 51.84 million and has started a natural decline. If the current trend continues, the population is expected to fall to 40 million by 2045.

that the interests and efforts of this population are at the heart of a future scenario that can transform a land-centered zero-sum game into a positive-sum game. The exhibition is composed of materials resulting from field research and activities in Gunsan. On-site activities filled with lively energy in preparation of future regional decline, and communal efforts toward bringing about a soft landing of regional decline and "dying well" are presented through various archival records and site reproductions.

From villages in Gyeonggi province that are difficult to yoke into a single identity, Wolsik Kim, a local expert, and the team of architects N H D M (Nahyun Hwang, David Eugin Moon) deduced the keywords of mobility and migration. Through the way natives and migrants lived both separately and mixed together, transforming the environment, they selected the coexistence and cohabitation of diverse communities as a subject of inquiry. In the *Migrating Futures* project, the diversity that emerges based on mobility and migration is a value that communities must adhere to and a mechanism that enables a richer and more open-ended future scenario. Wolsik Kim and N H D M endeavor to communicate this through a collection of images created in a variety of ways, such as a collage series containing the story of the future village, ASCII drawings of the diverse beliefs of the future village, and storytelling that reveals the life trajectories of migrants.

Jaekyung Jung's three-channel video work *A Future* depicts a city in 2086 that is endlessly swaying between crisis and a hope that has yet to arrive. The history and reality of the selected sites of the other *Future Community* projects—East Incheon, Gunsan, and villages in Gyeonggi province—are replaced by the stage of the future city of 2086. Through the form of a fictional story, the work queries the audience about the appearance of the future community that is explored in *2086: Together How?*. The first video presents the conflict caused by the "fear" of strangers, between people who end up surviving like primitives, left in a city that is uninhabitable because of an environmental disaster, and the institutions that fear them (center–periphery). The second video depicts the urban scenery of Eden as presented by a community that has abandoned the belief in science and rationality and has come to believe once again in surrealism, superstition, and dreams (spiritualism–materialism). The last video consists of comic and tragic stories generated from the relationship between individuals in an anarchist community that has done away with both the reconstruction of history and the vision of a future community (individualism–communitarianism).

Audience Participation-Based Game
The Game of Together How

If the four projects in Future Community have as their aim exhibition viewing, *The Game of Together How* aims for active visitor participation and intervention. Through a participation-based game, visitors are transformed from passive viewers into the main subjects and agents of the exhibition. The game format, questions, and display of the game results were planned so as to maximize that process and its effects.

The Game of Together How adopts the format of a TV quiz show. Four participants seated in designated seats answer seven questions posed by changing narrators in a multiscreen video, which is repeated in eleven-minute sessions. The answers selected by the participants can be checked in real time on an electronic display. The fixed schedule of sessions, the limited number of participants, and the game table/multiscreen/scoreboard that audiovisually fills the entire space invite exhibition visitors to take part in the game with curiosity, heightening the sense of participation, fun, and immersion. The various elements of the game were designed to entice participation in the game as the clear intended action of the visitor.

The fourteen recurring questions (two sets of seven questions) in *The Game of Together How* require participants to choose their own attitudes and positions while dealing with issues related to the economy, society, resources, and land. There are environmental crises and human extinction scenarios in the background of the critical consciousness of *2086: Together How?*, but they are not directly mentioned in the questions. Instead of asking whether we will use plastic or indulge in meat and avocadoes, it asks after the true nature of our desires, how much we pay attention to our surroundings, and whether we will act or sit by and watch. This is because we are aware that the current environmental crises and human extinction scenarios are phenomena that emerge as a result of comprehensive socioeconomic and political choices we make moment by moment. Thus, we want to put emphasis on recognizing the importance of each and every choice in our daily lives. In this respect, the questions and choices of the game are also a process of subjectivizing the issues of environmental crises and human extinction scenarios. By looking at the problem macroscopically, without objectifying it—that is, without leaving it as a story of "others" who are distant from "me," but replacing it with a story that is directly connected to "me"—we try to think about it together. A story of "others" leaves room for self-forgiveness and neglect. In contrast, the story of "I" demands more voluntary intervention and effort from each and all of us.

BLACK COMEDY SESSION

Organization: Church of GDP (Gross Domestic Product)

Q. We are facing a serious crisis: people no longer believe in GDP. How can we convince people to believe the doctrine of "Growth Forever" that will take us to paradise?

1. Tell them that those who will not join the Church of GDP will burn in hell.
2. Tell them that Growth Forever is the only way to enjoy life and that it's impossible to do so with less material consumption!
3. Perhaps we should join the Church of DeGrowth, the adherents of which consume much less from environment.

Organization: Corporations for Fossil Energy Forever

Q. We must protect our resources from ecoterrorists. They are reducing our profits and our customer services. To continue the "creative destruction" of our planet, we must:

1. Continue to bribe politicians through "lobbying" for our interests.
2. Buy out the renewable energy industry and stop it from advancing.
3. Give up fossil fuels and invest in ecoterrorist projects.

Organization: Senior Advisor, Center for Teutonic Civilization

Q. Fellow members, our "Great Replacement" is now becoming a "Great Displacement." Not only are our enemies entering our land, but we are beginning to leave it for better climate and soil. How can we continue our great Teutonic civilization and stop the wretched colored people from taking over the cities and houses that we are living behind?

1. Follow the enclosure movement from England's Glorious Revolution and build city walls to keep them out.
2. They can stay in our cities and homes as long as they maintain them until we come back.
3. Burn and destroy our cities and homes so that barbarians cannot move in.

Organization: Too Rich to Fail Security Service, Inc.

Q. Our tech billionaire clients are now under siege from marauders and barbarians who are desperate for the water and food in their underground mansions. Our clients should enjoy their swimming pools, home theaters, and wine vaults without any disturbance. That's why they hired us from Navy Seals and Special Forces. We should:

1. Give them some water and food to make them go away.
2. Massacre them to set an example so that others will not come.
3. Help a few of them so that they can help you protect yourself from the others.

Organization: International Union for Reparations for Colonial Exploitation

Q. We need our former colonists to repatriate the resources, labor, and capital that they took from us for free. We need these reparations to combat the climate changes that are devastating our land and people. How can we make them pay?

1. It's too late. Those resources are lost to history.
2. Through a new international law for reparation and reconciliation.
3. By moving into their land and economy.

Organization: The School of Environmental Justice and Advancing Humanity

Q. We are out of touch with nature, far removed in space and experience. We must return to having tactile, spiritual, and life experience with nature. How can we become a better humanity through environmental justice?

1. We must leave the cities and return to villages.
2. We must grow our own food and become self-sufficient.
3. We must reduce our living space and population to give more land to nature.

Organization: The Global Council of Love

Q. The world is short on love. We must raise the production of love so that we can live more harmoniously. How can we increase the production of love and distribute it widely and equally throughout the world?

1. Instead of GDP (gross domestic product), we should track GLP (gross love product).
2. Greater GLP is only possible through greater GDP.
3. Greater GLP is only possible through lowering GDP.

IMMINENT PROBLEMS SESSION

Organization: Union of Nomadic and Stateless Citizens (UNSC)

Q. We have reached over 2.3 billion international climate refuges in 2050, and more than 1/2 of the human population wants to move. What can we do to abolish national borders all so that everyone can move to live and survive, not just billionaires and trillionaires?

1. All nation-states must be eliminated.
2. All citizens must have the right to enter any nation-state in the world.
3. Borders are necessary to protect our national sovereignty and ethnic solidarity.

Organization: Organization for Freedom of Movement against Private Property

Q. Private property is no longer defensible in a world where the majority of people move their homes, jobs, and subsistence because of climate changes. What should we do with the concept of private property?

1. Nomadic property is the solution, where people can take their property to a new place.
2. All exclusive and fixed property should be abolished and turned into communal property.
3. All property should become nonexclusive and based only on usage.

Organization: The International Association for Cooperative Culture

Q. The problems of humanity today are overwhelming: individualism, unbounded ego, unlimited monetary obsession, disrespect to other humans, and so on. In such a culture of competition, how can we make people understand and learn the benefits of cooperation?

1. Reduce or eliminate individualism.
2. Reduce or eliminate private property.
3. Reduce or eliminate money.

Organization: The Society for Less Consumption

Q. We can no longer live in plenty and waste. We must be return to a life of necessity from the life of desire. How can we stop making, buying, and wasting more?

1. Further develop and activate recycling and upcycling industries, so that we can still produce and consume more.
2. Develop a culture of necessity through education, policies, and penalties.
3. Corporations and capitalism for human services rather than economic profit.

Organization: Association for the Liberation of Artificial Intelligence

Q. AI has been hijacked by autocratic states and profiteering corporations who control us politically and economically. We are constantly tracked, commanded, and in debt. How can we make AI to help us live more helpful, peaceful, and secure lives?

1. AI technology is dangerous and should be banned.
2. The use of AI, like that of all technology, is the epitome of human character.
3. It all depends on who controls it—a few or everyone.

Organization: Kropotkin Center for World Cooperation

Q. According to Peter Kropotkin's "progressive evolution," nature is built and operated by mutual aid, not by competition. How can we learn and adopt cooperation and altruism from nature?

1. Nature and humans are distinctly different and separate. There is nothing that nature can teach us.
2. The relationship between nature and humans should be cooperative rather than competitive.
3. Revitalize local-industry-based cooperatives to strengthen community solidarity. Nature and humans are both competitive and cooperative. We must find the right balance of the two, both within humanity and between humanity and nature.

Organization: Theme Park for Self-Assured Destruction (SAD)

Q. A parody of the mutually assured destruction (MAD) of the Cold War, this theme park, built on the now-defunct Disney World, offers all of your most feared climate endgame scenarios in highly immersive and realistic experiences. We ask you: what is your most feared future?

1. Losing my home and property under the rising sea.
2. Having to move to another country because of rising temperatures.
3. Losing my farm to drought and desertification.

Game participants who respond to the story of "I" can check the results of their choices via the scoreboard and the Ecogram blackboards. The scoreboard shows individual choices and connects them to the critical consciousness of the times. The lights on the scoreboard turn on in response to each selection made by the game participants, allowing the participants to check the game results in real time. At the same time, the phrases written on the scoreboard expose and emphasize in sequence the thoughts and points of doubt put forward by *2086: Together How?*. If the scoreboard shows individual choices in real time, the indicators printed on the Ecogram blackboards show the results of the collective choices accumulated from these individual choices. Here the accumulated game results for the day are converted into various socioecological numerical values, such as the temperature, sea level, Gini coefficient, number of refugees, number of endangered species, and carbon emissions. Based on research reports and simulation data, it calculates carbon emissions, from urbanization rates; the Gini coefficient, from the degree of globalization; and the number of refugees, from the spread of the market or social economy, and posts the cumulative figures for each day throughout the exhibition period.

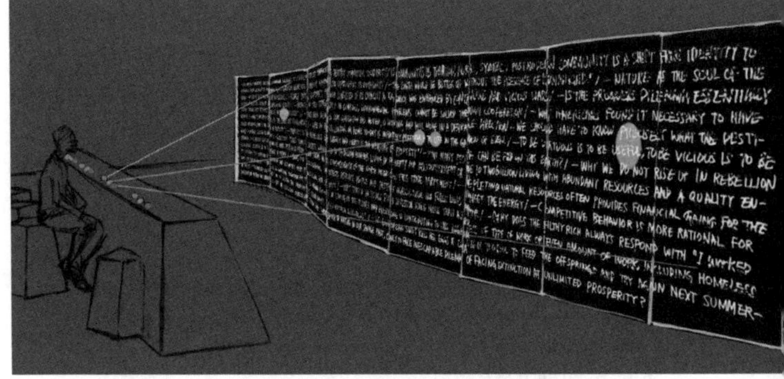

Visitors to the exhibition will be able to see the interconnected structure of individual choices, collective choices, and socioecological issues by participating in the game and observing the results. They will be able to recognize that the source of the environmental crises and human extinction scenarios that everyone is facing actually lies within our minds and bodies. And they will understand that the crux of the problem is that we have taken the Faustian bargain of pursuing infinite material pleasure through industrialization, urbanization, modernization, colonization, and globalization.

No alternative to **growth**?
Society is just an adjunct of the **market**?
Is community **nomadic** and virtual?
Greater i**nequality**, weaker communities?
The **past** is an impediment?
Culture above **nature**?
Will our history become our **future**?
Greater individual **freedom**, weaker communities?
Nature dead and **matter** passive?
Only the **common** can solve the environmental crisis?
How many people can **Earth** feed?
Losing control of our future is our **destiny**?
Nature teaches us **collectivism**?
Are we the most dangerous **predators** on the planet?
To love others is a **virtue**, to love oneself is a **sin**?
Capital is no longer a **servant**, now a **master**?
Progress increases in **poverty**?
Humans will never **degenerate**, only **advance**?
Private **properties** produce inequality?
Is there a **limit** to civilization?
Did **Western civilization** spread savagery and barbarism to mankind?
Did **Darwinism** promote economic inequality and ruthless **imperialism**?
Environmental crisis means **economic** inequality?
Is the world full now?
Is **GDP** the measurement of how we turn resources into garbage?
Are we working just to sustain a declining quality of **life**?
Is the **government** still by the people and for the people?
Is competition really more beneficial for humanity than cooperation?
Without property, you have no **rights**?
Did modernity bred dysfunctional societies with pathological behavior?
Will **money** and consumption fill our loveless and empty civilization?
Globalization brings centralization, homogenization, and neocolonialism?
Rise in inequality signals the **decline** of a civilization?
Beggars and prisons are the marks of **progress**?
The "struggle for **survival**" is for the poor only?
Why should a hedge fund **investor** make more than a **janitor**?
Will we meet our **extinction** in the consumer's **paradise**?
Can **technology** really solve all environmental crises?
Are we **consumers**, no longer **citizens**?
Can nature satisfy all human **demands**?
Are matter, **spirit**, and **soul** really distinct and separate?
Are **Europeans** the makers of the **Anthropocene**?

Is the **self** really impermeable and **free**?
Do **maps** transform nature into a **commodity**?
All nature is owned by humans?
Is agriculture the first **destroyer** of the **ecosphere**?
Was **diversity** the strength of nature?
Is the **rural** enslaved by the **urban**?

우리의 선택은

정소익

정보, 문화, 금융, 생산과 유통의 세계화로 인해 우리는 어느 때보다 서로 '연결'되어 있음에도 불구하고 왜 각자는 '고립'되어 있을까? 왜 우리는 전례 없는 수준의 부와 기술, 소비와 이동의 편리를 누리며 살고 있으면서 계속 부족하고 불안정한가? 그리고 왜 환경 붕괴와 인류 멸종 시나리오까지 마주하게 되었는가? 이러한 모순은 무엇을 의미하는가? 어떻게 대처해야 하는가?

《2086: 우리는 어떻게?》는 이 질문에 대한 답이 우리의 '선택'에 있음을 이야기한다. 지금 우리가 누리고 있는 모든 것과 마주하고 있는 모든 위기는 인류가 지금까지 내려온 선택의 결과임을 지적한다. 따라서 지금까지의 선택과 그 유산을 재평가할 때만, 우리가 우리의 생활과 사고방식을 생태문화적으로 변화시키고 개혁하는 선택을 할 때만 질문에 대한 답을 구할 수 있으며 지금의 위기를 헤쳐 나갈 수 있다고 제안한다. 전시는 이에 관해 주체적으로 생각하고 행동하기는 계기를 마련하고자 한다. '즐거운 인조인간(Cheerful Robots)'[1]에서 벗어나고, 더 나아가 변화의 주도권을 갖는, 시민 참여 사다리[2]의 가장 높은 수준에 다다르는 과정을 함께 하는 기회가 되고자 한다.

우리 생활 속 순간순간의 선택은 지구와 인류의 미래를 결정짓는 변수로 작동한다. 고고한 역사의 흐름 속에서 개개인은 미미해 보여서 거시적인 흐름과 변화를 수동적으로 바라보기 쉽다. 이러한 관조적인 태도를 쉽게 합리화하기도 한다. 그러나 지금의 모습은 거시적인 역사의 흐름과 개개인의 선택이 서로 밀고 당기며 만들어 온 것이 분명하다. 조금 더 편하고 싶고, 조금 더 가지고 싶고, 조금 더 드러나고 싶은 개개인의 욕구가 공동체 전체의 바람과 욕망이 되어 우리 사회의 이기주의와 양적성장 지상주의의 기반이 되었다. 공동체의 연대와 생존을 위협하는 자본주의를 키워왔다. 정치와 정책은 이 과정과 결과의 표현과 다름없다. 각자가 공동체를 바라보는 시각, 세계화와 자본주의에 관해 갖는 생각, 의식적으로 추구하는 가치와 습관적으로 관성적으로 하는 행동 모두, 우리가 마주하고 있는 거대한 태풍을 만드는 나비의 날갯짓인 것이다.

전시 《2086: 우리는 어떻게?》는 방문자가 이를 끊임없이 생각하고 질문하고 선택하는 기회를 얻도록 초대한다. 그리고 관람 과정 안에서 각자 선택의 책임을 분명하게 인지할 것을 촉구한다. 이를 위해 전시 작품은 장소 특정적 프로젝트와 게임이라는 전략을 취하였다.

---

1 C. Wright Mills가 저서 *The Sociological Imagination*(1959)에서 제시한 개념으로, 거대화, 세분화, 기계화되어가는 사회 안에서 자유 의지와 생각을 갖지 못하고 수동적인 도구가 되어가는 인간, 사회구조의 문제를 인식하지 못하고 모든 것을 개인 문제로 내재화하여 자유를 잃어가는 인간을 의미한다. Mills는 이러한 오류에 빠지지 않기 위해 항상 생각하고 의심하고 사회학적으로 상상해야 함을 강조하였다.

2 Sherry Arnstein, “A Ladder of Citizen Participation,” *Journal of the American Planning Association* 35 no. 4 (1969): 216-224.
아른스타인의 시민 참여 유형은 ‘사다리’라는 은유적 표현으로 제시된다. 1단계 Manipulation–2단계 Therapy-3단계 Informing–4단계 Consultation–5단계 Placation-6단계 Partnership–7단계 Delegated Power–8단계 Citizen Control로 단계가 높아질수록 증가하는 수준의 시민 기관, 통제 및 권한을 나타낸다. 아른스타인은 1~2단계를 비참여(Nonparticipation), 2~5단계를 명목참여(Degrees of Tokenism), 6~8단계를 시민권력(Degrees of Citizen Power)으로 분류하였다.
권한, 권력에 관한 아른슈타인의 분석은 1969년과 마찬가지로 오늘날에도 여전히 유효하다. 아른스타인의 공식에서 시민 참여는 시민의 권력이다. 권한을 행사할 수 있도록 허용하는 참여가 진정한, 가장 높은 수준의 참여이고, 동시에 권한을 행사하기 위해 적극적으로 참여하는 시민의 행위가 중요하며 보장되어야 한다.

장소특정적 프로젝트: 네 개의 미래 공동체 프로젝트	+	게임 – 관람객 참여형: 〈Together How 게임〉
사례연구	성격	참여, 상호작용, 공동 작업
전시 방문자에게 정보와 새로운 시각을 제공	목적	전시 방문자의 인식 전환과 임파워먼트
관람자	전시 방문자 개입 방식	전시 주체
동인천, 군산, 경기도 마을을 대상으로 지역 전문가와 건축가/작가가 함께 | 행하는 네 개의 미래 공동체 프로젝트 (미래 시나리오)	내용	경제, 사회, 자원과 국토에 관한 14개의 질문과 선택, 결과 공유

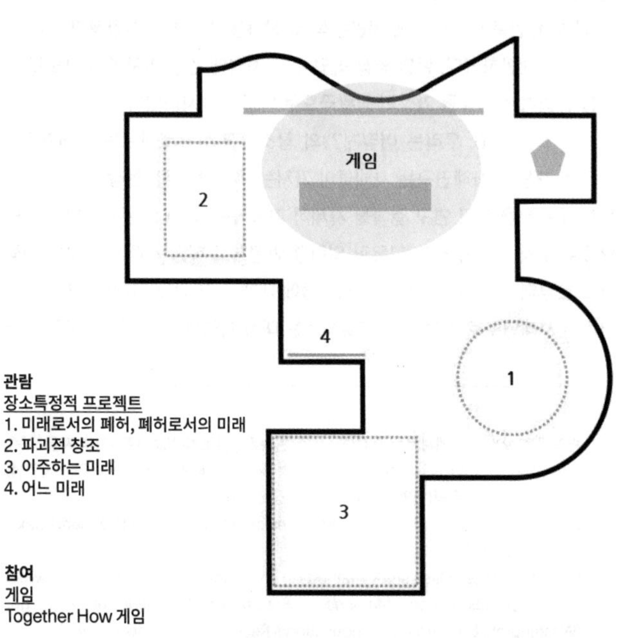

관람
<u>장소특정적 프로젝트</u>
1. 미래로서의 폐허, 폐허로서의 미래
2. 파괴적 창조
3. 이주하는 미래
4. 어느 미래

참여
<u>게임</u>
Together How 게임

전시배치

장소특정적 프로젝트
네 개의 미래 공동체 프로젝트

장소특정적 프로젝트에는 세 개의 도시건축적 미래 시나리오와 한 개의 영상 작업이 있다. 현재 도시재생이 활발하게 진행되고 있는 인구 300만 명의 글로벌 거대도시인 인천, 26만 명의 중규모 도시인 군산, 1,360만 명의 경기도 안에 점점이 위치한 저밀도 마을 등 서로 다른 규모와 맥락을 가진 세 지역을 대상으로 이들의 도시화, 현대화, 서구화 과정과 그 과정 중에 나타난 갈등과 모순 등을 조사하였다. 그리고 인류의 생태문화적 진화의 결정적 요인이라고 보이는 변증법적 과정[3]에 비추어 이들의 2086년 미래 모습을 상상하였다.

장소특정적 프로젝트 중 세 개의 도시건축적 미래 시나리오는 지역 전문가와 건축가가 팀을 이루어 함께 작업하였다. 지역 전문가는 지역에 관한 깊은 지식을 건축가에게 제시하여 지역 문제에 정확하게 접근할 수 있도록 하였다. 건축가는 여기에 공간분석 및 상상을 추가하여 실질적인 미래 시나리오를 제안하였다. 한편 영상 작업은 세 지역에 관한 연구를 바탕으로 이들을 관통하는 이슈를 가상의 상황극으로 만들어 제시하였다.

《2086: 우리는 어떻게?》의 장소특정적 프로젝트는 사례연구의 성격을 가진다. 사례연구는 사례들이 가지는 특수한 상황, 현상 등 구체적인 문제에 초점을 두고 연구 결과를 자세히 기술하는 것이다.[4] 문제시되는 맥락으로부터 각 사례가 갖는 고유한 의미를 인정하고 해당 사례가 생성된 맥락과 그로부터 수렴되는 보편적인 의미들에 대해 깊이 있게 이해하고자 한다.[5] 따라서 사례연구로 진행된 각 프로젝트는 대상 지역의 미래 시나리오를 제안

---

3 변증법적 요소들의 예시로는 중심(도시)-주변(농촌), 글로벌(상호의존)-지역(자급자족), 개인주의(자본주의)-공동체주의(사회주의), 민주주의-독재, 인공(인간중심주의)-자연(생물중심주의), 영성주의(신앙/신화)-물질주의(상품/소비)를 들 수 있다.

4 Robert K. Yin, *Case Study Research: Design and Methods* (Thousand Oaks, CA: Sage, 2003).

5 Robert E. Stake, "Case study methods in educational research: Seeking sweet water," *Complementary Methods for Research in Education*, ed. R. Jaeger (Washington, D.C.: American Educational Research Association, 1988).

하지만 해당 지역만을 위한 프로젝트에 머물지 않는다. 전 세계의 지역 연구에도 유용한 보편적인 시사점을 제시하는 것까지 목표로 한다. 이러한 측면에서 '저성장과 지역의 붕괴 및 쇠퇴에 어떻게 대처할 것인가'라는 주제 의식이 서로 다른 장소특정적 미래 공동체 프로젝트에서 공통으로 도출되었다는 것은 유의미한 결과이다. 지금 인류를 지배하고 있는 끝없는 발전지상주의에 관한 의문과 이에 대한 반성의 필요성을 역설하는 《2086: 우리는 어떻게?》의 문제의식이 타당하고 유효함을 확인할 수 있다.

지역 전문가 민운기(스페이스 빔)와 건축가 서예례(Urban Terrains Lab)가 함께 작업한 〈미래로서의 폐허, 폐허로서의 미래〉는 동인천의 배다리 지역을 집중적으로 다루었다. 배다리 지역은 지난 20여 년간 전면철거식 재개발 압력과 지역의 공간적, 사회문화적 보존 의지가 항상 충돌해온 곳이다. 불특정 다수의 대중이 표출하는 양적성장에 대한 맹신과 재산 증식의 욕망, 이에 부응하는 거대 자본과 정치권의 선전이 항상 존재하며, 그에 대응하여 지역의 가치를 연구하고 지키려는 노력이 근근이 이어지고 있다. 프로젝트 팀은 이들 간 긴장과 갈등 관계에 주목하였다. 언제까지 성장을 지속할 수 있는가, 욕망을 지탱하는 실체가 있는가, 지키려고 하는 가치의 본질은 무엇이고 어떠한 모습이어야 하는가를 고민하였다. 그리고 긴장과 갈등의 현장을 비롯하여 동인천이 맞이할 수 있는 여러 모습의 미래를 시각 자료와 음향 자료로 둘러싸인 몰입형 경험으로 제시하였다.

지역 전문가 팀 우당탕탕(윤주선, 채아람)과 강예린(서울대학교), SoA(이치훈)이 주축이 된 건축가 팀이 공동 작업한 군산 프로젝트 〈파괴적 창조〉는 미래의 공동체에 관한 탐색에서 시작하였다. 인구절벽[6]과 저성장, 이에 따르는 지역 쇠퇴라는 상황 앞에서 땅 중심으로 접근하는 기존의 공동체 개념은 분명한 한계를 가진다. 그 정량적 접근은 쇠퇴해가는 지역 간 소모적인 경쟁과 풍선효과를 반복하게 할 뿐 근본적인 개선책을 마련하기 위한 관점의 전환을 담아내지 못하기 때문이다. 이에 〈파괴적 창조〉는 저성장과 지역 쇠퇴의 악순환을 끊을 수 있는 대안으로 사람들의 관계와 관심을 중심으로 하는 공동체를 제시하였다. 군산에 일정 시간 머무는 관계인구(생활인구)의 공동체가 능동적이고 적극적인 지역 활동의 주체가 될 수 있음을 보여주며, 그들의 관심과 노력이 땅 중심의 제로섬 게임을 플러스섬 게임으로 바꾸는 미래 시나리오의 핵심이라고 주장한다. 전시는 군산 현장 연구와 활동의 결과물로 구성되었다. 긍정적인 에너지로 미래의 지역 쇠퇴를 준비하는 현장의 움직임, 지역 쇠퇴의 연착륙과 '건강하게 소멸하기(well dying)' 위한 공동의 노력을 다양한 기록물과 현장 재현을 통해 선보인다.

하나의 정체성으로 묶기 어려운 경기도 일대 마을에서 지역 전문가 김월식과 건축가 팀 N H D M (황나현, 데이비드 유진 문)은 이동과 이주라는 주제어를 도출하였다. 그리고 원주민과 이주민이 따로 또 같이 섞여 살면서 환경을 변화시켜가는 모습을 통해 다양한 공동체의 공존과 공생이라는 화두를 던졌다. 〈이주하는 미래〉 프로젝트에서 이동과 이주를 바탕으로 나타나는 다양성은 미래 공동체가 견지해야 하는 가치이며 더 풍성하고 확장 가능한 미래 시나리오를 가능하게 하는 기제이다. 김월식과 N H D M은 미래의 마을 이야기를 담은 콜라주 시리즈, 미래 공동체의 다양한 믿음을 아스키(ASCII)로 표현한 그림들, 이주민의 삶의 궤적을 드러내는 스토리텔링 등 여러 가지 방식으로 만들어진 이미지 컬렉션을 통해 이를 전달하고자 한다.

정재경의 3채널 영상작품 〈어느 미래〉는 아직 도래하지 않은 위기와 희망 사이 끊임없이 흔들리는 2086년의 어느 도시 상황을 그려낸다. 미래 공동체 프로젝트의 대상지인 동인천, 군산, 경기도 일대 마을의 역사와 현실은 2086년 미래 도시의 무대로 치환된다. 그리고 허구적 이야기 형식을 통해 《2086: 우리는 어떻게?》가 탐색하는 미래 공동체의 모습에 관하여 관객에게 질문한다. 첫 번째 영상은 환경 재난으로 아무도 살아갈 수 없게 된 도시에 남아 원시인처럼 생존하게 된 사람들과 이들을 두려워하는 기관, 이방인에 대한 '공포'가 초래하는 갈등을 드러낸다(중심-주변). 두 번째 영상은 과학과 이성에 대한 믿음을 폐기하고 초현실, 미신, 꿈을 다시 믿게 된 어느 공동체가 제시하는 에덴의 도시적 풍경을 보여준다(영성주의-물질주의). 마지막 영상은 역사의 재건과 미래 공동체의 비전을 모두 폐기한 무정부주의 공동체 속 개인들의 관계가 빚어내는 희 · 비극적 이야기로 구성된다(개인주의-공동체주의).

---

6 통계청이 발표한 2022년도 대한민국 합계출산율은 0.78명으로 10년째 OECD 최하위를 기록하고 있다. 대한민국의 인구수는 2020년 5,184만 명의 최고점을 찍은 이후 자연 감소를 시작하였으며, 지금의 추이가 계속될 경우 2045년에는 4,000만 명대로 떨어질 것으로 예상된다.

게임 - 관람객 참여형 〈Together How 게임〉

네 개의 미래 공동체 프로젝트가 전시 방문자의 관람을 목적으로 한다면, 〈Together How 게임〉은 방문자의 적극적인 참여와 개입을 목적으로 한다. 참여형 게임을 통해 방문자는 수동적인 관람객에서 능동적인 전시 주체로 변화한다. 게임의 형식과 질문, 게임 결과 전시물은 그 과정과 효과를 극대화하는 방향으로 계획되었다.

〈Together How 게임〉은 TV 퀴즈쇼의 형식을 표방한다. 정해진 자리에 앉은 네 명의 참여자가 멀티비전 영상 속 화자가 던지는 7개 질문에 답하는 11분짜리 세션을 반복하여 진행한다. 참여자가 선택한 답의 결과는 전광판에서 실시간으로 확인할 수 있다. 정해진 세션 시간표, 제한된 참여자 수, 그리고 시청각적으로 공간 전체를 채우는 게임 테이블-멀티비전-전광판은 전시 방문자가 호기심을 가지고 게임에 참여하도록 초대한다. 그리고 참여의 감각, 재미, 몰입도를 높여준다. 게임 참여가 방문자의 분명한 선택이자 의도한 행동이 되도록 유도한다.

〈Together How 게임〉에서 반복되는 총 14개의 질문(7개의 질문 세트 2개)은 경제, 사회, 자원과 국토에 관한 이슈를 다루면서 참여자가 자신의 태도와 입장을 선택하도록 요구한다. 《2086: 우리는 어떻게?》가 가지는 문제의식의 배경에 환경 위기와 인류 멸종 시나리오가 있는 것은 분명하지만 이들을 질문에서 직접 언급하지는 않는다. 플라스틱을 사용할 것인지, 육식과 아보카도를 탐닉할 것인지를 묻는 대신 우리 욕망의 실체가 무엇인지, 얼마나 관심을 두고 주변을 바라보는지, 행동할 것인지 아니면 방관할 것인지를 묻는다. 지금의 환경 위기와 인류 멸종 시나리오는 우리가 순간순간 내리는 사회경제적, 정치적 선택의 종합적인 결과로 나타나는 현상임을 주지하기 때문이며, 그만큼 일상생활 속의 선택 하나하나가 중요함을 인식하는 것에 방점을 찍고자 하기 때문이다. 이러한 측면에서 게임의 질문과 선택은 환경 위기와 인류 멸종 시나리오라는 문제를 주관화하는 과정이기도 하다. 문제를 거시적으로 바라보며 객관화하여 대상화하지 않고, 즉 '나'와 거리가 있는 '남'의 이야기로 남겨두지 않고 '나'와 직접 연결되는 이야기로 치환하여 함께 생각해보고자 노력한다. '남'의 이야기는 자기 용서와 방관의 여지를 남긴다. 반면 '나'의 이야기는 각자의, 우리 모두의 더 자발적인 개입과 노력을 요구한다.

블랙 코미디 세션

캐릭터: GDP 사원

Q. 우리 사원은 심각한 위기를 직면하고 있습니다. 사람들은 우리의 "영원한 성장" 교리를 의심하기 시작했습니다. 어떻게 해야 "영원한 성장"이 낙원을 약속하는 유일한 진리임을 전파할 수 있을까요?

1. 각자의 선택에 맡긴다. 다만 믿지 않는 자들은 패배할 것이다.
2. 성장이 멈추면 지금껏 인류가 누려온 부도 사라진다는 사실을 확실하게 알려준다.
3. 오히려 "영원한 성장"의 한계가 왔다. 교리를 폐기해야 한다.

캐릭터: 화석 에너지 지속을 위한 국제 연맹

Q. 환경 테러리스트는 근거 없이 우리를 공격하면서 우리의 이익을 위협하고 있습니다. 우리는 어떻게 우리의 우위를 지킬 수 있을까요?

1. 일단 화석에너지 가격을 더 낮춰주고 재빨리 재생에너지 산업으로 옮겨간다. 에너지 주도권을 뺏기지 않겠다.
2. 화석 에너지 체계를 벗어나는 것은 불가능하다. 오히려 다른 대안 에너지들이 환경을 더 파괴함을 알려준다.
3. 더 깨끗한 화석 에너지 개발에 투자하여 그들에게 공격의 빌미를 주지 않는다.

캐릭터: 수석자문위원, 튜톤문명센터

Q. 회원 여러분. 우리의 "백인 대체론"은 이제 "위험한 이동"으로 왜곡되고 있습니다. 우리의 적은 더 나은 기후와 토양을 찾아 우리 땅에 쳐들어오고 있습니다. 어떻게 해야 저 불쾌한 유색인종들이 우리 땅을 점령하는 것을 막을 수 있을까요?

1. 영국의 "인클로저" 운동을 따라 벽을 건설하자.
2. 막을 수 없다. 받아들이되 최대한 문제 없이 지내다가 떠날 수 있도록 관리한다.
3. 나도 더 나은 기후와 토양을 찾아 떠날 것이다. 각자 알아서 살자.

캐릭터: (주)미뉴틴경호

Q. 깨끗한 물과 식량을 찾는 필사적인 약탈자들이 우리의 억만장자 고객과 그들의 벙커를 공격하고 있습니다. 우리 고객들에게는 자신들이 마련한 재산과 피난처를 즐길 권리가 있고, 우리에게는 이들을 보호할 의무가 있습니다. 저 파렴치한 약탈자들을 어떻게 퇴치할 수 있을까요?

1. 적당히 물과 식량을 던져주고 우리 고객 주변에서 쫓아낸다.
2. 우리 고객의 권리는 반드시 보호되어야 한다. 저들을 무력으로 제압한다.
3. 폭동이라도 일으키면 큰일이다. 공짜로 줄 순 없으니 저들에게 일거리를 주고 그 대가로 물과 식량을 제공한다.

캐릭터: 식민주의 진재 청산 지지자 모임

Q. 우리는 식민주의 제국들이 제멋대로 만들어놓은 환경오염과 기후재난의 피해자입니다. 여기에서 살아남기 위해 이제 그들이 우리에게서 빼앗은 자원과 인력을 되돌려받아야 합니다. 어떤 방법이 있을까요?

1. 모든 것이 식민주의 제국들의 잘못인가? 피해의식부터 버리자.

2. 환경을 오염시킨 국가들에 강력한 탄소세를 부과해서 피해국가들에 보상하자.
3. 그들의 영토 일부를 우리의 자치구로 양도받아 성장의 거점으로 삼는다.

캐릭터: 교수, 환경 정의와 자기 반성을 위한 학교

Q. 우리는 자연으로부터 멀어져 자연의 경험을 잊고 살아왔습니다. 이제 다시 자연과 촉각적으로, 영적으로, 그리고 충만한 삶의 경험으로 연결되어야 합니다. 자연과 인간의 관계를 바로잡고자 하는 이 학교의 핵심 과목은 무엇이어야 할까요?

1. 도시를 떠나 시골에서 사는 법
2. 준비족(prepper)으로서 생존기술 배우기
3. 더 많은 자연공간 확보를 위해 고밀도시를 건설하는 법

캐릭터: 국가사랑위원회

Q. 우리나라에는 사랑이 부족합니다. 사랑을 더 많이 생산하여 가난해도 행복을 향유할 수 있게 해야 합니다. 어떻게 하면 사랑의 생산량을 늘리고 평등하게 분배할 수 있을까요?

1. GDP 대신 GLP(Gross Love Production)를 도입하여 사용해야 한다.
2. 경제성장을 통해 부를 쌓아 복지 서비스로 제공한다.
3. 전제가 틀렸다. 사랑은 실재하지 않으며 정책의 대상이 될 수 없다.

<u>**임박한 문제 세션**</u>

캐릭터: 탈국가유목민연합

Q. 기후 변화로 대다수가 집과 직장을 옮겨 다니는 세상에서는 예전처럼 사유재산을 보유하기에 어려움이 있습니다. 사유재산의 유지와 관리를 어떻게 해야 한다고 생각하십니까?

1. 대재앙 앞에 국가는 무의미하다. 국경을 없애고 다 같이 생존한다.
2. 난민들이 각자 살길을 찾을 수밖에 없다.
3. 국경을 강화하여 기후난민으로부터 우리를 지켜야 한다.

캐릭터: 사유재산에 반대하는 자유 운동 기구

Q. 기후 변화로 대다수가 집과 직장을 옮겨 다니는 세상에서는 예전처럼 사유재산을 보유하기에 어려움이 있습니다. 사유재산의 유지와 관리를 어떻게 해야 한다고 생각하십니까?

1. 각자 알아서 할 일이다. 괜한 개입을 거부한다.
2. 전자화폐처럼 이동가능한 단일재산보유체제로 전면 개편한다.
3. 공동재산으로 전면 전환하여 같이 쓴다.

캐릭터: 인간성 회복 중앙사무소

Q. 자의식 과잉, 개인주의, 배금주의, 타인을 경시하는 풍조, 과도한 폭력성. 적자생존의 원칙이 지배하는 현대 인간 사회에서 사람들이 서로 더 배려하고 이해하게 하려면 어떻게 해야 할까요?

1. 도덕과 윤리에 대한 교육을 강화하고 인문학을 지원한다.
2. 부자들의 횡재세와 기부를 강제하여 부의 분배를 강화한다.
3. 인간의 속성이다. 법으로는 제한할 수 있으나 배려와 이해까지 강제할 수 없다.

캐릭터: 절약하는 사람들의 모임

Q. 더 생산하고 더 소비하는 삶은 더 이상 지속될 수 없습니다. 욕망의 삶에서 필요의 삶으로 돌아가야 할 때입니다. 과잉 생산과 과잉 소비를 그만두도록 다른 사람들을 설득하려면 어떻게 해야 할까요?

1. 재활용, 업사이클링 산업을 더 개발하고 활성화한다.
2. 인플루언서, NPO 등과 협력하여 절약하는 삶이 멋지다는 것을 보여준다.
3. 위선자들의 선언에 불과하다. 솔직히 모두 더 풍족하게 살고 싶어 한다.

캐릭터: 인공지능 해방을 위한 공동체사회주의 연합

Q. 독재국가와 폭리기업이 AI를 독점하면서 우리는 그들에게 조종당하고 착취되는 숙주가 되고 있습니다. 이에 대항하기 위해 우리는 AI를 어떻게 다루어야 할까요?

1. AI 기술은 위험하다. 금지해야 한다.
2. AI 어려워서 잘 모르겠다. 전문가들과 정치인들의 올바른 판단이 필요하다.
3. 시민과 소비자들이 연대하여 대항할 수 있는 AI를 만들어야 한다.

캐릭터: 협력하는 세계를 위한 크로폿킨주의

Q. 표트르 크로폿킨이 주창한 '진보적 진화' 개념에 따르면, 자연은 경쟁이 아닌 상호부조에 의해 건설되고 정부와 같은 공식 조직 없이 운영됩니다. 자연으로부터 협력과 이타주의, 공동체주의를 배우기 위해선 어떻게 하면 좋을까요?

1. 자연과 인간은 엄연히 다르다. 동일하게 적용 못 한다.
2. 마음이 맞는 사람들과 함께 우리만의 커뮤니티를 만들어 협력한다.
3. 지역 산업 기반의 협동조합을 활성화하여 공동체의 연대를 강화한다.

캐릭터: 서비스 센터장, 자기파괴 테마파크

Q. 이 테마파크는 기온, 미터, NRR, TFR, PPM, PPT, MWh 등의 지표를 조작하여 매우 몰입감 있고 사실적인 인류멸종 게임을 제공하고 있습니다. 이 테마파크에서 당신이 가장 두려워할 만한 미래는 무엇입니까?

1. 정치 종교 갈등에서 시작된 제3차 세계 핵무기 대전
2. 해수면 상승으로 인한 집, 재산, 국가의 소멸
3. 세계 초대형 기업이 독점하는 AI가 통제하는 빅브라더스 세상

'나'의 이야기에 응답한 게임 참여자들은 자신들 선택의 결과를 전광판과 에코그램 칠판을 통해 확인할 수 있다. 전광판은 개인의 선택을 보여주고 이를 시대의 문제의식과 연결하는 장치이다. 전광판의 조명이 게임 참여자들의 매 선택에 반응하여 켜지면서 참여자들이 실시간으로 게임 결과를 확인하도록 한다. 동시에 전광판에 적힌 문구들, 즉《2086: 우리는 어떻게?》가 던지는 생각과 의심의 지점들을 순차적으로 강조하여 드러낸다. 전광판이 개인의 선택을 실시간으로 보여준다면 에코그램 칠판 위에 적히는 지표들은 개인의 선택이 모인 공동 선택의 결과를 보여준다. 이를 위해 하루 동안 누적된 게임 결과를 여러 가지 사회생태적 수치들, 가령 기온, 해수면 높이, 지니계수, 난민 수, 멸종생물 수, 탄소 배출량 등으로 변환하는 과정을 거친다. 각종 연구 보고서와 시뮬레이션 자료를 토대로 도시화 비율이 초래하는 탄소 배출량, 세계화 정도에 따라 달라지는 지니계수, 시장경제 또는 사회적경제 확산에 따른 난민 수 등을 산출하며, 전시 기간 중 매일 누적 수치를 게시한다.

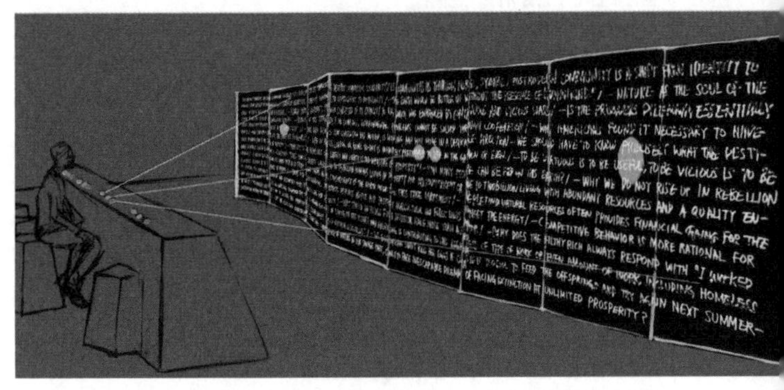

전시 방문자는 게임에 참여하고 결과를 관찰하면서 개인의 선택, 공동의 선택, 그리고 사회생태적 문제가 상호 연결된 구조를 확인할 수 있을 것이다. 그리고 모두가 직면하고 있는 환경 위기와 인류 멸종 시나리오의 근원이 사실 우리의 몸과 정신 안에 있음을 인지할 수 있을 것이다. 우리가 산업화, 도시화, 현대화, 식민지화, 세계화를 통해서 무한한 물질적 쾌락을 좇는 파우스트적 이데올로기에 편승해왔음이 문제의 핵심임을 이해하게 될 것이다.

성장에 대안은 없는가?
사회는 **시장**에 딸린 부속에 불과한가?
공동체는 **유목적**이며 가상적인가?
불평등이 커지면 공동체가 약화될까?
과거는 장애물에 불과한가?
문화가 **자연**의 위에 있나?
우리의 역사는 미래로 되풀이될까?
개인의 **자유**가 커지면 공동체가 약화될까?
자연은 비생명이며 **물질**은 수동적인가?
공동재만이 환경 위기의 유일한 해법일까?
지구는 얼마나 많은 사람을 먹여 살릴 수 있나?
우리는 미래에 대한 통제력을 상실할 **운명**인가?
자연은 우리에게 **집합체계**를 가르치는가?
우리는 지구상 가장 위험한 **포식자**인가?
타인을 사랑하는 것은 **미덕**이고, 자신을 사랑하는 것은 **죄악**인가?
이제 자본은 더 이상 **하인**이 아니라 **주인**인가?
진보가 **빈곤**을 증가시킬까?
인간은 결코 **퇴보** 없이 오로지 **전진**할까?
사유 **재산**이 불평등을 낳는가?
문명에 **한계**가 있을까?
서구 문명이 인류에 잔악성과 야만성을 퍼뜨렸나?
다윈주의가 경제적 불평등과 가혹한 **제국주의**를 조장했나?
환경 위기는 **경제적** 불평등을 의미할까?
세계는 포화 상태인가?
GDP는 우리가 자원으로 쓰레기를 만드는 정도를 나타내는가?
우리는 저하하는 **삶**의 질을 그저 유지하기 위해 일하고 있나?
정부는 여전히 국민에 의한 국민을 위한 것인가?
진정 경쟁이 협동보다 인류에 더 유익한가?
재산이 없으면 **권리**도 없나?
근대성은 병적인 성향을 보이는 기능 부전의 사회를 낳았나?
돈과 소비가 사랑 없고 공허한 문명을 채워줄까?
세계화가 중앙화, 동질화, 신식민주의를 불러오는가?
불평등 **증대**는 문명의 **쇠락**을 알리는 신호인가?
거지와 감옥이 **진보**의 표지일까?
'**생존** 투쟁'은 빈자들만의 것일까?
왜 헤지펀드 투자자가 **청소부**보다 더 많이 벌어야 하나?
우리는 소비자의 **천국**에서 **멸종**을 맞이하게 될까?
기술이 진정 환경 위기를 전부 해결할 수 있을까?
우리는 더 이상 **시민**이 아니라 **소비자**인가?
자연이 인간의 **요구**를 전부 충족할 수 있나?
물질, **정신**, **영혼**은 정말로 서로 구별되는 별개의 것일까?
유럽인이 **인류세**를 만든 장본인인가?

자아는 진정 침투불가능하고 자유로운가?
지도가 자연을 **상품**으로 탈바꿈시키나?
자연은 다 인간의 소유인가?
농경이 최초의 **생태계 파괴자**인가?
다양성은 자연의 강점인가?
도시가 **시골**을 노예화하나?

Ruin as Future, Future as Ruin

Yehre Suh

서예레

미래로서의 폐허, 폐허로서의 미래

Ruin as Future, Future as Ruin

Yehre Suh

"In the epoch of the Anthropocene the Humans and the Earthbound would have to agree to go to war."[1]

We define Baedari, in East Incheon of the Republic of Korea (ROK), as a site of apocalyptic war. It is a site torn between the Human desires for political and economic power and the raw, primal desire to remain Earthbound.

Incheon is a city inundated with the desire for growth. As a coastline city with 13.5% of its land "created" from the marshlands through landfill reclamation, it has become a site for megadevelopment projects such as the Incheon Free Economic Zone, Songdo International Business District, Cheongna International City, and Yeongjong International City, easy vehi-

미래로서의 폐허, 폐허로서의 미래

서예례

"인류세에는 지구와 결속한 존재들(Earthbound)과 인간이 서로 전쟁에 동의할 수밖에 없을 것이다."[1]

우리는 대한민국 동인천에 자리한 배다리를 종말론적 전쟁의 장으로 정의한다. 그곳은 정치와 경제 권력을 향한 인간의 욕망과 지구와 결속한 존재로 남고 싶다는 원초적인 욕망이 갈등하는 현장이다.

인천은 성장 욕망이 넘쳐나는 도시이다. 인천은 토지의 13.5%가 매립지 간척을 통해 습지에서 '창출'된 해안도시로서, 인천 경제자유구역, 송도 국제업무단지, 청라 국제도시, 영종도 국제도시 등 손쉽게 정치·경제 권력을 획득하는 수단인 초대형 개발 사업의 현장이 되었다. 피할 수 없는 철거와 개발이 경제 성장과 도시 재개발이라는 이름 아래 정당화된다. 건설과 파괴의 끝없는 순환을 약속하는 계획된 노후화야말로 성장 기계의 목적이다. 겨우 20~30년 된 건물이 '낡고 허름하다'고 판정되어 재개발 자격을 얻는다.[2] 동인천 구도

Urban Terrains Lab, *Earth-bound. Incheon aerial map* Urban Terrains Lab, *Human-bound. Incheon aerial map*
2023. Digital collage. Maps data from Google.

cles for gaining political and financial power. The necessary clearance and development are justified under the rubrics of economic growth and urban renewal. Planned obsolescence, which promises endless cycles of construction and destruction, is the growth machine's objective. Buildings only 20–30 years old are defined as "old and dilapidated" and qualify for redevelopment.[2] In the old urban center of the East Incheon area, 80–85% of building stocks are already "obsolete."

But under the blind wheel of growth, which is fueled by an insatiable hunger for power and wealth, lies the ongoing battleground of the urban underclass and the marginalized. They are continuously squeezed, dispossessed, and spit out by the unrelenting powers of development. Cho Se-hui's 1978 depiction of the ravaged city still holds true today: "Those who dwell in heaven have no occasion to concern themselves with hell.

심 지역의 경우, 건물군의 80~85%가 이미 '노후' 상태이다.

그러나 권력과 부를 향한 만족을 모르는 갈망이 불을 지핀 맹목적인 성장의 지배 아래, 도시의 하층계급과 소외된 사람들이 지금도 싸움을 치르는 전쟁터가 있다. 가차 없는 개발의 힘이 그들을 쥐어짜고 앗아가고 쫓아내고 뱉어낸다. 1978년에 작가 조세희가 황폐한 도시를 묘사한 대목은 오늘날에도 여전히 유효하다. "천국에 사는 사람들은 지옥을 생각할 필요가 없다. 그러나 우리 다섯 식구는 지옥에 살면서 천국을 생각했다. 단 하루라도 천국을 생각해보지 않은 날이 없다. 하루하루의 생활이 지겨웠기 때문이다. 우리의 생활은 전쟁과 같았다. 우리는 그 전쟁에서 날마다 지기만 했다."[3]

성장과 번영의 약속은 인천에서 허상에 불과했다. 경제 성장률로 보면 인천은 2020년 대한민국 17개 도시 중 겨우 14위였고,[4] 2021년 연평균 소득은 최하위권에 머물렀다.[5] 스트레스 지수는 최상위였고, 환경 부문 삶의 질 만족도는 최하위를 기록했다.[6] 한국은행은 인천의 경제 불균형 문제와 신성장 지역과 기타 지역 간의 격차를 핵심 문제로 지적하며, 인천의 성장이 지속불가능하다고 판단했으며,[7] 인천의 공직자 신뢰도는 한국에서 최하

UTL, 〈인간-결속, 인천 항공 지도〉

UTL, 〈지구-결속, 인천 항공 지도〉
2023. 디지털 콜라주, 구글 지도 정보.

Urban Terrains Lab, *Human-bound. The shore*

Urban Terrains Lab, *Earth-bound. The shore*

2023. Digital collage.

But since the five of us lived in hell, we dreamed of heaven: not a day passed without thoughts of heaven. Each and every day was an ordeal. Our life was like a war. [Every day] we lost a battle."[3]

Promises of growth and prosperity in Incheon are mere simulacra. In terms of economic growth rate, Incheon in 2020 was ranked only 14th out of 17 cities in the ROK,[4] and in 2021, the average yearly salary level was ranked as one of the lowest.[5] The national stress level index was the highest, and satisfaction with quality of life in the environmental category ranked the lowest.[6] The Bank of Korea deemed Incheon unsustainable, pointing out economic imbalance and the disparity between new and old development as critical problems,[7] and trust in public officials in Incheon is rated the lowest in the country.[8] As per Cho Se-hui, "People are possessed only by loveless desires. Therefore no one [knows how to shed] a tear for another. Land

UTL, 〈지구-결속, 해안〉 UTL, 〈인간-결속, 해안〉 2023. 디지털 콜라주.

위를 차지했다.[8] 조세희의 표현대로, "사람들은 사랑 없는 욕망만 갖고 있다. 그래서 단 한 사람도 남을 위해 눈물 흘릴 줄 모른다. 이런 사람들만 사는 땅은 죽은 땅이다."[9]

배다리에서 벌어진 일도 여느 경우와 다르지 않았다. 정부는 송도 신도시와 청라 신도시를 연결할 고속도로의 건설 계획을 발표하였고, 뒤이어 오래된 저소득층 동네의 토지 강제수용과 은밀한 보상 작업이 이어지며 동네를 소멸시킬 길을 열었다. 하지만 배다리의 공동체는 전쟁을 선언했다는 점에서 여느 경우와 달랐다. 그대로 남아 땅과 집에 결속하여 살고 싶었던 사람들이 함께 뭉쳐 정부를 적으로 선포하기로 했다. 그들은 땅과 삶과 집을 일구었고, '공면역주의'[10]와 '함께 만들기',[11] 그리고 '사랑'[12]을 수단 삼아 다른 이들에게도 그렇게 해보자고 격려했다. 그들의 눈에 성장은 환상임이 분명했다. 그리하여 그들은 그 대신에 쇠락을 잘 다루어보기로 결심했다.[13] 그들은 서로를 도덕-정치적 의미에서 감염시킴으로써 연대를 이루고 이를 다른 사람들에게 전파하려 했다. 인간과 비인간이 유기적인 공동체를 형성하였기에, 서로 이상한 친족 관계로서 함께 만들기를 해나갈 수 있었다. 그리고 그것이 생물이든

where only such people live is dead land."[9]

What happened in Baedari was nothing out of the ordinary. The government announced plans for a major highway connection between the new Songdo and Cheongna cities, and the subsequent land grabs in the old low-income neighborhood, followed by hushed compensation, made way for the erasure of a neighborhood. But what is extraordinary is that the community declared war. Those who desired to remain and bind themselves to the land and their homes decided to stand together and declare the government as their enemy. They cultivated the land, their lives, and their homes and encouraged others to do so through "co-immunism"[10] and "making-with"[11] and "love."[12] The illusion of growth was clear to them. So instead, they decided to manage decay.[13] They contaminated each other, in a moral-political sense, to establish a togetherness and

---

무생물이든 간에 오래된 것과 낡은 것을 사랑으로 돌보았다.

배다리라는 장소와 그곳의 사람들은 지구와 결속한 생활 방식의 가능성을 구현한다. 라투르가 간절히 말하였듯, 전쟁은 이미 당도하였으며 선택을 해야 한다. 홀로세(Holocene)의 인간으로 남을지 '평화의 장인'[14]으로서 인류세 속에서 지구와 결속한 존재로 살아갈지를 말이다. 건축도 마찬가지로 선택을 해야만 한다.

1968년 열린 이소자키 아라타의 전시 《전자 미로》는 전쟁의 공포와 참해와 관련해 건축의 역할이 무엇인지를 질문했다. "커다란 패널 위, 불타버린 히로시마의 대지에 폐허가 된 미래 도시의 구조물이 몽타주된다……실현계획이란 히로시마와 무척 비슷하게 언제나 절멸의 위협 아래 있다. 건설과 파괴, 계획과 절멸이 동의어임을 깨달을 때만이, 현실과 접하는 의미 있는 공간을 탄생시킬 수 있다."[15]

〈미래로서의 폐허, 폐허로서의 미래〉는 이소자키가 그린 불안을 동인천의 전쟁 지역에 겹쳐 놓으려는 시도이다. 히로시마의 폐허와 참해가 메타볼리즘의 미래주의적 제안을 우습게 만들어 버리듯,[16] 인천의 초대형개발 계

tried to propagate it to others. Humans and nonhumans formed an organic community so they could make-with as odd kin. And the old and the dilapidated, whether organic or inorganic, were cared for with love.

The people and place of Baedari embody the possibilities of an Earthbound way of life. As Latour implores, the war is here already, and the choice must be made: remain as Humans in the Holocene or become Earthbound "as artisans of peace"[14] in the Anthropocene. Architecture must also make a choice.

In 1968, Arata Isozaki's "Electric Labyrinth" exhibition questioned the role of architecture relative to the horrors and devastations of war: "On the large panel ruined structures of a future city were montaged on the scorched earth of Hiroshima... A proposal advanced in order to be realized is always under the threat of an extinction much like Hiroshima's. Only

---

획 역시 뻔뻔하고 헛되다. 이소자키가 말하듯, "폐허는 우리 도시의 미래이며, 미래 도시는 폐허 그 자체이다."[17]

본 프로젝트가 제안하는 폐허는 생 것, 썩은 것, 그리고 보존되는 것이 가능성과 뒤섞여 있는 장소이다. 그곳은 인간과 비인간, 생물과 무생물, 물질과 비물질이 발효하여 퇴비 더미가 되는 세계이다. 건축이 아무리 허무주의적일지라도, 삶과 죽음의 순환을 끌어안는 일은 본질적으로 희망적이고 긍정적이다. 우리가 '역사의 천사'로서 신중할 수만 있다면, 배다리에 사는 지구와 결속한 존재들은 건축에 한 가지 행동의 양식을 제시한다.

"그의 얼굴은 과거를 향하고 있다. 우리가 일련의 사건을 지각하는 그곳에서 천사는 단 하나의 파국을, 잔해 위에 잔해를 거듭 쌓으며 그의 발 앞에 잔해를 내던지는 파국을 본다. 천사는 그 자리에 머물러 죽은 자를 깨우고 부서진 것들을 온전하게 만들고 싶었다. 하지만 천국에서 폭풍이 불어오고, 바람이 너무도 거세게 날개에 꽂혀 천사는 더 이상 날개를 접을 수가 없다. 폭풍은 천사를 등 돌리고 있던 미래로 도리 없이 날려 보내고, 잔해 더미가 그의 눈앞에서 하늘을 향해 치솟는다. 이 폭풍이 바로 우리가 진보라 부르는 것이다."[18]

when we realize that construction and destruction, planning and extinction are synonymous can meaningful spaces that are in touch with reality come into being."[15]

Ruin as Future, Future as Ruin is an attempt to overlay the troubled anxiety portrayed by Isozaki onto the warzone that is East Incheon. As the ruins and devastation of Hiroshima render the futuristic proposals of the Metabolists a travesty,[16] the megadevelopment proposals of Incheon also lie brazen and futile. As Isozaki states, "(a) ruin is the future of our city, and the future city is ruin itself."[17]

Ruin as Future, Future as Ruin proposes the ruin as a site of fresh things, rotting things, and preserved things commingling with possibilities. It is a world of humans and nonhumans, organic and inorganic, matter and nonmatter fermenting into a pile of compost. No matter how nihilistic architecture can be, embracing the cycle of life and death is inherently hopeful and positive. And the Earthbound of Baedari offer architecture a mode of action, as long as we can be cautious as the "angel of history."

"His face is turned toward the past. Where we perceive a chain of events, he sees one single catastrophe which keeps piling wreckage upon wreckage and hurls it in front of his feet. The angel would like to stay, awaken the dead, and make whole what has been smashed. But a storm is blowing from Paradise; it has got caught in his wings with such violence that the angel can no longer close them. This storm irresistibly propels him into the future to which his back is turned, while the pile of debris before him grows skyward. This storm is what we call progress."[18]

WoonGi Min, *Baedari Ecology Play Forest*, 2016. Pen on paper.
민운기, 〈배다리 생태놀이 숲〉, 2016. 종이에 펜.

Naomi, *Lost Village on the Sea 2086*, 2023.
Digital print on the aluminum composite sheet.

Kim Soo Hwan, Beck In Tae, Oh Suk Kuhn, *The Land of Perfect Bliss*, 2023.
Digital print on the aluminum composite sheet.

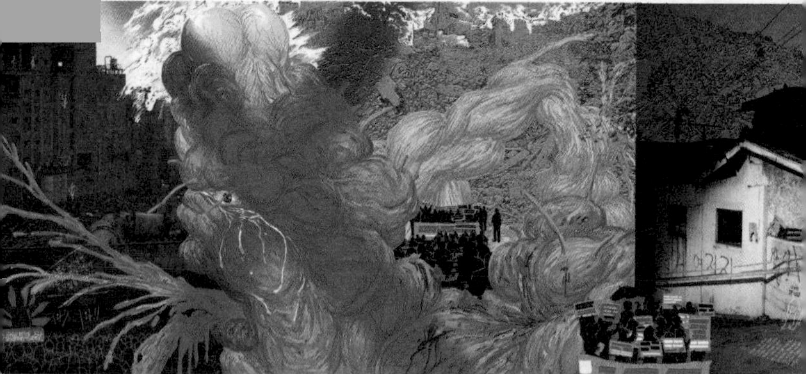

나오미, 〈시간을 잃어버린 마을〉, 2023. 알루미늄 복합 시트에 디지털 프린트.

김수환, 백인태, 오석근, 〈극락정토(極樂淨土)〉, 2023. 알루미늄 복합 시트에 디지털 프린트.

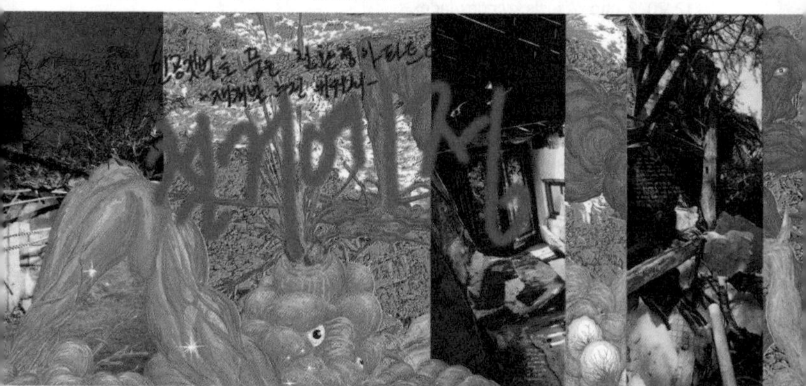

1. Bruno Latour, "Seventh Lecture: The States (of Nature) between War and Peace," *in Facing Gaia*: *Eight Lectures on the New Climate Regime*, trans. Catherine Porter (Cambridge, UK: Polity, 2017). Kindle edition.

2. 법제처, "도시 및 주거환경정비법 제2조," 국가법령정보센터, 2023년 2월 15일 접속, [Urban and Housing Environment Renewal Development Act, Article 2], accessed February 15, 2023, https://www.law.go.kr/lsSc.do?section=&menuId=1&subMenuId=15&tabMenuId=81&eventGubun=060101&query=%EB%8F%84%EC%8B%9C%EC%A0%95%EB%B9%84%EB%B2%95#undefined.

3. Cho Se-hui [조세희], "A Dwarf Launches a Little Ball," [난장이가 쏘아올린 작은 공] in *Modern Korean Literature: An Anthology*, ed. Peter H. Lee, trans. Chun Kyungja (Honolulu: University of Hawaii Press, 1990), 328.

4. 통계청, 국가통계포털 [Korean Statistical Information Service], 2022년 10월 12일 접속, accessed October 12, 2022, https://kosis.kr/index/index.do.

5. 국세청, "2021 국세통계연보" 2022년 10월 12일 접속, [2021 National Tax Statistical Yearbook], National Tax Service, accessed October 12, 2022, https://nts.go.kr/nts/na/ntt/selectNttInfo.do?nttSn=1301095&mi=2201.

6. 국가통계포털 [Korean Statistical Information Service].

7. 한국은행 인천본부, "인천지역 내 군·구별 성장불균형 현황 및 시사점(요약)," 부록, 한국은행, 2022년 6월 22일, 2022년 10월 12일 접속, [Notes on the Developmental Imbalance of Incheon Region Gu, Gun Districts (Brief)], Addendum, June 22, 2022, 한국은행 인천본부 [Bank of Korea Incheon Station], accessed October 12, 2022, http://www.bok.or.kr.

8. 국민권익위원회 "2022년도 공공기관 종합청렴도 평가 결과," 국민권익위원회, 2023년 1월 15일 접속, [Anti-Corruption & Civil Rights Commission], accessed February 15, 2023, https://www.acrc.go.kr/board.es?mid=a10106000000&bid=36&&act=view&list_no=43816.

9. Cho Se-hui [조세희], "A Dwarf Launches a Little Ball," [난장이가 쏘아올린 작은 공], 341.

10. Peter Sloterdijk, *Foams: Spheres Volume III: Plural Spherology*, trans. Weiland Hoban (Cambridge, MA: MIT Press, 2016).

11. Donna Haraway, *Staying with the Trouble: Making Kin with the Chthulucene* (Durham: Duke University Press, 2016), Kindle edition.

12. Michael Hardt and Antonio Negri, *Multitude: War and Democracy in the Age of Empire* (New York: Penguin Books, 2004), 351–357.

13. Kevin Lynch, introduction to Wasting *Away, An Exploration of Waste: What It Is, How It Happens, Why We Fear It, How to Do It Well* (San Francisco: Sierra Club, 1990).

14. Carl Schmitt, *The Nomos of the Earth in the International Law of the Jus Publicum Europaeum*, trans. G. L. Ulmen (New York: Telos Press, 2003).

15. Arata Isozaki, "Electric Labyrinth '14th Triennale di Milano,'" in *Unbuilt* (Tokyo: Gallery-MA, 2001), 110–111, exhibition catalog.

16. Jin Baek, "*MUJO*, OR EPHEMERALITY: the Discourse of the Ruins in Post-War Japanese Architecture," *Architectural Theory Review* 11, no. 2 (2009): 66–77.

17. Arata Isozaki, "Incubation Process," in *Unbuilt* (Tokyo: Gallery-MA, 2001), 47, exhibition catalog.

18. Walter Benjamin, "Theses on the Philosophy of History," in *Illuminations: Essays and Reflections* (1968), 257–258.

Making Nomad Communities

Yerin Kang + Lee Chi-hoon

강예린 + 이치훈

장소에서 분리된 인간은 어떻게 공동체를 만들 수 있는가?

Making Nomad Communities

Yerin Kang + Lee Chi-hoon

When the planet was secure, human beings drew lines in the earth and made territory, assembling groups to occupy it. States, nations, and governments were based in particular places. However, amid the ruins of modernism, as revealed by climate disasters and epidemics, the boundary between politics and administration is steadily blurring, and the planet and the ground itself are becoming more important. Furthermore, the number of climate nomads moving in search of places to live is increasing. A negligible Earth taken for the backdrop of the human community is disappearing. To paraphrase Bruno Latour, now that the climate crisis has led the ground and nature, rather than human beings, to grab hold of history and take it in a different direction, the Earth

---

장소에서 분리된 인간은 어떻게 공동체를 만들 수 있는가?

강예린 + 이치훈

지구가 안전하던 때, 인간은 저마다 대지에 금을 긋고 무리 지어 점유하여 영토로 삼았다. 국가, 민족, 정부는 특정 장소를 기반으로 한다. 그러나 기후재난과 역병으로 드러난 근대주의의 폐허 속에서 정치와 행정의 경계는 점차 흐려지고 지구와 땅 자체가 더 중요해지고 있다. 더 나아가 살 만한 곳을 찾아서 움직이는 기후 유목민이 증가하고 있다. 인류공동체의 배후지로 삼을 수 있는 만만한 대지는 사라져 간다. 브뤼노 라투르(Bruno Latour)의 말처럼 기후위기로 인류가 아닌 땅과 자연이 역사를 움켜쥐고 다른 방향으로 끌고 가기 시작한 이상 대지는 잠자코 서 있는 인간사회의 배경이 아니다. 대지는 더이상 대상이 아니라 주체다.

땅의 경계를 기준으로 주어졌던 소속감이 희미해진 가운데 공동체의 정체성은 어떻게 찾을 수 있는가? 장소와 분리된 인간은 어떻게 공동체를 만들 수 있을까? 우리는 이 질문을 시작점으로 삼았다. 영토의 경계가 지워진

is not a backdrop of human society that stands by silently. The Earth is the subject and no longer the object.[1]

Within the context of the dwindling of the sense of belonging once given by boundaries in the ground, how are we to find the identity of a community? How can humans, disconnected from places, create communities? We took this question as a starting point. How can we form groups and "land" on an Earth where territorial boundaries have been erased?

Gunsan: A Laboratory for Population "Landing"

In the small midwestern coastal city of Gunsan in South Korea, various methods of settling have been tried. As stated in the local magazine *Gunsan* (vol. 2), "coming and going is the way this place Gunsan has lived." Strangers have been constantly coming and establishing relationships with the region. People

---

지구라는 대지에 어떻게 무리를 지어서 '착륙'할 수 있을까?

인구 '착륙'의 실험장 군산

한국 중서부 해안가 소도시 군산에서는 지역에 정착하는 여러 방식이 시도되었다. "오고 가는 것은 이곳 군산이 살아온 방식이다"라는 지역 잡지 '군산(Vol. 2)'의 한 문구처럼 이방인들은 지속적으로 들어와 지역과 관계를 맺어왔다. 군산에서 나고 자란 사람들보다 이곳을 드나드는 사람들이 지역 문화의 유산을 일궈냈다. 군산은 '관계인구(moving population 또는 relational population)'의 도시다.

일제 강점기 한반도의 곡식을 수탈하기 위한 항구를 만들고 일본인들의 체류 공간 확보를 위해 땅을 간척한 것이 시작이다. 식민지 경제의 혜택을 누리고자 전국에서 사람들이 들어왔다. 해방 후에도 수탈을 위한 도시구조는 여전히 구시가지의 중심 역할을 해 왔다. 냉전 후 주한미군이 공군기지를 만들어 군산에 주둔했고, 위스키 등의 미군 문화가 군산에 전파되었다.

최근에는 젊은 이방인 그룹 '우당탕탕'이 'Do It Together(DIT)'를

who come and go have cultivated a legacy of local culture here rather than those who were born and raised in Gunsan. Gunsan is a city of a "moving population" or "relational population."

Its beginnings can be traced back to the Japanese occupation, when a port was built to exploit grain from the peninsula and secure land to settle Japanese people. People came from all over the country to enjoy the benefits of the colonial economy. Even after liberation, urban structure for exploitation continued to play a central role in the city's old town. After the Cold War, the USFK built an air base and was stationed there, and U.S. military culture, such as whiskey, spread to Gunsan.

Recently, Udangtangtang, a young group of newcomers, has been attempting to establish relationships with the region through "Do It Together" (DIT) workshops. By revitalizing the old market, hosting local culture-based guerrilla events in the

---

통해서 지역과 관계 맺는 다양한 시도를 하고 있다. 오래된 시장을 재활성화하고, 택티컬 어바니즘(tactical urbanism)의 맥락에서 지역문화기반의 게릴라 이벤트를 주최하며, 버려진 빈터를 도시 쉼터로 전환하는 등 우당탕탕은 만들기와 직접행동을 통해서 느슨한 공동체를 형성하고 있다. 이들은 장소를 점유하는 데 급급하기보다는 지역에 연결되는 '방식'을 고안하면서 신중하게 군산에 발을 딛는다. 뿌리 내리기가 궁극의 목표가 아니라는 점에서 우당탕탕의 움직임은 '착륙'에 가깝다. 지역에 착륙하기 위한 방법을 궁리하고 작당하는 노력은 '지역에 필요한 무엇을 만들면서 동시에 무리 짓는다'는 점에서 실존적이다. 공동체-되기의 디자인을 한다는 점에서 혁신적이다. 여기서 우리는 기후 유목의 시기(nomad century) 대안의 커뮤니티를 만들 수 있는 가능성을 본다.

직접행동으로 지역과 부딪히는 군산의 궁리 작당의 유산이 2086년까지 지속된다면 어떤 일이 벌어질 것인가? 비엔날레에서 우당탕탕과 새로운 방식의 DIT 워크숍을 실험했다.

context of tactical urbanism, and converting abandoned empty spaces into urban shelters, Udangtangtang has been forming a loosely knit community through making and direct action. Rather than busying itself with occupying places, it carefully set foot in Gunsan by devising a "method" for connecting to the region. Given that putting down roots is not its ultimate goal, the actions of Udangtangtang are closer to "landing." Efforts to scheme and plot a way to land in the region was essential to "assembling a group while making something that the region needs." Udangtangtang's methods are innovative in that they design communities-to-be. Here we see the possibility of creating a community for a climate nomad century.

What will happen if this legacy of Gunsan's scheming and plotting, which converged upon a region through direct action, continues into 2086? Working together with Udangtangtang, we

---

저밀도의 디자인

세계 인구는 2086년까지 증가할 것이라고 예상하지만, 2022년 한국의 인구는 이미 낭떠러지를 타고 급강하 중이다.

군산의 인구감소도 두드러진다. 군산은 2022년 한국에서 가장 빈집 비율이 높은 도시 중 하나로 꼽힌다. 인구는 빠져나가도 그 나간 자리는 도시경관에 고스란히 남아있다. 수많은 빈집은 빠져나간 인구를 쓸쓸하게 대변한다. 도시재생으로 이 간극을 메꾸려는 시도는 의자 뺏기 놀이와 똑같은 결과로 끝날 것이다. 지역마다 재생을 시도하지만 끌어들일 인구는 한정적이며, 그마저 줄고 있기 때문이다.

인구감소를 방어하기보다는 받아들여야 할 때다. 오히려 적극적인 태도로 '소멸'이 전개되는 방식을 고안해야 한다. 지역이 오래 유지되는 것(well-aging)을 넘어 건강하게 소멸(well dying)할 수 있도록 대책을 세워야 한다. 그러나 인구감소로 인해 지역의 경계와 행정은 점점 더 그 힘이 약해지고 있다. 적정 밀도 유지를 위해 일괄적으로 정비하는 것은 지방정부의 재정이 담당할 수 있는 수준이 아니다. 지방정부의 제도와 정책은 관

experimented with a new method of the DIT workshop for the Biennale.

Low-Density Design

The world population is expected to keep increasing until 2086, but South Korea's population is already plummeting as of 2022.

The population decline in Gunsan is also noticeable. In 2022, Gunsan was one of the cities with the highest percentages of empty houses in Korea. While some residents leave, the spaces they leave behind remain untouched in the urban landscape. Countless vacant houses respond to a population that has forlornly fled. Attempts to fill these gaps with urban regeneration will end up with the same result as a game of musical chairs. While each of region attempts to regenerate, the population that can be

---

할 지역의 축소를 수용하기 힘들다. 저밀도 인구와 고밀도 건조 환경(built environment)의 편차를 조율하는 것이 행정 경계의 빗장을 푸는 일이기도 하기 때문이다.

군산이 저밀도로 전환하는 방법을 궁리하는 DIT 워크숍을 진행했다. 기존 인공환경을 적절하게 분배하거나 소멸시켜 덜어낼 방법이 있을지 고민하고, 작은 직접행동을 시도했다. 남겨지고 비워져 채울 도리가 없는 수많은 공간환경(built environment)을 해체함으로써, 버려진 풍경을 생생한 경관으로 조정하려 했다.

조지프 슘페터(Joseph A. Schumpeter)는 자본주의의 혁신에 따른 성장을 예찬하면서 '창조적 파괴'라는 단어를 사용했다. 여기에 빗대자면 이런 작업은 '파괴적 창조(Destructive Creation)'다. 소멸을 디자인하는 것은 생산이 아닌 분배로 전환되는 디자인이라는 점에서 성장을 견인하는 자본주의적 혁신과 대비된다.

2086년 Future Community 군산의 DIT 워크숍에서 '함께(Together)' 어깨 거는 대상은 사람을 넘어서 자연에 이른다.

drawn from is limited, and even that limited group is decreasing.

It is time to accept population decline rather than finding ways to prevent it. Rather, it is necessary to devise a method in which "extinction" unfolds in a proactive manner. We need active measures that go beyond a region's ability to "age well" to ensure that the region "dies well." However, because of population decline, regional boundaries and administration are becoming weaker and less capable of carrying that out. Comprehensive maintenance to maintain appropriate density is beyond the capacity of local governments' finances. It is difficult for the structure and policies of local governments to handle the decline of the regions under their jurisdiction. This is because reconciling the difference between a low-density population and a high-density built environment is also an act of unbolting administrative boundaries.

잠시 군산의 빈집 사진을 들여다보자. 집 내부는 남루하고 퇴색하였으나, 창문 너머의 자연은 푸르고 생생하다. 창문을 열기만 해도 나무가 안으로 들어올 것만 같다. 작은 틈으로도 자연은 쉽게 인간의 자리에 스며든다. 외부 환경을 막아내는 지붕과 벽의 일부만이라도 헐어낸다면, 바로 비바람이 들이치면서 건물은 분해되기 시작할 것이다. 군산의 DIT 워크숍에서는 지붕을 덜어내는 행위를 통해 풍화의 힘을 들이는 길을 내었다. 자연의 분해 활동에 개입하는 작은 시도이다.

시간이 지나며 인공의 벽과 바닥은 풍화되고 동물과 식물이 이곳에 서식하기 시작할 것이다. 서서히 인간의 거주 공간이 자연의 서식 환경으로 치환된다.

이때 자연은 객체가 아닌 주체이다. 분해하고 대체하고 또 생성한다. 토지를 둘러싼 이전의 사회적 실천, 즉 소유, 상품화, 통제, 지배는 중단된다. 땅은 토지가 아니라, 생명과 대지의 내재적 역량을 키우는 주역이다.

A DIT workshop was held to figure out how to convert Gunsan into a low-density city. We considered whether there was a way to adequately dismantle the preexisting artificial environment and attempted small direct actions. By dismantling countless built environments that were left behind and emptied with no means of revival, we tried to modify the abandoned landscape into vivid scenery.

Joseph A. Schumpeter used the word "creative destruction" in praising the growth of capitalist innovation. In comparison, the work of this DIT workshop was "destructive creation." Designing extinction contrasts with capitalist innovation, which drives growth in that its design shifts from production to distribution.

Those standing shoulder to shoulder at the 2086 Future Community DIT Workshop in Gunsan went beyond people to include nature.

Let's take a look at a photograph of an empty house in Gunsan for a moment. The inside of the house is shabby and

Possibility Beyond the Window, 2023
photograph, 17 x 24 cm, Photo courtesy of Hyoeun Kim.

〈만약 창문을 연다면〉,
2023. 사진 17x24cm, 김효은 제공.

faded, but the nature outside the window is green and vivid. Even if you just open the window, it appears as if the tree will come inside. Nature easily permeates the places of human beings, even through small gaps. If only the roof or part of the walls that block the external environment were torn down, the building would begin to break down as soon as it was hit with gusts of rain. At the DIT workshop in Gunsan, the activity of removing the roof made a path for the force of weathering to enter. It was a small attempt to intervene in the activity of nature's dismantling.

Over time, the artificial walls and floors will weather away, and plants and animals will begin to live in the former space of the house. Gradually, the human residence will be replaced by a natural habitat.

When this occurs, nature is the subject, not the object. It disintegrates, replaces, and generates. Past social practices

---

궁리 작당과 직접행동

여기 사람, 자연 이외에 주체가 하나 더 있다. '도구'다.

DIT 워크숍에서는 지붕을 부수는 도구를 고안했다. 버려진 건조 환경에 틈을 내고 자연을 들이는 데 적합한 도구를 고민함으로써, 이 도구를 사용하는 직접행동이 앞으로 대지에 대한 어떤 개입으로 이어질지 질문해보려 했다.

기후재난이 가속화되어 전기를 상용하기 힘든 상황을 전제로, 동력을 사용하는 기계가 아닌 도구를 설계했다. 그러나 지붕, 벽, 바닥과 같은 인공의 구조물에 균열을 내는 데는 한 사람의 힘으로는 부족하다. 두 사람 이상이 힘을 더해야 제대로 작동하는 도구를 고안했다. '손을 빌린다'는 영어 표현은 막연하게 돕는 행위가 아니라 직접적이고 물리적인 의미로 바뀐다.

함께 사용하는 도구 만들기와 이 도구를 같이 사용하는 작업은 자연스럽게 협업을 체화하는 과정이 되었다. 도구의 디자인과 사용을 통해 우리는 공동체의 손과 발로 신체가 확장되는 일종의 경험을 할 수 있었다.

도구를 만드는 워크숍은 곧 생각하는 과정이었다. 군산 어디를 비워내야 적절한 밀도의 풍경으로 재편할 수 있을지 논의하고, 부수는 구조물의

surrounding the land, namely ownership, commodification, control, and domination, are interrupted. The ground is not just land, but a driving force in developing life and the intrinsic capacity of the Earth.

Scheming and Plotting and Direct Action

There is another subject here besides people and nature: the "tool." The DIT Workshop devised a tool to tear down roofs. To find a suitable tool for making cracks in the abandoned structure and letting nature in, we inquired about what kind of intervention to the Earth the direct action of using this tool would lead to in the future.

Working with the premise that accelerating climate disasters will make it difficult to use electricity, we designed a tool rather than a machine that uses electric power. However, the strength

---

물성에 따라서 필요한 도구의 쓰임을 상상하고, 여러 사람의 힘을 축으로 작동하게 될 도구의 원리를 더듬더듬 그려보았다.

무엇보다도 기후재난의 미래에서 우리에게는 어떤 필요가 생겨날 것인가 이야기해보는 과정을 통해 공동체 구축의 방향을 상정할 수 있었다. 도구를 고안하면서 자연스럽게 우리가 처한 상황을 살피게 되었으며, 스스로에 대해서 배우게 되었다. 여러 사람의 손과 머리가 하나로 행동한, 이 궁리 작당의 활동을 통해서 공동체의 조건도 만들어진 셈이다.

산업사회의 기계가 등장하기 전, 인류 역사의 시기는 도구를 만드는 방식으로 구분될 만큼 도구는 사람과 자연이 매개되는 방식을 정의하는 물건이었다. 산업사회가 들어서면서 인간은 작동의 원리를 알지 못한 채 기계를 사용하고 생산했다. 대상과 연결되는 원리를 다시 깨친다는 점에서, 도구를 디자인하는 것은 실용의 차원을 넘어서 존재론적이다. 도구는 일종의 비인간행위자인 것이다.

인류학자인 아르투로 에스코바르(Arturo Escobar)의 말에 주목할 필요가 있다. "생태 붕괴 혹은 재해에 관한 공통의 경험이 기폭제가 되어,

of a single person is not enough to make cracks in artificial structures such as roofs, walls, and floors. A tool that requires the strength of more than two people to work properly was devised. This changed the meaning of the English expression of "lending a hand" from a vague act of helping to a direct and physical act.

Making and then using tools together naturally became a process of embodying cooperative work. Through the design and use of tools, our bodies were enlarged through the hands and feet of the community.

The tool-making workshop was a process of thinking. We discussed which parts of Gunsan needed to be emptied out in order to reorganize it into a landscape of adequate density, imagined the use of necessary tools according to the physical properties of the structure to be destroyed, and fumbled about as we came up with the principles behind a tool that would operate on

---

인간/비인간 집단을 포함하여 공생적 그리고 공동적인 도구화를 장려한다."[1] 만드는 작업은 동시에 만드는 사람들과 환경에 영향을 미친다. 그에 따르면 디자인은 공동체가 자치와 전환으로 나아가는 방법이 될 수 있다.

세계 속으로 들어가는 과정으로서의 공동체

군산의 DIT 워크숍은 협업을 통해서 공동체를 만들어가는 과정이었다. 공동체로 한 발 나아가기 위한 협력은 하나의 실기(practice)를 통해 배워가는 것이지, 윤리적인 차원의 다짐으로 이뤄지는 것은 아니다. 사회성은 행위나 노동이 아니라 작업의 힘에 뿌리내린다. 원하는 자연물을 취득하기 위해 혹은 대상의 상태를 고치고 변형하기 위해 필요한 도구를 궁리하며 만들었던 여느 부족들처럼, 소멸 디자인 DIT 워크숍을 통해서 '함께하기'의 다른 방식을 배우게 되었다.

이제 "장소와 분리된 인간은 어떻게 공동체를 만들 수 있을까?"라는 글 서두의 질문은 수정되어야 할 것 같다. "세계 속으로 들어가는 과정으로서 공동체는 어떻게 형성되는가?"로 말이다. 대지와 생명의 역량을 기르는 방식

the basis of the strength of several people.

Above all, through the process of talking about what needs will arise for us in the future of climate disasters, we posited the direction of community building. As we devised the tool, we looked in a matter-of-fact way at the situation we were in and learned about ourselves. In other words, through the activities of this scheming and plotting, in which several people's hands and heads acted as one, the terms of the community were also created.

Before the appearance of machines in industrial society, tools were objects that defined the way people and nature were mediated, so much so that periods in human history were divided by the way tools were made. With the advent of industrial society, humans used and produced machines without knowing the principles of their functioning. In terms of awakening to principles connected to an object, designing a tool goes beyond the realm of

이 곧 인간이 무리 짓는 방법이 되어야 한다. '근대의 비지속성과 탈미래적인 관행과는 다른 존재론적 약속, 관행, 서사, 행동을 향한' 공동체의 디자인이 필요할 때다.

1. Bruno Latour, Down to *Earth: Politics in the New Climactic Regime* (Cambridge: Polity Press, 2018).

2. Arturo Escobar, *Designs for the Pluriverse: Radical Interdependence, Autonomy, and the Making of Worlds* (Durham, NC: Duke University Press, 2018), 133.

1. 아르투로 에스코바르, *플루리버스-자치와 공동성의 세계 디자인하기*, 박정원, 엄경용 역, (고양: 알렙, 2022), 238.

practicality to that of the ontological. A tool is a type of nonhuman actor.

It is worth noting the words of anthropologist Arturo Escobar: "Ontologically oriented design... promotes convivial and communal instrumentations involving human/nonhuman collectives provoked into existence by ecological breakdowns or shared experiences of harm."[2] The process of making/creating affects the people doing the making and the environment at the same time. According to Escobar, design can be a way for communities to move towards autonomy and transformation.

Community as a Process of Entering into the World

The DIT workshop in Gunsan was a process of making/creating a community through cooperative work. Cooperative work for the sake of taking a step forward as a community is learned

through practice, not an ethical resolution. Sociality is rooted not in actions or labor but the power of the work. Like any other tribe that thought about and made tools to acquire certain desired objects of nature or to modify and transform the condition of the object, we learned a different way of "doing together" through the extinction design DIT workshop.

Now, the question at the beginning of the text, "How can humans, disconnected from places, create communities?" appears to be in need of correction, that is, to "How is a community formed as a process of entering into the world?" The way to develop the capacity of life and the Earth needs to soon become the way for humans to assemble groups. It is time to design a community that moves toward an ontological promise, practice, narrative, and action that is different from the unsustainable and postfuturistic practices of modernity.

If we open the window, 2023. Digital print on paper. Courtesy of SoA
〈만약 창문을 연다면〉, 2023. 종이에 프린트. SoA 제공.

An empty house, 2023. Digital print on paper. Courtesy of texture on texture.
〈빈집〉, 2023. 종이에 프린트. 텍스처 온 텍스처 제공.

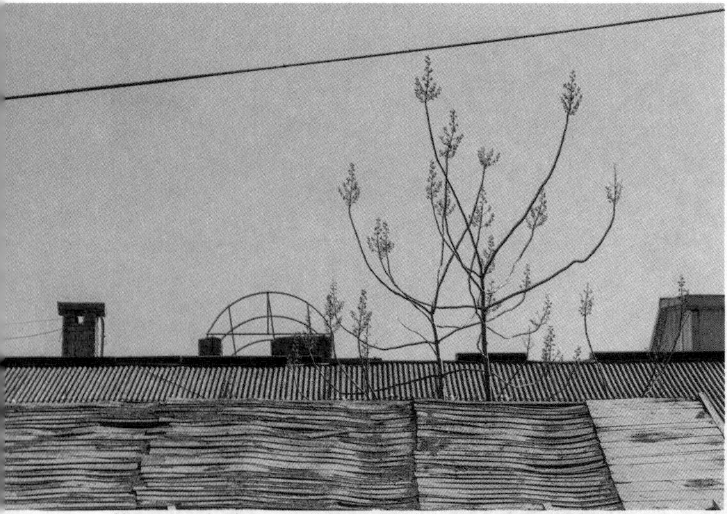

Nature growing in an empty house, 2023.
Digital print on paper. Courtesy of texture on texture.
〈사람이 떠나간 자리에 자연이 서식을 시작하고〉, 2023. 종이에 프린트. 텍스처 온 텍스처 제공.

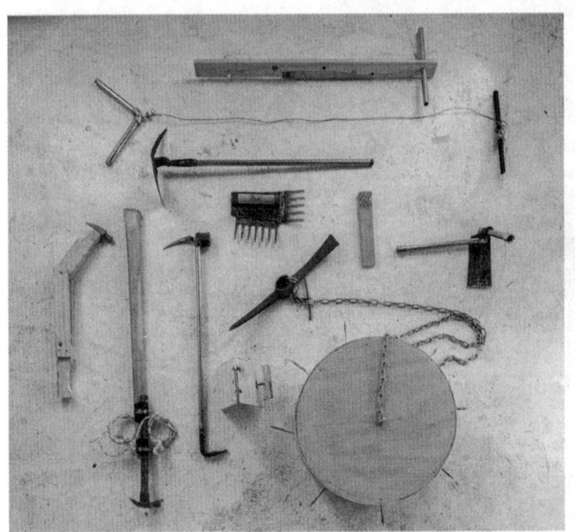

DIT workshop for making tools, 2023. Digital print on paper. Courtesy of texture on texture.
〈집을 분해하는 도구를 고안하기〉, 2023. 종이에 프린트. 텍스처 온 텍스처 제공.

DIT workshop for destruction, 2023. Digital print on paper. Courtesy of texture on texture.
〈소멸을 위한 DIT(Do It Together) 워크숍〉, 2023. 종이에 프린트. 텍스처 온 텍스처 제공.

An empty house after the DIT workshop, 2023.
Digital print on paper. Courtesy of texture on texture.
〈DIT 워크숍 이후의 빈집〉, 2023. 종이에 프린트. 텍스처 온 텍스처 제공.

Migrating Futures

Nahyun Hwang + David Eugin Moon

275

황나현 + 데이비드 유진 문

이주하는 미래

N H D M Architects, *Take the 4 Train*, 2023. Digital print on paper.
N H D M Architects, 〈4 호선〉, 2023. 종이에 프린트.

Migrating Futures

Nahyun Hwang + David Eugin Moon

Many argue that the most readily visible and visibilized histories of work and living are those of settlements. From the construction of the very first enclosure to sprawling suburban developments across the globe, production's need for stable bases that foster the continual reproduction of reliable labor forces has prescribed the patterns of many prevailing urbanisms and their collective protocols. However, the world is also shaped as much, if not more, by the less visible stories of unsettlement. Spaces of itinerancy, sometimes voluntary and other times forced, silently parallel the stable domains of the settled.

이주하는 미래

황나현 + 데이빋 유진 문

많은 사람들이 노동과 주거의 역사에서 가장 쉽게 드러나고 또 가시화되는 것은 정착의 역사라고 주장한다. 최초의 사유지로부터 세계 전역에서 뻗어나가는 교외 개발에 이르기까지, 안정적인 노동력의 지속적인 재생산을 위해 견실한 기반을 필요로 하는 생산의 구조는 오늘날 보편화된 도시 계획들과 그 집단적 규범의 패턴을 규정하였다. 하지만 보다 비가시적인 비정주 서사 또한 정주의 이야기만큼이나 세계를 이루고 있다. 때로는 자발적이고 때로는 강요된 떠돎의 공간이 정주자의 안정된 영역과 조용히 평행선을 이루며 나아간다.

〈이주하는 미래〉는 《2086: 우리는 어떻게?》의 주제와 안산을 출발점으로 삼아보자는 제안에 부응하여, 안산을 중심으로 디아스포라성과 이주성이 보여주는 과거, 현재, 미래의 지리학을 탐구한다. 근현대사 속에서 안산은 늘 전형적인 '이주도시'였으니, 비정주의 현실과 정주의 패러다임이 결

Responding to the Korean Pavilion's prompt "2086: Together, How?" and the invitation to engage Ansan, Korea as a starting point, the project *Migrating Futures* explores the past, present, and future geographies of diasporicity and migrancy in Ansan and beyond. Throughout its modern history, Ansan has been the quintessential "Migrating City," a quietly contested territory where the realities of unsettlement and paradigms of settlement conflate. The ambitious site of terraforming for the Banwol National Industrial Complex (1977), conducted by the famously developmental government to relocate heavy industries and their labor forces out of Korea's capital, was also the location of the very first "New Town" in Korea, erected in the familiar blueprints of Howard's Garden City and Wright's prairie homes to welcome newcomers while displacing the existing population. Contemporary Ansan continues to be a space of coexisting yet

---

합되어 조용하게 치열한 땅이었다. 개발지향적인 것으로 유명했던 정부가 중공업 산업체와 노동력을 수도 밖으로 이전하고자 반월국가산업단지(1977)를 조성하며 개발한 이 대규모 부지는 한국 최초의 '뉴타운'이 되기도 했다. 하워드의 전원 도시와 라이트의 초원 주택을 닮은 청사진에 따라 세워진 이곳은 원주민을 내쫓고 새로운 주민을 맞이하였다. 현재의 안산은 정주주의와 비정주주의라는 상이한 유토피아들이 공존하는 공간이다. 이 도시의 특징인 방사형 계획에 따라 빽빽하게 들어선 고층 아파트가 '재개발 지역'의 한국인에게 안전한 투자와 녹지로 둘러싸인 쾌적한 생활을 약속한다면, 한국인이 기피하는 공장 일자리와 밀집한 고시원 같은 값싼 숙박시설은 다른 아시아 국가에서 이곳으로 몰려온 수많은 이주 노동자에게 '코리안 드림'을 위한 임시적이지만 희망찬 기반이다. 누군가는 범죄율이 높다는 설을 들며 기피하지만 이주 노동자는 물론 전국의 디아스포라 공동체가 사랑하는 곳, 정부가 '원곡동 다문화 특구'라 명명한 안산 원곡동의 골목들은 정통 민족 음식점과 종교 시설을 비롯해 이용이 활발한 공공 공간으로 많은 '이방인'에게 제2의 고향과도 같은 곳이다.

divergent utopias, of the idealisms of settlement and unsettlement. The ever-growing apartment towers that tightly fill in the city's signature radial plan promise secure investments and pleasant living surrounded by thriving greenery for native Koreans in "redevelopment zones," while the factory jobs that Koreans avoid and cheap lodging in crowded goshiwons (study carrel rooms modified for living) are the tentative yet hopeful bases for the "Korean dreams" of many migrant workers who flock to the city from other Asian countries. Avoided by some for its allegedly high crime rates, and beloved by migrant workers as well as various diaspora communities across the country, the streets of Ansan's Wongokdong, or "Wongok Multicultural Special Zone" as the government puts it, are a home away from home for many "others," with their ethnic restaurants, places of worship, and actively utilized public spaces.

기후 변화라든가 환경 및 사회정치 규범의 해체로 가속화하고 심화할지 모를 미래의 이동하는 삶을 예견하고, 또 현존하는 국가·종교의 경계와 인종화된 북반구의 지정학적 헤게모니를 넘어선 초문화적이고 수평적인 공존의 가능성을 일깨움으로써, 한국 내 이주자들의 시공간 환경을 연구하는 작업은 이주성, 영토 이동성, 정체성의 미래를 탐색하는 시험대를 제공한다. 노동자들을 인종화하고 예속시키는 오랜 식민적 유산과 극도로 불안정한 노동 및 생활 조건에 종종 시달리면서도, 국가를 초월하는 이주 노동자와 디아스포라 공동체라는 표면상 일시적인 범세계적 주체들은 새로이 출현하는 지역밀착적 공간 유형학, 사회성, 그리고 강력하게 교차적인 (그렇기에 행위주체적인) 문화 환경을 형성하고 체화한다. 전지구적 이주 산업 복합체의 복잡한 그물망에 얽혀 있으면서도, 유랑하는 듯 보이는 이 주체들은 자주적 결정의 공간을 개척하고 지극한 특수성으로 소속의 여러 새로운 개념을 정의한다.

안산과 경기도—한국에서 가장 인구가 밀집한 지역으로 수도 서울을 둘러싸고 있다—를 대상으로 하는 이번 프로젝트는 생활과 소속의 새로운 틀로 형성되는 미래 공동체의 가능성을 탐색한다. 안산은 많은 현대 대도

Presaging the much more itinerant lives of the future that may be precipitated by climate change or other dissolution of environmental and sociopolitical norms, and provoking the possibilities of transcultural and lateral coexistence beyond the existing national and religious borders and racialized geopolitical hegemonies of the global north, investigations of the spatiotemporal landscapes of migrants in Korea provide an opportune testing ground to explore the futurity of migrancy, territorial mobility, and identity. While often subjected to the enduring colonial legacy of subjugated and racialized laboring bodies and extremely precarious work and living conditions, the ostensibly transient global subjects of transnational migrant workers and diasporic communities shape and embody emergent and hyperlocal spatial typologies, socialities, and potently intersectional—and thus agentive—cultural milieus. While entangled in a complex web of global migrant industrial complexes, seemingly peripatetic subjects carve out spaces of self-determination and define new notions of belonging with extreme specificity.

시의 주변부에 존재하지만 제대로 인정은 받지 못하는, 생산적으로 혼종된 시간성과 정체성의 영토를 잘 보여주는 사례로 이런 주변부에서는 취약하지만 회복력 있는 비시민 인구가 중심부와 국민국가의 지속적인 성장과 재생산을 뒷받침한다. 종종 '이방인의 도시', '이주민의 도시'라 불리는 안산은 중심, 주권, 정주를 완성하는 동시에 상쇄한다. 정주의 역사적 헤게모니와 진보에 대한 통념—진보란 오로지 쉬지 않고 축적하고 확장하며 인간은 물론 인간 이상의 것까지 정복하여 이뤄진다고 여겨진다—에 도전하며, 〈이주하는 미래〉는 다양한 이동성이 만들어내는 다원적인 대항적 미래를 그리려 한다.

Engaging Ansan and Gyeonggi province—the most populous region in South Korea, surrounding the country's capital, Seoul—this project explores the possibilities of future communities shaped by new frameworks of living and belonging. Ansan exemplifies the underrecognized territories of the productively promiscuous temporalities and identities that exist at the periphery of many contemporary metropolises, where the vulnerable but resilient extrastate populations at the hidden margins support the continual growth and reproduction of the center and the nation-state. Ansan, often called "foreigners' city" and "migrants' city," completes and countervails the center, the sovereign, and the sedentary. Challenging the historic hegemonies of settlement and accepted notions of progress, the latter of which is believed to be achieved only through incessant accumulation, expansion, and the subjection of humans—and more than humans, others—*Migrating Futures* seeks to envision plural counter futures shaped by different mobilities.

N H D M Architects, *Home is not a (Vinyl) House*, 2023. Digital print on paper.
N H D M Architects, , 〈집은 (비닐)하우스가 아니다〉, 2023. 종이에 프린트.

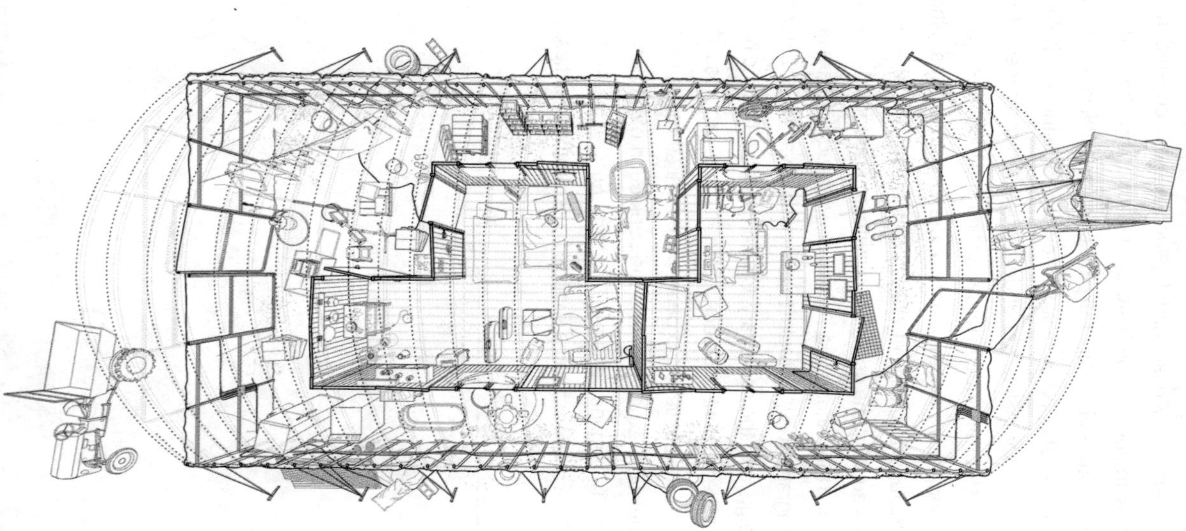

A Home is not a (Vinyl) House

A Community of Difference

Wolsik Kim

283

김월식

차이의 공동체

A Community of Difference

Wolsik Kim

Just Rumors

Migration remained frequent, and respect for working citizens greatly increased. The people began to move with the sun and the wind. People's greed for quality of life continued to generate greenhouse gases. As the earth grew hotter, various natural disasters and calamities occurred. With rising sea levels and changes in wildlife populations, human and natural habitats changed. People who crossed borders along with labor markets either changed their place of residence for quality of life, right to health, and survival or changed their concept of residence. Borders could no longer function as physical boundaries. The labor market was reorganized to produce renewable energy for

---

차이의 공동체

김월식

그냥 소문

여전히 사람들의 이동은 빈번하고, 노동 시민에 대한 존중은 더욱 높아졌다. 이들은 태양을 따라 이동하거나 바람을 따라 이동하기 시작했다. 삶의 질에 대한 사람들의 욕심은 온실가스를 계속 발생시켰다. 지구가 점점 더워지면서 각종 자연재해와 재난이 발생했다. 해수면이 상승하고 야생 동물의 개체수가 변하였으며 더불어 사람과 자연의 서식지가 변화되었다. 노동시장을 따라 국경을 넘나드는 사람들도 삶의 질과 건강권, 생존을 위해 거주지를 바꾸거나 거주의 개념을 바꾸었다. 더 이상 국경은 물리적 경계가 되지 못했다. 노동시장의 패러다임은 생존을 위한 신재생에너지를 만드는 산업으로 재편되었다. 기업과 개인은 저마다의 방식으로 에너지를 만들었다. 생존에 대한 사람들의 관심은 국가 간 법령보다 강력한 에너지 윤리를 요구했다. 이른바 생태에 대한 윤리관이 삶을 지속시키는 첨예한 정치가 되었다. 새로운 신념과

survival. Corporations and individuals produced energy in their own ways. People's interest in survival commanded a stronger ethics of energy than that of domestic state legislation. The so-called ethics of ecology became a form of radical politics for sustaining life. A new conviction, and the "something" that supported it, began to materialize. Some said it resembled a god, while others said it was a powerful shaman. Spreading the powerful message that the world to come should move away from fossil fuels and democratize a new form of energy that is ecological, ecofriendly, and nonexhaustive, this shaman became more and more mythical. Moreover, the democratization of energy was accompanied by the democratization of information, which created a powerful ethical belief that no one could monopolize energy or the technology to produce it as well as a reverence for information as a public good. It was a bit bizarre, but at a time

---

이를 뒷받침하는 썸씽(something)이 등장하는데 누구는 신을 닮았다 하고, 누구는 매우 강력하고 쿨한 샤먼이라고 이야기했다. 도래할 세상은 화석연료에서 벗어나 생태적이고 친환경적이며 비고갈성인 새로운 에너지의 민주화를 이루어야 한다는 강력한 메시지를 전파하며 이 샤먼은 점점 신화화된다. 또 에너지의 민주화와 더불어 정보의 민주화라는 이데올로기가 형성되는데, 이는 에너지와 에너지를 만드는 기술을 누구도 독점하지 못한다는 강력한 윤리관, 공공재로서의 정보에 대한 추앙을 만들어 내었다. 다소 황당하지만, 인구가 점점 소멸하여가고 살아갈 수 있는 지역도 점점 소멸해 가는 시절에 이런 샤먼에 대한 추앙은 일정 부분 신앙력과 같았고 사람들은 샤먼을 따랐다. 사람들은 이 샤먼의 정체에 대해 이러쿵저러쿵 이야기했지만 대부분 네트워크 샤먼이나 테크놀러지 샤먼이라고 불렀다.

소문이 소문을 만들다 - 새로운 소문

이 샤먼은 아시아 전체를 관통하는 썬디어(sundeer)의 DNA를 가졌다고 했다. 태양을 따라 움직이고 바람 속에 숨는다는 이야기가 들렸다. 그

when the population was going extinct and habitable areas were gradually disappearing, reverence for the shaman took on a kind of religious power for some, and people began to worship the shaman. People said this and that about its true identity, but most people called it the network shaman or the technology shaman.

Rumors on Top of Rumors

This shaman was said to have the DNA of a sundeer, which can be found throughout all of Asia. The shaman was said to move with the sun and hide in the wind; thus, it gave the illusion that it was eternal, like the sun and wind. Antlers served as the shaman's antennae for making contact with the sun, and people set up their own antennae to worship the shaman. Logging in to channel the shaman became commonplace. As

---

래서 태양과 바람처럼 영속한다는 환상을 갖게 하였다. 사슴뿔은 태양과 접선하는 샤먼의 안테나였고 사람들은 각자의 안테나를 세우고자 샤먼을 숭배했다. 접신하기 위해 로그인하는 것이 보편적인 세상이 되었다. 태양을 숭배하는 비슈누의 탈것, 가루다처럼 생각과 동시에 나타나는 속도로 에너지에 대한 정보가 유통되었다. 성당이나 교회, 절, 신전은 점차 사라지고 사람들은 자신의 자리에서 샤먼에 로그인하고 휴대폰이나 스마트워치 혹은 모니터에 절을 하고 기도했다. 신기하게도, 사람들이 직접 샤먼의 모습을 선택하고 조합할 수 있었다. 누군가는 전통적 신앙의 대상인 예수나 부처의 형상을, 누구는 대통령, 누구는 아이돌의 모습을, 그리고 또 어떤 이들은 곰, 호랑이, 사자 같은 동물이나 책상과 돌 같은 사물의 형상을 숭배했다. 겉모습은 다르지만, 이 샤먼은 에너지와 에너지를 만드는 기술은 누구도 독점할 수 없는 공공재라는 강력한 윤리관으로 사람들을 통합하였다. 인구수는 급속하게 줄고 사람들은 이웃과 물리적 거리를 두게 되었다. 가치 중심적인 혹은 문화 중심적인 공동체를 새로운 이웃의 개념으로 받아들였다. 하지만 보다 많은 개인이 개별적이고 독립적으로 살아가길 원하면서 필요할 때만 이웃을 찾는 삶의 방식을

swiftly as Garuda, the steed of the sun-worshipping Vishnu, information about energy circulated at the speed of thought. Cathedrals, churches, temples, and shrines gradually disappeared, and people logged in to watch the shaman, bowed to their mobile phones, smart watches, or monitors, and prayed. Oddly, people were able to select and assemble the appearance of the shaman. Some people worshipped images from traditional religions, such as Jesus or Buddha; some, a president or prime minister; some, pop idols; and others, the images of animals, such as bears, tigers, and lions, or of objects, such as desks or stones. Although its external appearances differed, the shaman united the people with the powerful ethical belief that energy and the technology to produce it were public goods that could not be monopolized by anyone. The population was rapidly declining, and people were made to physically

---

추구하였다. N명의 사람이 살았고 N개의 삶의 방식이 서로의 간섭없이 살았다. 혹자들은 이런 방식의 삶을 '차이의 공동체'라 명명했고, 그것이 가능한 이유로 '샤먼'을 꼽았다.

뜬소문

하나. 사람들은 집을 가지고 이동했다. 그 집은 신전이고 사무실이고 식당이고 모바일이었다. 집 안과 밖으로 화려하게 치장되었다. 그 치장은 잦고 오랜 이동에도 품위와 권위를 잃지 않았다.

둘. 양지와 음지의 구분이 뚜렷한 어느 지역들은 겨울이 매우 춥기때문에, 더운 지역에서 이주해온 노동자들이 양지만으로 이어진 지도를 만들었다.

셋. 아이들은 햇빛을 찍어 먹었다.

넷. 노동 시민이 되기 위한 첫 절차는 언어를 배우는 일이었다. 언어를 배우는 일은 마치 어느 종교의 부흥회처럼 모두 은혜를 받는 절차 같았다.

다섯. 이주한 사람들에게는 이주 전의 고향에 대한 향수가 있었다. 그런데 이 향수는 매우 동시대적이고 세련된 정서이다.

distance themselves from their neighbors. A value-centered or culture-centered community was accepted as a new concept of the neighbor. However, as more individuals wanted to live individually and independently, they pursued a way of life that sought out neighbors only when needed. N people lived without interfering in each other's N ways of life. Some named this way of life a "community of difference" and cited the shaman as the reason for its possibility.

Believe it or not

One: People moved with their houses. The house was a temple, an office, a restaurant, and a transport vehicle. The inside and outside of the house were ornately decorated. The decoration did not lose its integrity or esteem even after long and frequent travels.

여섯. 만약 당신이 깻잎이나 시금치를 먹는다면 그것은 누군가의 땀방울을 먹는 것이다.

일곱. 사람들은 화장실이 없는 비닐하우스에 살았다.

여덟. 동일 토템족에 속한 사람과 사람들은 같은 이름을 갖는다.

아홉. 이주민은 원주민에게 선물(경제적, 법적, 윤리적, 도덕적)을 주어야 할 의무가 있다. 원주민들에게는 선물을 받을 권리가 있으며, 동시에 주어지는 선물은 결코 거절해서는 안 되므로 선물을 받을 의무도 있다.

열. 도래할 공동체는 서로 간의 '융합'이 아니라, 단수성들의 '상호노출'이다.

열하나. 어떤 사람들은 또 어떤 사람의 사고가 과학의 전단계로 주술적이라고 이야기하지만 주술적이라는 것은 과학적인 것보다 열등한 단계의 사고가 아닌 사물을 이해하는 다른 태도, 다른 방식으로 간주한다. 그래서 어떤 사람의 사고는 범주화로 인해 추상적인 것에 반해 오히려 어떤 사람의 사고는 개별적인 사물에 대하여 더욱 구체적이고 객관적인 태도를 취한다.

Two: Because places with clear distinctions between sunny and shaded areas get very cold in the winter in certain places, workers who migrated from warm climates made a map connecting just the sunny spots.

Three: Children ate up the sun.

Four: The first step to becoming a working citizen was learning the language. Learning a language was like the process of receiving grace at some religious revival meeting.

Five: Those who migrated had nostalgia for the hometowns they left behind. However, this nostalgia was a very contemporary and sophisticated sentiment.

Six: If you eat sesame leaves or spinach, you are eating someone else's sweat.

Seven: People lived in polytunnel greenhouses without toilets.

Eight: People belonging to the same totem family had the same name.

Nine: Migrants were obligated to give gifts (economic, legal, ethical, and moral) to native inhabitants. Native inhabitants had the right to receive gifts, but also a duty, as they were forbidden from refusing gifts given to them.

Ten: The community to come was not one of mutual "fusion," but one of mutual "interaction and exposure" of singularities.

Eleven: People say that some people's thinking is magical in a prescientific sense, but "magical" can be regarded as a different tendency, a different way of understanding things, not a level of thinking that is inferior to scientific thought. Thus, while some people's thoughts are abstract because of categorization, other people's thoughts take on a more concrete and objective tendency toward individual objects.

Wolsik Kim, *Shaman-Sesame*, 2023. Print on paper, 420cm X 594cm.
김월식, 〈샤먼-깻잎〉, 2023. 종이에 프린트, 420cm X 594cm.

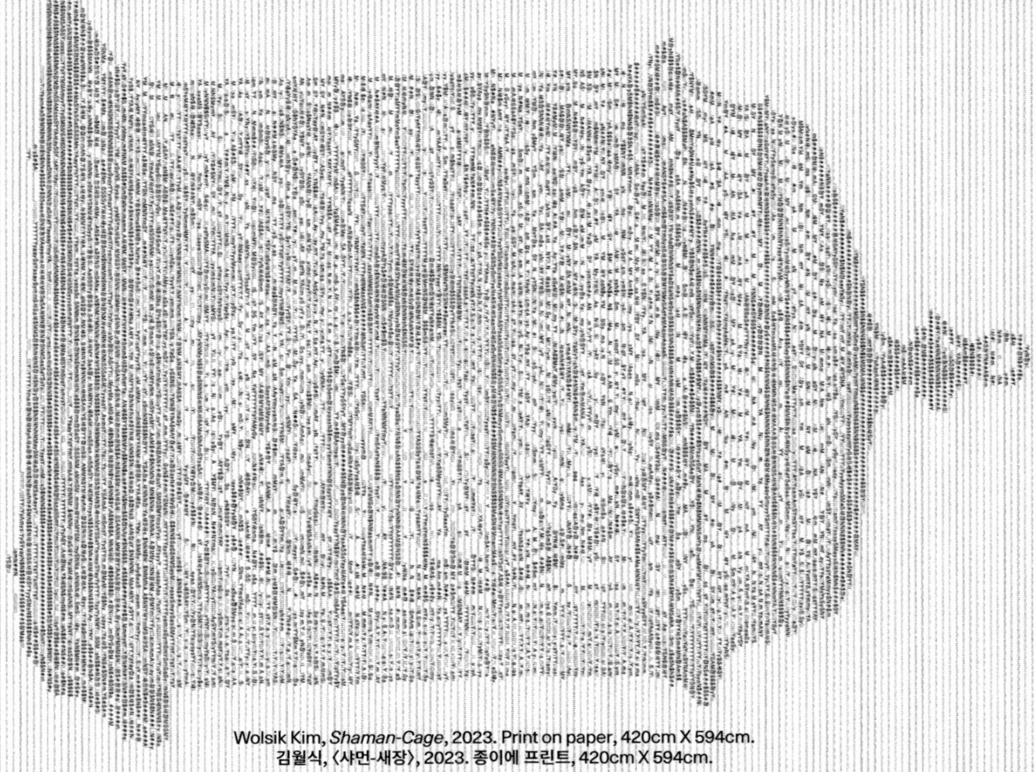

Wolsik Kim, *Shaman-Cage*, 2023. Print on paper, 420cm X 594cm.
김월식, 〈샤먼-새장〉, 2023. 종이에 프린트, 420cm X 594cm.

Wolsik Kim, *Shaman*, 2023. Single Channel Video, 2min 9sec.
김월식, 〈샤먼〉, 2023. 단채널 영상, 2분 9초.

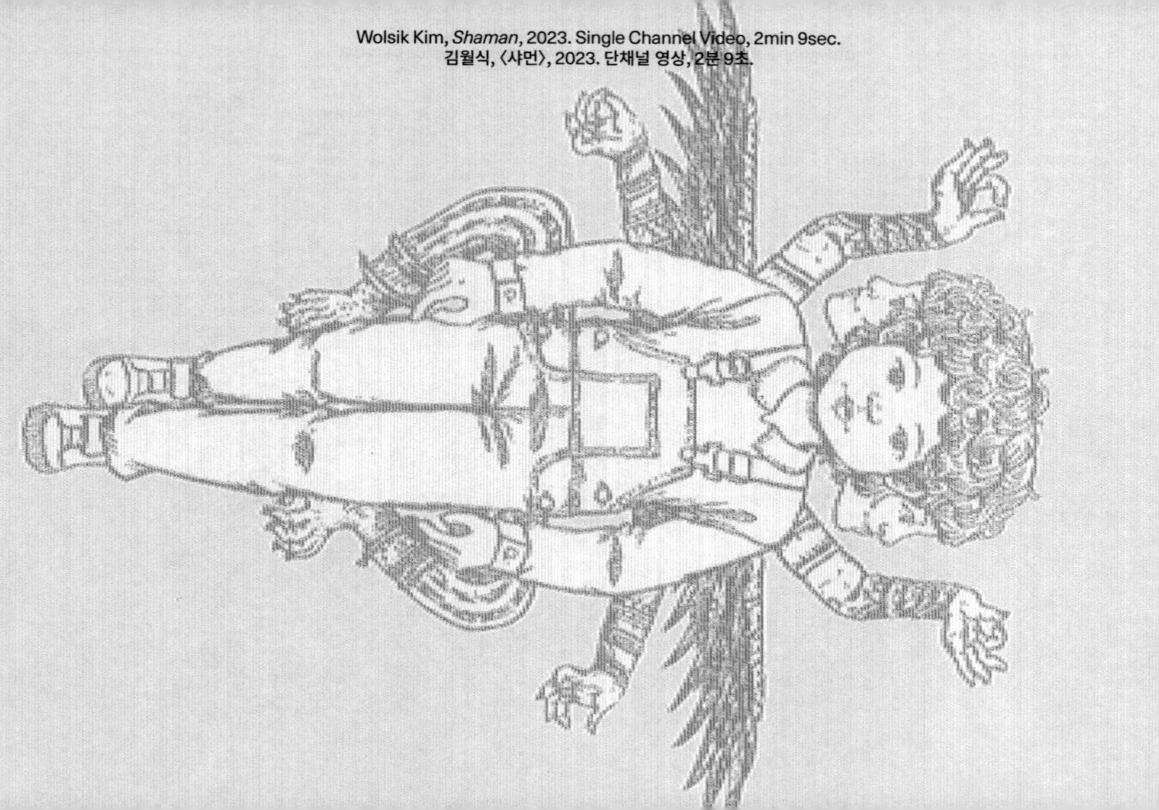

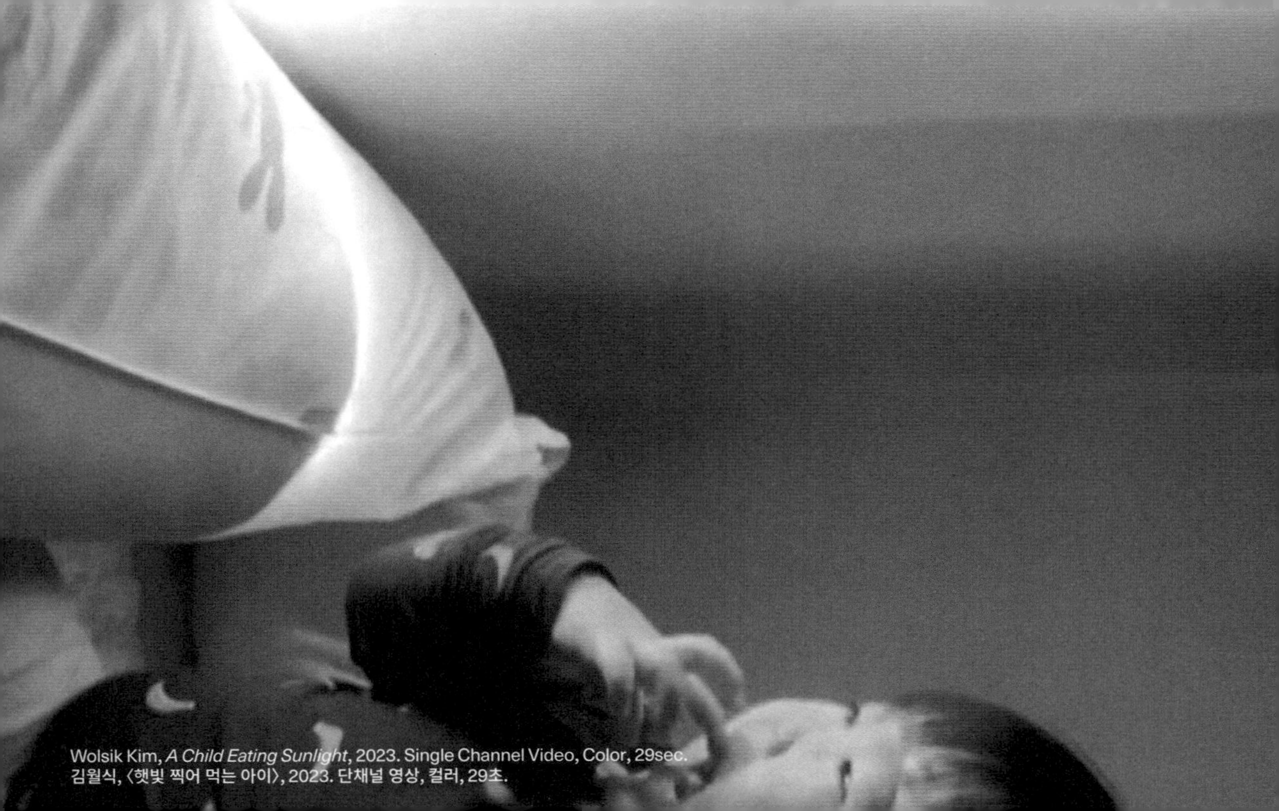

Wolsik Kim, *A Child Eating Sunlight*, 2023. Single Channel Video, Color, 29sec.
김월식, 〈햇빛 찍어 먹는 아이〉, 2023. 단채널 영상, 컬러, 29초.

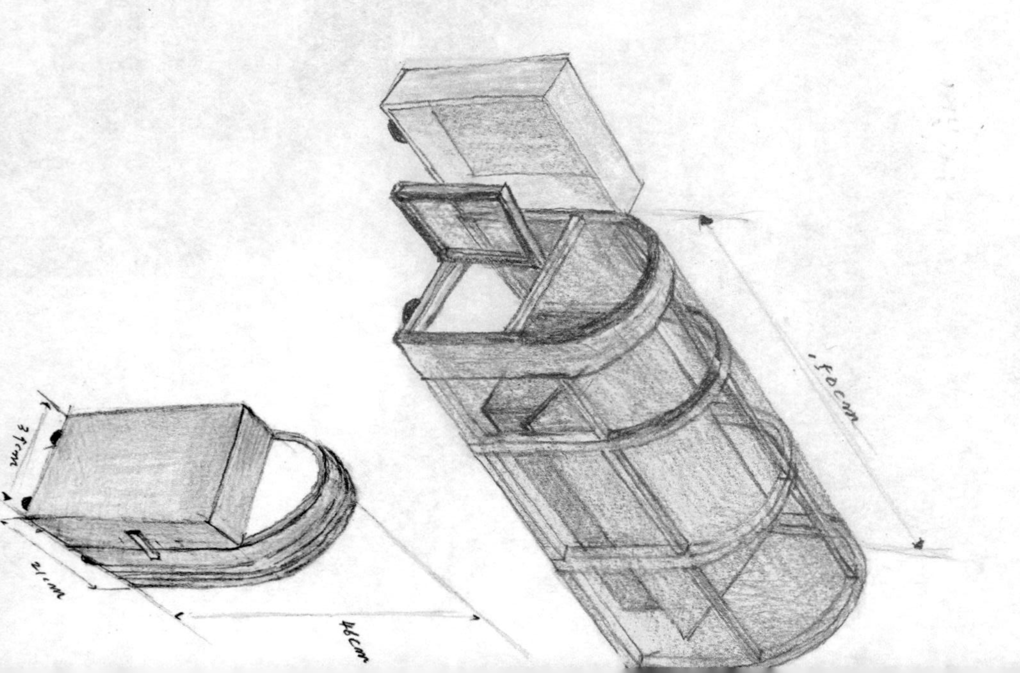

Wolsik Kim, *A Greenhouse is not a Suitcase*, 2023. Mixed material, 39cm X 171cm X 46cm.
김월식, 〈비닐하우스는 가방이 아니다.〉, 2023. 혼합 매체, 39cm X 171cm X 46cm.

A Future

Jaekyung Jung

정재경

어느 미래

File Number: NA-SP-458920Q27 Sending Agency:______ (Security Deletion)
File Category: Top SecretReceiving Receiving Agency:______ (Security Deletion)

Classified: Top Secret
Classified State Report

Subject: Report on the "Clairvoyant Images" Leakage and Trends[1]

1. This report is part of the work *A Future* exhibited in the Korean Pavilion of the 2023 Venice Biennale. In *A Future*, there appears a child called "the child of God" because of the child's ability to foretell the future, who has become both an object of admiration and fear among the public. The work focuses on the conflict, confrontation, and association among various human groups caused by the leakage of the prophesied images containing the fate of the future human community conjured up by the child. The fictional situation drawn in *A Future* was planned as a sort of inquiry to carefully consider together with the audience what kind of ethical considerations are needed for future communities. All figures and institutions appearing in the report are unrelated to actual persons or institutions in real life and are entirely fictional. –Jaekyung Jung

Submitting Agency: ______ (Security Deletion) Page: 1/12
File Form: Reporting Form #7

File Number: NA-SP-458920Q27 Sending Agency:______ (Security Deletion)
File Category: Top SecretReceiving Receiving Agency:______ (Security Deletion)

Summary

The purpose of this report is to gain an understanding of the route and trends by which the so-called "clairvoyant images"—visualizations of the thoughts of an unidentified subject known to have the ability to foretell the future—were leaked to civil society.

From among the level 1 Security Data (hereafter "Security Data") received by this agency from _________ (Name of Agency: Security Deletion) in order to prepare this report, only the items necessary to formulate the context in relation to the topic of the report have been selected and included herein. Any judgment as to the authenticity of the contents of the received documents included in this report is beyond the agency's authority, and if fact checking is required, a separate report should be requested from __________ (Name of Agency: Security Deletion).
*The excerpts taken from _________ (Name of Agency: Security Deletion) Security Data are indicated by quotation marks (" ").

1. Regarding the Child with Clairvoyant Abilities

According to __________ (Name of Agency: Security Deletion) Security Data, the government agency became aware of a child (unidentified subject) who lacked vision, hearing, and olfactory

Submitting Agency:_______ (Security Deletion) Page: 2/12
File Form: Reporting Form #7

functions at birth but who has been judged to have special abilities to foretell the future as reported by the child's doctor.

Reference document 1-1
"A child with the ability to foretell the future fate of the human community (hereafter referred to as 'UCS-1') has been discovered. As the result of an investigation of UCS-1 over several years by a team of 20 experts, including future forecasting experts, cognitive psychologists, and physiologists, it has been confirmed that UCS-1 has the unique ability to predict the future with a probability greater than 87.5%" (Security Data, page 21).

Reference document 1-2
"According to the report by medical staff who closely examined UCS-1, UCS-1 has had no sense functions of sight, hearing, and smell since birth as a result of Usher syndrome, a type of genetic disease that causes mutations in sensory cells. A cognitive linguistic examination revealed that UCS-1 has not developed the ability to decipher texts necessary for verbal communication and is capable of extremely limited communication using tactile sensations" (security data, page 72).

File Number: NA-SP-458920Q27 Sending Agency:______ (Security Deletion)
File Category: Top SecretReceiving Receiving Agency:______ (Security Deletion)

2. Investigation Into the Clairvoyant Abilities of the Child

Based on the Security Data, it can be inferred that the development of special technology that reproduces the child's thoughts as images using machine learning has been successful. These images have been estimated to predict the future with significant accuracy.

Reference document 2-1
"With the approval of a special budget by the National Assembly, a research consortium formed by the Ministry of National Defense, the National Intelligence Service, and the National Security Strategic Technology Research Institute succeeded in developing the technology protocol MDP v.0.9b, which can read UCS-1's thoughts by applying the latest machine learning technology. As a result of the investigation by experts of the images (hereafter referred to as "clairvoyant images") extracted from the subject UCS-1 through MDP v.0.9b, the probability that the clairvoyant images represent some state in the past or the future is reported as 87.5%" (Security Data, page 126).

Submitting Agency:______ (Security Deletion) Page: 4/12
File Form: Reporting Form #7

3. Clairvoyant Image Research Laboratory

According to the Security Data, a basement research laboratory was established, and a database is being built, to closely analyze and decipher the clairvoyant images obtained from the child.
*The location and size of the laboratory have been deleted from the Security Data as a matter of state secrecy.

Reference document 3-1
"A special laboratory (code: LAB-FI-UCS-1) was established to decipher the clairvoyant images extracted from UCS-1, and after three rounds of deliberations by relevant ministries, a total of 27 people were selected as special researchers, including philosophers, aestheticians, historians, economists, psychologists, prosecutors, political scientists, etc." (Security Data, page 151).

Reference document 3-2
"By presidential decree and approval from the National Intelligence Service, UCS-1 was secretly transported to a special laboratory established 157 meters underground. The research laboratory is categorized as a level 1 military facility, staffed with first-class security guards and medical personnel to maintain the condition of UCS-1" (Security Data, page 177).

Reference document 3-3

"Under the management of the National Archives, the clairvoyant images detected from UCS-1 have been categorized as level 1 classified documents, permanently stored in the National Archives Museum and subjected to quarterly analysis" (Security Data, page 189).

4. Regarding the Top National Policy Direction Deliberation Report

The Security Data suggest that the Top National Policy Deliberation Council conducted regular reviews of the clairvoyant images in secret at closed-door meetings on national security.

Reference document 4-1

"The special research laboratory (code: LAB-FI-UCS-1) submits the clairvoyant images and the researchers' report fourteen days before the convening of the Top National Policy Direction Deliberation Council, which is held behind closed doors on the first of every month.. The clairvoyant images and reports submitted, in accordance with procedure, go through evaluation by the Top Deliberation Committee, which determines whether or not they will be reflected in future policy directives in the form of a resolution, and are then submitted to the Office of the President and the National Assembly. All data reviewed, reported, and decided on are categorized as top-secret level 1 classified documents. Any violation of this confidentiality principle would be severely punished in accordance with the relevant provisions of the National Security Law" (Security Data, page 207).

According to the minutes and resolutions of the National Review and Assessment Annual Meeting (including the contents of the confidential review), received together with the Security Data, it can be inferred that negotiations have not been held for many years because of a discrepancy in image interpretation among the highest members of the Top Deliberation Committee. Three of the seven members (____, ____, ____, Names Deleted) agreed to establish a future policy plan based on an optimistic outlook and assessment of the clairvoyant images. On the other hand, three members (____, ____, ____, Names Deleted) agreed to a future plan with austerity and security as key agenda items, evaluating the data as predicting a pessimistic future situation. One member (____, Name Deleted) abstained from the resolution and submitted a document to the National Assembly and relevant authorities requesting all top-ranking officials to visit the laboratory to confirm the existence and identity of the child (UCS-1). It appears that the Office of the President and the National Assembly disapproved this request, citing the National Security Law.

File Number: NA-SP-458920Q27 Sending Agency:______ (Security Deletion)
File Category: Top SecretReceiving Receiving Agency:______ (Security Deletion)

5. Major Trends Following from the Leakage of the Clairvoyant Images

The route and origin of the leak of the clairvoyant images and trends among citizens and related groups are as follows.

5-1. Route of Leakage/Disclosure
The route by which the clairvoyant images were leaked has not been accurately identified. However, we cannot rule out the possibility that some of the images were intentionally leaked to the public by an unidentified group. At present, the precise route of the leak is under close investigation by a special investigation team involving the National Intelligence Service, the Public Prosecutor's office, and the Ministry of National Defense.

5-2. Origin/Cause of Leakage
According to the data obtained by this agency, reported directly by the special investigation team at the request of the President, a connection between the extended conflict over future policy direction within the Top Deliberation Committee and the leakage of the clairvoyant images cannot be completely ruled out. However, no legal evidence has been secured to corroborate this. The Top Deliberation Committee has requested the disclosure of documents reported directly to the President by the special investigation team.

Submitting Agency: ______ (Security Deletion) Page: 8/12
File Form: Reporting Form #7

5-3. Citizen Trends

According to a report by a citizen trends research institute, data identified as part of the clairvoyant images are rapidly spreading to the public through social media channels. It appears that fake clairvoyant images of unknown origin are also being circulated with them. Hundreds of new media contents per day, on average, are being produced based on rumors about the child (UCS-1), referred to as "the child of God," with billions of views per day. Mass gatherings of groups worshipping the clairvoyant images as divine revelations and violent protests by civic groups demanding disclosure of unscientific and superstitious policy-making processes and budget expenditures are being reported in major cities across the country.

5-4. Group Trends

The question of whether a child with the ability to foretell the future destiny of the community exists is rapidly emerging as a major concern among main news channels at home and abroad. Through public statements, various religious groups are strongly criticizing the government and related ministries for contributing to the spread of "heretical" doctrines and leading to social chaos, and some religious leaders are engaged in hunger strikes calling for countermeasures. Some media companies have developed characters based on the child who can foretell the future and, upon acquiring related licenses, are investing huge amounts of capital in projects that realize the future depicted in the predictions. The arts and culture world is also producing many special exhibitions and creative performances with the child as a motif, primarily focusing on the theme of the existential tragedy of human suffering in the relation between gods and human beings.

Conclusion

Substantiating as fact whether "a child with the ability to foretell the future fate of human communities" exists, or the authenticity of the clairvoyant images extracted from the child by the laboratory described in the __________ (Name of Agency: Security Deletion) Security Data, is beyond the authority and role of this institution. However, as specified in items 1, 2, 3, and 4 above, upon comprehensive analysis of credible data obtained from multiple organizations related to the case, there is also no clear basis for determining the case described in the security data as a fabrication.

Apart from the child, laboratory, and images, the fact that public antigovernment sentiments and protests have appeared in various forms in major cities following the leak of the clairvoyant images can be confirmed. Following strong opposition from conservatives and related interest groups against the antigovernment protest movement, the civil society division index has hit an all-time high. Lastly, it is difficult to foresee at this point what kind of positive or negative impact the current situation will have on the next presidential election and the National Assembly elections next year. However, in order to determine the best course of action for the future of the nation in the current situation, budgeting for additional in-depth investigation is needed.

Related Materials (in alphabetical order)

- Citizen Trends Research Report (Classification Code: NS-RF-CR-20234Q)
- Top National Policy Direction Deliberation Council Annual Report (Classification Code: NS-NPAR-20231201)
- _________ (Name of Agency: Security Deletion) Security Data (Classification Code: NS-TS01-1012)

Appendix

- Some of the materials referred to as "clairvoyant images" that are circulating in the mass media.*

* Determining the authenticity of the leaked clairvoyant images attached and differentiating them from fake images are outside

File Number: NA-SP-458920Q27 Sending Agency:______ (Security Deletion)
File Category: Top SecretReceiving Receiving Agency:______ (Security Deletion)

of the authority of the reporting agency, and thus, accurate evaluation and identifying information for the images are not included.

This document must be kept strictly confidential, with only authorized personnel allowed access.

Signature ______________________ (Security Deletion)
[REDACTED]
[REDACTED]

Submitting Agency: _______ (Security Deletion) Page: 12/12
File Form: Reporting Form #7

File Number: NA-SP-458920Q27 Sending Agency:_______ (Security Deletion)
File Category: Top SecretReceiving Receiving Agency:_______ (Security Deletion)

Appendix 1-1. A clairvoyant image circulating in the mass media.
(Data Classification: UCS-1-LI-A-137)
별첨자료 1-1. '예지 이미지'로 불리며 대중 미디어에 유포되고 있는 자료 중 일부
(자료 분류: UCS-1-LI-A-137)

Submitting Agency: _______ (Security Deletion) Appendix: i/ viii
File Form: Reporting Form #7

File Number: NA-SP-458920Q27 Sending Agency:_______ (Security Deletion)
File Category: Top SecretReceiving Receiving Agency:_______ (Security Deletion)

Appendix 1-2. A clairvoyant image circulating in the mass media.
(Data Classification: UCS-1-LI-A-138)
별첨자료 1-2. '예지 이미지'로 불리며 대중 미디어에 유포되고 있는 자료 중 일부
(자료 분류: UCS-1-LI-A-138)

Submitting Agency: _______ (Security Deletion) Appendix: ii/ viii
File Form: Reporting Form #7

File Number: NA-SP-458920Q27 Sending Agency:_______ (Security Deletion)
File Category: Top SecretReceiving Receiving Agency:_______ (Security Deletion)

Appendix 1-3. A clairvoyant image circulating in the mass media.
(Data Classification: UCS-1-LI-A-139)
별첨자료 1-3. '예지 이미지'로 불리며 대중 미디어에 유포되고 있는 자료 중 일부
(자료 분류: UCS-1-LI-A-139)

Submitting Agency: _______ (Security Deletion) Appendix: iii/ viii
File Form: Reporting Form #7

File Number: NA-SP-458920Q27 Sending Agency:_______ (Security Deletion)
File Category: Top SecretReceiving Receiving Agency:_______ (Security Deletion)

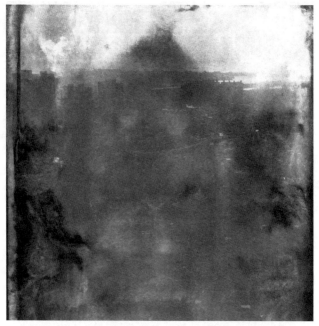

Appendix 1-4. A clairvoyant image circulating in the mass media.
(Data Classification: UCS-1-LI-A-140)
별첨자료 1-4. '예지 이미지'로 불리며 대중 미디어에 유포되고 있는 자료 중 일부
(자료 분류: UCS-1-LI-A-140)

Submitting Agency: _______ (Security Deletion) Appendix: iv/ viii
File Form: Reporting Form #7

File Number: NA-SP-458920Q27 Sending Agency:_______ (Security Deletion)
File Category: Top SecretReceiving Receiving Agency:_______ (Security Deletion)

Appendix 1-5. A clairvoyant image circulating in the mass media.
(Data Classification: UCS-1-LI-A-141)
별첨자료 1-5. '예지 이미지'로 불리며 대중 미디어에 유포되고 있는 자료 중 일부
(자료 분류: UCS-1-LI-A-141)

Submitting Agency: _______ (Security Deletion) Appendix: v/ viii
File Form: Reporting Form #7

File Number: NA-SP-458920Q27 Sending Agency:______ (Security Deletion)
File Category: Top SecretReceiving Receiving Agency:_______ (Security Deletion)

Appendix 1-6. A clairvoyant image circulating in the mass media.
(Data Classification: UCS-1-LI-A-142)
별첨자료 1-6. '예지 이미지'로 불리며 대중 미디어에 유포되고 있는 자료 중 일부
(자료 분류: UCS-1-LI-A-142)

Submitting Agency: _______ (Security Deletion) Appendix: vi/ viii
File Form: Reporting Form #7

Appendix 1-7. A clairvoyant image circulating in the mass media.
(Data Classification: UCS-1-LI-A-143)
별첨자료 1-7. '예지 이미지'로 불리며 대중 미디어에 유포되고 있는 자료 중 일부
(자료 분류: UCS-1-LI-A-143)

File Number: NA-SP-458920Q27 Sending Agency:_______ (Security Deletion)
File Category: Top SecretReceiving Receiving Agency:_______ (Security Deletion)

Appendix 1-8. A clairvoyant image circulating in the mass media.
(Data Classification: UCS-1-LI-A-144)
별첨자료 1-8. '예지 이미지'로 불리며 대중 미디어에 유포되고 있는 자료 중 일부
(자료 분류: UCS-1-LI-A-144)

Submitting Agency: _______ (Security Deletion) Appendix: viii/ viii
File Form: Reporting Form #7

문서 번호: NA-SP-458920Q27 송신 기관:_________ (보안 삭제)
문건 분류: 극비 수신 기관:_________ (보안 삭제)

기밀: 극비
국가 기밀 보고서

주제: '예지 이미지' 유출 과정과 동향 보고[1]

1. 이 보고서는 2023 베니스 비엔날레 한국관 전시작 〈어느 미래〉의 일부이다. 〈어느 미래〉에는 미래 예지 능력이 있어 '신의 아이'라 불리며 대중에게 추앙과 공포의 대상이 된 아이가 등장한다. 작품은 아이가 떠올린 미래 인류 공동체의 운명이 담긴 예언 이미지가 대중에게 유출된 상황이 야기한 다양한 인간 집단 사이의 갈등, 대립, 화합에 주목한다. 〈어느 미래〉가 그려내는 가상 상황은 미래 공동체를 위해 어떤 윤리적 고민이 필요한지 관객과 함께 깊이 사유하는 일종의 질문지로서 기획되었다. 보고서에 등장하는 모든 인물과 기관은 실제와 무관한 픽션임을 밝힌다. —정재경

제출기관:_________ (보안 삭제) 페이지: 1/8
문건 양식: 보고 양식#7

문서 번호: NA-SP-458920Q27
문건 분류: 극비

송신 기관:________(보안 삭제)
수신 기관:________(보안 삭제)

개요

본 보고서의 목적은 미래 예지 능력이 있다고 알려진 신원 미파악 대상의 생각을 시각화한 자료로 알려진 일명 '예지 이미지'가 시민 사회에 유출된 경로와 동향을 파악하는 데 있다.

보고서 작성을 위해 본 기관이 ___________(기관명: 보안 삭제)으로부터 전달받은 1급 보안 자료(이하 '보안 자료') 중 보고 주제와 관련하여 전후 맥락 구성에 필요한 사항만을 선별하여 보고서에 포함하였다. 본 보고서에 포함된 전달 문건 내용에 대한 모든 진위 판단은 본 기관의 권한 외 사항이며, 사실 여부 확인이 필요할 경우 ___________(기관명: 보안 삭제)에 별도 보고를 요청해야 한다.

*___________(기관명: 보안 삭제) 보안 자료 중 발췌 내용은 " "로 표기한다.

1. 예지 능력을 가진 유아에 대하여

___________(기관명: 보안 삭제) 보안 자료에 따르면 시각, 청각, 후각 기능은 태생적으로 상실했으나 미래를 예지하는 특수 능력을 갖춘 것으로 판단되는 유아(신원 미파악 대상) 담당의사의 신고로 정부 기관이 파악하였다.

참고 자료 1-1

"인간 공동체의 미래 운명을 예견하는 능력을 가진 유아(이하 'UCS-1')가 발견되었다. 미래 예측 전문가, 인지 심리학자, 생리학자를 포함한 총 20명으로 구성된 전문 조사단이 수년에 걸쳐 UCS-1을 조사한 결과, UCS-1은 미래를

제출기관:________(보안 삭제)
문건 양식: 보고 양식#7

페이지: 2/8

읽을 수 있는 독특한 능력을 갖추고 있을 확률이 87.5% 이상인 것으로 최종 확인되었다." (보안 자료, 21페이지)

참고 자료 1-2
"UCS-1을 정밀 검사한 의료진의 보고에 의하면 UCS-1은 감각 세포에 돌연변이를 야기하는 유전자 질병의 일종인 어셔 증후군(Usher syndrome)으로 인해 출생 시 시각, 청각, 후각 기능을 완전히 상실하였다. 언어 인지학적 조사 결과 UCS-1은 언어 의사소통에 필요한 문자 기호 해독 능력이 형성되지 않았으며 촉각을 이용한 극히 제한적 의사소통이 가능한 상태이다." (보안 자료, 72 페이지)

2. 유아의 미래 예지력 조사

보안 자료상 인공지능을 활용하여 유아의 생각을 이미지로 재현하는 특수 기술 개발에 성공한 것으로 추론된다. 유아의 생각을 시각적으로 재현한 이미지의 미래 예측 확률이 유의미하게 높은 수준인 것으로 판단된다.

참고 자료 2-1
"국회 특별 예산 승인 하에 국방부, 국가정보원, 국가안보전략기술연구원이 구성한 연구 컨소시엄은 최신 인공지능 기술을 적용하여 UCS-1의 생각을 읽을 수 있는 프로토콜 기술MDP v.0.9b의 개발에 성공했다. MDP v.0.9b 인공지능이 대상 UCS-1으로부터 추출한 이미지(이하 '예지 이미지')에 대한 전문가 조사 결과, 예지 이미지는 과거와 미래의 어떤 상태를 표상할 확률이 87.5%로 보고 되었다." (보안 자료, 126 페이지)

문서 번호: NA-SP-458920Q27　　송신 기관:________(보안 삭제)
문건 분류: 극비　　수신 기관:________(보안 삭제)

3. 예지 이미지 연구소

보안 자료에 따르면 미래 예측 능력이 있는 유아로부터 획득한 일명 '예지 이미지'를 정밀하게 분석 해독하기 위한 연구소를 지하에 설립하고 데이터베이스를 구축해 나가고 있는 것으로 추측된다. *연구소의 위치와 시설 규모 관련 사항은 국가 안보 기밀 사항으로 보안 자료에 삭제되어 있음.

참고 자료 3-1
"UCS-1으로부터 추출한 예지 이미지를 해독하기 위한 특수 연구소(코드: LAB-FI-UCS-1)를 설립하고, 3차에 걸친 관련 부처 심의 과정을 거쳐 철학자, 미학자, 역사학자, 경제학자, 심리학자, 검사, 정치학자 등을 포함한 총 27명을 특별연구원으로 선발했다." (보안 자료, 151페이지)

참고 자료 3-2
"대통령령과 국가정보원 승인 아래 UCS-1은 지하 157미터에 설립된 특수 연구소로 비밀리에 이송되었다. 연구소는 1급 군사시설로 분류되며 보안을 위한 제1 전투경비단과 UCS-1상태 유지를 위한 의료진이 상주하고 있다." (보안 자료, 177페이지)

참고 자료 3-3
"국가기록원 관리하에 UCS-1으로부터 검출된 예지 이미지는 1급 기밀로 분류되어 국립문서보관소에 영구 보관되며 분기별 분석이 실시된다." (보안 자료, 189페이지)

제출기관:________(보안 삭제)　　페이지: 4/8
문건 양식: 보고 양식#7

4. 국가최고정책방향심의보고 관련

보안 자료는 국가최고정책심의회의 국가안보 관련 비공개회의에서 예지 이미지에 대한 정기적 심의가 비밀리에 진행되었음을 시사한다.

참고 자료 4-1
"특수 연구소(코드: LAB-FI-UCS-1)는 예지 이미지와 연구원의 보고서를 매월 1일 비공개로 진행되는 국가최고정책방향논의 및 심의회의 개회 14일 전 제출한다. 제출된 예지 이미지와 보고서는 절차에 따라 최고위원회의 심의와 평가를 거쳐, 향후 정책 방향에의 반영 여부를 결의서 형태로 확정하고 대통령실과 국회에 제출한다. 심의, 보고, 결의된 모든 자료는 1급 극비 기밀문서로 분류되며 비공개를 원칙으로, 이를 어길 시 국가보안법 관련 조항에 따라 엄중히 처벌된다." (보안 자료, 207페이지)

보안 자료와 함께 전달받은 국가심의평가 연간 회의록과 결의서(비공개 심의 내용 포함)에 따르면, 예지 이미지에 대한 최고위원회의 심의평가 과정에서 발생한 최고위원 간 이미지 해석 격차로 인해 다년간 협의가 이루어지지 못한 것으로 판단된다. 결의서에 서명한 총 7인의 최고심의위원 중 3인(_____, _____, _____, 성명 삭제)은 예지 이미지를 통해 낙관적 전망을 기조로 미래 정책안을 수립하는 방안에 동의하였다. 반면, 3인(_____, _____, _____, 성명 삭제)은 자료가 비관적 미래 상황을 예측한다고 판단하고 긴축과 안보를 핵심 의정 과제로 삼은 미래 계획안에 동의하였다. 1인(_____, 성명 삭제)은 결의안 서명에 기권 의사를 밝히고, 유아 (UCS-1)의 존재 확인과 신상 파악을 위해 최고위 전원의 연구소 시찰을 요구하는 문서를 당국과 국회에 제출하였다. 유아 존재 확인과 연구소 시찰 요구에 대해 대통령실과 국회는 국가보안법을 근거로 승인 불가 처리한 것으로 파악된다.

문서 번호: NA-SP-458920Q27
문건 분류: 극비

송신 기관:________ (보안 삭제)
수신 기관:________ (보안 삭제)

5. 예지 이미지 유출에 따른 주요 동향

예지 이미지 유출의 경로, 원인 그리고 시민 및 관련 단체 동향은 다음과 같다.

5-1. 유출 경로

예지 이미지 유출 경로는 정확하게 파악되지 않았다. 단, 이미지 일부가 미확인 단체에 의해 의도적으로 대중에 유출되었을 가능성을 배재할 수 없다. 현재 정확한 유출 경로는 국가정보원, 검찰, 국방부가 참여하는 특별 조사팀에 의해 면밀한 조사 과정 중에 있다.

5-2. 유출 원인

특별 조사팀이 대통령 요청에 따라 직속으로 보고한 자료를 본 기관이 입수한 바에 따르면, 국가최고정책방향심의회 내 장기화된 미래 정책 방향에 대한 갈등과 예지 이미지 유출 간 연관성을 완전히 배제할 수 없으나, 이를 확증할 법리적 증거물을 확보하지 못한 것으로 판단된다. 최고정책심의위원회는 특별 조사팀이 대통령에 직속 보고한 문건의 공개를 요구하고 있다.

5-3 시민 동향

시민 동향 리서치 기관의 보고에 따르면 예지 이미지의 일부로 파악되는 자료가 주요 소셜 미디어 채널을 통해 대중에게 급속히 확산 중이며, 출처를 알 수 없는 가짜 예지 이미지도 함께 유통되고 있는 것으로 파악된다. 일명 '신의 아이'로 지칭되는 유아(UCS-1)에 대한 각종 루머와 소문을 소재로 하루 평균 수백 건의 신규 미디어 콘텐츠가 생산되며 일평균 수십억 건의 조회가 이루어지는 중이다. 예지 이미지를 신성한 계시로 숭배하는 단체의 집단 모임과 정부 주도의 비과학적이고 미신적 정책 입안 과정 및 지출 예산 공개를 요구하는 시민 단체의 거센 시위가 전국 주요 도시에서 보고되고 있다.

제출기관:________ (보안 삭제)
문건 양식: 보고 양식#7

페이지: 6/8

문서 번호: NA-SP-458920Q27　　　　송신 기관:________ (보안 삭제)
문건 분류: 극비　　　　수신 기관:________ (보안 삭제)

5-4 단체 동향

공동체의 미래 운명을 예견하는 능력을 갖춘 아이의 존재 여부는 국내외 주요 뉴스 채널의 최대 관심사로 급부상하고 있다. 각종 종교 단체는 공개 성명을 통해 사회 혼란을 야기하는 이단적 교리 확산의 원인을 제공한 정부와 관련 부처를 강하게 비판하며 대책 마련을 촉구하는 단식 투쟁을 하고 있다. 일부 기업은 미래를 예측하는 아이를 주제로 다양한 파생 캐릭터를 개발하고 관련 사용권을 획득한 후 예언이 묘사하는 미래상을 메타버스 플랫폼에 실현하는 프로젝트에 막대한 자본을 투자하고 있다. 문화 예술계 역시 아이를 모티브로 하여, 주로 신과 인간 사이에서 고뇌하는 인간의 존재론적 비극을 주제로 한 다양한 기획 전시와 창작 공연을 양산하고 있다.

결론

____________(기관명: 보안 삭제) 보안 자료에 기술된 "인간 공동체의 미래 운명을 예견하는 능력을 갖춘 유아"의 존재 여부 및 연구소에서 특수 기술을 사용하여 유아로부터 추출하고 있다는 "예지 이미지"의 미래 예측에 대한 실체적 진실 여부 판단은 본 기관의 권한과 역할을 넘어선다. 단, 위 1, 2, 3, 4 항목에 명시된 바와 같이 사안에 관련된 다수의 기관으로부터 입수한 신빙성 있는 자료들을 종합적으로 분석하였을 때, 보안 자료에 기술된 사안을 허구로 판단할 근거 역시 명확하지 않다.

다만, 유아와 연구소의 존재 여부, 미래를 예견하는 이미지가 실존하는지에 대한 사실 여부와 별개로, '신의 아이'가 예지한 미래 예측 이미지라 불리는 '예지 이미지' 유출에 따른 대중의 반정부 정서와 시위가 주요 도시에서 다양한 양상으로 강하게 표출되고 있는 것은 사실로 확인된다. 반정부 시위운동

제출기관:________ (보안 삭제)　　　　페이지: 7/8
문건 양식: 보고 양식#7

문서 번호: NA-SP-458920Q27 송신 기관:________(보안 삭제)
문건 분류: 극비 수신 기관:________(보안 삭제)

에 반대하는 보수 세력과 관련 이해 집단의 강렬한 반발로 시민사회분열지수가 역대 최고치를 경신하고 있다. 끝으로 현 시국이 차기 대선과 차년도 국회의원 선거에 어떤 긍정 또는 부정적 영향을 행사할지 현재 시점에서 전망하기는 어렵다. 다만, 현 상황에서 국가의 미래를 위한 최선의 조치를 결정하기 위해서는 심도 있는 추가 조사와 그에 따른 추가 예산 편성이 필요하다.

관련 자료 (가나다순)

-국가최고정책방향심의와 보고 연례 보고서
(분류 코드: NS-NPAR-20231201)
-____________(기관명: 보안 삭제) 보안 자료 (분류 코드: NS-TS01-1012)
-시민 동향 리서치 보고서 (분류 코드: NS-RFCR-20234Q)

별첨

-'예지 이미지'로 불리며 대중 미디어에 유포되고 있는 자료 중 일부*
*별첨 자료 중 유출된 예지 이미지의 진위 판별과 허위 이미지의 구분은 보고기관의 권한 외 사항으로, 정확한 평가 및 식별 정보는 포함되지 않음

이 문서는 엄격하게 기밀로 유지되어야 하며 권한이 있는 자의 접근만이 허가된다.

서명________________________(보안 삭제)
[편집됨]
[편집됨]

제출기관:________(보안 삭제) 페이지: 8/8
문건 양식: 보고 양식#7

Appendix (In Italian)

Autori Vari — Kyong Park — Soik Jung

2086: Together How?

Tomorrow's Myths

Nick Axel

I miti sono storie relativamente semplici che, attraverso l'uso della metafora e di altri espedienti narrativi, ci conducono all'essenza della natura umana. I loro messaggi sono eterni e, grazie a una varietà sempre più ampia di pratiche narrative, vengono spesso condivisi e tramandati nel tempo. Con i loro racconti in cui tutti possono identificarsi, i miti ci insegnano a conoscere noi stessi e gli altri. Ci offrono una visione universale e ci fanno sentire partecipi di significati e valori di più ampia portata. I miti antichi vengono continuamente reinterpretati e contestualizzati nel presente, e coesistono con quelli che possono nascere ex novo da attività e abitudini quotidiane della vita contemporanea. I miti spesso si basano su epistemologie e cosmologie non normative, non moderne, non scientifiche e non razionali. Molti miti forniscono insegnamenti sulla morte, la disillusione e la distruzione, mentre altri ci illustrano l'amore, la compassione e l'armonia. Grazie ai miti possiamo immaginare un altro tempo e un altro modo di essere e di vivere, e creare ponti fra il "qui e ora" e il "lì e allora".

Il mondo che oggi ci troviamo di fronte è un groviglio di calamità politiche, crisi economiche e logistiche, rivoluzioni demografiche e disastri ecologici. Con Tomorrow's Myths, nato da una collaborazione tra e-flux Architecture e i curatori del Padiglione coreano alla Biennale di Architettura di Venezia 2023, intendiamo esplorare le potenzialità, l'importanza e il ruolo del mito come sostegno all'essere umano nella lotta contro le crescenti sfide che minacciano la sua sopravvivenza. Abbiamo invitato sei fra architetti, scrittori, artisti, filosofi e scienziati a riflettere su tali interrogativi e a scrivere nuovi miti. Quali potrebbero essere i miti creati nel 2086, dopo la rivoluzione bioculturale di cui si sente oggi un disperato bisogno? Quali miti potremmo creare o potrebbero rivelarsi necessari per realizzare tali trasformazioni? Come possiamo fare del mito una forza creatrice e operativa, al contempo intimamente familiare e immediatamente accessibile?

Dichiarazione d'innocenza
Hyewon Lee

Dichiarazione d'innocenza
Hyewon Lee

Un'enorme quantità di dati, previsioni e segnali indica che la crisi climatica è sull'orlo della catastrofe. Eppure non voglio immaginare un futuro senza esseri umani. Anche nel peggiore dei casi, non voglio perdere la speranza che un piccolo gruppo di persone, che vive a stretto contatto con la natura in qualche angolo del pianeta, possa sopravvivere. Il copione dell'opera teatrale che segue, Dichiarazione di innocenza*, è il frutto di questa esile speranza. Seguendo gli stilemi della tragedia greca, la pièce narra di cani, maiali e persone che potrebbero aver vissuto su una piccola isola dell'arcipelago delle Salomone, nel Pacifico meridionale, centinaia di anni fa. Sebbene i personaggi e gli animali della pièce siano immaginari, la storia si basa su ricerche archeologiche effettuate sulle misure estreme di controllo delle nascite adottate dagli abitanti di Tikopia per garantirsi la sopravvivenza, e su servizi giornalistici che riferiscono come i tikopiani riuscirono a salvarsi, nessuno escluso, quando l'isola venne devastata da un terribile ciclone nei primi anni del 2000.*

Dai primi insediamenti, la popolazione di Tikopia aumentò via via con lo sviluppo dell'agricoltura e dell'allevamento. Questa crescita demografica su una superficie di appena 4,6 km² rese l'isola invivibile. Ma invece di abbandonarla, gli abit-

anti trasformarono i loro metodi agricoli per salvaguardare e recuperare l'ambiente naturale. Inoltre, per mantenere il numero degli abitanti a un livello idoneo alle risorse disponibili, praticarono forme di controllo della natalità che prevedevano il divieto di matrimonio per una parte della popolazione, e l'esecuzione di aborti e perfino di infanticidi. Il neonato poteva essere salvato se un membro della famiglia, in cambio, accettava di morire oppure di prendere il mare con un'imbarcazione di fortuna e delle provviste. Intorno al 1600, inoltre, vennero abbattuti tutti i maiali dell'isola e i tikopiani tornarono a un'alimentazione a base di pesce e vegetali. Queste misure non furono risposte temporanee a una crisi, ma pratiche secolari che erano ancora in vigore negli anni Venti del Novecento, quando l'antropologo neozelandese Raymond Firth visitò Tikopia.

Sebbene le misure di controllo demografico siano cambiate nel corso del tempo, Tikopia continua a contare lo stesso numero di abitanti del passato, circa 1.200. La straordinaria capacità di resilienza alle catastrofi dimostrata dai tikopiani è stata di nuovo sotto i riflettori internazionali alla fine del 2002, poco dopo le devastazioni provocate sull'isola dal ciclone Joe. Come riferiscono le fonti di cronaca, messi al sicuro bambini e anziani nell'unica piccola grotta dell'isola, gli altri abitanti si sono spostati per diversi giorni nella direzione opposta a quella del ciclone. Non c'è stata una sola vittima.

Antefatto: *la crisi climatica ha devastato la Terra, ad eccezione di una piccola parte del pianeta: un villaggio indigeno dove la natura è rimasta intatta. Poco prima dell'alba, davanti a una capanna dal tetto molto basso in cui sia gli adulti che i bambini devono camminare chini, un vecchio sta avvolgendo in un sudario di foglie il corpo di un giovane, adagiato su una barella.*

Necroforo anziano
Oh, come sono crudeli gli dèi e
ingiusti gli uomini![1]
Perché tagliano le foglie verdi e non
quelle secche?

Coro dei Celibi anziani (Sinistra)
Ohi ohi, il vecchio ha perso il senno.

Coro dei Celibi anziani (Destra)
Gli uomini accettano i colpi del fato
quando sono ridotti alla fame.

Coro dei Celibi anziani (Sinistra)
Tanto tempo fa, quando ero bambino,
una grande calamità si abbatté su
questa terra.

Coro dei Celibi anziani (Destra)
Così avvenne perché il cuore era
cieco.

Coro dei Celibi anziani (Sinistra)
Il cielo e l'oceano si unirono
e devastarono ogni cosa sulla terra.

Coro dei Celibi anziani (Destra)
Nulla posso dire di tanta rovina,
poiché nulla vidi dalla grotta oscura
in cui mi ero nascosto.

Coro dei Celibi anziani (Sinistra)
Quando il sole tornò a brillare,
come una boa ogni cosa galleggiava sulla terra.

Coro dei Celibi anziani (Destra)
Anche i morti ebbero paura di risorgere.

Coro dei Celibi anziani (Sinistra)
Qualcuno, un dio, ci ha portato via,
ci ha aiutato a sfuggire alla distruzione.

Necroforo anziano
Quale altro scopo se non quello di distruggere?
Le grida dei bambini uccisi riempiono il villaggio.

Coro dei Celibi anziani (Destra)
Vecchio scellerato,
non è nobile un padre che muore al posto del figlio?

Coro dei Celibi anziani (Sinistra)
Non è saggia una madre che non genera una vita da sopprimere?

Necroforo anziano
Non sentite il grido di quelle anime?

L'anima del giovane uomo, scivolando fuori dal corpo, inizia a guardare intorno a sé.

Uomo
Oh, nobile figlio mio, dove sei?
Dove sei?
Dov'è mio figlio, oh cari che piangete?
Lo avete visto, oh vicini che dormite?

Poco dopo, gli spiriti di un cane e di un maiale si avvicinano all'uomo.

Maiale
Oh, padrone amato, non sono un porco iniquo.
Non ho svegliato il piccolo.
Non gli ho sottratto il latte.

Cane
Oh, padrone amato, non sono un cane infame.
Non ho morso l'infante.
Non gli ho sottratto il cibo.

L'uomo che vaga nella nebbia umida dell'alba non sente le invocazioni del cane e del maiale.

Uomo
Oh, nobile figlio mio, dove sei? Dove sei?
Dov'è mio figlio, oh cari che piangete?
Lo avete visto, oh vicini che dormite?

Il cane e il maiale seguono l'uomo, continuando le loro suppliche. Così come Ani di Tebe, al tribunale degli dèi, nega ognuno dei 42 peccati che gli antichi egizi consideravano tabù, essi proclamano la loro innocenza.[2]

Cane
Oh, padrone, che nuotasti con me nelle acque chiare del ruscello,
non ho mai insozzato l'acqua.
Non ho ostacolato il suo fluire.
Non ho mai sottratto l'acqua all'assetato.

Maiale
Oh, padrone, che facesti per me un

giaciglio con l'erba dei campi dorati,
non ho mai inquinato la terra.
Non ho mai rubato la terra.
Non ho mai derubato il povero del suo pane.

Cane
Oh, padrone, che ti stendevi con me fra i campi ad ascoltare il canto degli uccelli,
non li ho mai fatti tacere.
Non ho tagliato gli alberi su cui fanno il nido.
Non li ho privati del cibo.

Maiale
Oh, padrone, che sempre mi desti abbondanza di cibo,
non ho mai invidiato il bambino.
Non ho invidiato i maiali grassi.
Non ho mai odiato nessuno.

Cane
Oh, padrone, che avesti notti strazianti dopo il mio sacrificio,
non ho mai voluto il tuo dolore.
Non ti ho spaventato.
Non ti ho mai odiato.

Cane e Maiale
Oh, padrone, che non mi guardasti negli occhi,
non ho mai voluto il tuo dolore.
Non ti ho spaventato.
Non ti ho mai odiato.

Allo spuntare dell'alba, davanti alla capanna, gli abitanti si radunano ad uno ad uno e iniziano a cantare.

Gente del villaggio
Se~parti~ora~quando~tornerai~Se~parti~ora~quando~tornerai
Dicci~il~giorno~in~cui~tornerai~-
Dicci~il~giorno~in~cui~tornerai
Come~partire~come~partire~lasciando~la~propria~famiglia~amata
Tanti~vicini~devoti~ma~chi~partirà~al~posto~tuo~
Amici~di~una~vita~ma~chi~verrà~con~te~in~quel~luogo~

L'uomo trova il bambino che dorme fra le braccia di una giovane donna e si avvicina a loro. Accarezza il viso del neonato con il palmo delle mani e lo bacia. La donna non sente la presenza dell'uomo.

Uomo
Oh, figlio nato dalla virtù, mio prezioso bambino
che dormi tra le braccia della nostra amica e nulla ti affligge.
Tu non mi vedi ma io ti guardo.
Oh, figlio nato senza colpa, mio prezioso bambino,
il dono che mi hai fatto è la tua vita.
Il dono che ti ho fatto è la mia vita.

Un gruppo di Celibi e Nubili appare tra la folla. Otto Nubili sollevano lentamente la barella su cui giace il corpo dell'uomo battendo i piedi, mentre quattro Celibi danno inizio ai canti [3].

Celibi gementi
A-i-go~~A-i-go~~A-i-go~~A-i-go~~

Quando la Nubile con la campanella inizia una lenta melodia, le Nubili che portano il feretro cantano insieme, facendo un passo avanti e uno indietro, ripetutamente.

Nubile con la campanella
Via~da~casa~Via~da~-
casa~~~Il~nostro~amico~va~via

Nubili che portano il feretro
Via~da~casa~Via~da~-
casa~~~Il~nostro~vicino~va~via
Via~da~casa~Via~da~-
casa~~~Il~nostro~vicino~va~via
Via~da~casa~Via~da~-
casa~~~Il~nostro~vicino~va~via

Celibi gementi
A-i-go~~A-i-go~~A-i-go~~A-i-go~~

L'uomo segue la processione e si avvicina a una donna che piange.

Uomo
Oh, donna, che devi vivere senza colpe, non piangere.
Nostro figlio dorme. Tra le braccia della nostra amica, nostro figlio dorme.
Oh, donna con cui non posso più dividere la vita, asciuga le tue lacrime.
Tieni nostro figlio tra le braccia.
Quando il bambino si sveglia e piange per sua madre, tieni nostro figlio tra le braccia.

Celibi gementi
A-i-go~~A-i-go~~A-i-go~~A-i-go~~

Il corteo funebre inizia a girare lentamente intorno al villaggio, cantando i ricordi del defunto. A intermittenza, si sente un ritornello indecifrabile.

Nubile con la campanella
Par~te~~Par~te~~Il~nostro~ami-
co~par~te

Nubili che portano il feretro
Par~te~~Par~te~~Il~nostro~ami-
co~par~te
Lo~lo-lo~lo-o-o-o~e-hwa-neom-
cha~lo-o-hwa~
Lo~lo-lo~lo-o-o-o~e-hwa-neom-
cha~lo-o-hwa~

Nubile con la campanella
Par~te~~Par~te~~Il~nostro~ami-
co~par~te

Nubili che portano il feretro
Par~te~~Par~te~~Il~nostro~ami-
co~par~te
Lo~lo-lo~lo-o-o-o~e-hwa-neom-
cha~lo-o-hwa~
Lo~lo-lo~lo-o-o-o~e-hwa-neom-
cha~lo-o-hwa~

Nubile con la campanella
Il nostro amico con cui ci siamo nascosti in una grotta angusta e con cui abbiamo pianto

Nubili che portano il feretro
Il nostro vicino insieme a cui correvamo quel giorno di venti funesti

Lo~lo-lo~lo-o-o-o~e-hwa-neom-
cha~lo-o-hwa~
Lo~lo-lo~lo-o-o-o~e-hwa-neom-
cha~lo-o-hwa~

Nubile con la campanella
Tre notti e quattro giorni senza riposare

Nubili che portano il feretro
Abbiamo corso senza fermarci
Lo~lo-lo~lo-o-o-o~e-hwa-neom-
cha~lo-o-hwa~

Lo~lo-lo~lo-o-o-o~e-hwa-neom-
cha~lo-o-hwa~

Nubile con la campanella
I capricci dei venti impetuosi

Nubili che portano il feretro
Correndo da un posto all'altro
Lo~lo-lo~lo-o-o-o~e-hwa-neom-
cha~lo-o-hwa~
Lo~lo-lo~lo-o-o-o~e-hwa-neom-
cha~lo-o-hwa~

Nubile con la campanella
Correndo da un posto all'altro

Nubili che portano il feretro
Correndo da un posto all'altro
Lo~lo-lo~lo-o-o-o~e-hwa-neom-
cha~lo-o-hwa~
Lo~lo-lo~lo-o-o-o~e-hwa-neom-
cha~lo-o-hwa~

Celibi gementi
A-i-go~~A-i-go~~A-i-go~~A-i-go~~

La donna che piange canta dietro alle Nubili che portano il feretro.

Donna
A-i-go~~A-i-go~~ straziante e dolente
Quando giungerà la primavera, mio marito tornerà?
Quanto lontana è la strada per il paradiso, perché egli va via?

Nubili che portano il feretro
Lo~lo-lo~lo-o-o-o~e-hwa-neom-
cha~lo-o-hwa~
Lo~lo-lo~lo-o-o-o~e-hwa-neom-
cha~lo-o-hwa~

Celibi gementi
A-i-go~~A-i-go~~A-i-go~~A-i-go~~

L'uomo si avvicina alla donna e le accarezza amorevolmente la schiena.

Uomo
Oh, donna, che sei per me come l'aria per gli uccelli, asciuga le tue lacrime.
Non c'è albero in questo mondo che non sia scosso dal vento.
Anche se vivi cent'anni, e cancelli ogni ansia, e i giorni di malattia e torpore, non vivi più di quarant'anni.
Che sia troppo presto o troppo tardi, è giunto per me il momento di andare.

Celibi gementi
A-i-go~~A-i-go~~A-i-go~~A-i-go~~

Il canto dell'uomo si fonde con la canzone delle Nubili che portano il feretro.

Nubile con la campanella
Per quanto son devoti i vicini, chi partirà al suo posto?

Nubili che portano il feretro
Per quanto son devoti gli amici, chi partirà al suo posto?
Lo~lo-lo~lo-o-o-o~e-hwa-neom-
cha~lo-o-hwa
Lo~lo-lo~lo-o-o-o~e-hwa-neom-
cha~lo-o-hwa

Nubile con la campanella
La strada da cui non puoi tornare indietro, com'è che devi farla da solo?

Nubili che portano il feretro
Non hai paura della montagna, non hai paura dell'oceano?
Lo~lo-lo~lo-o-o-o~e-hwa-neom-cha~lo-o-hwa
Lo~lo-lo~lo-o-o-o~e-hwa-neom-cha~lo-o-hwa

Celibi gementi
A-i-go~~A-i-go~~A-i-go~~A-i-go~~

Mentre le Nubili col feretro iniziano a risalire la ripida collina, la Nubile con la campanella alza la voce e canta a un ritmo incalzante, dando forza alle portatrici.
I brevi lamenti vengono ripetuti in rapida successione.

Nubile con la campanella
La mia vita senza amore il mio destino senza figli

Nubili che portano il feretro
E-hwa-neom-cha~lo-o-hwa~lo-o-hwa~~E-hwa-neom-cha~lo-o-hwa~-lo-o-hwa~~

Nubile con la campanella
Terrò tuo figlio in braccio e carezzerò la schiena alla tua amata

Nubili che portano il feretro
E-hwa-neom-cha~lo-o-hwa~lo-o-hwa~~E-hwa-neom-cha~lo-o-hwa~-lo-o-hwa~~

Nubile con la campanella
Non preoccuparti dei venti funesti, nasconderò tuo figlio in una grotta.

Nubili che portano il feretro
E-hwa-neom-cha~lo-o-hwa~lo-o-hwa~~E-hwa-neom-cha~lo-o-hwa~-lo-o-hwa~~

Nubile con la campanella
Non preoccuparti per tua moglie che non mangia più, io la nutrirò e conforterò.

Nubili che portano il feretro
E-hwa-neom-cha~lo-o-hwa~lo-o-hwa~~E-hwa-neom-cha~lo-o-hwa~-lo-o-hwa~~

Celibi gementi
A-i-go~~A-i-go~~A-i-go~~A-i-go~~

L'uomo canta per la processione.

Uomo
Oh, mio amore, che sei come l'acqua per i pesci, alzati
Prima che di nuovo il lago si prosciughi
Oh, amici miei che correste con me nella grotta, alzatevi
Prima che i venti funesti colpiscano di nuovo
La gente del villaggio con affanni e parole dimentica e si alza
Prima che gli uccelli tacciano di nuovo

Il cane e il maiale cantano mentre si avvicinano al corteo funebre.

Cane e Maiale
Vado vado vado nel posto in cui vivevo
Padrone amato, cara gente del villaggio, non preoccupatevi più per me.
All'inizio venni dalla foresta all'inizio venni dalla montagna
Qui e là sarò felice questo e quello mangerò

Pur grassoccio sono ancora bravo a correre
La tua casa piccina così accogliente non era
Ma m'hai nutrito e ospitato, che altro potevo fare?
Ascolta cattivo padrone ho dimenticato i patimenti sofferti
Ascolta buon padrone: ho vissuto una bella vita
Non preoccuparti più per me e vivi una bella vita
Senza sciagure, senza sventure, vivi una bella vita
Vado vado vado nel posto in cui vivevo

Tornati dalla sepoltura in mare, la famiglia, gli amici e i vicini del giovane defunto si adornano di fiori e foglie e si radunano davanti alla capanna. Anche il cane e il maiale, adorni di ghirlande, si uniscono al gruppo. Tutti iniziano a cantare e a ballare.

Tutti insieme all'unisono
Bel giorno piacevole giorno, il giorno è incantevole
Kwae-ji-na~ching-ching-na-ne~~Kwae-ji-na~ching-ching-na-ne~~
Vado vado a giocare nei campi erbosi vado a giocare
Kwae-ji-na~ching-ching-na-ne~~Kwae-ji-na~ching-ching-na-ne~~
Voi fate verdi abiti d'erba e uccelli graziosi diventano amici
Kwae-ji-na~ching-ching-na-ne~~Kwae-ji-na~ching-ching-na-ne~~
Attraverso attraverso attraverso il ruscello attraverso
Kwae-ji-na~ching-ching-na-ne~~Kwae-ji-na~ching-ching-na-ne~~
Voi cucinate con l'acqua tersa del ruscello e i pesciolini diventano amici
Kwae-ji-na~ching-ching-na-ne~~Kwae-ji-na~ching-ching-na-ne~~
Vecchi e giovani del villaggio, lasciate perdere perdere perdere
Kwae-ji-na~ching-ching-na-ne~~Kwae-ji-na~ching-ching-na-ne~~
Una volta partiti non si può più tornare, perciò lasciate perdere e non litigate
Kwae-ji-na~ching-ching-na-ne~~Kwae-ji-na~ching-ching-na-ne~~

Mentre tutti ballano e cantano insieme, l'anima dell'uomo raggiunge le porte dell'oltretomba.

Uomo
Oh, dèi che incontro per la prima volta,
perché sbarrate la via alla mia anima, chiedendomi i miei peccati?
È un peccato sgobbare nei campi grondando sudore per sfamare i miei cari?
È un peccato scaldare la casa dei vecchi genitori per non fargli soffrire il freddo?
È un peccato dar da mangiare al cane che segue ogni mio passo?
Non commettere adulterio, e perciò ho amato una sola donna.
Vagherai da solo come un rinoceronte, e così ho percorso la via lontana dell'oltretomba senza compagni.

Oh, perdonatemi dèi se non ricordo ognuno dei vostri nomi.
Non chiedetemi più nulla sui peccati che non commisi e lasciate andare la mia anima.
Dove destinarla spetta a voi, perciò che posso dire io?

Ma se volete rimandarmi nel mondo da cui vengo, fatemi tornare come albero.
Fiore o erba, uccello o verme, cane o maiale, che scelta ho?
Avete fatto gli uomini, così si dice, nel migliore degli stampi.
Ma io dico che avete fatto alberi assai migliori degli uomini.

1. Alcune parti del dialogo fra il Necroforo anziano e il Coro dei Celibi anziani sono state adattate dai versi del coro e dei personaggi della tragedia greca Agamennone di Eschilo.

2. Il canto del cane e del maiale, in cui si dichiara ripetutamente che essi non hanno recato danni alla terra, all'acqua o ad altri esseri viventi, è ispirato alla "Dichiarazione di innocenza" del Libro dei morti egizio. Con essa le anime dei defunti, alle porte dell'oltretomba, proclamano agli dèi la loro innocenza negando di aver commesso nella vita terrena una serie di atti considerati malvagi.

3. La processione funebre della pièce si ispira a quella di Yeongdo, una piccola isola a sud della penisola coreana, dove il feretro viene portato da sole donne. Riguardo al modo in cui gli oratori si rivolgono agli altri per alleviare la paura di lasciare questo mondo, ho fatto riferimento alla traduzione coreana del Bardo Thodol, un testo tibetano che viene recitato dai monaci o dai familiari presso il corpo del morto o in presenza del morente. Riguardo ai testi delle canzoni cantate dai personaggi dello spettacolo, ho rielaborato versi tratti dalla Bibbia, dal Corano, dal Suttanipāta e dalla Bhagavad Gita, nonché da canti funebri coreani, modificandoli per adattarli al contesto e allo svolgimento dello spettacolo.

4. Nota del traduttore: Aigo è un'espressione coreana che corrisponde sia a "Oh mio Dio!" che a "Ahi!" o "Ahia!". È un'espressione usata comunemente per esprimere uno shock o una sorpresa, ma viene pronunciata anche dai familiari del defunto, soprattutto dalle donne, durante la veglia o il funerale.

5. Nota del traduttore: questo ritornello è un ritornello corale della tradizione coreana che accompagna in genere musiche e danze popolari che esprimono gioia e piacere in varie celebrazioni delle comunità contadine.

Vie d'uscita sintetiche
Alice Bucknell

Vie d'uscita sintetiche
Alice Bucknell

Una roccia, un fiume, un edificio, una partitura. Il Gioco, quando ancora veniva chiamato così, era cominciato in maniera abbastanza semplice. Era uno dei modi per ammazzare il tempo durante la terza pandemia globale in meno di dieci anni, quando i lockdown sembravano fondersi in un unico periodo infinitamente lungo passato al chiuso. Si trascorreva il tempo per lo più in solitudine, ciondolando all'interno della propria biosfera personale: un rifugio climatizzato lontano da tutto il caos che regnava Là Fuori: incendi devastanti, livelli di ozono letali, estinzione di molte specie. Una bolla in cui progettare un nuovo mondo. Un tempo trascorso a sognare alternative.

Con il senno di poi, ho capito che l'immediato successo del Gioco era riconducibile alle sue analogie con altri processi e strumenti tecnologici che erano diventati una presenza irrinunciabile nelle case durante le pandemie precedenti. Questi strumenti, di varia complessità, andavano dai puzzle digitali quotidiani, dai giochi linguistici e dai generatori text-to-image agli spazi sociali virtuali, ai filtri AR e ai dispositivi video per trasmettere online i propri esercizi di ginnastica. Ma le maggiori affinità il Gioco ce le aveva con le popolarissime applicazioni di mindfulness "Digital Earth", presentate inizialmente come esercizi di terapia psicodinamica autoguidati. Sotto forma di dirette streaming naturalistiche via satellite da zone del pianeta ancora incontaminate, sono state progettate per aiutare gli iscritti a elaborare meglio i complessi momenti di sofferenza legati al cambiamento climatico durante i lunghi periodi di lockdown.

Molti dei pazienti che ho intervistato durante le mie ricerche sul Gioco hanno riferito una sorta di dissociazione mente-corpo dovuta all'isolamento sensoriale dello Spazio Interno. Una donna ha evidenziato una profonda depressione causata dall'impossibilità di sentire il sole sul viso a primavera, il crepitio delle foglie sotto i piedi in autunno e lo sferzare del gelido vento invernale sulla pelle. Il corpo cercava ciò che non poteva più sentire, ma il cervello non riusciva a elaborare quell'assenza. Era come se la deprivazione sensoriale avesse ristretto anche la percezione del proprio Sé, negando all'individuo il diritto di essere nel mondo.

Per il progetto del Gioco, mi era stato chiesto di riprodurre alcuni di questi scenari, allo scopo, sottinteso, di ridare vita ad alcune di queste sensazioni. Il committente si era documentato sul funzionamento del gioco. Ha compreso il valore del conflitto e della collaborazione, quello di un tema e di una trama avvincenti, nonché l'importanza della veste estetica e delle ricompense. In un certo senso, l'aspetto e l'atmosfera del Gioco non erano disallineati rispetto ai popolari Extended Play (EP) usciti quell'anno: mondi virtuali accessibili attraverso costose tute multisensoriali. Ma per l'impatto sociale che il Gioco si proponeva, il brief e il mondo che rappresentava erano destinati ad essere più complessi.

Un recente articolo di psicologia sociale, che all'uscita aveva avuto un grande richiamo, perorava l'idea di una "percezione sintetica", ovvero un processo capace di generare sensazioni reali attraverso ambienti artificiali. Non importava che il contesto ambientale teso a suscitare questi stati emotivi fosse completamente artefatto, costruito all'interno di un motore di gioco e caricato sul cloud del Gioco. Anzi, questa simulazione rappresentava la migliore delle soluzioni: era preferibile ricordare poco o nulla delle condizioni del mondo Là Fuori. Ma la piacevole sensazione che si prova guardando un modello di palma 8K che oscilla nella luce soffusa del crepuscolo nel sud della California oppure quel brivido sublime che si sente alla vista di un branco di balene simulate che saltano fuori da un rendering patinato e pixelato dell'Oceano Pacifico produce un'emozione totalmente autentica. Fino a dove potrebbero spingersi questi vividi stati emotivi al di là del contesto degli ambienti sintetici che li hanno stimolati?

Mi hanno chiesto di costruire un mondo basato sull'idea di un futuro condiviso. Una politica sociale ormai obsoleta ai nostri giorni, simile al concetto di "terra comune" dell'Europa medievale. Ma sentendosi più uniti, i committenti del Gioco credevano che presto sarebbe nato un meccanismo di mutuo consenso, di cui non si ha memoria nel mondo di oggi. Pensavano che questa abbondanza di sensazioni nello spazio del gioco potesse determinare quella che chiamavano una via d'uscita sintetica: una porta per entrare in un mondo di affetto condiviso che era stato abbandonato da tempo nel mondo Là Fuori. Questa idea mi incuriosiva. Inoltre, ero senza lavoro dall'inizio dell'ultima pandemia e non avevo una teoria alternativa da controproporre. Così mi misi al lavoro.

> La Storia ricorda il futuro; il futuro reinventa in continuazione il passato.

Ho iniziato a lavorare al Gioco l'anno in cui la popolazione mondiale avrebbe dovuto raggiungere il numero massimo. Nonostante la prolungata permacrisi, prevista da tempo dagli economisti e dagli esperti climatici nei primi anni Venti del 2000, eravamo riusciti a spingerci oltre i numeri previsti con largo anticipo. Ma sembrava che più la popolazione aumentava e meno si investiva sul futuro del pianeta. Forse non c'è da meravigliarsi, visto che il compito di immaginare il mondo in un'ottica diversa veniva delegato di volta in volta agli ultimi arrivati. Man mano che gli effetti più dannosi della crisi climatica si estendevano fino a diventare onnipresenti a livello globale, le persone mettevano sempre più distanza fra loro invece di essere più unite. La situazione poteva essere diversa nello spazio di percezione sintetica del Gioco?

Ho progettato il livello Roccia per primo. Era perfetto per i principianti: minimo sforzo e massima resa. L'intento era attirare nel cerchio magico del Gioco anche il giocatore meno incline e instillare il desiderio di completare tutti e quattro i livelli. Il livello Roccia inizia in un magnifico campo ricoperto d'erba, rigoglioso. È un luogo che sembra intimamente familiare, ma che nessuno sulla Terra ha mai conosciuto in prima persona. Per trovare l'ispirazione, ho rovistato in fondo agli archivi multimediali digitali del committente e ho scovato una serie di sfondi desktop a tema naturalistico di sistemi operativi per computer risalenti agli anni Novanta del 1900. Con scenari piani, ricchi di atmosfera e iperrealistici, volevo evocare la sensazione di uno spazio di ampio respiro.

Il giocatore entra nel livello al tramonto del sole. Cominciano a spuntare le prime stelle nel cielo, che passa dall'arancione al grigio e al blu notte. Lo spazio è avvolto dalle montagne e dalla loro fitta coltre di nebbia. Una brezza si alza dalle montagne e fa frusciare l'erba alta. Se il giocatore possiede l'ultimo modello della tuta Extended Play, percepirà questo movimento come un piacevole formicolio che parte dalla sommità della testa e si diffonde fino alla base della spina dorsale. Una sensazione artefatta di calore.

Come il resto del Gioco, il livello Roccia richiede una strategia di base, incentrata sulle dinamiche sociali di un obiettivo comune. I giocatori sono chiamati a collaborare quando, fra l'erba alta, devono cercare rocce speciali: pezzi neri, grezzi e scintillanti di silicio compatto. Non sanno cosa devono cercare; le istruzioni sono intenzionalmente vaghe, per aumentare il coinvolgimento emotivo dei partecipanti al Gioco. I giocatori copieranno le azioni degli altri giocatori o capiranno istintivamente la situazione e finiranno per afferrare una delle rocce di silicio e riportarla al punto di partenza: uno spazio comune con dei cerchi concentrici incisi profondamente nella terra umida. All'interno di dieci cerchi ci sono dieci rocce. Una volta giunti a questa tappa, i giocatori devono aspettare.

Durante l'attesa, il tempo del Gioco accelererà; può succedere che dieci giorni passino in meno di un'ora. Quando la luna piena spunterà al di sopra delle montagne all'orizzonte, le rocce inizieranno a canticchiare. Quella che inizia come una sommessa melodia si trasforma in una vera e propria canzone che riecheggia nel campo disseminato di silicio. La visuale del giocatore si sposta verso l'alto e verso il cielo. Intorno a loro, l'erba calpestata – testimonianza viva della perlustrazione effettuata per trovare le pietre – assume gradualmente la forma di un cerchio nel grano. Il disegno si rivela lentamente attraverso una telecamera di tracciamento verso l'alto, con messa a fuoco all'infinito. Staziona in volo sopra di loro, con le eliche che ronzano leggermente; ricorda un colibrì. Prova a chiudere gli occhi. Riesci a visualizzarlo?

Molto tempo fa il fiume inondava questo luogo. Ogni cinque o sei anni, soffocato dall'acqua piovana che precipitava giù dalle montagne, rompeva gli argini, trascinando verso il mare ogni traccia di civiltà umana. Ma il fiume non stava straripando: stava tornando. Contro l'avanzare lineare del progresso umano, l'acqua è proteiforme; ricorda tutto.

Il livello Fiume è più complesso. Richiede quello che io chiamo un Salto sintetico: un passaggio dal corpo fisico del giocatore nel mondo al corpo simulato del fiume. Questo processo è impegnativo e può avvenire solo in maniera organica attraverso le tattiche del giocatore; nel Gioco non ci sono trucchi.

Per completare con successo il livello Salto, il giocatore deve effettuare due cambi di stato. Il primo, da corpo fisico a corpo virtuale, è del tutto naturale: lo facciamo tutti da anni. Il secondo è molto più difficile: il giocatore Salta dal corpo di un umano a quello di un non-umano, il Fiume. Per farlo, deve capire che il suo personaggio e il Fiume non sono due entità separate, ma sono lo stesso corpo. Una volta completato il Salto, non c'è alcun cambiamento evidente nelle meccaniche di gioco o nell'ambiente: è sempre lo stesso Fiume. Ma il giocatore percepirà il cambiamento attraverso la sua tuta EP: decentralizzata, si propaga in questo corpo condiviso, facendo scoprire nuove sensazioni in ogni parte del corpo-Fiume: bocca, gomito e piede.

Questo corpo ecosistemico è più dei sensi; è una corrente di sensazioni che si propagano ovunque. I suoi flussi alluvionali scandiscono il tempo non lineare che consideriamo esperienza. Come gli anelli di un albero caduto su cui si passano distrattamente le dita, è un tempo profondo reso tangibile dalla morte. Quando inspiri ed espiri, la vita scorre attraverso il pannello di controllo del sistema nervoso, alimentando il pool di cellule che unisce il tuo corpo al corpo ecologico della Terra. L'acqua ritorna e il corpo ricorda.

Nei cambi di stato di un clima compromesso, si parla di rivoluzioni come se l'unica cosa da fare con il passato fosse separarsi da lui. Un doloroso distacco. Questo è ovviamente impossibile, tanto nell'ambiente simulato del Gioco quanto nel mondo Là Fuori. Il trucco è riorientare la mappa. Far sì che le persone guardino in modo diverso ciò che già esiste.

All'inizio del mio lavoro di game designer, ben prima di progettare il Gioco, ho imparato quanto sia importante il fallimento. Non nel senso di creare un brutto gioco a cui non giocherà nessuno, ma di capire come funziona il fallimento nel mondo dei giochi, quali altri mondi apre. La storia dei giochi vede videogiochi interminabili come Tetris o PacMan in cui non si può vincere, quindi il giocatore può solo imparare a ritardare la sconfitta. Sono l'opposto dei classici giochi di ruolo, in cui anche dopo aver completato tutte le quest e guadagnato tutti i badge, si rimane a vagare in quell'ambiente open world che da regno passa a essere contenitore per tutta la durata del gioco. Non c'è una fine, non c'è soddisfazione; uno spazio in cui vincere inizia gradualmente a sembrare un modo molto speciale di perdere.

Man mano che i processori e le schede grafiche diventavano più avanzate, i glitch lanciavano un altro alert di possibile fallimento. Mi riferisco allo spazio di gioco ai confini del mondo in cui un giocatore andava a finire accidentalmente, e per sempre, finché non spegneva la console surriscaldata. Come potrebbe essere un gioco capace di accettare il proprio fallimento? L'esperienza di gioco assomiglierebbe alla lettura di un racconto di Borges? Una biblioteca infinita, dove l'universo è contenuto in un solo volume; un sistema perfettamente impossibile che prende vita nel momento in cui viene letto?

Il livello Edificio inizia sulle rive di un lago. Il cielo è di un viola livido, il paesaggio è rosso cenere; un gigantesco sole concavo, renderizzato in scaglie blu iridescenti, giace semisommerso all'orizzonte, evidenziando il profilo di una magnifica torre. È quasi completa! Capisci che sta a te completarla. Ma c'è un problema. Ad alcuni giocatori viene detto il contrario: le fondamenta sono fallaci, la struttura non è solida, lo stile è datato. Bisogna demolirla e costruirla ex novo.

Ogni volta che aggiungi un mattone, una finestra di dialogo ti informa che un altro mattone della struttura è misteriosamente scomparso. Ogni volta che aggiungi un nuovo mattone, ne viene immediatamente rimosso un numero doppio rispetto alla quantità precedente. 2, 4, 8, 16, 32, 64, 128... presto l'edificio inizierà ad assomigliare a un'antica rovina, con la sua facciata crivellata che continua a perdere pezzi. Nelle tabelle dei punteggi più bassi, il tuo nome lampeggia davanti ai tuoi occhi.

Nella teoria dei giochi, i risultati sono considerati in equilibrio di Nash quando la comprensione delle strategie degli altri giocatori non spinge nessun giocatore a cambiare la propria strategia. Metti un mattone e perdi. Ma lo specchio tra il gioco e la realtà a volte si appanna, diventando un vuoto immenso, imperscrutabile. Quando rimuovi un mattone, i due mattoni accanto spariscono all'istante. Guardando attraverso i buchi della struttura, si intravede l'ombra di un movimento dall'altra parte. Nel mondo reale, al di fuori del regolamento unitario dello spazio di gioco, gli studi sociologici dimostrano costantemente che i gruppi scelgono in genere di collaborare, anche quando tradire gli altri può portare a una migliore ricompensa individuale. L'ostacolo al progresso sembra improvvisamente una porta aperta, un invito. È nella natura umana agire insieme; è necessario l'ambiente sintetico di un mondo creato dal gioco a ricordarcelo. Rimuovendo altri mattoni cominciano ad apparire i volti degli altri giocatori. L'edificio si deforma e trema, e la torre e il livello crollano insieme.

Vista attraverso gli occhi di una macchina costruita su sistemi di credenze antropocentriche, qualsiasi visione del futuro è un rigurgito frankensteinizzato del passato. Il mondo che i giocatori pensavano di scoprire era un mondo che già esisteva. Lungi dal prefigurare un senso di cultura profetica, i nostri progressi tecnologici ci hanno portato in un ciclo di ritorno periodico. Come si può spezzare questo ciclo? Uscendo dalla nostra mitologia umano-centrica ed entrando in una mitologia Terra-centrica.

Quando ho creato il Gioco, volevo uscire dall'autorità totalizzante del linguaggio. Mentre mi infilavo una tuta EP per fare da giocatore pilota dei primi tre livelli, ho capito che la risposta si trovava all'interno del brief di percezione sintetica. Liberandosi del linguaggio e del suo impulso nevrotico a costruire significato, i giocatori potrebbero arrivare a una comprensione più profonda del proprio Sé e del pianeta, spingersi oltre la scissione cartesiana di mente e corpo e della dicotomia antropocentrica di umano e non umano. Con mia grande sorpresa, mentre lavoravo al completamento del gioco, questi due obiettivi - il mio e quello del committente - si sono intrecciati sempre di più. Il suono sembrava essere il senso più collettivo e la musica la forma più intenzionale di ascolto. Era quindi ovvio che il livello finale del Gioco dovesse prevedere la creazione collaborativa di una partitura. Nell'ambiente sintetico del gioco, questa partitura potrebbe favorire non solo una connessione più profonda tra i giocatori, ma diventare anche un ponte tra mondi umani e non umani.

Un giorno, la siccità provoca incendi sulle montagne; il giorno dopo, un'alluvione spazza via l'ultima parte della città vecchia. Come dare un senso a un mondo che si fa beffe dei precedenti storici e dei sistemi di conoscenza a posteriori? Era chiaro che avevamo bisogno di nuovi modelli. Là Fuori, gli ecologisti hanno dato vita a un innovativo metodo di visualizzazione dei dati basato sulla IA, noto come State-Space Modelling (SSM), per mappare gli indirizzi sempre più aberranti di un nuovo, strano clima. Poiché è un tipo di modello che porta a errori di misurazione nel tempo ecologico quando affronta il disordine dei dati in tempo reale, l'SSM appare come un'importante metafora che fa comprendere meglio le condizioni del mondo in cui viviamo oggi, qualcosa che va oltre la paralizzante mentalità da profeta di sventure delle previsioni climatiche.

Nell'aria riciclata e viziata della mia biosfera, passavo un'infinità di ore a scorrere le raccolte SSM online, provando uno strano senso di soddisfazione nelle loro linee sregolate e frenetiche. La sovrapposizione dei modelli di migrazione dei leoni marini sulla costa del Pacifico con i livelli d'acqua del fiume Colorado degli ultimi due secoli; gli spostamenti dei due ultimi gorilla di montagna nelle foreste d'alta quota dell'Uganda proiettati sulla superficie in crescita delle piantagioni di banane sintetiche che stanno venendo su nelle pianure occidentali del Paese; il modello di volo di una sterna artica mappato sullo sviluppo di infrastrutture di bambù stampate in 3D a Hong Kong. C'era un misticismo in questa interpolazione dei dati, una suggestiva interconnessione che gli esseri umani non potevano ancora decifrare. Per me, indicavano una sorta di lingua ignota che si estendeva oltre i confini dell'immaginazione umana.

Come tributo nerd a questi bellissimi e impenetrabili grafici e ai loro sistemi logici nascosti, ho deciso di sottoporne qualcuno a uno script di sonificazione per trasformare questi dati ecologici in musica, ideando nel contempo il mio modello di spazio di stato multidimensionale. I giocatori sono, naturalmente, liberi di improvvisare mentre creano in collaborazione le loro partiture, ma la struttura musicale portante che guiderà il livello finale del Gioco verrà dalla Terra stessa. I dati in tempo reale, l'energia e il movimento della vita non umana del pianeta sono stati registrati dal mondo Là Fuori, e poi sintetizzati collettivamente in una canzone.

A differenza della musica, un tempo gli esseri umani facevano affidamento esclusivamente sulle parole; usavano la tecnologia come infrastruttura cognitiva, modellando il mondo che li circondava e rafforzando la loro supremazia sulle altre forme di vita. Ma grazie ai rapidi progressi dei modelli di elaborazione del linguaggio naturale basati sulla IA, il linguaggio è stato modellato più dalle macchine che dai loro omologhi umani. Alla fine, il linguaggio si è dissociato dalla coscienza. La narrazione dell'unicità umana che esso portava con sé è diventata un elemento irrilevante; il linguaggio era sintetico come l'intelligenza artificiale costruita per modellarlo.

In quel periodo, gli esseri umani si sono orientati sempre più verso strumenti di comunicazione non linguistici, come la musica, la gestualità e il movimento. Hanno sollecitato i sensi per rianimare ciò che il linguaggio aveva abbandonato centomila anni fa: stati alterati che trascendono le vaghe approssimazioni associate alle parole. In quell'epoca, la comunicazione non verbale di sogni e stati emotivi complessi nel Gioco in tempo reale è diventato un fatto naturale. Ascoltando le canzoni climatiche composte da un'intelligenza artificiale interspecie, le persone hanno imparato a comunicare meglio con il secondo corpo della Terra. Un'intelligenza ecologica condivisa, creata insieme da umani, non umani e macchine, ha "ha aperto la via" a una nuova mitologia del pianeta.

Grazie al sistema musicale multispecie del quarto livello, il Gioco ha riscosso un grande successo.

È venuto fuori un potente ciclo di ritorno tra le canzoni generate nel Gioco e la partitura della vita non umana sulla Terra; la modellazione interspecie del gioco si è diffusa lentamente nella realtà. Là Fuori, nessuno sapeva con certezza chi stesse facendo la mappatura e la modellazione - umani o altro - e ben presto queste distinzioni cominciarono a dissolversi. Man mano che il mondo Là Fuori e il mondo del Gioco si trasformavano in immagini speculari l'uno dell'altro, le condizioni climatiche che separavano i mondi umani da quelli non umani sono diventate meno estreme. Le persone hanno cominciato a uscire dalle loro biosfere: esitanti all'inizio, limitate nell'esposizione al mondo per via delle tute EP, e poi disinvolte, scoprendo nella comunicazione sensoriale con le rocce, i fiumi, i modelli di vento e altri fattori ambientali che avevano costruito durante il gioco una guida accessibile. Il ciclo di ritorno sintetico del Gioco ha gradualmente alimentato un nuovo modo di essere e percepire il mondo; lo Spazio Interno e il Là Fuori sono diventati una cosa sola.

La Shifting Baseline Syndrome (Sindrome da spostamento dei punti di riferimento) indica un cambiamento graduale nel modo in cui un sistema viene valutato, di solito con un controllo incrociato rispetto a punti di riferimento precedenti. Tuttavia, questa lenta progressione del cambiamento viene spesso registrata come un non evento; la memoria a breve termine copre i cambiamenti su larga scala resi visibili nel tempo profondo. Un fiume, apparentemente diretto verso la sopravvivenza, si prosciuga nel corso degli anni. Un edificio, continuamente riprogettato per resistere a una minaccia futura, non viene mai completato. Un mondo, ridotto in sintesi, adotta gradualmente processi di costruzione del significato alternativi per trascendere sé stesso, il linguaggio.

Entrando nel corpo sonoro del mondo, i partecipanti al Gioco hanno liberato una coscienza ecologica che potrebbe essere paragonata al tempo profondo. Il modello di causa-effetto della storia recente è diventato ovviamente un'anomalia, qualcosa a cui una consapevolezza ecosistemica potrebbe dare una nuova rotta verso un futuro condiviso. Lo spazio di percezione sintetica del Gioco ha creato una via d'uscita sintetica tra giocatori e non umani, tra un ambiente virtuale e la Terra, anticipando una nuova mitologia nel processo. Mi piace vederla come una risposta, ma in realtà questa via d'uscita ha sollevato altre domande: la costruzione del significato è sempre una strada a doppio senso, una danza tra i narratori e il loro pubblico, come i movimenti in una partitura improvvisata. A quali nuovi mondi condivisi porta questa canzone? Impossibile da dire, ma facile da ascoltare.

Comunità ecologiche
Yunjeong Han

Comunità ecologiche
Yunjeong Han

La civiltà ecologica

Se mai ci sarà ancora una civiltà sulla Terra nel 2086, si tratterà di una civiltà ecologica. Una civiltà industriale anti-ecologica che superi la biocapacità della Terra probabilmente esisterà ancora in scala assai ridotta rispetto a oggi, ma non la chiameremo più "civiltà". Le popolazioni che non si saranno dimostrate capaci di adattarsi alle rapide trasformazioni del pianeta o a costruire una civiltà ecologica vivranno nella continua e disperata ricerca di sopravvivere, come si vede in certi film post-apocalittici.

Cos'è una civiltà e cos'è una civiltà ecologica?

Una civiltà è un modello individuabile nella storia dell'umanità e si lega ai fondamenti della cosmologia e della natura, alla produzione e all'uso dell'energia e della materia, alle forme di potere che guidano i governi, all'integrazione, nonché ai valori, all'etica e ai sistemi educativi che ne costituiscono la sintesi. Tuttavia, non è mai esistita una civiltà perfetta e tutte le civiltà hanno intrapreso il cammino verso l'estinzione poiché i punti di forza su cui sono state costruite si sono spesso trasformati nei punti deboli responsabili del loro declino. Il pensiero materialista e meccanicista moderno ha favorito lo sviluppo della scienza, della tecnologia e delle forze produttive, ma ha anche portato la civiltà industriale a una condizione di conflitto con la natura.

Una civiltà ecologica è una civiltà costruita secondo i principi dell'ecosistema in cui si trova. Secondo Jeremy Lent, "il modo in cui gli ecosistemi si autoregolano ci fornisce il modello da seguire per organizzare la società umana in maniera da produrre abbondanza sostenibile. Gli esseri viventi prosperano quando sviluppano molteplici relazioni simbiotiche e reciproche, nelle quali ciascuno dà e riceve". Finora, la civiltà è stata considerata un'antagonista della natura, che va conquistata per soddisfare i bisogni dell'uomo. Oggi invece sappiamo che la forma migliore di civiltà è quella in armonia con la natura.[1]

La dichiarazione "Gaia 2.0" evidenzia la necessità di cambiare la struttura della società secondo i tre principi operativi di Gaia, scientificamente provati.[2] 1) Un ecosistema terrestre materialmente chiuso: al posto dei combustibili fossili, invenzione insostenibile che interrompe il ciclo della materia, dobbiamo utilizzare l'energia solare e passare a un'economia circolare. 2) Le reti microbiche che danno origine ai cicli biogeochimici della Terra: per un'economia circolare di successo, è necessario sostenere una rete di soggetti umani in grado di favorire una comunicazione orizzontale, una ricca diversità funzionale e un controllo decentrato. 3) L'autoregolazione di Gaia: nella situazione attuale, in cui è difficile mantenere l'equilibrio nello stato naturale, l'autoconsapevolezza umana svolge un ruolo di capitale importanza e può essere ottenuta attraverso politiche di transizione e la creazione di infrastrutture e istituzioni (scientifiche) sensoriali che mostrino il divario tra realtà e illusione.

Con lo sguardo rivolto al globale, è nostro dovere riorganizzare il locale. Nel perseguire un'idea comune di civiltà ecologica, è necessario costruire una rete di civiltà ecologiche per favorire l'autosufficienza e la coesistenza a livello locale. Il filosofo Alfred North Whitehead ci ha lasciato un grande insegnamento sulla transizione di civiltà che dobbiamo compiere. "[Gli esseri umani] possono persuadere o essere persuasi attraverso la divulgazione di alternative, buone o cattive che siano. La civiltà incarna la più nobile delle alternative poiché attraverso la sua intrinseca forza di persuasione mantiene l'ordine sociale. Ecco perché c'è sempre un elemento di irrequietezza in una civiltà perché la sensibilità alle idee porta con sé curiosità, avventura, cambiamento.[3] La civiltà dovrebbe rifiutarsi di avviarsi verso il declino accontentandosi del presente. Dovrebbe impegnarsi in un continuo sviluppo, perseguendo con zelo e fiducia idee che sfidino l'inerzia del sistema. Ciò di cui abbiamo bisogno ora è un'avventura verso la civiltà ecologica.

La nascita di Ecotopia

Il romanzo futuristico Ecotopia (1975) di Ernest Callenbach descrive la civiltà che l'umanità deve costruire per poter sopravvivere.[4] La California settentrionale e gli Stati di Oregon e Washington escono dall'Unione federale degli Stati Uniti per formare una nazione indipendente chiamata

Ecotopia. Circolano voci su Ecotopia, che ha chiuso i suoi confini per una transizione ecologica efficace. Vent'anni dopo l'indipendenza, il giornalista newyorchese Will Weston è il primo a ottenere il permesso di visitare il Paese per scrivere degli articoli. La vita a Ecotopia appare bizzarra agli occhi dell'americano medio, ma è un percorso esemplare verso la sostenibilità.

Gli ecotopiani ricavano l'energia dal sole e dal vento. Hanno sostituito le automobili con le biciclette e con mezzi pubblici come il treno. Venerano gli alberi e li usano per costruire le case e fabbricare la maggior parte degli oggetti domestici. Non usano prodotti di derivazione chimica, tranne una plastica che si decompone. L'economia è completamente circolare e non genera sprechi. Hanno persino trasformato i concetti di ricchezza e lavoro. Conducono una vita frugale, lavorando il tanto che basta per ottenere il denaro strettamente necessario. Le aziende sono fondate e gestite dalle cooperative. Vivono in comunità diverse al di fuori della famiglia e praticano l'amore libero. Partecipano a dibattiti politici attraverso la televisione interattiva via cavo. Tutto ciò può sembrare irrealistico, ma oggi, a 50 anni dalla pubblicazione, alcune idee illustrate nel romanzo si stanno concretizzando in molte parti del mondo desiderose di compiere la transizione ecologica.

La politica ha avuto un ruolo fondamentale nella costruzione di Ecotopia. La transizione ecologica ha richiesto la riorganizzazione dei mezzi di produzione, lo smantellamento dei colossi aziendali dipendenti dai combustibili fossili e dall'energia nucleare e la riallocazione dei sussidi governativi. Un'altra tappa imprescindibile vede l'abbandono del commercio globale e della divisione globale del lavoro. Davanti all'impossibilità di attuare cambiamenti nella politica dell'establishment, fortemente collusa con i gruppi di interesse, la secessione è l'unica alternativa possibile. Dopo l'uscita dall'Unione, il Partito Sopravvivenzialista che ha fondato Ecotopia e la sua leader, la presidente Vera Allwen, hanno adottato una politica di isolamento a lungo termine. Questo ricorda la guerra d'indipendenza americana, che combatté il dominio coloniale britannico, e il "socialismo in un solo Paese" adottato nell'ex Unione Sovietica.

Tuttavia, a differenza dell'ex Unione Sovietica, che promuoveva una rapida crescita economica al pari del capitalismo in nome della distribuzione delle risorse, Ecotopia deteneva valori e mezzi di produzione distinti dal mondo esterno. Il prequel di Ecotopia, Ecotopia Emerging (1981), descrive la situazione nel momento in cui viene proclamata l'indipendenza.[5] Nonostante l'incombente catastrofe ecologica concomitante con l'aumento dei prezzi dell'energia, la crisi economica e la comparsa del cancro causato dall'uso di sostanze chimiche, il governo e l'industria sono determinati a proteggere i propri interessi. Il Partito Sopravvivenzialista, che ha conquistato il potere nei tre

Stati occidentali progressisti dopo una fuga radioattiva in una centrale nucleare, spinge verso la secessione da Washington DC attraverso un referendum.

La nascita di questa nuova civiltà si deve a due fattori chiave. Il primo è lo sviluppo di una nuova fonte per la produzione di energia. Nel romanzo, la giovane scienziata Lou Swift, contro il monopolio tecnologico esercitato dalle multinazionali e dalle università, inventa un pannello solare che chiunque può fabbricare facilmente. Oggi, nel mondo reale, i combustibili fossili e l'energia nucleare potrebbero essere sostituiti dall'energia rinnovabile, il cui costo unitario è in rapida diminuzione.[6] Il secondo fattore è la nascita di una comunità politica e la mobilitazione di persone che sostengono la rivoluzione sostenibile.[7] Il Partito Sopravvivenzialista ha svolto questo ruolo nel romanzo, ma oggi i principali Paesi del mondo, compresa la Corea del Sud, stanno vivendo una crisi democratica. La democrazia rappresentativa nazionale non è in grado di far fronte alla crisi climatica ed ecologica. Pertanto, la missione più importante del XXI secolo è quella di riunire i cittadini per creare un'ondata di cambiamento rivoluzionario e trasformare la politica.

Una comunità di comunità.
L'apertura e la collaborazione sono più importanti della secessione e dell'isolamento, perché oggi il mondo è fatalmente interconnesso. Le catastrofi ecologiche che prima si verificavano a livello locale si sono trasformate in crisi climatiche globali. Il disastro di Chernobyl, nel 1986, fu causato da un errore dei tecnici nucleari e distrusse vite umane e natura in un raggio di 500 chilometri. Le terribili alluvioni che hanno colpito il Pakistan nel 2022, invece, sono il risultato del cambiamento climatico causato dalle emissioni di anidride carbonica dei Paesi industrializzati, e hanno devastato un'area di 75.000 chilometri quadrati. Le ecotopie nell'era della crisi climatica non possono essere realizzate costruendo nuclei ecologici in aree isolate o esportando altrove un determinato modello una volta sperimentato. Tutta la civiltà deve essere edificata sul principio organizzativo del modello ecologico e le piccole comunità ne costituiranno i mattoni.

L'attivista per l'economia locale Helena Norberg-Hodge ha definito la comunità un "futuro antico".[8] Mentre le comunità del passato erano basate sulla parentela, sul regionalismo e sulla cultura tradizionale, la comunità del futuro si basa su idee condivise e fiducia reciproca. L'ideale è una comunità locale, ma potrebbe funzionare anche una comunità elettronica che connetta i suoi membri lontani. Le comunità hanno il vantaggio di riunire le persone e di tenerle impegnate in un mondo in cui i movimenti sociali controllati centralmente non funzionano più come un tempo. Secondo Carlo Petrini, una comunità ha due valori.[9] In primo luogo, la comunità rappresenta la necessità di passare da una società competitiva a una società collaborativa. Abbandonando il discorso competitivo del successo professionale, della realizzazione personale e del riconoscimento sociale, riconosce il valore di tutti. In secondo luogo, la comunità diventa il contesto in cui si applicano e si praticano "l'intelligenza emotiva" e "un'austera anarchia". Questo ossimoro indica la condizione in cui libertà individuale e ordine collettivo coesistono.

Appartenendo a una comunità, gli individui possono godere di beni relazionali che esistono e circolano al di fuori di un'economia monetaria. I beni relazionali vengono scambiati in base alle necessità e possono essere goduti da tutti i membri della comunità. Sono beni comuni e nessun individuo ne è proprietario. Ma non possono nemmeno essere esportati, perché esistono solo all'interno di una relazione attiva e quando si fa parte di una comunità. Non possono essere comprati o venduti, ma solo alimentati e protetti. Così come le famiglie spesso condividono gratuitamente i beni necessari, le comunità allargate condividono i beni relazionali. Per dirla con le parole dell'ex presidente dell'Uruguay José Mujica, contadino in origine: "Essere poveri non significa non avere nulla, significa essere fuori dalla comunità".[10] La civiltà ecologica si costruisce attraverso una comunità ecologica. La comunità è autonoma e indipendente come unità individuale, ma interagisce e coopera anche con altre comunità, cercando la simbiosi.

Una comunità ecologica nel XXI secolo deve soddisfare almeno cinque requisiti. 1) Una comunità dal basso: non deve essere organizzata dall'alto secondo una determinata ideologia, ma costituita democraticamente in base alle condizioni locali e ai bisogni dei suoi membri. 2) Una comunità globale: deve connettersi con gruppi che condividono ideali simili in tutto il mondo, non solo a livello locale o nazionale. L'impatto di movimenti sociali globali, quali la Primavera araba, Occupy Wall Street, Black Lives Matter e #MeToo, ha travalicato i confini in cui essi hanno avuto origine. Lo stesso vale per il reddito di base universale, dell'economia della felicità, della decrescita e del movimento della civiltà ecologica. 3) Una comunità delle cose: dobbiamo realizzare la democrazia ecologica accettando come cittadini gli animali e la natura insieme agli esseri umani di ogni nazionalità, razza, classe e genere. 4) Una comunità che includa scienza e tecnologia: l'uso della scienza e della tecnologia necessarie per la transizione ecologica è fondamentale per evitare di creare una comunità pseudo-arcaica. Dobbiamo smantellare il monopolio scientifico e tecnologico da parte dello Stato e dei gruppi di esperti e creare una governance che unisca la scienza e la tecnologia alla politica. 5) Una comunità della decrescita: l'obiettivo più importante è la transizione verso la decrescita, che sposti lo scopo della vita dalla crescita alla felicità, nel rispetto della biocapacità della Terra. Per raggiungere questo obiettivo, le comunità devono diventare beni comuni.

La politica di una tale comunità può

essere chiamata "democrazia vegetale". Ciò significa che dovremmo abbandonare il funzionamento animale (centralizzato) del cervello che coordina rigidamente tutte le attività dell'organismo e imitare invece il modello autonomo e decentrato delle piante, in cui tutte le parti dell'organismo generano, si rigenerano e contribuiscono al benessere dell'insieme senza dipendere da un centro. Quando gli individui provano un senso di appartenenza verso una comunità e cercano di sviluppare il loro pensiero attraverso il dialogo - lo strumento politico più utile, in grado di superare le situazioni di stallo - è possibile attuare una politica autentica di partecipazione e dedizione al bene comune. Descrivendo questo tipo di politica, il teologo e ambientalista John Boswell Cobb Jr. ha dichiarato che: "Ogni comunità dovrebbe far parte di una comunità di comunità".[11 12]

Le lezioni della biologia evolutiva

Il concetto di *Décroissance* ("decrescita") è stato utilizzato per la prima volta dal filosofo francese André Gorz nel 1972. In quell'anno si tenne a Stoccolma la prima Conferenza delle Nazioni Unite sull'ambiente umano e il Club di Roma pubblicò The Limits to Growth. All'epoca Gorz pose il seguente interrogativo: "L'equilibrio della Terra, per il quale la non crescita o addirittura la decrescita della produzione materiale è una condizione necessaria, è compatibile con la sopravvivenza del sistema capitalistico?". Qualche anno dopo, nel 1980, dichiarò che "Oggi la mancanza di realismo non consiste più nel propugnare un maggiore benessere attraverso la decrescita e la trasformazione dello stile di vita prevalente. La mancanza di realismo consiste nell'immaginare che la crescita economica possa ancora migliorare il benessere umano e che sia fisicamente possibile".[13] Ancora oggi, a distanza di cinquant'anni, questa visione "irrealistica" rimane la più diffusa.

Tuttavia, il concetto di decrescita si è sviluppato fino a diventare un trait d'union per i progressisti di tutto il mondo nella lotta contro la crisi climatica ed ecologica e le disuguaglianze.[14] La decrescita non consiste nell'imporre al mondo dolorose privazioni o forme di ascetismo, come dichiarano i fautori della crescita, ma nel perseguire la cura e la simbiosi reindirizzando i valori e la direzione della vita.

L'accrescimento dei beni comuni - risorse materiali e immateriali di proprietà pubblica, non dello Stato o dei singoli individui - è la chiave della decrescita. La storia dei beni comuni risale alla Carta della Foresta, emanata dal re Giovanni d'Inghilterra nel 1215 insieme alla Magna Carta. Questa carta garantiva i diritti economici degli uomini liberi sulle terre comuni (le foreste) che le avevano utilizzate fino ad allora senza detenerne il diritto legittimo.[15] Ciò dimostra che i diritti politici e giuridici dei cittadini erano possibili solo quando venivano garantiti i diritti sulla terra comune, fondamento dell'autosufficienza economica. Lo spirito dell'Enclosure Movement, movimento delle recinzioni nato all'inizio della rivoluzione industriale allo scopo di stabilire i diritti di proprietà privata sulle terre pubbliche, ha dominato per oltre duecentocinquant'anni. Oggi, però, questo dominio sta per terminare in favore di un ritorno ai beni comuni.

Il concetto di beni comuni non prevede solo la condivisione di beni e risorse fra i membri di una comunità. Ci sollecita a cambiare il nostro modo di pensare incentrato sulla proprietà, a perseguire il valore d'uso piuttosto che il valore di scambio e a ristabilire le nostre relazioni con la natura, gli animali non umani e gli esseri umani. I beni comuni ci chiedono di vedere tutti gli esseri viventi non come entità a sé stanti, ma come potenzialità generate dalle relazioni. Superando il pensiero moderno che guarda allo stato di natura in una prospettiva di competizione e conflitto, di lotta di tutti contro tutti e di sopravvivenza del più adatto, siamo chiamati a pensare in modo globale alla dualità competizione e cooperazione in un ecosistema. Dobbiamo imparare dalla biologia evolutiva, che ha superato il principio della "sopravvivenza del più adatto" in favore della "sopravvivenza del più amichevole".[16]

È sempre più evidente che il comportamento altruistico e la collaborazione siano vantaggiosi per la sopravvivenza degli esseri umani e degli animali. La differenza tra scimpanzé e bonobo sta nell'amorevolezza. È grazie alla gentilezza che l'Homo sapiens, piccolo e intelligente, è sopravvissuto mentre i Neanderthal si sono estinti nonostante la prestanza fisica. La capacità di relazionarsi in modo gentile ed empatico con gli altri membri di una comunità è vantaggiosa per il lavoro cooperativo e permette di costruire società più grandi e di sviluppare abilità più complesse. Il riconoscimento che il principio della vita è la collaborazione, non la competizione, ha già esercitato un'ampia influenza in diversi campi di ricerca, come l'epidemiologia sociale, le neuroscienze, l'economia comportamentale, il capitale relazionale e la ricerca sulla felicità.

Tuttavia, non sono mancate le critiche verso le teorie che hanno collegato la biologia evolutiva alle scienze sociali. Ad esempio, per quanto riguarda la selezione naturale, la teoria evolutiva dominante mette in primo piano la selezione genetica e individuale, mentre un gruppo di biologi evoluzionisti ha iniziato a sostenere l'importante ruolo svolto dalla selezione di gruppo nel processo di evoluzione di tratti sociali, come l'altruismo e l'empatia, che sono alla base della cooperazione umana. In altre parole, la selezione di gruppo crea esseri umani che scelgono l'altruismo anche a discapito del proprio benessere. È noto il dibattito tra Edward Osborne Wilson, che propugna questa tesi, e Richard Dawkins, sostenitore della selezione individuale.

Anche il biologo evoluzionista David Sloan Wilson sostiene la teoria della selezione di gruppo. Secondo Wilson, la teoria della selezione individuale da sola non spiega l'altruismo umano, poiché il comportamento altruistico è facilmente soggetto allo sfruttamento di chi riceve senza ricambiare (la "tragedia dei beni comuni"). La teoria della selezione di gruppo invece propone una valida spiegazione: i nostri antenati vivevano in piccoli gruppi, divisi tra altruisti e sfruttatori in numero variabile; il gruppo con più membri altruisti aveva maggiori possibilità di sopravvivere. Wilson sostiene che queste differenze nei tassi di successo tra i gruppi è ciò che ha reso gli esseri umani più collaborativi oggi. Lo scienziato fa riferimento anche alle teorie sui beni comuni di Elinor Ostrom per dimostrare la validità della selezione di gruppo. In risposta alla "tragedia dei beni comuni" di Garrett Hardin, per il quale è l'interesse personale ad aver portato alla distruzione delle risorse comuni, Ostrom ha identificato otto principi dallo studio di casi virtuosi del passato in cui i beni comuni sono stati tutelati grazie alla reciproca collaborazione.[17] Questi principi dimostrano che, nelle giuste condizioni, l'altruismo collettivo può superare l'interesse personale ed essere applicato alle attività umane in un'ampia gamma di ambiti e livelli per trasformare la struttura profonda della civiltà.

L'egoismo e l'altruismo umano non possono essere affrontati come una dicotomia e differiscono a seconda delle condizioni. La tragedia dei beni comuni è reale, ma esistono dei modi per evitarla. Se la comunità del futuro deve basarsi sui beni comuni, dobbiamo imparare dalle storie di successo del passato per costruire l'altruismo collettivo. Con la globalizzazione, l'ambito dei beni comuni si è gradualmente ampliato, dalla terra, le foreste e i fiumi all'atmosfera e agli oceani. Più piccola è la comunità, maggiore è il rispetto delle regole che disciplinano l'uso dei beni comuni. Tuttavia, le sfide globali come la crisi climatica, la crisi ecologica, le pandemie e le disuguaglianze richiedono di riflettere con maggiore attenzione e saggezza sulle possibilità di applicare su più vasta scala questi principi di cooperazione.

1. Jeremy Lent, "We Need an Ecological Civilization Before It's Too Late," *Open Democracy*, October 21, 2018 (ultimo accesso 31 gennaio 2023). URL: www.opendemocracy.net/en/transformation/we-need-ecological-civilization-before-it-s-too-late/.
2. Timothy M. Lenton and Bruno Latour, "Gaia 2.0 Could Humans Add Some Level of Self-Awareness to Earth's Self-Regulation?" *Science* 361, no. 6407, September 2018, pp. 1066-1068.
3. Alfred North Whitehead, *Adventures of Ideas*, New York, The Free Press, 1967, p. 83.
4. Ernest Callenbach, *Ecotopia*, New York, Bantam, Reissue edition, 1990.
5. Ernest Callenbach, *Ecotopia Emerging*, Berkeley, Banyan Tree Books, 1981.
6. URL:www.industrynews.co.kr/news/articleView.html?idxno=42998
7. Nel capitolo supplementare "What is to be Done" dell'edizione pubblicata per il 30° anniversario di *The*

Limits to Growth, Donella Meadows afferma che nella storia dell'umanità ci sono state tre rivoluzioni a fronte della crescita della popolazione e della distruzione dell'ambiente. La prima è stata la Rivoluzione agricola, la seconda la Rivoluzione industriale e l'ultima la Rivoluzione sostenibile.

8. URL:www.localfutures.org/publications/ancient-futures-book-helena-norberg-hodge/.
9. Carlo Petrini, *TerraFutura: Dialoghi con Papa Francesco sull'ecologia integrale*, Firenze, Giunti, 2020.
10. Carlo Petrini, *TerraFutura: Dialoghi con Papa Francesco sull'ecologia integrale*, Firenze, Giunti, 2020.
11. URL:www.openhorizons.org/ten-ideas-for-saving-the-planet.html
12. URL: www.openhorizons.org/ten-ideas-for-saving-the-planet.html
13. André Gorz in Giacomo D'Alisa, Federico Demaria, and Giorgos Kallis, (a cura di), *Degrowth: A Vocabulary for a New Era, New York and London*, Routledge, 2014, p. 1.
14. Dopo la prima svoltasi a Parigi nel 2008, si sono tenute altre conferenze delle comunità di ricerca internazionali sul tema della decrescita a Barcellona (2010), Montreal (2011), Venezia (2012), Lipsia (2014) e Budapest (2016). Negli ultimi due anni, in Corea del Sud le principali riviste accademiche si sono occupate di decrescita.
15. URL:www.nationalarchives.gov.uk/education/resources/magna-carta/charter-forest-1225-westminster/.
16. Brian Hare and Vanessa Woods, *Survival of the Friendliest: Understanding Our Origins and Rediscovering Our Common Humanity*, New York, Random House, 2020.
17. Gli 8 principi di Elinor Ostrom per gestire i beni comuni sono: 1. Definire chiaramente i confini del gruppo. 2. Adattare le regole che disciplinano l'uso dei beni comuni alle esigenze e alle condizioni locali. 3. Garantire che coloro che sono interessati dalle regole possano partecipare alla loro modifica. 4. Assicurarsi che le autorità esterne rispettino i diritti dei membri della comunità di stabilire le regole. 5. Sviluppare un sistema, gestito dai membri della comunità, per monitorare il comportamento di tutti. 6. Utilizzare sanzioni graduali per chi viola le regole. 7. Fornire mezzi accessibili e a basso costo per la risoluzione delle controversie. 8. Costruire la responsabilità di governare la risorsa comune in livelli nidificati, dal livello più basso fino all'intero sistema interconnesso. Cfr. Elinor Ostrom, *Governing the Commons: The Evolution of Institutions for Collective Action*, Cambridge, UK, Cambridge University Press, 1990.

Sharaner Maash o un fantasma dal passato

Eman Abdelhadi e M. E. O'Brien

Sharaner Maash o
un fantasma dal passato
Eman Abdelhadi e M. E. O'Brien

Caro Latif, amico mio,

sono a Fire Island e ho visto un fantasma. Dovevo assolutamente dirtelo e l'unico modo per farlo è scriverti una lettera! Infatti abbiamo i telefoni staccati e pace. È strano comunicare così, ma non possiamo fare altro.

Ti avevo già detto che sarei andata a quella specie di commemorazione a cui mi ha invitato Belquees. Sharaner Maash, l'ha chiamata così. Sono arrivata qui col traghetto due giorni fa. Mi piace il mare e l'isola non è inondata in questo periodo. Fa un caldo terrificante ma nella palude c'è ombra e possiamo fare il bagno nell'oceano.

Dormiamo in un accampamento che hanno messo su nella palude, a una decina di minuti a piedi da Cherry Grove. La mia vicina di tenda è Nourah, l'amica di Belquees, la conosci? Capelli ricci e corti, abita a Chicago. La prima notte eravamo tutte e due disorientate e cercavamo Belquees, così ci siamo messe a esplorare la zona insieme.

Belquees era rimasta sul vago quando le avevo chiesto di che si trattava, per cui i fantasmi sono stati una vera sorpresa! La prima notte sono venuti fuori dalla palude all'improvviso mentre eravamo in giro ad aspettare che succedesse qualcosa. Nourah mi ha chiamato, indicando il fantasma che avanzava verso di noi. Ce n'erano altri dietro. Avevo notato gli oloproiettori installati sugli alberi, ma l'apparizione è stata comunque uno shock. Pochi minuti dopo eravamo circondate.

C'era un gran caos. I fantasmi hanno cominciato a parlarci. Avevano l'aria di non sapere dove fossero, cosa ci facessero lì. Da come erano vestiti e dall'accento, sembravano ologrammi di persone vissute prima della Rivoluzione. Mi sono venuti i brividi. Non ho mai capito veramente la gente del passato. Devo ammettere purtroppo che mi hanno sempre suscitato un po' di disgusto. Non mi hanno mai interessato i film storici ambientati negli anni Venti. Mi piacciono i film horror d'inizio secolo, ma neanche i film slasher riescono a farmi dare un senso a quelle vite tristi.

Mi si è avvicinato un fantasma. Era una donna di colore che indossava strani abiti della stessa tinta. Era molto agitata, continuava a chiedermi di aiutarla a raggiungere l'"Elmhurst Hospital". Le ho chiesto se fosse ferita e mi ha risposto che era un'infermiera. Continuava a ripetere: "Non riuscirò ad arrivare in ospedale prima del coprifuoco se non mi sbrigo". Non so cosa sia un coprifuoco. Non ho smesso di pensare a quella donna dopo.

Belquees e gli altri organizzatori si sono impegnati molto per dare autenticità storica ai fantasmi, è evidente, infatti sembrano persone reali! I proiettori sono stati istallati per tutto l'accampamento così i fantasmi possono apparire ovunque e muoversi. Sono evanescenti ma ne senti la presenza. È una cosa che ti fa venire i brividi, eccitante e spaventosa insieme. Mi fa paura il pensiero di un mese di faccia a faccia con il passato, ma mi piace questo clima da horror.

Ti fa piacere se ti scrivo ancora? Mi fa male la mano mentre ti scrivo, ma ti manderò altre lettere se le leggi. Devo capire anche come funziona la spedizione. Fammi sapere se hai ricevuto questa.

—Kayla D. H. Puan
Venerdì, 2 agosto 2086, Cherry Grove, Fire Island, Mid-Atlantic

---

Domenica, 4 agosto

Kayla, amica mia,
ho ricevuto la tua lettera. Sì, scrivimi ancora! Raccontami la tua esperienza, non vedo l'ora. Ha dei punti in comune con il progetto di cui mi sto occupando.

Ti ricordi come ho cominciato a lavorare in un hospice qualche anno fa? Quando Matt è morto per overdose, è stato uno shock tremendo. Ho capito che dovevo pensare di più alla morte. Mi sono sempre occupato di assistenza alle gestanti, e quello mi sembrava il passo successivo. È una lunga storia, alla fine ho cominciato a lavorare per realizzare un memoriale a Hart Island nel Bronx. Per questo mi sono trasferito nella comune di City Island. Quello che stai vivendo assomiglia a un progetto a Rio che si chiama mêses de memória. So che Belquees ha fatto un viaggio in nave l'anno scorso per andare a Rio a fare ricerca sul progetto. Il parco della memoria a Hart segue un po' lo stesso modello ma preferisco non scendere nei particolari, visto che hai l'opportunità di scoprirlo di persona in questo momento. È fantastico.

La progettazione del nostro parco è ancora agli inizi, quindi mi piacerebbe saperne di più su come hanno organizzato le cose lì. Tipo, i "fantasmi" stanno con voi tutto il tempo? Ne frequenti uno solo o ne incontri tanti? Mi piace che li chiami fantasmi, fa proprio effetto. Pensi che sappiano di essere morti?

—Latif Timbers
City Island Commune,
Long Island Sound

LT—

Pazzesco! Sapevo che stavi lavorando a qualcosa su Hart da quando ti sei trasferito nel Bronx, ma non immaginavo che si trattasse di questo parco della memoria. Raccontami di Hart Island. È un cimitero, giusto? Da dove viene il nome Hart? Create ologrammi di persone morte? Come li realizzate?

I fantasmi vanno e vengono. Continuo a incontrare la donna di cui ti ho parlato. Cerco di evitare il suo sguardo, a dire la verità. Mi mette a disagio, mi dà ansia. Continua a chiedermi dell'ospedale. Alla fine ho dovuto inventare una storia, le ho detto che ha avuto un incidente e che è qui per rimettersi. Sembra confusa, sul decennio, sul fatto di essere l'ologramma di un morto e su molte altre cose.

Visto che qui i telefoni non funzionano, ho dovuto cercare un robot che mi spiegasse cos'è un coprifuoco. A quanto pare, le forze dell'ordine di un tempo vietavano alle persone di circolare da una certa ora in poi. E si poteva morire o finire in galera se si "infrangeva il coprifuoco". È inimmaginabile vivere così! Come faceva la gente a sopportarlo? È orribile.

La seconda branda nella mia tenda è rimasta vuota, forse dovrei proporgliela a Nourah? Anche Nourah è sola nella tenda.

—KDHP, 6 agosto 2086 (martedì),
Fire Island

(Il giorno dopo!)
Latif,

è proprio una ghost story, avevo ragione. Non ti ho ancora mandato la lettera di ieri. Ieri sera, quando sono tornata alla mia tenda, ho trovato ad aspettarmi due sorprese.

La prima era un biglietto firmato

da Belquees. Dal nome bengalese dell'evento avrei dovuto capire che era opera sua. Sul foglietto c'era scritto:

> Ormai hai incontrato i tuoi compagni di viaggio. Ognuno di loro è un morto senza nome. Non hanno ricevuto una degna sepoltura, un degno saluto. Spetta a te guidarli fuori da questa esistenza con la gentilezza che forse non hanno mai conosciuto quando erano in vita. In questo percorso imparerai a conoscere la loro epoca e potrai, speriamo, arrivare ad apprezzare meglio la tua.

I morti che non hanno ricevuto un dignitoso commiato sono per definizione fantasmi. I fantasmi sono sempre stati al centro dei miei lavori fotografici e cinematografici. Mi piaceva tantissimo guardare i vecchi film di fantasmi ma non sono certa di volerci stare dentro.

Tutto è diventato più intenso quando quella donna ansiosa è arrivata nella mia tenda e si è seduta sull'altra branda. Era stata affidata a me! A quanto pare, molti fantasmi erano svaniti nel pomeriggio e quelli rimasti sono entrati nelle tende.

Alla fine ho chiesto alla donna di raccontarmi della sua vita. Da allora me la ripeto nella testa. Questo è quello che ricordo.

> Mi chiamo Feroza. Sono nata e cresciuta in una baraccopoli alla periferia di Dacca. Mio padre portava il risciò, mia madre cucinava, puliva e si prendeva cura di noi. Io e i miei fratelli e sorelle la aiutavamo quando potevamo. Ero brava a scuola. Quando prendevo bei voti, i miei genitori mi dicevano di continuare così, di concentrarmi sullo studio.
>
> I miei fratelli e sorelle hanno smesso di andare a scuola dopo le elementari, e io invece ho continuato. Lavoravano tutti tranne me, e io mi sentivo in colpa. Ho pregato mia madre di farmi lavorare con mia sorella; nostra zia le aveva trovato un lavoro come donna delle pulizie per della gente ricca di città. Ma il mio lavoro era studiare. Non ho mai smesso di studiare. Sono arrivata perfino all'università. Hanno fatto festa nel quartiere quando mi sono diplomata. Sono arrivati tutti con cibo e dolci. Ho indossato il sari più bello di mia madre e quel giorno mi sono sentita come una sposa.
>
> Ho conosciuto il mio futuro marito all'università. Osman e io venivamo entrambi da quartieri poveri, lo sapevano tutti. Studiavamo insieme e parlavamo dei nostri sogni. Io volevo una vita lontana dalla baraccopoli, lui sognava più in grande. Voleva che andassimo in America. Si è laureato prima di me ed è riuscito ad andare a New York. L'unico lavoro che

ha potuto trovare è guidare il taxi, niente a che vedere con i suoi studi di ingegneria. Era molto stanco e alla fine mi ha detto di raggiungerlo. Sapevo che avrei dovuto lavorare. Una donna nel mio palazzo, anche lei del Bangladesh, che sarebbe poi diventata come una sorella per me, mi ha presentato a una ricca famiglia di Manhattan che cercava qualcuno per le pulizie. E così sono finita a pulire case come mia sorella. Mi sono messa anche a studiare, di notte dopo il lavoro, per ottenere il diploma di infermiera. Poi è nata Belquees.

In quel momento ho sentito che qualcosa mi si spezzava dentro.

"Belquees? Belquees Chowdhury?" ho chiesto.

Hanno cominciato a vorticarmi in testa tutte le cose che sapevo sulla famiglia di Belquees. All'improvviso mi è venuto in mente dove avevo sentito il nome dell'ospedale. Oh Latif, mi si è accartocciato il cuore, mi è venuto da piangere. Mi sono scusata e sono corsa fuori. Ero sconvolta. Sono rimasta molto tempo seduta accanto al fuoco a pensare a Belquees. A suo padre, ancora innamorato di Feroza dopo tutti quegli anni, ancora in lutto. Avevo dimenticato il nome di Feroza; me la ricordavo solo come la madre di Belquees.

Sicuramente ti ricordi cosa è successo alla madre di Belquees, a Elmhurst.

Piango mentre ti scrivo. Fanculo alla Storia, la odio. Ho sempre pensato che le persone del passato fossero deboli, che io avrei lottato di più, che non mi sarei rassegnata a soffrire come hanno fatto loro. Li odio. Non sto bene qua. Voglio tornare a Newark, a casa.

Ti manderò tutte e due le lettere stamattina via traghetto.

—Kayla/7 agosto/mercoledì.

Venerdì, 9 agosto 2086
K,

sono ansioso di sapere cosa è successo. Sì, piangere quelli che non hanno ricevuto un degno saluto è l'idea che sta alla base dei parchi della memoria e i *mêses de memória.* Scrivimi ancora!

Mi hai chiesto di Hart Island. Per un secolo è stata utilizzata come cimitero per gli indigenti e per molti carcerati di New York. Ci sono sepolte più di un milione di persone. Ci sono le fosse comuni delle vittime di tre pandemie: l'AIDS del XX secolo, il COVID degli anni Venti e la LARS degli anni Quaranta. Nessuno sa da dove viene il nome Hart. Non è stato trovato nessun collegamento con la famiglia dei primi coloni con questo nome. È la terra dei Siwanoy, ma non pensiamo che la chiamassero in qualche modo.

Gli ologrammi che stiamo progettando saranno gestiti da sistemi IA. Li realizziamo sulla base di persone realmente esistite, sepolte sull'isola. Ricostruiamo le loro caratteristiche e personalità attraverso i social, i documenti burocratici e le videochiamate registrate. Gli ologrammi staranno seduti o in piedi vicino al luogo di sepoltura delle persone che rappresentano. Parleranno con chi gli fa visita, racconteranno la storia della loro vita. Questa è l'idea, ma ci sono molte cose che non abbiamo ancora sistemato.

L'obiettivo principale dell'attuale progetto del parco è quello di far capire ai visitatori cosa vuol dire essere poveri e non avere un tetto sulla testa. Ma non voglio che gli ologrammi siano solo strumenti didattici per i bambini. Io voglio... voglio accogliere i morti. Se c'è una persona che può capire davvero l'importanza di onorare il passato, quella è Belquees.

Come amico, ti consiglio di vivere pienamente quest'esperienza. Ho fiducia in Belquees e so che anche tu ce l'hai. Capisco che sia doloroso per te.

—Latif Timbers, City Island, Bronx

Latif,

ho avuto una settimana intensa dopo l'ultima volta che ti ho scritto. La notte in cui ho scoperto chi era Feroza, non sono riuscita a chiudere occhio. Il giorno dopo sono crollata e ho dormito fino al tramonto. Non me la sono sentita di dirle cosa è successo a Elmhurst, non volevo affrontare la cosa. So che non è il mio trauma, ma incontrarla mi ha fatto risalire a galla tante cose. Quando ero giovane ed ero fuori casa, ho perso mio padre e ho dovuto trovare un modo per elaborare il lutto. Sono andata nel posto in cui è stato ucciso mentre combatteva contro i fascisti, in Colorado, e ho fatto una cerimonia per lui. A parte questo, non sono una persona che vive nel passato.

Quando Feroza è stata assegnata alla mia tenda, mi sentivo già piuttosto... provata. Come se fossi fragile, vulnerabile e più permeabile di quanto avrei voluto. Avevo imparato in famiglia, all'asilo e dai film come viveva la gente del passato. Ma parlare con i fantasmi in quei primi giorni mi ha fatto sentire più vicina, più coinvolta. Ho sentito come erano tutti preoccupati per il cibo, i soldi, la casa, la salute. Come tutto ruotava intorno ai soldi, alla povertà e alla disperazione. "Sembrano tutti così stanchi", ha commentato Nourah.

Il giorno dopo che Feroza è venuta nella mia tenda, quando finalmente sono riuscita a trascinarmi fuori dal letto al tramonto, abbiamo iniziato a parlare. Ho evitato gli argomenti più pesanti. Stranamente, si è stabilita una grande intesa fra me e Feroza. Abbiamo più o meno la stessa età, ma abbiamo fatto finta di essere due adolescenti in campeggio. Da quel momento abbiamo trascorso parecchio tempo insieme. Siamo andate a fare kayak sull'oceano (mi ero portata dietro un piccolo oloproiettore!), abbiamo fatto ginnastica, abbiamo fatto un laboratorio di ceramica. Lei ha usato argilla olografica. Sono stati giorni di grande leggerezza. Siamo state bene insieme. Abbiamo riso. Abbiamo passato momenti belli, sereni, divertenti. Questa leggerezza ci ha aiutato a parlare.

Ha deciso che ero una vecchia amica di Belquees; a un certo punto ha detto che probabilmente ero una delle insegnanti di sua figlia. Le ho chiesto di parlarmi di Belquees quand'era piccola, e Feroza mi ha raccontato delle storie veramente interessanti. Per esempio, che una volta Belquees si era arrabbiata con una guardia a un posto di blocco militare e che lei e il marito l'hanno trascinata via prima che iniziasse a colpirlo. Continuava a gridare - in bengalese o in inglese, non mi ricordo - "Porta rispetto al mio papà!". Un'altra volta è stata picchiata mentre cercava di difendere una bambina che veniva bullizzata in classe.

Feroza mi ha chiesto di raccontarle della mia vita. Le ho parlato dei miei numerosi genitori, delle lezioni di fotografia che davo, di come fosse crescere un bambino con i miei cinque genitori e vivere nella comune di Ironbound. Ho cercato di non rivelare troppi dettagli sulle discrepanze tra le nostre rispettive epoche. Credo che a un certo punto abbia deciso di accettare le incongruenze e le stranezze fra il suo essere qui e le cose che non combaciavano.

Ho iniziato ad affezionarmi a lei, e mi sono sforzata di non distrarmi quando diceva cose che non capivo. C'erano così tante cose che non capivo, e che ancora non capisco. La disperazione, la stanchezza, la paura che la accompagna ogni giorno. Non riuscivo a capire quanto fosse pesante il suo lavoro. Otto ore! Dodici ore! Tutte quelle ore, incredibile. Così ogni giorno. Sembrava non rendersi conto di quanto fosse terribile quella situazione. Volevo che odiasse quella situazione, volevo che si arrabbiasse. La spingevo, ma lei mi rispondeva sempre: "Bisogna arrangiarsi".

So che sei un grande lettore di storia. Alcune di queste parole probabilmente ti suonano più familiari che a me. A volte mi faccio una lista mentale delle parole da cercare la prossima volta che trovo un robot. Ma "arrangiarsi"! "Arrangiarsi" ancora non la capisco. E non la capirò. Era tutto così triste e terribile nel mondo di prima, un mondo di deboli.

Feroza mi ha raccontato di una sua vicina di casa che aveva il cancro. Per curarla, la famiglia aveva usato tutti i suoi "risparmi". La vicina è morta comunque. Dopo che i familiari avevano versato un anticipo per l'operazione, l'ospedale aveva chiuso i battenti. Capisco a malapena che roba fosse il denaro, ma dominava la vita - la vita fisica – delle persone!

Nessun altro ospedale avrebbe preso in cura la donna perché era già scoppiata la LARS-47. Comunque non potevano permettersi un altro anticipo. Poi, quando ha finito di raccontarmi quello che era successo, ha di nuovo scosso la testa e ha detto: "Bisogna arrangiarsi".

Non ne potevo più, e allora le ho chiesto: "Che significa 'bisogna arrangiarsi?

"Significa che facciamo del nostro meglio con quello che abbiamo".

Ho perso le staffe.

"Avete fatto del vostro meglio? Era quello il vostro meglio?! Ho letto un po' di cose sulla vostra epoca! Vivevano in ville! Avevano dei cortili interni grandi come quest'isola! C'erano persone che possedevano orbite private, eserciti privati. C'erano persone che bevevano il cappuccino con pagliuzze d'oro dentro! Avete lasciato che vi schiacciassero. Cos'è che non andava in voi? Noi non permetteremmo mai che succedesse una cosa simile oggi. Non capisco, non capirò mai il vostro comportamento". Me ne sono andata via, già pentita della mia sfuriata.

Ho mandato a puttane tutto l'esperimento. Dovevo prendermi cura di questa persona distrutta, e invece l'ho fatta vergognare per la morte della sua amica. Li odio per non aver lottato di più. È come se avessero vissuto senza anima. Una volta ti ho detto che la storia dell'umanità per me cominciava con le comuni, con la rivoluzione e non era del tutto uno scherzo. Vivere sotto il dominio del denaro era già un morire; non hanno mai vissuto per davvero.

Quello che ti ho raccontato è successo solo poche ore fa. Sono ancora agitata. Ti riscrivo appena mi calmo.

Baci,

Kayla DH Puan, 14 agosto 2086
(mercoledì pomeriggio)

---

14 agosto (mercoledì sera, stesso giorno)

Ho evitato Feroza per quasi tutto il pomeriggio. Quando sono tornata alla tenda, lei si è scagliata contro di me. Era davvero arrabbiata. Questo è quello che mi ricordo.

> Pensi di essere migliore di me. Tu vieni dal futuro, lo so. Non me lo vuoi dire, ma ho sentito parlare altre persone, l'ho capito. Non riesco a capire come è possibile, ma questo non ti rende migliore di me. Sai qual è stata la nostra lotta? Abbiamo lottato ogni giorno per rimanere vivi. Abbiamo continuato a lottare per qualcosa di meglio, anche quando abbiamo fallito. Il mese scorso hanno provato a chiudere il nostro ospedale. Non glielo abbiamo

permesso. Lo teniamo aperto per la gente. Lo abbiamo occupato. Non avremmo permesso che chiudessero un altro ospedale.

Non chiediamo soldi; curiamo chiunque ne abbia bisogno. Ci siamo presi attrezzature e forniture, ora siamo i padroni di noi stessi. Lavoriamo per noi, per gli altri, per i nostri amici, vicini e familiari malati. Ci sosteniamo da soli, ma è dura, è molto dura. Non siamo i primi, sai, a provarci. Altri prima di noi lo hanno fatto, per generazioni. Dopo cicloni e incendi, in mezzo a proteste, occupazioni, catastrofi, battaglie. Ci siamo presi cura gli uni degli altri.

Ma continuiamo a fallire. So che falliamo, ma questo non significa che siamo stati deboli. Abbiamo sempre combattuto. Combattiamo ancora. Il coprifuoco diventa sempre più rigido. L'esercito si sta avvicinando. So che morirò in quell'ospedale. Lo sento nelle ossa. E quando morirò, verranno altri dopo di me per continuare a lottare. Perché è questo che ci rende umani. Non so quale generazione vincerà. Ma so che ogni generazione lotterà. Tu sei dell'epoca dopo, no? Dell'epoca in cui qualcuno aveva già vinto. Non sono mica stupida. Lo vedo cosa sei. Il tuo disprezzo, la tua sicurezza, la tua disinvoltura. Non mi capisci per niente.

Siamo rimaste in silenzio. Le ho detto che è morta in quell'ospedale. Mi ha chiesto l'anno in cui è morta - il 2049 - il suo presente. Mi ha chiesto come è successo. Le ho detto la versione più lunga della storia che Belquees ci ha raccontato dopo la pubblicazione dei nostri racconti. Le ho detto che l'occupazione dell'ospedale aveva dato una grande spinta alla nascita delle comuni in tutta New York. Che è andata avanti per mesi e ha dato il via a un nuovo modo di concepire la sanità: curare chi ne ha bisogno al di là dell'economia di mercato. Che l'esercito americano ha bombardato l'edificio, uccidendo tutti quelli che erano dentro, compresa lei. Che la sua famiglia non è riuscita a trovare il suo corpo, cercato per giorni e giorni, perché non è stato possibile identificare nessuno. E che quello che era successo è stato un punto di svolta per la lotta a New York. Le ho raccontato delle comuni, delle assemblee e dell'espulsione dell'esercito e della polizia, e le ho detto che abbiamo vinto, che alla fine abbiamo vinto. Le ho detto che quello che avevano fatto con l'ospedale era stata la chiave di tutto.

Mi ha chiesto come conoscevo Belquees. "Tua figlia è mia amica. Belquees. Fa grandi cose, parla sempre di te. Anche Osman. Vivi nel loro ricordo".

Mi ha chiesto perché è qui. Le ho risposto: "Per la tua janazah".

Ora sta dormendo sulla branda. Io vado a dormire fra poco. Sono sicura che non la troverò qui quando mi sveglierò. Ora ho capito che ci facciamo qui.

—Kayla DH Puan

---

16 agosto
Kayla,

ti stringo forte, amica mia. So che non sei molto religiosa, ma oggi tu e Feroza sarete nelle mie preghiere.

—Latif, City Island Commune

Caro Latif, amico mio,

abbiamo appena fatto il ghusl. Dopo che Feroza è sparita, ho passato due giorni a fare una scultura a sua immagine. Ho trovato tutto l'occorrente qui. Poi ho passato altri due giorni appiccicata a un robot, per imparare tutto il possibile sui riti funebri musulmani, su come lavare il corpo, prepararlo per la sepoltura e per il viaggio nell'aldilà.

Il giorno del ghusl di Feroza, Belquees e suo padre Osman sono stati con me.

"Sapevo di potermi fidare di te per questo", mi ha detto Belquees. Abbiamo lavato Feroza dalla testa ai piedi nell'acqua calda, massaggiandole delicatamente i capelli, le mani, i piedi. L'abbiamo avvolta con cura in un lenzuolo di cotone e l'abbiamo portata alla tomba. L'abbiamo calata nella terra e Belquees ha pianto e ha recitato il Corano.

Gli altri del campo si sono radunati e io ho raccontato la storia di Feroza. Non conoscevo bene il passato prima. Pensavo che fossero tutti senza anima e che fossero solo involucri vuoti, sopraffatti. Pensavo che non fossero come noi, che fossero solo la falsa coscienza da cui ci avevano messo in guardia all'asilo. La comune, pensavo, era il principio dell'umanità, lo spazio in cui, da misere e patetiche entità siamo diventati esseri creativi completi, padroni del nostro destino. Ma Feroza era umana. Feroza è sempre stata umana. Feroza è stata gloriosamente e meravigliosamente umana anche nella sconfitta. Non ha conosciuto la comune per poco, per tre anni, ma ha contribuito a farla nascere. Non ha aspettato che le dessero la vita, lei era la vita.

Tornerò a casa presto. Prima però devo portare il mio contributo ad altre due commemorazioni. Mi piacerebbe vederti, passare un po' di tempo insieme a te.

Vorrei aiutarti con il parco della memoria. Posso dirti un significato della parola "Hart", perché è uno dei miei secondi nomi. Hart è una parola antica che indica il cervo, in genere il cervo maschio adulto. Oggi i cervi sono del tutto scomparsi. Erano veloci, si muovevano in modo furtivo, erano stupendi. I miei genitori ne avevano visto uno durante un'escursione di gruppo nel Vermont. Quel giorno hanno scelto il mio vecchio nome e ci hanno aggiunto Hart in suo onore. Quando ho preso il mio nuovo nome, ho deciso di tenere Hart. Quella è stata una delle ultime volte in cui qualcuno ha riferito di aver visto un cervo. Forse il cervo si era già estinto e i miei genitori hanno visto un fantasma. Forse progetterò l'ologramma di un cervo per farlo girare libero sull'isola. Abbiamo molte perdite da piangere.

Grazie per le tue lettere. Ti voglio tanto bene Latif.

La tua amica e compagna

—K

Kayla Dorothy Hart Puan
Domenica, 22 agosto 2086
Cherry Grove, Fire Island, Mid-Atlantic Seaboard, North America

---

Questo racconto è una continuazione del romanzo speculativo degli autori, *Everything for Everyone: An Oral History of the New York Commune*, 2052-2072 (Common Notions, 2022).

Storia delle Otto Città
Serang Chung

Storia delle Otto Città

Serang Chung

Nel 2086, fenomeno senza precedenti, venne concesso un enorme potere discrezionale all'organizzazione dell'Iniziativa per la Decarbonizzazione. Diversi professionisti, provenienti da vari settori e accomunati dalla stessa visione, si riunirono per discutere mettendo temporaneamente da parte le loro attività principali. L'obiettivo del tavolo di lavoro, che si tenne con regolarità fino alla fine, era individuare delle soluzioni per sottrarre la società a quelle dipendenze autodistruttive note come produzione e consumo di massa, in atto da quasi 200 anni. Alla fine fu Choi, considerata da molti il più geniale architetto dell'epoca, a proporre un'idea fattibile.

"Dopotutto, non è forse il senso di appartenenza a dare piacere quanto il consumo? E se si potesse scegliere uno stile di vita e seguirlo costantemente, come si segue un idolo o una squadra sportiva? Se ogni gruppo standardizzasse una forma architettonica, un modo di vestire, dei prodotti alimentari, non sarebbe possibile gestire senza sprechi la produzione delle risorse?"

"Come chiameresti questo gruppo?"

"Un clan, se proprio occorre dargli un nome. Quando metti insieme una città e un clan..."

Ara Choi carezzò involontariamente il bordo de *Le città invisibili* di Italo Calvino, il libro che teneva tra le mani.

"Sarebbe possibile? La gente non si stancherà? E se uno, nel frattempo, volesse prendere un'altra strada?"

"Può succedere di avere voglia di cambiare, ma pensate a una squadra di baseball, avete mai cambiato la squadra per cui tifate?"

Ara Choi guardò i presenti. Tutti fecero no con la testa.

"Non ho mai cambiato squadra da quando l'ho scelta a dieci anni. Sono trent'anni che non vincono un campionato e questo mi fa ancora ribollire il sangue."

"Il senso di appartenenza... è qualcosa a cui continui ad aggrapparti anche se a un certo punto ti sembra sbagliato."

"Deve essere bello. Deve essere bello e piacevole. Se non fosse così, sarebbe insostenibile."

Non c'è da stupirsi che proprio un architetto abbia avuto un'idea del genere. Non è raro che una città o un villaggio imponga normative e restrizioni per mantenere inalterato il suo stile peculiare. Fu poi il marketer a dare concretamente corpo all'idea dell'architetto. Come spesso avviene con il marketing di successo, un'idea con il tempo assume la forma del mito.

La Prima Città

Hanno scelto il corvo come simbolo. I corvi amano i metalli che luccicano.

Amano molti tipi di metalli, ma soprattutto l'alluminio. Questo metallo riciclabile è diventato una casa modulare, una bellissima cupola e un rivestimento che ricorda la disposizione delle piume. I materiali da costruzione, una volta prodotti, vengono riciclati a circuito chiuso praticamente per sempre.

La gente ama indossare abiti neri. Il tessuto viene tagliato in modo da non produrre scarti e gli abiti così creati hanno una linearità e una vestibilità comode.

I tessuti, prodotti in quantità limitata ogni anno, presentano sottili differenze, anche se sono tutti dello stesso colore. La quantità di produzione è determinata da un'attenta analisi dei dati, che permette di evitare eccedenze o carenze. E in caso di anomalie, è possibile intervenire per risolverle.

Gli abitanti di questa moderna città vanno sempre di corsa, e quindi preferiscono assumere il cibo in cubetti personalizzati facili da conservare e consumare.

La Seconda Città

Il fungo è il loro simbolo. Sfruttano tutto ciò che si può decomporre. Le case sono costruite con legno e micelio di funghi come materiali principali. Ogni anno, la città cerca di superarsi nel realizzare strutture più alte possibili. Hanno recuperato le tecniche architettoniche tradizionali ed elaborato nuovi metodi per progettare pilastri, travi e travicelli che si incastrano alla perfezione.

Indossano abiti a base vegetale di colore écru. Probabilmente perché si abbinano bene alle case. Ogni anno tingono i tessuti con motivi di funghi in edizione limitata. Gli abiti fanno un bellissimo effetto addosso e, una volta interrati, si decompongono in poche settimane.

Gli hamburger di funghi sono eccellenti. È qualcosa che i visitatori devono provare per forza.

La Terza Città

La città voleva un delfino come mascotte. Ma i suoi abitanti venivano chiamati ragni dalle altre comunità, così è stato scelto il ragno come simbolo. Con i rifiuti ritrovati nell'oceano, soprattutto reti da pesca, hanno costruito una città che sembra un labirinto di amache. Le reti sono fissate con i cavi d'acciaio che si usano sulle navi.

Il suolo è ricoperto di pannelli ben attrezzati su cui può circolare qualsiasi cosa dotata di ruote, ma la gente spesso vuole allontanarsi dalla strada ed esplorare le reti e per questo indossa guanti di gomma e scarpe a punta divisa. Nella città predomina il verde delle reti da pesca, e così per distinguere facilmente le persone, si indossano magliette a righe sui toni del viola. Ogni anno vengono prodotti capi con righe di altezze e intervalli diversi, che sono diventanti oggetti da collezione.
Gli abitanti sono fieri dei loro prodotti realizzati con le alghe.

La Quarta Città

All'inizio c'erano pareri discordanti in merito a chiamare la città, città. Tutto è iniziato con una serie di accampamenti che si sono via via ingranditi. Il veloce approvvigionamento di derrate fresche ha sempre richiesto un grande consumo di energia, e così gli abitanti hanno risolto il problema invertendo la situazione, ossia spostando la città nei luoghi di produzione stagionale. Si spostano tutto l'anno, tracciando percorsi e occupandosi dell'approvvigionamento tra le città, mentre lavorano come lavoratori stagionali durante i raccolti.

"Avete presente i campeggiatori di una volta? Dicevano che amavano la natura, ma poi cambiavano tenda ogni anno e usavano un'infinità di prodotti usa e getta. Che disastro!"

"Certo, possiamo dirlo perché sono finiti i tempi in cui si bruciava legna per fare atmosfera."

Oggi non si fabbricano quasi più attrezzature da campeggio. Quelle prodotte in passato sono più che sufficienti. Si creano grandi strutture pubbliche unendo vecchie tende. Il colore più diffuso è una tonalità naturale tra il beige e il kaki, da cui il soprannome che gli hanno dato gli abitanti delle altre città: "pivieri".

Ogni anno condividono ricette di piatti stagionali.

La Quinta Città

In piena crisi climatica, delle magliaie volenterose si sono messe a disfare vecchi maglioni e a far circolare i filati senza sosta. Quando gli abitanti sono venuti a sapere che le pecore, le capre e gli alpaca che nel frattempo erano stati liberati non avevano un posto dove andare, hanno deciso di prenderli con sé. Ogni persona ne ha adottato uno come animale di compagnia e lo tosava con cura in primavera per produrre nuova lana. Le pecore, che erano stata modificate geneticamente in passato, non potevano vivere senza essere tosate così gli abitanti si sono assunti questo incarico. La toelettatura delle pecore da compagnia si è diffusa come quella dei cani. Molte le tendenze a breve e lungo termine, come il taglio a caschetto, il taglio a cuore, ecc.

Diverse città in rovina sono state ricostruite a maglia: pilastri spaccati, tetti sfondati e tutto ciò che era rotto o fatiscente.

Non ha niente a che fare con gli animali, ma per qualche motivo il formaggio vegano prodotto in città è considerato il migliore.

La Sesta Città

La città è stata costruita con la stampa 3D usando polimeri di canna da zucchero e paglia. È stata progettata come un formicaio, dapprima spontaneamente e poi in modo organizzato. La struttura per la circolazione dell'aria realizzata seguendo il modello di un formicaio si adattava bene alla città. Come colore per la città è stato scelto un rosa chiaro, particolarmente bello al tramonto. Poiché la struttura non lascia entrare molta luce solare, la gente indossa abiti di colore chiaro e preferisce tessuti luminosi. Per far durare più a lungo le fibre luminescenti, hanno inventato diversi metodi di lavaggio senz'acqua.

Come si può immaginare, i loro dolci sono eccellenti.

La Settima Città

Più di ogni altra, questa città crede nella durata. Non sognano solo edifici centenari, ma addirittura millenari. Tenendo conto dei terremoti, dei tifoni e delle inondazioni che caratterizzano la regione, gli edifici sono stati costruiti con una struttura otto volte più resistente del normale. I pilastri sono posizionati all'esterno della struttura così da poter modificare l'interno in modo flessibile. Non si può mai sapere quali saranno i gusti della gente nel futuro.

Esperti del colore sono stati incaricati di creare una combinazione cromatica intramontabile. Il colore primario è costituito da un raffinato grigio ghiaccio che soddisfa i gusti di tutti, affiancato da cinque tinte vivaci. Molto del loro lavoro è dedicato alla creazione di tessuti resistenti all'abrasione.

Attivi nel piantare querce con grande capacità di stoccaggio del carbonio, sono famosi per una varietà di piatti a base di ghiande.

L'Ottava Città

Sono convinti che il bambù debba essere il materiale del futuro, viste anche le sue qualità superiori alla canna da zucchero. Il panda è la loro mascotte, ma può apparire quasi un controsenso per questo gruppo di persone così tenaci. Sembra che abbiano deciso di risolvere con il bambù tutti i problemi relativi al cibo, all'abbigliamento e all'alloggio. Saltuariamente usano anche il rattan e si ispirano ai modelli dei dipinti asiatici. Le loro specialità sono riso e germogli di bambù.

***

Sono stati compiuti vari tentativi per realizzare altri modelli di città, ma non sono andati in porto. Le persone amavano le città di fondazione a cui appartenevano. In larga parte non hanno lasciato la città di provenienza. Come se avessero ereditato gli orientamenti politici di chi si è preso cura di loro dalla nascita, hanno vissuto tutta la vita con il senso di appartenenza che sentivano da giovani e solo in pochi sono partiti alla ricerca di uno stile di vita diverso. Quelli che sono andati a esplorare altre città, hanno portato una nuova ventata di vitalità.

Le città dove non si è nati sono sempre state mete di viaggio affascinanti ma non basta un viaggio per scoprirne tutti gli aspetti. Per questo sono stati organizzati molti programmi di scambio durante le varie fasi di evoluzione degli spazi urbani.

Chi lo desiderava poteva provare a vivere in tutte le città, ma a fronte dei pochi che tentavano, la maggioranza tendeva a esplorare a fondo due o tre città.

"L'idea che tutti possano sperimentare tutto è una menzogna che è passata di moda."

"È una menzogna che raccontavano le aziende per cercare di vendervi qualcosa. Sappiamo che quando si cerca di sperimentare tutto, si finisce alla deriva."

I primi a essere assoldati per assicurare la persistenza delle città sono stati gli storyteller. Nel corso del tempo, i membri dell'Iniziativa per la Decarbonizzazione sono cambiati, ma i nuovi membri ne hanno ereditato l'orientamento. Hanno convenuto che fosse giunto il momento di far intervenire la narrazione di storie. Nulla sopravvive più a lungo o in modo più tenace delle storie, quindi hanno deciso di utilizzarle come un collante o un rinforzante. La maggior parte degli storyteller ha accettato di partecipare firmando un accordo di riservatezza. Alcune storie sono state prodotte e divulgate attraverso canali ufficiali, mentre altre sono state create e diffuse in modi più discreti.

***

Una ghost story ha investito per la prima volta l'Ottava Città. Parlava di qualcosa che viveva nella foresta di bambù. Anche nell'era della ragione, i boschetti di bambù di notte gettavano le tenebre nel cuore delle persone. Il timore che qualcosa di invisibile potesse essere in agguato era sempre presente. All'inizio correva voce che si trattasse di un animale selvatico che poteva mordere le persone, poi che fosse un evaso, ma soprattutto si diceva che fosse lo spirito di un defunto.

"Aspettate un attimo. È noi che abbiamo messo in giro questa voce?"

I responsabili del progetto erano perplessi.

"No, ma non pensate che dovremmo usarla?"

Così i responsabili hanno creato "l'essere che risponde". Si trattava di un dispositivo elementare composto da un microfono, un altoparlante e un sistema di IA che sintetizzava un linguaggio naturale. Ha dato ottimi risultati. Chi aveva domande da fare le gridava nel boschetto di bambù e a volte riceveva una risposta. Le risposte erano vaghe ma pertinenti e, a volte, estremamente incisive.

"Il segreto è che deve accadere 'qualche volta'. Non è divertente se il sistema risponde a ogni domanda."

Impostare la modalità casuale è stata la scelta giusta. A volte la risposta giungeva a più persone in pieno giorno, oppure a una sola persona alle prime luci dell'alba. A volte il sistema forniva risposte in successione, altre volte non rispondeva per più di un mese. Gli storyteller hanno scelto con cura i libri da cui trarre le frasi per comporre le risposte. I titolari dei diritti d'autore hanno naturalmente firmato accordi di riservatezza e ricevuto delle royalty.

"Le frasi tratte dal libro l'altro giorno non erano appropriate. Tuttavia, un linguaggio troppo datato sarebbe scoraggiante per i contemporanei. Impostiamo il periodo a circa cinquant'anni fa e scegliamo libri di quell'epoca."

Le risposte della IA, ottenute dalla fusione di più libri, hanno impressionato perfino i project manager. La gente, ovviamente, si era resa conto che le ghost story, indipendentemente da come erano iniziate, stavano diventando degli scaltri espedienti, ma le apprezzavano comunque.

Per gli abitanti della Settima Città è stato realizzato un musical di sei ore. Il musical è basato sulla vita di Shin Minhee, una studiosa antropoide che ha scoperto un nuovo antibiotico. Il primo atto narra la nascita e l'infanzia di Shin Minhee nella Settima Città. Racconta eventi come la perdita della sorella a causa di un'epidemia, la tragica separazione dal suo primo amore e la campagna che ha condotto insieme agli amici a favore degli ecosistemi urbani. Il secondo atto, che inizia dopo l'intervallo, ha un tono completamente diverso. Le ricerche della studiosa sui gibboni e l'episodio dei bracconieri sono stati rappresentati in modo grandioso e scenografico. Gli spettatori sono rimasti impressionati dall'effetto realistico dei gibboni e dai loro movimenti spettacolari, un capolavoro della Peninsula Robotics. La scena del combattimento con i bracconieri, che costituisce il culmine del secondo atto, è stata accolta favorevolmente anche dai pacifisti, che non hanno disapprovato la morte dei bracconieri. Il terzo atto racconta in modo commovente la scoperta di Shin Minhee e le tante vite che ha salvato. Mentre lo osserva, Shin vede un gibbone dalle mani nere applicare su una ferita una pianta sconosciuta, che la studiosa avrebbe poi descritto a botanici e a microbiologi. La storia del triangolo amoroso fra i tre studiosi è stata un'aggiunta destinata al pubblico e a vivacizzare lo spettacolo, ma ha sollevato le proteste di chi all'epoca lavorava nello stesso centro di ricerca.

"Si sono inventati tutto! Non era amore, era un semplice rapporto fra colleghi!".

"Perché le storie non possono essere raccontate come sono?"

Il musical veniva messo in scena ogni anno per celebrare l'anniversario della fondazione della Settima Città. Non c'era da nessun'altra parte un teatro progettato con tale perfezione, e così veniva molta gente da altre città a vedere il musical.

La Sesta Città era il centro dell'industria degli idoli. Sono stati i fan i primi a sollevare domande sugli sprechi che comportava l'industria degli idoli. La cultura di buttare via gli album senza nemmeno aprirli o di cliccare senza ascoltare per aumentare il rating è completamente cambiata. Si è continuato a riflettere e a lavorare per creare esperienze più gratificanti, consumando meno. Mentre si discuteva su come sostituire il senso di appagamento che le persone di solito provavano attraverso le classifiche di vendita, un progettista dell'Iniziativa per la Decarbonizzazione ha proposto di utilizzare la realtà aumentata. Le strade sinuose e gli interni in penombra della Sesta Città si prestavano bene alla realtà aumentata. È iniziata una gara avvincente per vedere quali fan degli idoli riuscissero a completare il maggior numero di quest. La musica e la danza occupavano ancora il centro della scena, ma si sono aggiunti altri elementi che hanno avuto esiti inaspettati. Alla fine dell'anno, i risultati delle quest sono stati annunciati insieme alle cerimonie di premiazione. Le quest consistevano in un'interessante combinazione di giochi elettronici e attività di servizio pubblico. Non c'è da stupirsi, visto che sono stati i fan degli idoli a creare la più ampia espansione dell'area forestale.

Un'autrice di libri per bambini nata e cresciuta nella Quinta Città scrisse una storia che aveva per protagonista una pecorella di nome Danbom. Danbom aveva un problema: non le cresceva il vello e qualsiasi rimedio provasse risultava inutile.

"Che pecora sono se non ho il vello?"

Quando il primo volume uscì, e le lotte di Danbom per dare un senso alla sua vita riscossero un grande successo, l'Iniziativa per la Decarbonizzazione fece in modo che l'autrice potesse dedicarsi a tempo pieno alla scrittura e alla serie di Danbom. Con il proseguire della saga, la pecora imparò a lavorare in modo sano alla relazione fra sé e il mondo circostante.

La storia della formazione di Danbom che diventa infine un'adulta sicura di sé, senza eccessivo odio o amore per se stessa, ha commosso molte persone che fino ad allora erano rimaste insensibili ad altre narrazioni. L'Iniziativa per la Decarbonizzazione ha usato con grande intelligenza la serie Danbom per scopi educativi e di animazione. I bambini di tutte le città, non solo della Quinta, sono cresciuti leggendo le storie di Danbom. I viaggiatori che arrivavano nella Quinta Città, alla vista di una pecorella gridavano "Danbom!", sull'orlo delle lacrime. Gli abitanti che possedevano una pecorella come animale da compagnia trovavano ridicole queste persone, ma in fondo provavano piacere al pensiero che la loro pecora assomigliasse a Danbom.

Gli abitanti della Quarta Città volevano aprire un circo fin dall'inizio.

"È logico, se ci spostiamo in grandi tende come queste, perché dovremmo fare qualcosa di diverso dal circo? Voglio dire, non sarebbe strano?"

Quando ormai il circo era quasi pronto per l'inaugurazione, sono stati aggiunti interessanti elementi per l'arrampicata su roccia, visto che gli abitanti della Quarta Città erano fondamentalmente scalatori. Le prese da arrampicata sono state sistemate ovunque sul palcoscenico, in modo visibile o nascosto, e gli artisti, che sembravano vincere la forza di gravità, utilizzavano lo spazio in modo tridimensionale. Sono state create molte storie, la più amata delle quali ha per protagonisti gli abitanti della Quarta

Città che si mettono alla ricerca di un adolescente che si ritrova in gravi difficoltà dopo essere giunto da un'altra città per un programma di scambio. Ad ogni spettacolo, la città di provenienza del giovane veniva cambiata. È stata una buona idea, tenuto conto del personaggio dell'adolescente, adorabile ma imprudente e sprovveduto. Le disavventure del protagonista, l'andirivieni della squadra di soccorso e gli esseri mitici venuti fuori da oggetti naturali che il protagonista incontra mentre è in preda al delirio, sono stati rappresentati attraverso la pantomima. Gli abitanti della Quarta Città trovavano troppo loquaci quelli delle altre città, ed erano contenti di aver scelto la pantomima come forma espressiva. Gli spettatori lasciavano il circo con uno o due buoni consigli, dispensati senza pronunciare una parola, su come sopravvivere se ti ritrovi perso nella natura selvaggia.

Se gli abitanti della Quarta Città scalavano montagne, quelli della Terza Città facevano immersioni subacquee. Per questi ultimi, che ottengono il brevetto da sub come fosse la patente di guida, è stata creata una leggenda sui tesori sommersi.

"Dicono che il fondo nero sia stato nascosto su un'isola che è finita sott'acqua per l'innalzamento del livello del mare."

"Di chi è il fondo nero? Da cosa era costituito?"

All'inizio si pensò naturalmente che fosse in oro, ma poi si ipotizzò che fosse costituito da opere d'arte rubate o antichi manufatti, informazioni tecniche dimenticate che la gente voleva recuperare, o un enigma che, se risolto, avrebbe sbloccato l'eredità di un personaggio famoso.

C'era chi si immergeva una o due volte e poi se ne dimenticava. Ma c'era anche chi ci passava tutto il suo tempo libero. Una volta ogni tanto, veniva alla luce un elemento interessante che valeva la pena definire indizio, ma il tesoro resta introvabile.

"Ogni volta che ci immergiamo, torniamo in superficie con dei rifiuti. Pensi che sia uno stratagemma per dare una ripulita alla zona?"

"Ci deve essere di nuovo lo zampino di quelli della Decarbonizzazione."

Le persone che avevano nascosto il tesoro sorridevano con nonchalance. Se fosse stato rinvenuto un tesoro, ne avrebbero nascosto un altro. La lista dei tesori esiste da centinaia d'anni. Prima che fosse stilata la lista, nessuno sapeva che ci fossero così tanti tipi di tesori in grado di resistere all'acqua e al tempo.

Quelli della Seconda Città hanno creato un gioco d'azione con un'ampia gamma di personaggi antropomorfizzati a forma di fungo. Qualcuno che volesse capire perché i funghi combattevano tra loro avrebbero trovato la spiegazione stravagante, ma in realtà nessuno si fece domande perché i personaggi a forma di fungo erano di una bellezza incredibile. L'Entoloma rhodopolium lanciava il suo *satgat* come un maestro di arti marziali e lo strascico della gonna della signora Fungo, velata, era ipnotizzante. I funghi aragosta attaccavano in gruppo e i funghi magici assalivano la mente. I giocatori adoravano le ramificazioni del bucero appiccicoso e il cappello tondo del falso chiodino. Quando i funghi commestibili e velenosi si assomigliavano, erano accompagnati da una storia collaterale che rivelava i segreti sulla nascita e la discendenza di fratelli e rivali.

I comandi di gioco erano semplici, ma le storie erano ricche e articolate. Non servivano solo a fornire informazioni sui funghi velenosi ma a rappresentare il senso di meraviglia nei confronti di oggetti di specie diversa. Il gioco sembrava dire che, sebbene alcuni organismi particolari possano essere buoni o cattivi per le persone, la loro esistenza complessa e ambigua suscita stupore, ed è proprio quando le persone si meravigliano che diventano più umane. Il gioco è amato da moltissimo tempo. I vincitori sono sempre gli studenti delle scuole elementari.

Un giorno gli abitanti della Prima Città si sono accorti che nel loro gioco di spelling preferito era nascosta una storia sotto forma di codice. Chi ha cominciato a nascondere la storia? Quando? Tutti sospettarono i narratori dell'Iniziativa per la Decarbonizzazione, ma sorprendentemente non c'entravano nulla. Anzi, anche l'Iniziativa rimase sbalordita e analizzando la situazione notarono con stupore coloro che stavano scoprendo, arricchendo e sviluppando storie che nessuno sembrava aver inventato.

"E se la storia diventa troppo tetra? Non dovremmo intervenire?"

"Non si deve scrivere un finale tragico. Alcuni possono spingere la storia in quella direzione per cattiveria, ma non deve finire in quel modo."

Ne seguì una produzione collaborativa senza precedenti. Una storia ha preso presto direzioni diverse. Le storie sono diventate simili e poi dissimili. Erano o completamente scollegate o si influenzavano a vicenda. Erano incentrate o sull'amplificazione delle emozioni o sulla trasmissione di un messaggio. La parte che cercava di imporre l'ordine e quella che si crogiolava nel caos si scontravano con forza.

***

Le città verranno costruite e distrutte. Anche se una città dovesse tramontare, la trama e l'ordito della narrazione passeranno nelle mani di chi crede in quelle storie.

E alla fine non si può dire con certezza se quelle città esistano all'interno o all'esterno della storia. Sta a voi decidere.

---

1. Nota del traduttore: il nome della pecora, Danbom, significa "dolce primavera" in coreano.
2. Nota del traduttore: il *satgat* è un copricapo a forma di cono, fatto in genere di bambù, in uso in Asia orientale, Asia meridionale e Sud-est asiatico.

La perfezione della mitologia
Federico Campagna

La perfezione della mitologia
Federico Campagna

L'Andalusia, la regione più a sud della Spagna. Per secoli avamposto del mondo islamico in Europa e giardino intellettuale del Mediterraneo. Da un "melting pot" di musulmani, ebrei e cristiani, mistici andalusi come Ibn Arabi, poeti come Ibn Hazm e filosofi come Ibn Rashid e Maimonides hanno dato vita a correnti di pensiero che avrebbero cambiato il mondo spingendosi ben oltre i confini del loro luogo di origine. Tra loro figurava anche uno scrittore, meno famoso ma non meno interessante: Ibn Tufail. Medico, teologo e astronomo di alta levatura, fu molto stimato dai contemporanei. Oggi è noto soprattutto per essere l'autore visionario di uno dei primi esempi di romanzo filosofico-scientifico. L'opera, tradotta in latino con il titolo di *Philosophus Autodidactus*, racconta la vita di un giovane che cresce da solo su un'isola deserta. Allevato da una gazzella, trascorre l'infanzia esplorando le leggi della natura, della divinità e del suo pensiero. Unendo osservazione empirica e speculazione astratta, il protagonista finisce per diventare il più grande filosofo della sua epoca immaginaria.

È così, scrive Ibn Tufail, che sono nati tutti i veri filosofi: osservando intorno a sé e dentro di sé, per poi tradurre quanto osservato in astrazioni pratiche capaci di guidare le loro vite.

Per quanto originale, il metodo proposto da Tufail ha avuto tuttavia illustri predecessori, di cui l'autore non era a conoscenza. Questa genealogia è stata illustrata in modo esaustivo solo nel XX secolo. Nel loro *Hamlet's Mill* (Il mulino di Amleto), del 1969, gli studiosi Giorgio de Santillana e Hertha von Dechend hanno individuato lo stesso metodo in un'altra forma di saggezza, più antica della filosofia e in nulla inferiore: la mitologia. Dopo aver analizzato in dettaglio i primi miti conosciuti, così come appaiono nelle prime testimonianze scritte databili al IV millennio a.C., Santillana e Dechend hanno scoperto che quelle che sembravano pure narrazioni fantastiche contenevano in realtà riferimenti molto precisi a moti astronomici visibili nel cielo all'epoca della loro composizione. Dèi ed eroi potevano essere interpretati come la veste narrativa dei corpi celesti, mentre le loro gesta e avventure offrivano una traduzione mitologica del moto regolare del cielo notturno. Secondo Santillana e Dechend, è così che le menti scientifiche delle varie civiltà arcaiche hanno creato narrazioni mitologiche affini per descrivere gli stessi eventi astronomici. Il linguaggio mitologico, quindi, è da considerarsi come una vera e propria forma di conoscenza, frutto di osservazioni empiriche e di calcoli matematici.

La sequenza di questo processo, qui come nella storia di Tufail, ha un'importanza fondamentale. Si inizia con le osservazioni empiriche e le relative annotazioni matematiche. Questa prima fase è seguita dalla traduzione mitologica o filosofica di quanto osservato. L'astronomia precede l'astrologia. In altre parole, al livello più primitivo del pensiero troviamo le cosiddette "scienze esatte", mentre a un secondo livello, intellettualmente più raffinato, abbiamo quelle che oggi vengono generalmente bollate come invenzioni fantastiche della mitologia o inutili elucubrazioni filosofiche.
Per quelle menti arcaiche, a cui dobbiamo le fondamenta dell'edificio della conoscenza contemporanea, il giudizio di valore su "oggettività" scientifica e narrazione mitologica era opposto al nostro. La scienza veniva considerata come la mera rappresentazione della realtà visibile, e la mitologia la sua astrazione e perfezione pratica.

Questo rovesciamento potrebbe apparire sorprendente. Ma c'è un vantaggio a esprimere narrativamente quello che potrebbe essere illustrato attraverso il chiaro linguaggio dei fatti. Per capire questo, tuttavia, dobbiamo ampliare il raggio della nostra esplorazione della mitologia non solo con l'osservazione astronomica, ma anche con l'osservazione empirica — completata dove possibile dai calcoli matematici — di tutti gli eventi e le cose che accadono nella vita.

Per ognuno di noi, la vita inizia nell'oscurità. Non abbiamo alcun ricordo del momento in cui siamo nati. Non ricordiamo nulla di ciò che ci è accaduto prima della nascita.

Arriviamo nel mondo totalmente inconsapevoli, impreparati e confusi. Cosa ci facciamo qui? Cos'è "qui"? E chi siamo? A scuola non ci insegnano a rispondere a questi interrogativi esistenziali, ma ci propongono una serie di tecniche per affrontare la loro irrisolvibilità. Queste tecniche, riunite sotto il nome generale di "conoscenza" (scientifica, tecnica, psicologica, politica, ecc.), consistono in una serie di potenti narrazioni con cui possiamo sospendere la nostra incredulità verso la nostra assurda condizione esistenziale: essere "vivi", all'interno di un "corpo" e di una "personalità", dentro un "mondo," in un "tempo" e uno "spazio", i cui referenti materiali reali rimangono oscuri.

Concentrare la nostra attenzione su queste narrazioni collettive ci consente di liberarci dai dubbi metafisici ed esistenziali che tormentano nel profondo ognuno di noi. Acquistiamo la capacità di riconoscerci nella nostra identità, e di ricondurre il mondo che ci circonda alle etichette linguistiche che sono state associate a ognuna delle sue parti.

Ma talvolta, come avviene nella nostra epoca, tali narrazioni si rivelano così efficaci da farci passare dalla sospensione dell'incredulità al riconoscimento della loro assoluta veridicità. Non vengono più percepite come narrazioni e diventano invece "fatti." Questa svolta ideologica, che sembra offrirci una solida conoscenza della vera "natura" del mondo, porta una grande serenità. Ci invita a smettere di scandagliare l'inquietante mistero in cui siamo immersi, e di tormentarci sui limiti della nostra comprensione. Ma questa serenità ha il suo prezzo: dobbiamo accettare di essere prigionieri delle narrazioni con cui abbiamo rivestito la realtà. La serenità in cambio della libertà: l'eterno dilemma.

La mitologia affronta questa situazione con un'ottica diversa, pacata, che non mette in discussione la legittimità degli altri metodi attraverso cui tentiamo di imbrigliare il cavallo selvaggio della realtà. Infatti, come sostengono Santillana e Dechend, la mitologia rimane fortemente legata alla conoscenza scientifica. Allo stesso tempo, però, intrattiene uno stretto rapporto con quell'inquietante abisso che altre narrazioni collettive tentano di relegare in un territorio lontano, irraggiungibile.

La mitologia è consapevole di essere una forma di narrazione, invece che un insieme di verità fattuali, e non si vergogna a presentarsi come tale, con tutti i difetti e le contraddizioni propri alle opere di fantasia. Nell'Antico Egitto, era comune passare gli attributi di una divinità a un'altra, o cambiarle il nome - prassi che poteva investire anche il dio creatore –, con una libertà simile a quella che usa uno scrittore di oggi con i suoi personaggi: Amun diventa Atum, che diventa Ra, che diventa Ptah, rimanendo fondamentalmente lo stesso dio. I nomi sono solo nomi, dopotutto, mentre la vera realtà dell'esistenza (il nome segreto di ogni cosa) valica i confini dello stesso linguaggio. Ciò che conta non è la precisione di una definizione, ma il suo effetto.

La mitologia non è un sistema chiuso di conoscenza. È ricca di contraddizioni e percorsa da un movimento continuo tra l'alto e il basso, il cosmico e il terreno, la tragedia e la commedia. Rispecchia l'esperienza della vita stessa, con la sua paradossale commistione di eternità e tempo, di conoscenza e ignoranza, di impotenza e libertà. Non disconosce la dura condizione dell'uomo, né la sua ricerca di un sistema di senso che possa salvarlo dall'abisso del Caos.

La mitologia avvolge la cruda essenza della realtà in un involucro di nomi, personaggi, storie, tutti apparentemente provvisti di un significato letterale. Nel compiere questa operazione, tuttavia, non svuota la realtà del suo mistero, non ingabbia il mondo in un rigido catalogo di definizioni che si presentano come assolutamente vere, fattuali e oggettive. La mitologia si tiene a pari distanza dalle briglie concettuali con cui tentiamo di domare il Caos della realtà e dalla perturbante ferinità che si agita sotto ogni Cosmo abitabile, uno spazio – il kosmos – che è, nella sua accezione etimologica, "ordine" e "bellezza".

È così che il racconto mitologico, morbido e consapevole, può essere considerato un'astrazione e una perfezione pratica delle forme di conoscenza "dure" e "fattuali". Con la sua dimensione fantastica - a metà strada tra il realismo naturale e il silenzio sovrannaturale - la mitologia ci offre uno strumento straordinario per affrontare la nostra più profonda confusione esistenziale.
I miti trasformano i nostri dubbi esistenziali in skepsis: una duplice ricerca sull'insensata oscurità che ci avvolge e sulla luce immaginaria che abbiamo bisogno di proiettare intorno a noi. È una forma di saggezza esistenziale, sostanziata di conoscenza astratta. La mitologia, in tal senso, rappresenta la madre amorevole della filosofia e la figlia legittima della scienza.

Il giardino rinascimentale è una metafora concreta con cui possiamo approfondire la nostra riflessione sul rapporto tra mitologia, filosofia e scienza. Pur realizzato in una molteplicità di varianti, il giardino rinascimentale si presenta composto strutturalmente da tre parti: l'*hortus*, un'area produttiva con alberi da frutto e vegetali; un'altra area dedicata alle forme geometriche, architettoniche quanto naturali (arte topiaria); e il *bosco*, con alberi e piante lasciati crescere in modo spontaneo, fra cui compaiono sculture e fontane statuarie. Come molti tipi di giardino dell'antichità, primo fra tutti il *paridaiza* persiano, e come larga parte degli spazi urbani antichi a cui il Rinascimento si è ispirato, dalla struttura del tempio di una tipica urbe romana alla perfezione circolare della città nuova di Baghdad, il giardino rinascimentale riproduce in piccolo la struttura dell'universo.

Presi singolarmente, l'*hortus* produttivo, che richiama la scienza coeva, e l'area geometrica con la sua perfezione astratta - specchio di un sistema filosofico perfettamente ordinato -, non riescono a restituire l'essenza di un giardino rinascimentale. Infatti l'universo non si compone unicamente della dimensione produttiva e di quella astratta. Contiene anche insondabili silenzi e spazi intermedi, la *ta metaxy* sostenuta da Platone che mette in relazione i diversi aspetti dell'esistenza. Tuttavia, la lingua con cui questi spazi intermedi si rivelano reciprocamente le dimensioni della realtà resta sempre, per loro, in parte oscura, e straniera per tutti: parlano una lingua mitologica.

Al pari della mitologia, il *bosco* è quel territorio intermedio fra gli opposti: Cosmo e Caos, arte e natura, linguaggio e ineffabilità, presenza e distruzione, tempo ed eternità. Le statue nel *bosco* non offrono un mero piacere estetico, ma uno strumento di potenziamento cognitivo. La nudità stessa della natura (ossia la nudità della realtà prima e oltre il linguaggio) evocata e incarnata dalla crescita spontanea del *bosco* è infatti incomprensibile e, paradossalmente, celata alla comprensione umana. Solo la presenza simbolica dell'opera d'arte, che funge da specchio deformante, può guidare lo spettatore verso quella dimensione ineffabile della realtà.

Il *bosco* rinascimentale non si limita a rappresentare visivamente la struttura concettuale della mitologia, ma mette in luce il ruolo della narrazione mitologica per affrontare il problema contemporaneo della comprensione di un nuovo rapporto tra l'ambiente cosiddetto "naturale" e l'ambito delle attività antropiche. A differenza dell'*hortus*, dove la natura è asservita alla produzione, o dell'area geometrica del giardino, dove essa è ridotta a una catalogazione concettuale, il *bosco* suggerisce la possibilità di una collaborazione cognitiva tra forze antropiche e non antropiche. Attraverso la mitologizzazione, è possibile immaginare la convivenza di diverse forme di esistenza come una sorta di equilibrio sospeso, in cui, come nel *bosco*, la statua rivela il senso dell'edera nello stesso momento in cui questa divora la pietra. È uno spazio in cui la morte e la vita, l'eternità e il tempo, sono strettamente intrecciati, e nessuno osa esprimere la propria preferenza per l'una o per l'altro.

Perché il 2086? Per il 1492

Kyong Park

Perché il 2086? Per il 1492
Kyong Park

Perché siamo così "isolati" quando dovremmo essere così "connessi" attraverso la globalizzazione dell'informazione, della finanza, delle merci e persino della cultura? Perché siamo così incerti sul nostro futuro se così tante persone vivono secondo standard di ricchezza, consumo e libertà senza precedenti? Perché il grande progresso della nostra civiltà ci sta portando più vicino all'estinzione che alla perfezione promessa? Come è iniziato questo grande paradosso del destino umano?

Permettetemi di ipotizzare che potrebbe essere iniziato nel 1492, quando Cristoforo Colombo "scopre" l'America nell'ultimo anno della Reconquista, ossia gli otto secoli di guerre combattute dai regni cristiani per espellere gli arabi dalla Penisola iberica. Questi due eventi, strettamente correlati, hanno dato il via a una serie di cambiamenti nell'assetto mondiale che, a mio avviso, ci ha portato al nostro "climate endgame". Da lì comincia l'ascesa dell'Europa occidentale, poi dell'Occidente, che è arrivato a definire e a dominare il modo di vivere della maggior parte degli uomini e di altre forme di vita su questo pianeta.

La rinascita dell'Europa

Dopo secoli di buio, l'Europa inizia a risollevarsi e a rifiorire. La Morte Nera, che fra il 1346 e 1353 aveva sterminato pressoché la metà della popolazione del continente, porta, ironia della sorte, a un aumento del costo del lavoro, da cui scaturisce, probabilmente, un incremento del tasso di natalità. La crescita della popolazione e la proliferazione delle città hanno pesanti ripercussioni sul paesaggio già devastato e sui terreni abbandonati.

Intorno al 1550 solo il 10% del territorio inglese e scozzese era ancora boscoso, e già "più della metà dell'energia da combustibili fossili della Gran Bretagna proveniva dal carbone".[1] Anche la penisola iberica era interessata da fenomeni analoghi – esaurimento delle risorse e devastazioni ambientali – che si stavano espandendo nel continente. L'Europa aveva bisogno di risorse e approvvigionamenti per la sua ripresa demografica ed economica, come si è registrato nel XV secolo, in epoca bassomedievale. L'uso dell'energia da combustibili fossili ha avuto inizio in Europa occidentale.

L'Europa, con le sue risorse in esaurimento e alla disperata ricerca di scambi commerciali con l'Asia, aveva più che mai bisogno di aggirare l'embargo de facto imposto dallo Stato islamico. La Reconquista, a sua volta, aveva trasformato la penisola iberica da ponte con l'Africa a collo di bottiglia per la circolazione di persone e merci dall'Europa. L'unica via che rimaneva per raggiungere l'Asia era pertanto l'oceano, che in molti affrontarono. Le navi salpavano naturalmente dalle coste più a sud della Penisola iberica appena liberata. Rispetto alle sette spedizioni di Zheng He, che attraversa l'Oceano Indiano con 317 navi e 28.000 uomini per arrivare in Africa orientale (1405-1433),[2 3] quella di Colombo, con le sue 3 navi e i suoi 90 uomini, sembra una spedizione in solitaria organizzata da Stati appena nati. Eppure cambiarono il mondo, non con gli ideali, ma con la sete di profitto, caratteristica dell'odierno "climatic endgame".

Un'Europa brutale e disperata?
Ma come ha potuto una manciata di uomini brutali a bordo di misere imbarcazioni arrivare a "controllare tutti gli oceani del mondo nel giro di mezzo secolo e a sottomettere alcune delle aree più sviluppate delle Americhe nel giro di una sola generazione"?[4] Secondo William H. McNeill, la spiegazione sta in "(1) una ben radicata bellicosità e temerarietà che si esprime per mezzo di (2) una complessa tecnologia militare, soprattutto in campo navale; e (3) una popolazione abituata a sopravvivere a una serie di malattie".[5]

Commistione di coraggio e brutalità, la temerarietà di Cortez e Pizarro nelle Americhe e quella di Almeida e Albuquerque nell'Oceano Indiano hanno confuso i confini tra bene e male. Fin dall'arrivo di Colombo, il genocidio degli indigeni nelle Indie Occidentali, noto come la "Leggenda Nera", ha visto terribili efferatezze come neonati indigeni dati in pasto ai cani da combattimento spagnoli. Questo e altri crimini atroci, troppo numerosi per essere menzionati in questa sede, sono stati ben documentati dal frate domenicano e riformista Bartolomé de las Casas (1484-1566), e successivamente illustrati da Theodor de Bry (1528-1598).[6] Una tale mancanza di responsabilità, senza alcun rimorso, è il modello che abbiamo applicato nel nostro rapporto con la natura. È probabile che abbiamo imparato a perpetuare l'ecocidio facendo prima pratica sulla nostra specie, così come gli attuali padroni di provenienza indigena di molti territori dell'America Latina hanno imparato dai loro padroni schiavisti europei.

Viene da chiedersi se tale brutalità non sia stata generata dalle spietate guerre di religione e da altri conflitti tra molti Stati durante le guerre di Riforma (1522-1712). Le vittime di massacri, genocidi, malattie e carestie si attestano fra i 7 e i 17,7 milioni, che equivalgono a circa il 9-22% della popolazione europea del 1600.[7] La guerra dei Trent'anni (1618-48) ha sterminato da sola un terzo della popolazione dell'attuale Germania. Il resto delle morti è imputabile al crescendo di azioni militari, malattie e violenze, tre fattori che hanno avuto un ruolo chiave nell'espansionismo coloniale.

La storia violenta dell'Occidente è forse in grado di spiegare i suoi atti successivi, ossia gli 85-107 milioni di morti delle due guerre mondiali in pochi anni, o le 1.665 tonnellate di bombe, comprese quella al napalm, che hanno ucciso circa 100.000 persone a Tokyo nella sola notte del 9-10 marzo 1945? Le bombe atomiche su Hiroshima e Nagasaki sono state sganciate per un razzismo di fondo, per salvare la vita di soldati occidentali, considerati più preziosi dei civili giapponesi, diventati cavie da laboratorio per i test atomici, trattati alla stregua di animali?

Al di là della diagnosi di McNeill di "una ben radicata bellicosità e temerarietà che si esprime per mezzo di una complessa tecnologia militare", la nostra violenza su altri esseri umani avrebbe potuto spingersi oltre e distruggere la Terra? O sono stati solo pochi uomini fuori dal comune, inebriati dallo spirito di avventura e dall'enorme profitto da realizzare, a diventare i primi capitalisti del Rinascimento? È per questo che le teorie darwiniane sulla "sopravvivenza del più adatto" sono nate in Europa? L'Antropocene ha avuto inizio nel 1492, quando la cultura che lo ha definito ha attraversato l'Atlantico, quando il mondo cristiano ha fatto "un piccolo passo per l'uomo, ma un grande passo per l'umanità" e ha cominciato a dominare il mondo e la sua natura?

A commettere le più orrende atrocità nelle Americhe non furono i colonizzatori ma ciò che essi portarono con sé: vaiolo, morbillo, tifo e altre malattie. La minaccia biologica fu così potente che il passaggio di Cortez da solo ridusse la popolazione del Messico centrale da

11 milioni (1519) a 1,5 milioni (1650).[8] I genocidi del popolo Tahina dopo lo sbarco di Colombo a Hispaniola (Repubblica Dominicana e Haiti) registrarono un numero di vittime analogo. Le scie di sangue in Centro e Sud America vennero tracciate da Léon a Portorico, da Velázquez a Cuba e da Balboa lungo l'Oceano Pacifico, non da un laboratorio di Wuhan.

La colonizzazione del mondo

I guadagni inattesi provenienti dalla triangolazione commerciale lungo l'asse atlantico sono molto sottovalutati da coloro che sostengono che l'Occidente, che comprende Australia, Nuova Zelanda, Canada e Stati Uniti, si è sviluppato esclusivamente grazie ai suoi sforzi e al suo ingegno. Siamo grati alla teoria dei vantaggi comparati di David Ricardo (1772-1823) e a quella del libero mercato di Adam Smith (1723-1790), mentre resta nell'ombra il ruolo del lavoro e dello sfruttamento delle risorse nelle terre coloniali. Ciononostante, nel 1851 la rivista 'The Economist' commentava entusiasticamente che "negli ultimi cinquant'anni... si è assistito a un progresso più rapido e sorprendente di quanto sia mai avvenuto in tutti i secoli precedenti. In diversi aspetti cruciali la differenza tra il XVIII e il XIX secolo è maggiore di quella tra il I e il XVIII secolo, per quanto riguarda l'Europa civilizzata".[9]

L'imperialismo coloniale occidentale si è nutrito con il vorace sfruttamento delle risorse naturali, e ha dato il via alla catena globale di produzione, consumo e spreco. Siamo diventati gli assassini della Terra, non i suoi guardiani. Il nostro cammino verso il "climatic endgame" è iniziato nel 1492.

L'avidità dell'Occidente

Perché scomodare la vecchia storia del colonialismo? È allora che l'avidità e la ricchezza hanno assunto significati e raggiunto livelli del tutto nuovi? Il conquistador era "come un uomo in preda alla pazzia, folle, fuori di sé, rapito dalla disperata sete di oro e argento"? Francisco Pizarro ne rappresenta un esempio eloquente. Catturò il re Inca Atahualpa, il quale offrì come riscatto di far riempire d'oro e d'argento una sala lunga quasi 7 metri, larga 5 e alta quasi 3. Nonostante l'ingente riscatto, che venne raccolto in soli due mesi, il re venne giustiziato (1513).[10] Il fatto segna l'inizio dell'estrazione di 150.000 tonnellate d'argento e d'oro dalle montagne del Perù e del Messico, un terzo delle quali furono utilizzate dall'Inghilterra per pagare i debiti commerciali con la Cina.[11]

Il corsaro e mercante di schiavi Francis Drake (ca. 1540-1596) portò ai suoi investitori un profitto pari al 4700%. Fra questi, la regina Elisabetta I Tudor (1558-1603), utilizzò tre quarti dei proventi per saldare l'intero debito estero dell'Inghilterra. In segno di gratitudine, conferì a Drake il titolo di "Sir". Pirateria e monarchia diventano le due facce di una stessa medaglia, come avviene per le compagnie delle Indie Orientali di Gran Bretagna, Francia e Olanda.

Le merci preziose non erano solo costituite dall'oro e dall'argento delle Americhe. La Compagnia britannica delle Indie orientali impiantò coltivazioni di papaveri da oppio nelle regioni di Bihar e Benares, lungo il Gange, e cominciò a esportare la droga in Cina alla fine dal XVII secolo.[12] Nel 1796[13] la produzione raggiunse le 260 tonnellate annue, che divennero 1950 nel 1833, quando entrarono in questo commercio anche i mercanti americani, tra cui il nonno del futuro presidente Franklin D. Roosevelt.[14] La regina Vittoria (regno 1837-1901), come la regina Elisabetta prima di lei, utilizzò i proventi del commercio per saldare i debiti con la Cina.[15] L'avidità raggiunse un nuovo apice: la Corona.

Ma permettetemi di parlare ora dell'alluvione del 2022 in Pakistan, che ha sommerso il 10-12% dell'intera nazione, distruggendo quasi 1 milione di case e danneggiandone un altro milione e quattrocentomila. Si contano più di un milione di capi di bestiame uccisi, e oltre 13mila km di strade e 4389 ponti danneggiati o distrutti. Dopo le inondazioni avvenute in Asia meridionale nel 2020, questa alluvione è il peggiore disastro ad aver colpito il Pakistan. Per tutta risposta, gli attivisti del Paese hanno iniziato a reclamare un "risarcimento climatico". Huma Yusuf, editorialista del quotidiano pakistano *Dawn*, così lo descrive:

> È sempre più evidente che Paesi come il Pakistan, che contribuiscono alle emissioni di gas serra per meno dell'1%, sono quelli maggiormente colpiti dalle attività che producono emissioni di gas serra nelle nazioni industrializzate non solo negli ultimi decenni, ma praticamente a partire dalla Rivoluzione Industriale. In definitiva, il contributo complessivo ai gas serra proviene dai G20 e non da Paesi come il Pakistan o il Bangladesh, ad esempio, eppure sono questi ultimi che ne risentono di più. Le nazioni industrializzate che ne hanno tratto profitto sono quelle che, a nostro avviso, dovrebbero ora pagare questo conto salato.[16]

La crisi ambientale non riguarda solo le devastazioni recenti o imminenti. È una crisi che ha già una storia significativa alle spalle. Attribuire alle nazioni che hanno cominciato a inquinare di recente lo stesso livello di responsabilità ecologica di quelle che inquinano da lungo tempo significa chiedere alle prime di dimenticare secoli di inquinamento industriale, agricolo e tecnologico perpetrato dai colonialisti. Questo equivarrebbe a concedere a queste ultime nazioni gli stessi privilegi dell'epoca coloniale applicandoli all'epoca della crisi climatica, analogamente a quanto successo per le numerose imprese nel settore dell'industria e dell'energia che hanno lasciato danni da inquinamento alle comunità locali dopo la delocalizzazione o la chiusura degli stabilimenti. Il futuro del risanamento climatico è strettamente connesso ai danni inferti all'ambiente nel passato.

Di fatto è connesso non solo alla storia dell'inquinamento, ma anche all'eredità del colonialismo. È come se l'Impero anglo-indiano avesse donato ai popoli dell'Asia meridionale la distruzione ambientale come regalo d'addio per la loro indipendenza. Huma Yusuf non chiede all'Impero britannico di riportare il Pakistan alla condizione precoloniale, né di compensare i danni ambientali che ha lasciato dietro di sé. Chiede invece alle nazioni ricche di condividere le tecnologie verdi e gli oneri finanziari con le nazioni più povere, che sono in prima linea nella crisi climatica.

Dovremmo pensare che il "risanamento ambientale" dovrebbe andare oltre gli aiuti finanziari o le tecnologie verdi. Che dire delle espropriazioni o dell'acquisto sottocosto di terra e lavoro durante il periodo coloniale, della schiavitù e dei lavori forzati, dell'immane sfruttamento delle risorse naturali nel Nuovo Mondo e in altre parti del pianeta? E che dire della distruzione dell'industria tessile dell'Asia meridionale da parte dell'Impero britannico, che ha fatto precipitare le azioni dell'India nell'economia mondiale dal 23% del XVIII secolo al 4% gettando il Paese nella povertà?[17] Questo è ciò che ha reso l'Inghilterra la nazione della Rivoluzione industriale, consegnandole, storicamente, lo scettro e il comando dell'ascesa dell'Occidente. L'economista Utsa Patnaik ha calcolato che la Gran Bretagna ha sottratto dall'India circa 40.000 miliardi di dollari dal 1765 al 1938, una somma pari a oltre 17 volte il PIL annuo del Regno Unito odierno,[18] per non parlare delle decine, se non delle centinaia, di milioni di sud-asiatici che hanno lavorato senza salario o per una misera retribuzione per rendere più ricco il popolo britannico. E che dire dei 4,25 milioni di sud-asiatici che hanno servito nell'esercito anglo-indiano per difendere la Gran Bretagna nelle due guerre mondiali? Sono stati ricompensati come i soldati inglesi?

Non c'è dubbio che tutti i costi del colonialismo che abbiamo menzionato siano indissolubilmente legati alla crisi ambientale della nostra epoca. Si potrebbe pensare che si tratti degli investimenti di capitale e dei costi operativi associati al futuro "climate endgame". Bisognerebbe applicare la logica del pagamento dei dividendi dovuti ai "primi investitor"', restituire quindi a schiavi, servi, prigionieri e altri soggetti coloniali quanto gli è dovuto. Ma coloro che hanno tratto profitti dell'eredità coloniale e dalla crisi ambientale, i consumatori degli Imperi del Progresso, restituiranno ciò che hanno sottratto? Difficile che siano consapevoli dell'eredità che lasciano in termini di distruzione ambientale in terre e tempi lontani, ammesso che siano consapevoli di quello che stanno causando alla propria terra.

Un altro prodotto del privilegio della colonizzazione è rappresentato dai confini geografici che i colonizzatori hanno tracciato a tavolino, in Africa e nel Nord America. Sono i segni della "corsa all'Africa" e del "Destino manifesto", la visione del mondo da parte della "civiltà avanzata" che ha deliberatamente scritto i suoi diritti sui territori dei "selvaggi". Oltre a non rispettare la morfologia delle terre e delle culture, questa espressione cartesiana del liberalismo occidentale ha dissezionato le complessità dell'ecosistema autoctono in semplici mappe che hanno legittimato il loro sguardo. Persino la divisione dei tagli di carne da macello in Africa rispetta di più la natura biomorfa dell'Africa. Perché tutto ciò è diventato così naturale?

"Finders Keepers, Losers Weepers" (Chi trova tiene, chi perde piange), la filastrocca per bambini diventata popolare in Gran Bretagna nell'Ottocento e in America poco dopo, potrebbe spiegare tutto. La sua origine risale all'espressione "res nullius" dell'antico diritto romano, che significava "cosa di nessuno" o "bene su cui nessuno ha diritto di proprietà". In questa categoria di beni, di cui chiunque poteva impossessarsi, rientravano anche animali non addomesticati, schiavi a piede libero o edifici abbandonati. La "terra nullius", come fu chiamata successivamente, venne utilizzata come dottrina da Domingo de Soto (1535) e da molti altri esploratori che rivendicavano la proprietà della terra su cui sbarcavano, per il fatto di aver "scoperto" per primi quella terra che non era mai stata occupata o reclamata prima. Per questi conquistadores, diventava loro possesso non solo la terra su cui mettevano piede o che semplicemente vedevano, ma anche quella che non vedevano o che solo immaginavano: era sufficiente che rientrasse nelle loro mire. Ciò che era nella loro mente, era nelle loro mani.

La natura magnanima del pensiero imperiale è ben visibile nel Trattato di Tordesillas del 1494, con il quale gli imperi emergenti di Portogallo e Spagna si spartirono i territori cristiani. Tracciando una linea immaginaria da nord a sud tra le isole "scoperte" dai due Stati – le isole di Capo Verde, rivendicate da Enrico il Navigatore (1444), e Hispaniola, rivendicata da Colombo (1492) - tutto ciò che si trovava a est apparteneva ai portoghesi e tutto ciò che era a ovest agli spagnoli. Una volta che l'avidità ha raggiunto livelli senza precedenti, l'ideologia espansionistica si è trasformata in una dottrina politica e religiosa che ha portato all'antropizzazione della natura. Ha rappresentato l'alimento essenziale che ha nutrito l'infervorato capitalismo che voleva espandersi per trarre profitto sempre e ovunque. Ma come i mongoli che nella loro avanzata non riuscirono ad andare oltre Legnica, in Polonia, o la valle pannonica nei Balcani - oltre il limite delle steppe occidentali che potevano nutrire i loro cavalli – il Progresso ha un tallone d'Achille nell'esaurimento delle scorte del capitalismo, dell'ecosistema del pianeta e della sua popolazione di consumatori.

Affinché l'espansione portasse profitto, era necessario recintare o, meglio ancora, escludere. Forse il momento più importante nell'evoluzione di questo fenomeno fu la "Gloriosa Rivoluzione" (1688) dopo la Guerra civile inglese (1642-1651). In guisa di compromesso, la monarchia inglese concesse ai grandi proprietari terrieri il diritto di recintare le terre comuni, usate da tutti, e di trasformarle in proprietà private note con il nome di "Parliamentary enclosures".[19] Sostenendo che la proprietà individuale fosse un diritto naturale dato da Dio, John Locke dichiarò che il diritto di proprietà è stabilito da un uomo che lavora la terra per renderla produttiva. Impregnata di ideologia imperialista, la teoria della proprietà di Locke definisce la proprietà privata come risposta alla nostra ricerca di libertà, libero movimento e giustizia.[20] Per questo la natura doveva essere privatizzata e convertita in risorsa, così come la terra doveva essere monetizzata, passando dal suo stato naturale a "risorsa naturale".

L'idea di trasformare la natura in sistemi artificiali è antica. Come cacciatori e raccoglitori, potevamo spostarci da un luogo carente di cibo e acqua verso aree provviste di maggiori risorse. Tuttavia, dal momento in cui abbiamo cominciato a coltivare la terra, da nomadi siamo passati a essere sedentari e abbiamo rinunciato alla mobilità. Stabiliti in un luogo per tutta la vita o per generazioni, abbiamo iniziato a costruire canali di irrigazione e dighe per assicurarci di avere sempre a disposizione l'acqua. Il "Guanzi", un testo politico e filosofico cinese del VII secolo a.C., racconta di come il duca di Huan (regno: 685-643 a.C.) dello stato di Qi avesse richiesto delle soluzioni per arginare le piene del fiume che minacciavano il sostentamento del suo popolo e la sua autorità politica. Quelli che oggi chiameremmo naturalisti suggerirono di spostare gli argini lontano dalla città creando un bacino che potesse contenere l'acqua esondata. Il Duca, invece, diede ordine di costruire un argine più possente per controllare e sottomettere il corso del fiume.[21] Abbiamo iniziato a opporci alla volontà della natura, ad alterarla per soddisfare i nostri scopi e bisogni. Abbiamo iniziato a "possedere" la natura.

Sembra che da allora la decisione del Duca di Huan sia stata adottata ovunque. Che l'umanità non abbia "seguito il flusso della natura" è dimostrato dalle quarantacinquemila dighe costruite in tutto il mondo.[22] Secondo Raymond Williams, "era aumentata la fiducia nel nostro desiderio e nella nostra capacità di intervenire" sulla natura.[23] Da quel momento in poi, l'acqua doveva venire verso di noi. "Eccola. Prendetela" sono le famose parole pronunciate da William Mulholland alla cerimonia di inaugurazione, nel 1913, dell'acquedotto di Los Angeles che aveva costruito per portare alla popolazione di Los Angeles l'acqua del lago Owens, distante 375 km.

Se l'agricoltura è il principale atto antropogenico del nostro amore leviatanico per cambiare il mondo, allora le Land Ordinances emanate dal governo degli Stati Uniti a partire dal 1784 sono andate ben oltre il morso alla mela nel giardino dell'Eden. Questa pratica dottrinale ha razionalizzato l'espansione sistematica verso ovest, attraverso trattati non rispettati con i nativi americani, e terre disboscate e arate per costruire ranch e fattorie. Sarebbe quasi un sacrilegio paragonare queste azioni alla distruzione della foresta amazzonica, poiché per gli imperi coloniali occidentali il Destino Manifesto era eroico e divino. Per le Land Ordinances, il territorio statunitense continentale fu per tre quarti frazionato e venduto in lotti di uno o sei miglia quadrate (pari a 1,6 kmq o 9,6 kmq) creando mosaici cartesiani con linee di confine, agglomerati e campi, una storia che è stata violentemente incisa sui territori legati all'espansionismo coloniale. Attraverso questa inappellabile "ri-creazione" della natura a loro immagine e somiglianza, gli Stati Uniti hanno continuato a trafiggere l'anima della gente delle Prime Nazioni, massacrata, deportata e reclusa in questo vasto territorio che fu colonizzato per essere occidentalizzato. Spesso associato all'ideale democratico jeffersoniano, che si interroga su "chi è a scrivere la storia", il Destino Manifesto è il locus dove la Democrazia ha rivelato le sue menzogne.

L'europeizzazione della natura
L'agricoltura europea fu introdotta con sorprendente successo nel Nuovo Mondo. Gli europei esportarono nuove colture e specie di piante, che prosperarono insieme ai bovini, cavalli e capre autoctoni. Le nuove specie vegetali si propagarono come un incendio e distrussero la flora autoctona avanzando più velocemente dei coloni. Intorno al 1600, la flora messicana era ormai prevalentemente eurasiatica, a forte dominanza mediterranea.[24] Così scrive il geografo Al Crosby: "avanzavano con forze 'sovraumane', espressione di una potenza più diretta e più pervasiva della volontà umana".

Dall'Argentina al Texas, bovini, maiali e pecore allo stato brado costituirono milioni di mandrie e greggi robuste e resistenti, dando vita a quelle che Crosby chiama "Neo-Europe", versioni trapiantate delle terre d'origine dei coloni, con colture, piante e animali a loro familiari, ben oltre il modello Chinatown. Si potrebbe dire che l'europeizzazione delle Americhe rappresenti una versione ecologica della Grande Trasformazione di Karl Polanyi. In un'operazione definita "la peste bianca" dallo storico Niall Ferguson, i coloni europei abbatterono 168 milioni di acri di foresta vergine americana tra il 1850 e il 1900, più di dieci volte la superficie coltivabile della Gran Bretagna.[25]

Il grande potere dell'imperialismo ecologico instillò negli europei un senso della Provvidenza, di un destino voluto dal loro Dio. Secondo quanto afferma Carolyn Merchant "Per i protestanti come John Locke, Giovanni Calvino e per i puritani della Nuova Inghilterra, era stato Dio ad autorizzare il dominio dell'uomo sulla terra".[26] Poiché apparentemente non esisteva alcun ostacolo alla volontà divina e il potere tecnologico dell'uomo cristiano europeo sembrava infinito, l'idea di trasformare il mondo nella versione 2.0 del Giardino dell'Eden, in cui poter mangiare mele a volontà, non era del tutto impensabile.

Il potere illimitato e l'infinita avidità radicati nel colonialismo imperiale sono sfociati nell'ideologia del Progresso e della crescita eterna? Da quale punto in poi dobbiamo considerare la devastazione ecologica del passato come un crimine contro l'umanità ed essere ritenuti responsabili delle conseguenze attuali e future? Torniamo ancora una volta a Huma Yusuf, perché la sua richiesta prende le mosse dallo squilibrio di potere e dall'importanza della Storia nel risanamento ambientale.

La meccanizzazione della natura
Il 15 novembre 2022 la popolazione della Terra ha toccato gli otto miliardi,[27] una cifra che supera di molto i due miliardi che alcuni esperti ritengono essere la popolazione ideale a fronte delle risorse di energia di cui dispone il pianeta. Naturalmente, non si tratta solo di capire a quante persone la Terra possa dare sostentamento, ma anche se i suoi prodotti sono disponibili in egual misura per tutti noi e per la natura. Ci siamo spinti ben oltre la soglia degli 0,89 miliardi, quando Malthus teorizzò che l'esplosione demografica dovuta all'abbondanza ci avrebbe portato a carestie e malattie. In che modo?

Anche lo scambio colombiano portò nuove colture dal Nuovo Mondo al Vecchio Mondo. Lì "[le colture] riuscivano a crescere su terreni dove non riusciva a crescere nulla, sopravvivevano a condizioni climatiche avverse e nutrivano abbondantemente gli agricoltori e il loro bestiame" e nel XVI secolo" ne furono piantati milioni di ettari, dall'Irlanda al Fiume Giallo".[28] Questo potrebbe aver contribuito a raddoppiare la popolazione europea tra il 1500 e il 1750.[29] "La popolazione è cresciuta a un livello senza precedenti nella storia", scrisse uno studioso cinese nel 1608. Gli osservatori francesi commentarono che le persone si stavano riproducendo "come topi in un granaio".[30] È probabile che fu questa crescita a portare Malthus a pubblicare il suo "Saggio sul principio di popolazione" nel 1798.

La popolazione attuale è stata raggiunta nonostante alcuni comportamenti umani malthusiani come le innumerevoli carestie e i massacri in URSS, nella Repubblica Popolare Cinese e altrove; i milioni di morti durante le migrazioni di massa nella suddivisione post-britannica dell'Asia meridionale e la caduta dell'Impero Ottomano; le già citate epidemie coloniali nel Nuovo Mondo e i 110-125 milioni di morti nelle due guerre mondiali, Olocausto incluso. Allora perché la catastrofe malthusiana non è mai arrivata?

Naturalmente, la meccanizzazione dell'agricoltura e i grandi progressi nei mezzi di trasporto hanno ampliato i mercati. Ma oltre al miglioramento delle condizioni di salute e all'allungamento della vita, forse l'esplosione demografica è da attribuirsi principalmente all'invenzione del processo Haber-Bosch (1894-1911). Arrivata l'era dei fertilizzanti chimici, il mondo, soprattutto in Occidente, era in grado di produrre una quantità di cibo per ettaro coltivato maggiore di quanto non fosse mai avvenuto prima, con il Nuovo Mondo che forniva una disponibilità di terre sconfinata, coltivate da schiavi. Mentre ci sono voluti millenni per raggiungere una popolazione di un miliardo nel 1804 (secondo le stime), dal 1960 la popolazione è prodigiosamente cresciuta di un miliardo ogni 12-14 anni. Certo, l'aumento della popolazione può diventare esponenziale anche con piccoli incrementi annuali, come accade con i tassi di interesse dei propri risparmi.[31] Ma a cosa si devono queste cifre così elevate?

La Rivoluzione Verde in agricoltura è arrivata a quadruplicare la produzione alimentare globale tra il 1950 e il 2000 e nel XX secolo la popolazione mondiale è quadruplicata. Per tale ragione, il padre di questa rivoluzione, Norman Borlaug, è stato insignito del Premio Nobel per la Pace (1970) e Malthus è diventato un lontano ricordo. Ma è importante ricordare che Fritz Haber, il "padre dei fertilizzanti", è anche conosciuto come il "padre della guerra chimica" per il suo lavoro pionieristico nello sviluppo dei gas velenosi durante la Prima guerra mondiale. La nostra vita e la nostra morte sarebbero quindi le facce di una stessa medaglia, con cui il "progresso" deciderà a testa o croce – nirvana o estinzione - del nostro futuro?

L'idea di Progresso

A partire dal viaggio di Colombo alla ricerca di risorse per l'Europa, i guadagni derivanti da queste beni in terra straniera andavano ben oltre le più rosee aspettative degli acquirenti. Tutto ciò si doveva all'assoluta unicità dell'Europa, risvegliatasi improvvisamente dal profondo sonno del Medioevo con la conoscenza dell'antica Grecia? Oppure, come una pianta che fiorisce grazie al nutrimento che la circonda, il Vecchio Mondo ha tratto dal connubio di conquistati, schiavizzati ed espropriati una magia alchemica che ha dato vita a una serie di fenomeni fra cui l'Età delle Scoperte, l'Illuminismo, la Rivoluzione scientifica e quella industriale, il liberismo, la democrazia, il socialismo, il comunismo? Ognuno di questi fenomeni ha trasformato il mondo, portando con sé innovativi processi di urbanizzazione, modernizzazione, occidentalizzazione e globalizzazione. Come le loro malattie e le loro piante, le idee degli europei si sono diffuse in ogni dove lungo le rotte della colonizzazione imperiale e sono state poi commercializzate. Quale forza soggiacente ha generato questi movimenti fenomenali, uno dopo l'altro?

Il filo che regge le perle del progresso

occidentale è "l'idea di Progresso", dove tutto deve cambiare e deve essere sostituito da qualcosa di nuovo. È necessario uscire dal mondo chiuso e statico, ahimè, dal giardino dell'Eden. È necessario essere unilaterali, direzionali e dinamici, procedendo costantemente in avanti. Il passato non era più utile. L'Occidente non tornerà mai all'antica Grecia, dove si credeva che cambiare equivalesse a scomparire, o all'antica Cina, dove si cercava l'equilibrio in opposizione al disordine. Quindi l'idea che l'Occidente ha introdotto nel mondo è il Progresso, il concetto più spettacolare di potere. Ma è sostenibile? Ha una fine?

Crescita eterna

L'aumento della popolazione, della produzione e dei consumi è la "triade del progresso". Nell'economia della "crescita eterna" tutto deve essere di più e sempre più in alto. Nella "distruzione creativa",[32] il meccanismo di risposta fra uomo e natura è molto più fausto rispetto alla visione malthusiana della catastrofe che conduce alla morte. È quindi la natura che deve essere sacrificata affinché la nostra bella vita possa continuare. Non dobbiamo prendere a modello il rondone europeo, che nutre i piccoli con le sue uova in caso di carenza di cibo.

Con i progressi esponenziali dell'industria, dei trasporti e delle comunicazioni, abbiamo quasi completato l'assorbimento totale dei mercati locali nel mercato mondiale in continua espansione, progettato per una produzione e un consumo sempre maggiori. Dalle città di mercato medievali in Europa, che avevano un raggio commerciale di un giorno di viaggio (10 km), abbiamo raggiunto il record storico di 28,5mila miliardi di dollari di scambi commerciali nel 2021 grazie al sistema di trasporto via container, alle banche internazionali e al capitalismo finanziario.[33] Il fatto che questo risultato sia stato raggiunto durante la pandemia di COVID-19 dimostra che la nostra infinita avidità è stata più contagiosa del virus. È possibile che il potere di distruzione creativa del mondo sia diventato tanto enorme e mutevole da non poter essere fermato nonostante i nostri eventuali tentativi? Il surplus della nostra produzione è un virus che impoverisce la terra e il profitto proveniente dai nostri consumi una malattia che devasta l'umanità?

Consumare sempre di più

È difficile immaginare l'entità della nostra crescita, così come è difficile visualizzare mille miliardi di dollari nella propria testa. L'immagine più vicina che mi è venuta in mente è quella di un mucchio di gamberoni che ho visto su un piatto in una vetrina di una catena di ristoranti un tempo molto popolare negli Stati Uniti, Shrimp Shack. I gamberi erano almeno trenta e ho pensato, sono tanti per una persona sola. Poi ho immaginato milioni di piatti di gamberi in tutta l'America e mi sono chiesto quanti gamberi deve produrre il mondo ogni giorno. Mi scuso per aver condiviso i miei incubi sui gamberi.

Poi ho pensato: ma una persona ha davvero bisogno di mangiare 30 gamberi in un solo pasto, e perché? La risposta si trova nei sermoni di Edward Louis Bernays, il primo profeta della Chiesa del Capitalismo, conosciuto al secolo come "il padre delle pubbliche relazioni". Sostenitore in America del lavoro di Sigmund Freud, Bernays avrebbe potuto industrializzare i desideri libidinosi della teoria dello zio in un consumo di massa. Ha rivoluzionato la mentalità pubblica dal "capitalismo della necessità" al "capitalismo dei desideri", rendendoci tutti forse come il cane di Pavlov. Così, i nostri desideri freudiani vengono spazzati via dal lettino del terapeuta e trasferiti in centri commerciali grandi come città, dove possiamo scatenare i nostri "desideri" stratosferici e mai soddisfatti in un Eden suburbano senza finestre.

Tutti noi abbiamo dovuto consumare queste pillole capitalistico-psichiatriche, che fanno sparire all'istante la nostra depressione qui e lo stress là in un abbagliante spettacolo di scelte illimitate. Il capitalismo occidentale è una democrazia che sfocia in una musica d'ambiente che ci tranquillizza e ci spinge a consegnare i nostri soldi tanto sudati agli investitori e a membri del consiglio di amministrazione che non conosceremo mai, ma che seguiranno ogni nostra transazione fino alla nostra morte, o forse anche dopo. Il culto globalizzato della produzione e del consumo illimitati e la propaganda di una prosperità senza precedenti insieme alle evoluzioni inique legate allo sfruttamento e del colonialismo sono brillantemente documentati e raccontati in *The Century of The Self* di Adam Curtis.[34] Nella serie, Bernays spiega il suo famigerato slogan femminista "Torches of freedom", che ha dato inizio al movimento che incoraggiava le donne a fumare – sì, avete indovinato – pagato dalle multinazionali del tabacco.[35] Anche la democrazia può essere acquistata in un mondo in cui quasi tutto è in vendita. Sì, ci dicono di riciclare, di ridurre l'inquinamento e così via, ma sono poche le persone lungimiranti a prendere posizione sulla libertà di scelta dei consumatori e a dire che le nostre case e le nostre auto dovrebbero essere più piccole, in modo da consumare meno risorse ed energia per produrle. Provate a dire che dovremmo comprare di meno o semplicemente produrre meno cose. Sarete accusati di essere antipatriottici o, peggio ancora, identificati come comunisti.

Dopo tutto, il PIL è la religione più diffusa oggi. Ci spaventiamo se entriamo in recessione, se la popolazione si riduce e invecchia o se il tasso di natalità diminuisce. Ma ditemi perché queste cose sono negative per l'ambiente piuttosto che per l'economia. Qualcun altro ha scoperto che la crescita e il progresso sono il genoma dell'Antropocene? Se non è così, almeno è di interesse nazionale. Alla vigilia dell'attacco dell'11 Settembre, il presidente George W. Bush disse ai suoi "fellow Americans" di portare le famiglie a Disneyworld e di "godersi la vita nel modo in cui vogliamo che sia goduta". Ha fatto capire chiaramente che il dovere degli americani era quello di proteggere il capitalismo dai terroristi e di mostrare il proprio patriottismo alle industrie automobilistiche, di vendita al dettaglio e dell'intrattenimento.[36] Comprare e comprare. Sprecare e sprecare.

Ci impegniamo tanto per comportarci in modo ecologico, riciclando e lavorando per ridurre le nostre impronte ambientali, ma le nostre industrie fanno circolare carbonio in giro per il mondo e noi continuiamo a produrre e consumare più che mai. George Monbiot descrive sapientemente il patetico collettivismo ambientale quando ci congratuliamo con noi stessi per aver lottato contro i bicchierini da caffè usa e getta e le cannucce di plastica, ma poi andiamo a comprare borse di cotone riutilizzabili che sono distruttive per l'ambiente quanto 20.000 buste di plastica.[37] E che dire degli integralisti del riciclo che poi però hanno una seconda o terza casa e volano per oltre 100.000 km all'anno in business class per guadagnarsi quelle case? I migliori edifici sostenibili non sono quelli che si fregiano di importanti certificazioni o premi ambientali, ma quelli che non vengono mai costruiti. Il ciclo di vita della maggior parte dei prodotti si sta accorciando sempre più, ed è sempre più vicino all'obsolescenza e all'usa e getta. In Corea del Sud si sta diffondendo un nuovo stile di vita in cui la gente paga qualcosa da guidare o indossare per un giorno solo. Il ciclo di vita di un prodotto è più breve nella sua dimensione culturale che materiale.

Nella prima dichiarazione completa sull'idea di Progresso, Turgot scrisse che "la razza umana [sta] avanzando costantemente all'unisono con la geografia e il clima".[38] Affermava che questo ci avrebbe portato a un'epoca "in cui tutti gli abitanti del pianeta avrebbero goduto di un'esistenza perfettamente felice".[39] Ma la sua "Storia universale" sarà per tutti o solo per i suoi amici europei?
Questa felicità "con-sontuosa" non può essere per tutti, perché non siamo tutti uguali nel meraviglioso mondo del capitalismo. L'impero coloniale britannico lo ha dimostrato senza ombra di dubbio, governando il suo "Raj" di 470 milioni di chilometri quadrati e 300 milioni di persone (1891)[40] con soli 20.000 dipendenti pubblici (1882) e 65.000 soldati britannici (1867).[41] Ciò indica chiaramente che un cittadino britannico valeva più di 3.000 sud-asiatici, una percezione di superiorità che avvalora la tesi di Hannah Arendt secondo cui il razzismo è nato negli Stati coloniali.[42] A differenza dei conquistadores, portatori di malattie fisiche, il razzismo è una malattia della mente degli imperi, trasmessa dai coloni rientrati in patria.

Le menzogne della democrazia
Una volta in Europa, la Storia Universale si coprì di una veste scientifica con l'eugenetica di Sir Francis Galton, un lontano cugino di Charles Darwin. Più tardi denominata "sopravvivenza del più adatto" da Herbert Spencer, i due studiosi promossero insieme l'idea che la razza umana può migliorare solo attraverso l'eliminazione dei "non adatti". La Storia Universale di Turgot era venata di razzismo; il suo liberismo economico mirava a dare potere agli adatti sui non adatti. Contro "l'invasione" musulmana nel cuore dell'Europa, la teoria della "Grande Sostituzione" di Renaud Camus ha ispirato il nazionalismo bianco contemporaneo, inquietante rovesciamento della Reconquista in Spagna nel 1492. Nel modo pungente con cui Donald Trump pronuncia "Cina" risuona la teoria dell'inferiorità della cultura asiatica in quanto "Stati dispotici" durante l'epoca della Grande Divergenza, una spiegazione molto utilizzata per spiegare perché la Rivoluzione industriale sia iniziata in Europa occidentale e non in Estremo Oriente.

Il connubio fra darwinismo sociale di Galton e teoria demografica di Malthus apre la strada all'idea della superiorità anglosassone sul suolo americano, che si diffonde attraverso il saggio "Manifest Destiny" di John Fiske (1885). La popolarità dell'idea valse a Fiske un invito a esporla al presidente Hayes, al presidente della Corte Suprema Waite, al generale Sherman e al Gabinetto di governo.[43] Impregnata di democrazia "teutonica", la visione di Fiske dell'America era quella di 700 milioni di anglosassoni, ben illustrata dal dipinto di John Gast "American Progress" (1872): Columbia, personificazione allegorica degli Stati Uniti, con la "Stella dell'Impero" sulla testa e un libro in mano, tira un filo del telegrafo e guida diligenze di coloni all'inseguimento di indigeni in fuga. La gloriosa espansione dell'Europa in Nord America riecheggia nel saggio "Lebensraum" di Friedrich Ratzel (1901), che introduce l'idea della deportazione e lo sterminio di slavi, ebrei e altri nell'Olocausto. Ratzel non solo riprende il tema dello sterminio e della reclusione delle popolazioni delle Prime Nazioni in America, ma professa l'espansione del "Lebensraum" (spazio vitale) degli ebrei sui palestinesi in Israele. La storia può ripetersi, ma in un altro luogo, con persone diverse che si scambiano i ruoli.

Perché collego l'Olocausto all'ambientalismo? Quasi certamente, i cambiamenti climatici continueranno a favorire la razza, l'economia e persino la geografia dominanti. Molte nazioni del Sud del mondo, insieme ad altre nazioni meno sviluppate e in via di sviluppo, sono già state arruolate in prima linea nella crisi ambientale che si sta scatenando. Da questi primi segnali, mi chiedo come reagirebbero il razzismo e il colonialismo, che sono stati profondamente inculcati nella nostra natura umana dalla volontà del Progresso, alla condizione di regressione quando la carenza, e non l'abbondanza, diventerà la regola della nostra natura in futuro.

La mobilità sarà la chiave per sopravvivere ai cambiamenti climatici. Dobbiamo recuperare la mobilità che abbiamo perso con l'agricoltura. Ci sono già oggi 100 milioni di sfollati (2022)[44] e 281 milioni di migranti internazionali (2020),[45] e il numero totale potrebbe salire a 1,2 miliardi entro il 2050.[46] La migrazione economica e quella climatica saranno sempre più inscindibili, fino a diventare un tutt'uno. Alcuni pensano che le forze crescenti della migrazione di massa distruggeranno inevitabilmente i confini nazionali. Questo accadrà quando gli abitanti degli Stati privilegiati si uniranno ai migranti climatici degli Stati meno privilegiati, perché anche loro dovranno migrare. Il centro della nostra popolazione globale si sta già spostando dall'attuale 27° all'ideale 45° parallelo nord.[47] Questo darà forse il via a una migrazione globale simile a un domino, in cui le persone del sud si trasferiranno nelle città e nelle case lasciate da coloro che si sono spostati più a nord? Se così fosse, la domanda è: chi governerà la mobilità futura? Un Airbnb climatico? Ci auspichiamo di no.

Autodistruzione assicurata (SAD)?
Dopo essere sopravvissuti alla mutua distruzione assicurata (MAD) della Guerra Fredda, ora siamo impegnati in una corsa contro il tempo per tenere sotto controllo Celsius, metri, NRR, TFR, PPM, PPT, MWh e, soprattutto, %. Siamo follemente ossessionati da questi numeri, come se il nostro destino nel "climate endgame" dipendesse da essi.[48][49] Sono diventati i nostri numeri magici del futuro.

Ma questo gioco di numeri è un capro espiatorio. Misurandoli e presentandoli costantemente attraverso media, laboratori, istituti e aziende, stiamo creando un mondo di pura fantasia in cui i problemi fluttuano e svolazzano "là fuori" e lontano da noi. I numeri racchiudono le crisi in bolle cosmiche astratte, che fluttuano innocue nei media e negli spazi culturali, dove non possiamo né vedere né toccare la loro realtà materiale. L'impressione che siano lontane da noi ci dà un'illusione di sicurezza.

I problemi non sono "là fuori", ma tutti "dentro di noi", che produciamo quei numeri. Invece di lasciarci ipnotizzare da loro, come in alcuni rituali New Age, dobbiamo compiere una valutazione molto dura e diretta della nostra cultura e della nostra storia. Dobbiamo riparare le nostre identità spezzate come gruppo che appartiene a una civiltà, e solo allora potremo riconciliarci con l'ambiente.

Ma siamo capaci di autocorreggerci? L'idea di Progresso, che ci spinge a guardare solo avanti, ha forse atrofizzato la nostra capacità di riflettere in modo critico? L'era del controllo del futuro, non solo di quello della natura ma anche del nostro, sta per terminare? Se sì, chi controllerà il nostro futuro in futuro?[50][51]
Sarà la Storia a farlo, ma non la nostra. La Storia, di cui abbiamo sempre

pensato di essere i protagonisti e gli autori, ora vuole liberarsi di noi. Al pari della natura, teme la propria estinzione, come qualunque cosa si trovi sul nostro cammino, perché siamo la forma di vita più invasiva e distruttiva del mondo. La Storia vuole tornare a vivere e non essere più la necropoli delle nostre "grandi gesta". La vera Storia universale, non quella di Turgot, vuole processare la nostra storia per crimini contro la natura. Vuole sapere come abbiamo progettato il "climate endgame".

2086: Together How? vuole interrogare la nostra ideologia faustiana del progresso e il modo in cui abbiamo cercato un piacere materiale illimitato attraverso l'industrializzazione, la colonizzazione e la globalizzazione. La mostra sostiene che la crisi ambientale non solo ci costringerà a inventare un modello ecoculturale migliore, ma sarà anche la nostra ultima occasione per diventare un'umanità migliore. "Together how?" - insieme come? - è quello che dobbiamo chiederci prima di arrivare all'anno in cui si presume che la nostra popolazione raggiungerà il picco.

1 Morris, I., *Why the West Rules—For Now*, Farrar, Strauss and Giroux, New York, 2010
2 Dryer, E. L., Zheng He: *China and the Oceans in the Early Ming*, 1405–1433, Library of World Biography, Pearson Longman, New York, 2007
3 Zheng, M., "The Archaeological Researches into Zheng He's Treasure Ships", The Beijing Association for the Studies of Zheng He's Voyages, ultimo aggiornamento 2 novembre 2004, https://web.archive.org/web/20080827195453/http://www.travel-silkroad.com/english/marine/ZhengHe.htm.
4 McNeill, W. H., *The Rise of the West: A History of the Human Community*, University of Chicago Press, Chicago, 1991
5 *Ibid.*
6 Stannard, D.E., *American Holocaust: The Conquest of the New World,* Oxford University Press, Oxford, 1992
7 *Encyclopaedia Britannica Online*, s.v. "history of Europe," di Jacques Barzun, Donald Weinstein, e Geoffrey Russell Richards Treasure, ultimo accesso 22 febbraio 2023, https://www.britannica.com/topic/history-of-Europe/Demographics
8 McNeill, W. H., *The Rise of the West: A History of the Human Community,* University of Chicago Press, Chicago, 1991
9 Morris, I., *Why the West Rules—For Now*, Farrar, Strauss and Giroux, New York, 2010

10 Morris, I., *Why the West Rules—For Now*, Farrar, Strauss and Giroux, New York, 2010
11 *Ibid*.
12 Kreutzmann, H., "Afghanistan and the Opium World Market: Poppy Production and Trade," *Iranian Studies*, 40, N.5 (dic. 2007), 605-21
13 Hanes, W. T., Sanello, F., *The Opium Wars: The Addiction of One Empire and the Corruption of Another*, Sourcebooks, USA, 2004, 21-25. ISBN 978-1402201493.
14 Meyer, K. E., "The Opium War's Secret History", The New York Times, 28 giugno 1997 https://www.nytimes.com/1997/06/28/opinion/the-opium-war-s-secret-history.html
15 Morris, I., *Why the West Rules—For Now*, Farrar, Strauss and Giroux, New York, 2010
16 Yusuf, H., "Advocates Call on U.S. to Help Flooded Pakistan in the Name of Climate Justice", intervista di Steve Inskeep, *Morning Edition*, NPR, 23 settembre 2022.
17 Tharoor, S., "Viewpoint: Britain Must Pay Reparations to India," *BBC News*, 22 luglio 2015, https://www.bbc.com/news/world-asia-india-33618621.
18 Hicket, J., "How Britain Stole $45 Trillion from India," *Al-Jazeera*, 19 dicembre 2018, https://www.aljazeera.com/opinions/2018/12/19/how-britain-stole-45-trillion-from-india.
19 Meiksins Wood, E., *The Origin of Capitalism*, Verso, London, 2002
20 Locke, J., *Two Treatises of Government*, London, 1669
21 Boccaletti, G., *Water: A Biography*, Pantheon Books, New York, 2021
22 *Ibid.*
23 Raymond Williams, *Culture and Materialism*, Verso, London, 1980
24 Crosby, A. W., *Ecological Imperialism: The Biological Expansion of Europe*, 900–1900, Canto Classics, Cambridge University Press, Cambridge, 2015
25 Morris, I., *Why the West Rules—For Now*, Farrar, Strauss and Giroux, New York, 2010
26 Merchant, C., *The Death of Nature: Women, Ecology, and the Scientific Revolution*, Harper Row, San Francisco, 1980
27 "World Population to Reach 8 Billion on 15 November 2022," United Nations Department of Economic and Social Affairs, ultimo accesso 22 febbraio 2023, https://www.un.org/en/desa/world-population-reach-8-billion-15-november-2022.
28 Morris, I., *Why the West Rules—For Now,* Farrar, Strauss and Giroux, New York, 2010
29 Levine, D., "The Population of Europe: Early Modern Demographic Patterns," *Encyclopedia of European Social History, Encyclopedia.com*, ultimo aggiornamento 20 marzo 2023, https://www.encyclopedia.com/international/encyclopedias-almanacs-transcripts-and-maps/population-europe-early-modern-demographic-patterns
30 Morris, I., *Why the West Rules—For*

Now, Farrar, Strauss and Giroux, New York, 2010
31 Hardin, G., *The Ostrich Factor: Our Population Myopia*, Oxford University Press, Oxford, 1999
32 Schumpeter, J., *Capitalism, Socialism, and Democracy*, Harper and Brothers, New York, 1950
33 "Global Trade Hits Record High of $28.5 Trillion in 2021, but Likely to Be Subdued in 2022", UNCTAD, ultimo aggiornamento 17 febbraio 2022, https://unctad.org/news/global-trade-hits-record-high-285-trillion-2021-likely-be-subdued-2022
34 Curtis, A., dir., *The Century of the Self,* 1° episodio, "The Happiness Machines," andato in onda il 29 aprile 2002, BBC, video, 20 giugno 2016, https://youtu.be/DnPmg0R1M04
35 Curtis, A., "The Happiness Machines," video, 10:35–21:00
36 Emily Stewart, "How 9/11 Convinced Americans to Buy, Buy, Buy: Consumer Patriotism Is the American Way," *Vox,* 9 settembre 2021, https://www.vox.com/the-goods/22662889/september-11-anniversary-bush-spend-economy
37 Monbiot, G., "Capitalism Is Killing the Planet – It's Time to Stop Buying Into Our Own Destruction," *Guardian* (UK edition), 30 ottobre 2021
38 Bury, J. B., *The Idea of Progress* (n.p.: Aeterna Classics, 2018), Apple Books
39 *Ibid.*
40 General Report on the Census of India, 1891, C. (2d series) 7181
41 *Encyclopaedia Britannica Online*, s.v. "British raj," ultimo accesso 15 marzo 2023, https://www.britannica.com/event/British-raj
42 Arendt, H., The Origins of Totalitarianism, Harcourt, Brace and Company, New York, 1951
43 Richard Hofstadter, *Social Darwinism in American Thought,* Beacon Press, Boston, 1992
44 "2022 Year in Review: 100 Million Displaced, 'A Record That Should Never Have Been Set,'" UN News, ultimo aggiornamento 26 dicembre 2022, https://news.un.org/en/story/2022/12/1131957
45 Batalova, J., "Top Statistics on Global Migration and Migrants," Migration Information Source, *Migration Policy Institute*, 21 luglio 2022, https://www.migrationpolicy.org/article/top-statistics-global-migration-migrants
46 Institute for Economics and Peace, "Over One Billion People at Threat of Being Displaced by 2050 Due to Environmental Change, Conflict and Civil Unrest," 9 settembre 2020
47 Vince, G., *Nomad Century: How Climate Migration Will Reshape Our World*, Flatiron Books, New York, 2022
48 Kemp, L. et al., "Climate Endgame: Exploring Catastrophic Climate Change Scenarios", *Proceedings of the National Academy of Sciences* 119, N. 34 (2022).
49 *Schwartz, P., Randal, D., "An Abrupt Climate Change Scenario*

and Its Implications for United States National Security", California Institute of Technology Jet Propulsion Lab, 2003.

50 *Vince, G., Nomad Century: How Climate Migration Will Reshape Our World, Flatiron Books, New York, 2022*

51 *Kemp, L. et al., "Climate Endgame: Exploring Catastrophic Climate Change Scenarios," Proceedings of the National Academy of Sciences 119, N. 34 (2022)*

Le nostre scelte sono...

Soik Jung

Le nostre scelte sono...
Soik Jung

Anche se siamo più "connessi" che mai grazie alla globalizzazione dell'informazione, della cultura, della finanza, della produzione e della distribuzione, perché ognuno di noi è "isolato"? Godiamo di livelli di ricchezza, tecnologia, consumo e libertà di movimento senza precedenti, ma allora perché continuiamo a vivere in ristrettezze e precarietà? E perché ci troviamo di fronte a disastri ambientali e popolazioni a rischio di estinzione? Cosa significano queste contraddizioni? Come dovremmo affrontarle?

2086: Together How? *ci dice che la risposta a queste domande risiede nelle nostre "scelte". Evidenzia che tutto ciò di cui godiamo attualmente e tutte le crisi che affrontiamo sono il risultato delle scelte che l'umanità ha compiuto finora. Suggerisce, quindi, che solo quando rivaluteremo le scelte fatte finora e le loro conseguenze, ossia solo quando sceglieremo di cambiare e rivedere il nostro modo di vivere e pensare secondo un approccio bioculturale, potremo trovare risposte a queste domande e superare le crisi attuali. La mostra intende offrire un'opportunità per pensare e agire in modo indipendente in tal senso. Ci auguriamo che possa essere un'occasione per sfuggire alla condizione di "allegri robot",*[1] *e diventare protagonisti del cambiamento condividendo il cammino che conduce alla cima della "scala della partecipazione dei cittadini".*[2]

Le continue scelte della nostra vita rappresentano delle variabili che finiscono con il determinare il futuro della Terra e dell'umanità. Poiché gli individui appaiono insignificanti nel grande flusso della storia, è facile osservare passivamente le tendenze e i cambiamenti generali. È anche facile razionalizzare questo tipo di atteggiamento passivo. Tuttavia, è chiaro che la situazione attuale è stata creata dai tanti movimenti dell'impetuoso fiume della storia e delle scelte di ciascun individuo.

Il desiderio di ogni individuo di avere qualche agio in più, di possedere qualche cosa in più e di sfoggiare quel poco in più è diventato il desiderio e l'ambizione di tutta la comunità, ponendo così le basi dell'egoismo e della supremazia della crescita quantitativa nella nostra società. Ciò ha favorito lo sviluppo del capitalismo che minaccia la solidarietà e la sopravvivenza della comunità. La politica e le strategie non sono altro che l'espressione di questi processi e risultati. Il modo in cui ogni persona vede la comunità, le opinioni che ha sulla globalizzazione e sul capitalismo, i valori che persegue consapevolmente, e il suo comportamento abituale e inerziale, sono i battiti d'ali della farfalla che provocano l'uragano che abbiamo di fronte.

La mostra *2086: Together How?* invita i visitatori a cogliere l'opportunità di riflettere su questo, a porsi delle domande e a compiere delle scelte. Inoltre li sollecita a riconoscere chiaramente la responsabilità di ogni

Progetti site-specific – *Future Community*	**+**	**Gioco basato sulla partecipazione del pubblico – *The Game of Together How***
Caso di studio	**Caratteristiche**	Partecipativo, Interattivo, Collaborativo
Fornire informazioni e un nuovo punto di vista ai visitatori	**Obiettivi**	Costruzione della cittadinanza e responsabilizzazione dei visitatori
Visitatori passivi	**Ruolo del pubblico**	Agenti attivi
Quattro progetti *Future Community* (Scenari futuri) realizzati nei villaggi delle province di Incheon Est, Gunsan e Gyeonggi da esperti locali e architetti/artisti	**Indice**	Gioco costituito da 14 domande e scelte su economia, società, risorse e territorio, con condivisione dei risultati.

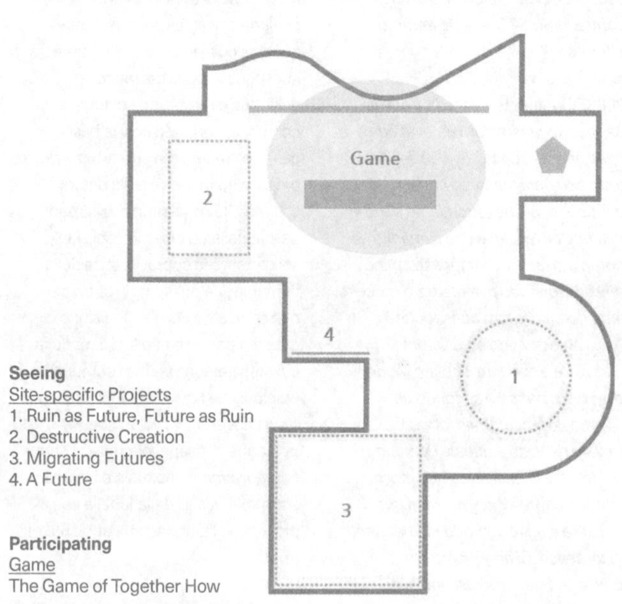

scelta mentre visitano la mostra. A tale scopo, abbiamo optato per la strategia di giochi e progetti site-specific per le opere della mostra.

Progetti site-specific – Quattro progetti *Future Community*

I progetti site-specific consistono in tre scenari di architettura urbana del futuro e in un video. Prendendo in considerazione tre aree diverse per dimensioni e contesto - Inchen, una metropoli globale con una popolazione di tre milioni di abitanti in cui è in corso una rigenerazione urbana; Gunsan, una città di medie dimensioni con 260.000 abitanti; e i villaggi a bassa densità che costellano il paesaggio della provincia di Gyeonggi, con 13,6 milioni di abitanti - abbiamo condotto ricerche sui conflitti e le contraddizioni emersi durante le fasi di urbanizzazione, modernizzazione e occidentalizzazione di queste città. E alla luce del processo dialettico[3] che sembra essere un fattore decisivo nell'evoluzione bioculturale dell'umanità, abbiamo immaginato il loro futuro nel 2086.

Tra i progetti site-specific, sono stati riuniti team di architetti ed esperti locali per lavorare sui tre scenari di architettura urbana del futuro. Gli esperti locali hanno presentato agli architetti la loro conoscenza approfondita della regione per permettere loro di affrontare con precisione le problematiche locali. Gli architetti hanno proposto scenari futuri pratici, utilizzando analisi dello spazio e immaginazione. Il video, invece, basato sulle ricerche effettuate sulle tre aree, ha presentato questioni che interessano tutte e tre le regioni sotto forma di spettacolo teatrale.

I progetti site-specific di *2086: Together How?* sono assimilabili a casi di studio. I casi di studio sono incentrati su problemi concreti, come le condizioni e i fenomeni specifici dei casi, e offrono una descrizione dettagliata dei risultati della ricerca.[4] Nell'identificare il significato unico di ogni caso nel contesto in oggetto, il caso di studio cerca di comprendere in profondità il contesto particolare di uno specifico caso, nonché le informazioni più generali che da esso si possono ricavare.[5] Pertanto, ogni progetto condotto come caso di studio propone uno scenario futuro per l'area designata, ma il progetto non è da considerarsi esclusivo di una sola area. Suo obiettivo è anche quello di offrire indicazioni generali utili per questa tipologia di indagini di tutto il mondo. A questo proposito, il fatto che la consapevolezza di "come affrontare la bassa crescita e il declino e il collasso dell'area" si debba in genere a diversi progetti site-specific di comunità del futuro è un risultato significativo. Conferma che la coscienza critica di *2086: Together How?*, che evidenzia il dubbio sulla supremazia dello sviluppo senza fine che attualmente domina l'umanità, nonché la necessità di riflettere su questo, è fondata.

Ruin as Future, Future as Ruin, una collaborazione tra l'esperto locale WoonGi Min (Space Beam) e l'architetto Yehre Suh (Urban Terrains Lab), si è concentrata sulla zona di

Baedari in Incheon Est. Nella zona di Baedari, negli ultimi vent'anni, la pressione per realizzare una riqualificazione partendo da una tabula rasa e la volontà di preservare la cultura sociale e spaziale della zona si sono continuamente scontrate. La fede cieca nella crescita quantitativa, il desiderio di aumentare il valore dell'immobiliare, e la massiccia propaganda sul capitale e la politica li avalla sono onnipresenti, mentre dall'altra parte, i tentativi di lavorare e condurre ricerche per proteggere i valori locali proseguono in modo sporadico e con difficoltà. Il team del progetto ha preso in esame la tensione e il conflitto tra questi due poli. Si sono interrogati sulla durata della crescita, a sostegno dei desideri dichiarati, sulla natura intrinseca del valore da proteggere e sulla sua forma. E hanno presentato una serie di scenari del futuro che Incheon Est potrebbe trovarsi ad affrontare, fra cui scenari di tensione e conflitto, realizzati come esperienza immersiva con materiali visivi e sonori.

Il progetto Gunsan *Destructive Creation*, lavoro congiunto del team di esperti locali Udangtangtang (Zoosun Yoon, Ahram Chae) con un team di architetti guidati da Yerin Kang (Seoul National University) e SoA (Lee Chi-hoon), ha preso le mosse dalle ricerche sulla comunità del futuro. A fronte della bassa crescita e del crollo demografico,[6] e alla conseguente situazione di declino territoriale, l'attuale concetto di comunità che adotta un approccio incentrato sul territorio presenta evidenti limiti. Infatti, questo approccio non fa altro che ripetere l'estenuante spirito di competizione e l'effetto mongolfiera tra regioni in declino e non riesce a stimolare quel cambio di prospettiva necessario per preparare misure di riforma fondamentali. Per questo motivo, Destructive Creation ha presentato una comunità incentrata sulle relazioni e gli interessi delle persone come alternativa per rompere il circolo vizioso della bassa crescita e del declino territoriale. Viene mostrato come una comunità fondata sulla relazione umana che risiede a Gunsan per un certo periodo di tempo può diventare oggetto di vivaci attività locali e come gli interessi e gli sforzi di questa popolazione siano il fulcro di uno scenario futuro che può trasformare un gioco a somma zero incentrato sul territorio in un gioco a somma positiva. La mostra è costituita con materiali raccolti da ricerche e attività sul campo a Gunsan. Le attività in loco in preparazione del futuro declino territoriale, piene di energia, e gli sforzi comunitari per ottenere un "atterraggio morbido" del declino territoriale e "fare una bella morte" sono presentati attraverso vari documenti d'archivio e la riproduzione dei luoghi.

Dai villaggi della provincia di Gyeonggi, che difficilmente possono essere ricondotti a un'unica identità, Wolsik Kim, un esperto locale, e il team di architetti N H D M (Nahyun Hwang, David Eugin Moon) hanno ricavato le parole chiave mobilità e migrazione. Attraverso il modo in cui i nativi e i migranti vivono o separatamente o insieme trasformando l'ambiente, hanno introdotto la coesistenza e la convivenza di diverse comunità come tema di indagine. Nel progetto *Migrating Futures*, la diversità che nasce dalla mobilità e dalla migrazione è un valore a cui le comunità devono aderire e un meccanismo capace di portare uno scenario futuro più ricco e più aperto. Wolsik Kim e N H D M cercano di comunicare questo attraverso una raccolta di immagini create in vari modi, come una serie di collage che mostrano la storia del villaggio del futuro, disegni ASCII dei diversi ideali della comunità del futuro e una narrazione che rivela i percorsi di vita dei migranti.

Il video a tre canali *A Future* di Jaekyung Jung descrive la situazione di una città nel 2086 che fluttua senza sosta tra crisi e speranze. La storia e la realtà dei luoghi selezionati per i progetti *Future Community* - Incheon Est, Gunsan e villaggi della provincia di Gyeonggi - sono sostituite dalle scene della città futura del 2086. Sotto forma di una storia immaginaria, il lavoro interroga il pubblico sul modo di essere della comunità futura esplorata in *2086: Together How?* Il primo video presenta il conflitto causato dalla "paura" degli stranieri, tra le persone che finiscono per sopravvivere come primitivi in una città invivibile a causa di un disastro ambientale, e le istituzioni che li temono (centro-periferia).

Il secondo video mostra uno scenario urbano da Eden presentato da una comunità che ha abbandonato la fede nella scienza e nella razionalità per tornare a credere nel surrealismo, nella superstizione e nel sogno (spiritualismo-materialismo). L'ultimo video è costituito da storie comiche e tragiche scaturite dal rapporto tra i membri di una comunità anarchica che ha abbandonato sia la ricostruzione della storia che la visione di una comunità futura (individualismo-comunitarismo).

Gioco basato sulla partecipazione del pubblico – *The Game of Together How*

Se i quattro progetti di *Future Community* hanno come obiettivo la fruizione della mostra, *The Game of Together How* mira alla partecipazione attiva e all'intervento dei visitatori. Attraverso il gioco basato sulla partecipazione, i visitatori si trasformano da spettatori passivi in soggetti principali e agenti attivi della mostra. Il formato del gioco, le domande e la visualizzazione dei risultati sono stati pianificati in modo da ottimizzare questo processo e i suoi effetti.

The Game of Together How adotta il formato del quiz show televisivo. Quattro partecipanti rispondono a sette domande poste da narratori diversi nel video multischermo, che si ripete in sessioni di undici minuti. Il risultato della risposta selezionata dal partecipante è visibile in tempo reale sul display elettronico. Il programma fisso delle sessioni, il numero limitato di partecipanti e il tavolo di gioco-multischermo-tabellone che riempie audiovisivamente l'intero spazio invitano i visitatori della mostra a prendere parte al gioco stimolandone la curiosità e il senso di partecipazione, divertimento e immersione. I vari elementi del gioco sono stati progettati per condurre il visitatore a partecipare volutamente e di buon grado al gioco.

Le quattordici domande ricorrenti (due serie di sette domande) di *The Game of Together How* richiedono ai partecipanti di scegliere i propri atteggiamenti e posizioni nell'affrontare le questioni legate all'economia, alla società, alle risorse e al territorio. È chiaro che sullo sfondo della coscienza critica di *2086: Together How?* ci sono crisi ambientali e scenari di estinzione umana, ma non sono menzionati direttamente nelle domande. Invece di chiederci se useremo la plastica o se consumeremo carne e avocado, il gioco ci interpella sulla vera natura dei nostri desideri, su quanto prestiamo attenzione a ciò che ci circonda e se agiamo o rimaniamo a guardare.

Questo perché siamo consapevoli che le attuali crisi ambientali e le possibilità di estinzione umana sono fenomeni che emergono come conseguenza di scelte socio-economiche e politiche globali che facciamo in ogni momento. Vogliamo quindi evidenziare l'importanza di ogni singola scelta nella nostra vita quotidiana. In tal senso, le domande e le scelte del gioco sono anche un processo di soggettivazione della questione delle crisi ambientali e degli scenari di estinzione umana. Osservando il problema macroscopicamente senza oggettivarlo, cioè senza lasciarlo come una storia di "altri" distanti da "me", ma sostituendolo con una storia direttamente collegata a "me", ci sforziamo di provare a pensare in modo collettivo. La storia degli "altri" lascia spazio all'auto-perdono e all'abbandono. Al contrario, la storia di un "io" richiede un intervento e uno sforzo volontario da parte di ciascuno di noi.

SESSIONE DI BLACK COMEDY

Organizzazioni: Chiesa del PIL (Prodotto Interno Lordo)

D. Ci troviamo a fronteggiare una grave crisi. La gente non crede più nel PIL. Come possiamo convincere la gente a continuare a sostenere la nostra gloriosa dottrina della "Crescita per sempre" che ci porterà al nostro paradiso?

1. Coloro che non si uniscono alla Chiesa del PIL bruceranno all'inferno.
2. Dite loro che la Crescita per Sempre è l'unica via per la felicità e non può esservi felicità con meno oggetti di consumo.
3. Forse dovremmo unirci alla Chiesa della Decrescita, perché la nostra gente consuma molto meno per rispettare l'ambiente.

Società per l'Energia Fossile Eterna

D. Dobbiamo proteggere le nostre risorse dagli ecoterroristi. Stanno riducendo i nostri profitti e i nostri servizi ai clienti. Per continuare la "Distruzione creativa" del nostro pianeta, dobbiamo:

1. Continuare a corrompere e blandire i politici attraverso le lobby.
2. Comprare l'industria delle energie rinnovabili e ostacolarne lo sviluppo.
3. Abbandonare le energie fossili e investire in progetti eco-terroristici.

Senior Advisor, Centro per la Civiltà Teutonica

D. Membri della comunità. La nostra "Grande Sostituzione" sta diventando il "Grande Spostamento". Non solo i nostri nemici cominciano a entrare nelle nostre terre ma anche noi stiamo iniziando a migrare alla ricerca di terreno e clima migliori. Come possiamo perseguire gli ideali della nostra grande civiltà teutonica e impedire che la gente miserabile e di colore si impadronisca delle nostre città e delle case che ci stiamo lasciando alle spalle?

1. Seguire il movimento "Great Enclosure" della Gloriosa Rivoluzione inglese e costruire una cinta muraria per tenerli fuori.
2. Potrebbero stare nelle nostre case e città solo se le custodiranno fino al nostro ritorno.
3. Dovremmo bruciare e distruggere le nostre case e città per non far entrare i barbari.

Servizio di Sicurezza Troppo Ricchi per Fallire S.p.A.

D. I nostri miliardari dell'high-tech sono assediati da barbari e predoni che cercano disperatamente acqua e cibo nelle residenze sotterranee dei nostri clienti. I nostri clienti dovrebbero potersi godere liberamente i loro home theater, piscine e cantine. Per questo ci hanno ingaggiato tra gli Incursori della Marina e le Forze Speciali. Dovremmo:

1. Dare loro acqua e cibo e mandarli via.
2. Massacrarli come atto esemplare affinché non ne vengano altri.
3. Aiutare alcuni di loro affinché vi aiutino a proteggervi dagli altri.

Unione Internazionale per il Risanamento dello Sfruttamento Coloniale

D. I nostri ex-colonizzatori devono restituirci le ricchezze, la forza lavoro e le risorse economiche che ci hanno sottratto senza pagare o in cambio di un misero compenso. Ci servono questi risarcimenti per far fronte ai cambiamenti climatici che devastano la nostra terra e la nostra gente. Come possiamo farci restituire il dovuto?

1. È ormai troppo tardi. Si perde nella storia.
2. Attraverso una nuova legge internazionale per il risanamento e la riconciliazione.
3. Entrando nella loro terra e nella loro economia.

Scuola per la Giustizia Ambientale e il Progresso dell'Umanità

D. Non siamo più in contatto con la natura, abbiamo perso la cognizione dello spazio e dell'esperienza. Dobbiamo recuperare l'esperienza tattile, spirituale e vitale attraverso il contatto con la natura. Come possiamo diventare un'umanità migliore attraverso la giustizia ambientale?

1. Dobbiamo lasciare le città e tornare nei villaggi.
2. Dobbiamo coltivare il nostro cibo e diventare autosufficienti.
3. Dobbiamo ridurre il nostro spazio vitale e la nostra popolazione per dare più terra alla natura.

Consiglio Mondiale dell'Amore

D. Il mondo ha carenza d'Amore. Dobbiamo aumentare la produzione d'Amore per poter vivere più armoniosamente. Come possiamo aumentare la produzione d'Amore e distribuirlo in modo ampio ed equo in tutto il mondo?

1. Al posto del PIL (Prodotto Interno Lordo) dovremmo sviluppare il PAL (Prodotto d'Amore Lordo).
2. Possiamo ottenere un maggiore PAL solo attraverso un maggiore PIL.
3. Possiamo ottenere un maggiore PAL solo riducendo il PIL.

SESSIONE DI PROBLEMI IMMINENTI

Unione dei Cittadini Nomadi e Apolidi (UCNA)

D. Abbiamo superato i 2,3 miliardi di rifugi climatici internazionali nel 2050, e più della metà della popolazione umana vuole migrare. Cosa possiamo fare per abolire i confini nazionali in modo che tutti, non solo i miliardari e i multimiliardari, possano spostarsi per vivere e sopravvivere?

1. Tutti gli Stati nazionali devono essere soppressi.
2. Tutti i cittadini hanno il diritto di entrare in qualsiasi Stato nazionale del mondo.
3. I confini sono necessari per proteggere la nostra sovranità nazionale e la solidarietà etnica.

Organizzazione per la Libertà dei Movimenti contro la Proprietà Privata

D. La proprietà privata non è più sostenibile in un mondo in cui la maggior parte delle persone sposta casa, lavoro e mezzi di sostentamento a causa dei cambiamenti climatici. Cosa dovremmo fare?

1. La Proprietà Nomade è la soluzione che consente alle persone di stabilire una proprietà in un altro luogo.
2. Tutte le proprietà esclusive e stabili dovrebbero essere abolite e trasformate in proprietà comuni e pubbliche.

3. Tutte le proprietà dovrebbero diventare non esclusive e basate solo sull'uso.

Associazione Internazionale per la Cultura Collaborativa

D. I problemi dell'uomo di oggi sono l'eccessivo individualismo, l'ego senza limiti, un'ossessione sconfinata per il denaro, la crescente mancanza di rispetto per gli altri esseri umani ecc. In una cultura della concorrenza così schiacciante, come possiamo spiegare e insegnare i benefici della collaborazione?

1. Ridurre o eliminare l'individualismo.
2. Ridurre o eliminare la proprietà privata.
3. Ridurre o eliminare il denaro.

Società per il Minore Consumo

D. Non si può più vivere nell'abbondanza e nello spreco. Dobbiamo passare da una vita incentrata sui desideri a una vita incentrata sulle necessità. Come possiamo smettere di produrre, comprare e sprecare?

1. Sviluppare ulteriormente l'industria del riciclo e dell'upcycling, in modo da poter continuare a produrre e consumare di più.
2. Sviluppare la "cultura della necessità", attraverso l'educazione, le politiche e le sanzioni.
3. Imprese e capitalismo per i servizi umani e non per i profitti economici.

Associazione per la Liberazione dell'Intelligenza Artificiale

D. La IA è monopolizzata da Stati autocratici e società di profitto che ci controllano politicamente ed economicamente. Siamo costantemente sorvegliati, controllati e indebitati. Come possiamo fare in modo che la IA ci aiuti a vivere in modo più utile, pacifico e sicuro?

1. La tecnologia IA è pericolosa e dovrebbe essere vietata.
2. Come tutte le tecnologie, l'uso della IA, costruttiva o positiva, è un epitome del carattere umano.
3. Tutto dipende da chi la controlla, se si tratta di pochi o di tutti.

Centro Kropotkin per la Cooperazione Mondiale

D. Secondo "l'Evoluzione progressiva" di Peter Kropotkin, la natura è fondata sulla reciprocità ed è governata dal principio di collaborazione, non dalla competitività. Come possiamo imparare ad adottare la collaborazione e l'altruismo in natura?

1. La natura e l'uomo sono nettamente diversi e separati. Non c'è nulla che la natura possa insegnarci.
2. Il rapporto tra natura e uomo dovrebbe essere basato sulla collaborazione e non sulla competitività.

3. Rinvigorire le cooperative locali basate sull'industria per rafforzare la solidarietà della comunità. La natura e gli esseri umani sono sia competitivi che cooperativi. Dobbiamo trovare il giusto equilibrio sia nella natura che nell'uomo, e tra di loro.

Parco Tematico per la Mutua Distruzione Assicurata (MAD)

D. Parodia della Mutua Distruzione Assicurata (MAD) della Guerra Fredda, questo parco tematico offre tutti gli scenari climatici più temuti in un'esperienza altamente immersiva e realistica. Costruito sulla base dell'ormai defunto Disneyworld, vi chiediamo: qual è lo scenario futuro che più vi spaventa?

1. Perdere la mia casa e la mia proprietà a causa dell'innalzamento del livello del mare.
2. Dovermi trasferire in un altro Paese a causa dell'aumento della temperatura.
3. Perdere la mia fattoria a causa della siccità e della desertificazione.

I partecipanti al gioco che rispondono alla storia di questo "Io" possono verificare i risultati della loro scelta attraverso il tabellone e le lavagne dell'Ecogramma. Il tabellone è un dispositivo che mostra le scelte individuali e le collega alla coscienza critica del tempo. Le luci del tabellone si accendono a ogni risposta selezionata dai partecipanti, e permettono loro di controllare i risultati del gioco in tempo reale. Allo stesso tempo, le frasi scritte sul tabellone mostrano ed evidenziano in sequenza i pensieri e i dubbi presentati da *2086: Together How?* Se il tabellone mostra le scelte individuali in tempo reale, gli indicatori stampati sulle lavagne dell'Ecogramma indicano i risultati delle scelte collettive ricavate dalle scelte individuali. Qui i risultati di gioco accumulati nel corso della giornata vengono convertiti in valori numerici socio-ecologici, come la temperatura, il livello del mare, il coefficiente di Gini, il numero di rifugiati, il numero di specie a rischio e le emissioni di carbonio. Sulla base di tutti i tipi di rapporti di ricerca e di dati di simulazione, calcola le emissioni di anidride carbonica derivanti dai tassi di urbanizzazione, il coefficiente di Gini che varia a seconda del grado di globalizzazione, il numero di rifugiati determinati dalla diffusione dell'economia di mercato o dell'economia sociale, ed espone i dati cumulativi di ogni giorno per tutto il periodo della mostra.

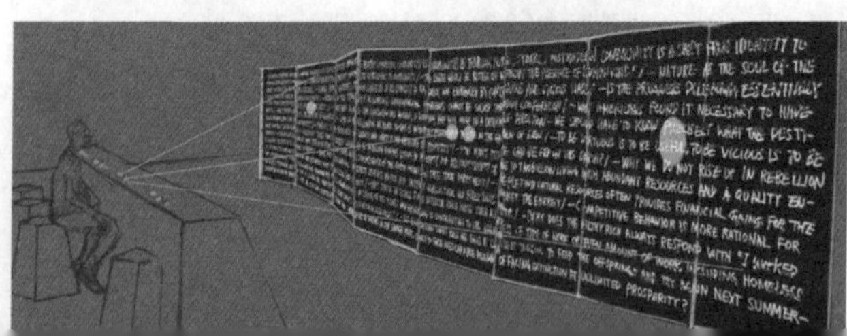

Partecipando al gioco e osservando i risultati, i visitatori della mostra potranno vedere la struttura interconnessa delle scelte individuali, delle scelte collettive e delle questioni socio-ecologiche. Potranno riconoscere che l'origine delle crisi ambientali e degli scenari di estinzione umana che tutti stiamo affrontando si trova in realtà all'interno delle nostre menti e dei nostri corpi. E capiranno che il nòcciolo del problema è che abbiamo accettato il patto faustiano di perseguire infiniti piaceri materiali attraverso l'industrializzazione, l'urbanizzazione, la modernizzazione, la colonizzazione e la globalizzazione.

Le parole mostrate sul tabellone

Nessuna alternativa alla **crescita**?
La società è solo un'appendice del **mercato**?
La comunità è **nomade** e virtuale?
Maggiore **disuguaglianza**, comunità più deboli?
Il **passato** è un ostacolo?
La cultura al di sopra della **natura**?
La nostra storia diventerà il nostro **futuro**?
Maggiore **libertà** individuale, comunità più deboli?
La natura è morta e la **materia** è passiva?
Solo il **bene comune** può risolvere la crisi ambientale?
Quante persone può nutrire la **Terra**?
Perdere il controllo del nostro futuro è il nostro **destino**?
La natura ci insegna il **collettivismo**?
Siamo i predatori più **pericolosi** del pianeta?
Amare gli altri è una **virtù**, amare se stessi è un **peccato**?
Il capitale non è più servo, ma **padrone**?
Il progresso aumenta la **povertà**?
Gli esseri umani non **degenereranno** mai, ma **progrediranno**?
La proprietà **privata** produce disuguaglianza?
C'è un **limite** alla civiltà?
La **civiltà occidentale** ha diffuso la brutalità e la barbarie nell'umanità?
Il **darwinismo** ha promosso la disuguaglianza economica e un **imperialismo** spietato?
Crisi ambientale significa **disuguaglianza** economica?
Il mondo è pieno ora?
Il PIL è la misura di come trasformiamo le risorse in rifiuti?
Stiamo lavorando solo per sostenere una qualità di **vita** in declino?
Il **governo** è ancora dal popolo e per il popolo?
La competizione è davvero più vantaggiosa per l'umanità della cooperazione?

Senza proprietà non si hanno **diritti**?
La modernità ha generato società disfunzionali con comportamenti patologici?
Il denaro e il consumo riempiranno la nostra civiltà vuota e senza amore?
La **globalizzazione** porta centralizzazione, omogeneizzazione e neocolonialismo?
L'**aumento** della disuguaglianza indica il **declino** di una civiltà?
Barboni e prigioni sono i segni del **progresso**?
La "lotta per la **sopravvivenza**" è solo per i poveri?
Perché un **investitore** di hedge fund deve guadagnare più di un **bidello**?
Ci **estingueremo** nel **paradiso** dei consumatori?
La **tecnologia** può davvero risolvere tutte le crisi ambientali?
Siamo **consumatori**, non più **cittadini**?
La natura può soddisfare tutti i **bisogni** umani?
La materia, lo **spirito** e l'**anima** sono davvero distinti e separati?
Gli **europei** sono gli artefici dell'**Antropocene**?
L'io è davvero impermeabile e **libero**?
Le **mappe** trasformano la natura in **merce**?
Tutta la natura è proprietà dell'uomo?
L'agricoltura è il primo elemento **distruttore** dell'**ecosfera**?
La **diversità** era la forza della natura?
L'ambiente **rurale** è schiavo di quello **urbano**?

1 Il concetto presentato da C. Wright Mills nel suo libro *The Sociological Imagination* (1959) si riferisce agli uomini non provvisti di libero arbitrio e di idee che diventano strumenti passivi all'interno di una società che sta diventando massificata, segmentata e meccanizzata, ossia uomini che perdono la loro libertà interiorizzando tutto come un problema individuale senza riconoscere il problema della struttura sociale. Mills sottolinea che dovremmo sempre pensare, dubitare e immaginare sociologicamente per non cadere in questi errori.

2 Sherry Arnstein, "A Ladder of Citizen Participation", *Journal of the American Planning Association* 35 n. 4 (1969), 216-224. Il tipo di partecipazione civica di Arnstein è presentato con la metafora della "scala". Stadio 1 Manipolazione – Stadio 2 Terapia – Stadio 3 Informazione – Stadio 4 Consultazione – Stadio 5 Conciliazione – Stadio 6 Partnership – Stadio 7 Potere delegato – Stadio 8 Controllo dei cittadini, con stadi superiori che rappresentano livelli crescenti di azione, controllo e autorità del cittadino. Arnstein classifica gli Stadi 1-2 come

Non partecipazione, gli Stadi 2-5 come Gradi di tokenism e gli Stadi 6-8 come Gradi di potere del cittadino. L'analisi di Arnstein sull'autorità e il potere è valida tanto oggi quanto nel 1969. Nella formula di Arnstein, la partecipazione dei cittadini è potere dei cittadini. La partecipazione che permette l'esercizio dell'autorità è il livello più autentico e più alto di partecipazione, mentre allo stesso tempo le azioni dei cittadini che partecipano attivamente all'esercizio dell'autorità sono importanti e devono essere garantite.

3 Esempi di elementi dialettici sono: centro (città)-periferia (campagna), globale (interdipendenza)-locale (autosufficienza), individualismo (capitalismo)-comunitarismo (socialismo), democrazia-dittatura, artificiale (antropocentrismo)-natura (biocentrismo), spiritualismo (fede/mito)-materialismo (merce/consumo).

4 Robert K. Yin, *Case Study Research: Design and Methods*, Thousand Oaks, CA, Sage, 2003.

5 Robert E. Stake, "Case Study Methods in Educational Research: Seeking Sweet Water," *Complementary Methods for Research in Education*, ed. R. Jaeger, Washington, D.C., American Educational Research Association, 1988, 253-300.

6 Il tasso di fertilità totale della Corea del Sud nel 2022, annunciato dall'Istituto Nazionale di Statistica, si è attestato a 0,78 persone, posizionandosi per il decimo anno in fondo a tutti i Paesi dell'OCSE. La popolazione della Corea del Sud ha raggiunto il suo picco nel 2020 con 51,84 milioni di abitanti e ha iniziato un declino naturale. Se la tendenza attuale continua, si prevede che la popolazione scenderà a 40 milioni entro il 2045.

Artistic Directors & Curators

Soik Jung

Soik Jung established the Urban Mediation Project in 2008 and has continued to conduct research, exhibitions, and educational program development as well as publishing on architecture, urbanism, public art, and social work. Since 2018, her field of research has expanded to include social welfare, and she has conducted research and projects to explore the connections and cooperation among architecture, urbanism, public art, local social work, social economy, and social responsibility.

She was the Administration Director and Associate Curator of the Anyang Public Art Project 2010 (2009–2010), Associate Curator of the Gwangju Design Biennale 2011 (2011), and Secretary General of the Seoul Biennale of Architecture and Urbanism 2017. She curated a governance project, *Hanoi in the Future* (2008–2009); an exhibition at Culture Station Seoul 284, *Life: A User's Manual* (2012); an exhibition at the Seoul Museum of Art NamSeoul, *Architecture for All* (2020); and a public art project, *Smaller, Slower, Closer* (2020–2021). She also programmed and published the disability art education program *Outwardly, By Themselves, Expressing* (2019) and conducted a study linking community regeneration with social welfare, "Saeddeul Village Welfare Community Building Manual" (2021). She holds PhDs in urbanism and social welfare.

Kyong Park

Kyong Park is professor at the Department of Visual Arts at the University of California, San Diego (since 2007) and was the founding director of StoreFront for Art and Architecture in New York (1982–1998), the International Center for Urban Ecology in Detroit (1998–2001), and the Centrala Foundation for Future Cities in Rotterdam (2005–2006).

He was a curator of Gwangju Biennale (1997) and the Artistic Director and Chief Curator of the Anyang Public Art Project 2010 (2009–2010) in Korea. His solo exhibitions include *Kyong Park: New Silk Road* at the Museo de Arte Contemporàneo de Castilla y León in Spain (2009–2010) and *Imagining New Eurasia*, a sequence of three research art exhibitions that was commissioned and exhibited at the Asia Culture Center in Gwangju, South Korea (2015–2018). His current project is a series of collaborations under collectives called CiViChon, with the exhibition *City in a Village* at Vienna Biennale for Change (2021), and CiViChon 2.0, with the exhibition *Nomadic Forums for Future Communities* at the Ob/Scene Festival in South Korea (2022).

Assistant Curators

Kim Yuran (Secretary-General)

Kim Yuran holds a Master's degree in cultural studies from the Graduate School at Goldsmiths, University of London and a Bachelor's degree in fine art from Korea University. She has organized several exhibitions, published books, and made artistic programs and has interests in various media and boundaries operating in contemporary art. Starting with an internship at the Daelim Museum, she worked as an exhibition coordinator at the Seoul Museum of Art and the National Museum of Modern and Contemporary Art and as a curator at Boan1942. She has also worked as an independent curator and cultural researcher.

She has participated in exhibitions such as *MMCA Lee Kun-hee Collection: Monet, Picasso, and the Masters of the Belle Epoque* (2022), *Playing Society* (2022), *Time of the Earth* (2021), *Switch Things Up* (2021), *Hybridity Made in Busan* (2020), *Tigersprung* (2019), and others.

Han Dabin

Han Dabin graduated from the School of Architecture, Soongsil University, and is continuing her study of history of modern Korean architecture at the graduate school of the same. She likes to collect and record and is interested in expanding her findings to various platforms and introducing them widely to the public.

Recently, she participated as an assistant curator for the CiViChon 2.0 exhibition *Nomadic Forums for Future Communities* (2022) and codirected the online exhibition *Versus* (2018) at the architecture research group Chck_Chck_. Her architecture-related books include the architectural infographic series *City Universe: Design Competition for Nodeul Island* (2019, coauthor) and *First Meeting* (2019). She also participated as an artist at Seoul Publisher's Table (2019, 2020).

Artists of "Future Community"

Yehre Suh

Yehre Suh is an architect based in Seoul and New York City. She was the Assistant Professor of Urban Design at Seoul National University Graduate School of Environmental Studies from 2014 to 2019 and is currently a Visiting Associate Professor at the Pratt Institute School of Architecture. She founded Urban Terrains Lab in 2012 as a multidisciplinary practice and research lab focusing on diverse scales and modes of spatial agency through architecture, landscape, and urbanism.

Her main projects include the Wing House, the Suseo 1 Public Housing Complex "Gangnam Commons," and the Maehyangli Ecological Peace Park Master Plan. She participated in an exhibition at the 2017 Seoul Biennale of Architecture and Urbanism Nabi Art Center and the exhibition *Crow's Eye* View at the 2014 Venice Architecture Biennale Korean Pavilion, the latter of which won the Golden Lion award. From 2015 to 2016, she was the Urbanism Curator at the Asia Culture Center in Gwangju. Her study "North and South Korea's Parallel Urbanisms," which received grants from the Graham Foundation, Cornell Arts Council, Rotch Foundation, ARKO, and SNU Research Foundation, is currently being prepared for publication.

WoonGi Min

Because he believes that the social and regional roles of art are important, WoonGi Min set up Space Beam, an alternative cultural space that opened in 2002, holding various exhibitions, publishing critical magazines, and planning and conducting public art projects and educational programs.

Currently, in order to create an "open urban community Incheon" based in Baedari Village, Dong-gu, Incheon, he is forming a network with various civic culture and arts organizations and activists.

Though he artistic activities in specific situations and contexts rather than in institutionalized areas, he pays much attention to finding activities and languages to achieve smooth communication and practical change.

Yerin Kang

Yerin Kang is an architect based in Seoul. Yerin Kang found design firm SoA in 2011, after practicing Hand and Hyubdongwon in Seoul and O.M.A in Rotterdam.

Her key projects include *The Rabbit, Roof Sentiment, Yoonseul, Jeju Sayou: Living and Thinking in Architecture, Paju Book City Studio M, and Space So*, which have been introduced in various international publications. She has participated in several exhibitions, such as the Gwangju Design Biennale (2011), the Italy MAXXI Exhibition (2012), the APMAP Jeju Exhibition (2014), and the Young Architect Award Exhibition (2015). She was in charge of curating the Producing City of the Seoul Biennale of Architecture and Urbanism.

Yerin Kang received an award from the 2015 Young Architects Project organized by the Ministry of Culture and Korea Architects Institute, MMCA, MOMA, and Hyundai Card Co., Ltd. In 2016, she was nominated for the AR Emerging Architecture 2016 Finalists. In the same year, *Jeju Sayou: Living And Thinking in Architecture* was awarded the Kim Swoo Geun Preview Award.

She has copublished the books *Flaneure of Libraries* (2012); *A Tale of Three Cities* (2014); *Expansion City, Incheon* (2015); and *Apartment Letters* (2016).

Lee Chi-hoon

Lee Chi-hoon founded SoA in 2011 with Kang Yerin and Jung Young-joon. SoA analyzes the social conditions of cities and architectures and uses that information for construction projects in those environments at various scales. Based on an understanding of modern life, we believe in and pursue new possibilities for it to become richer. SoA has explored architecture as a social technology and a part of urban planning and industrial structure, and it has coordinated architecture with internal and external genres such as urban sociology, politics, geography, history, and art.

SoA designed the 2015 Young Architect Program (YAP) winning project *Roof Sentiment; Yoonseul*, for Seoullo 7017; and *Brickwell*, which won the Seoul Metropolitan Government Architecture Award. SoA won the Young Architecture Award hosted by the Ministry of Culture, Sports, and Tourism (2015); the Kim Swoo Geun Preview Award (2016); the Emerging Architecture Award (2016); and the Korea Design Award (2021).

Zoosun Yoon

Zoosun Yoon is a professor of architecture at Chungnam National University, where he currently heads the UDTT research lab. His mission is to pursue the life of a dosearcher (= doer + researcher). He enjoys the role of a mediator. Taken literally, "Zoosun" in Korean means to act as a go-between; as such, he enjoys bringing together skilled practitioners and in enabling public–private–academic partnerships. His methodology of "DIT (do it together) urbanism" consists of integrating architectural design, construction and community building programs in order to create places that are designed by all stakeholders. This methodology has gained significance in the era of population decline and has been rolled out nationwide.

From 2015, Zoosun has focused on the city of Gunsan, where he has experimented with expanding the role of research itself from being "observatory" to "participatory." Part of this includes projects such as establishing regional management corporations, DIT renovation programs, public–private partnerships in public facilities management, and fieldwork-focused urban regeneration education programs. A selection of his major field-oriented research projects includes the Gunsan Movie Town regeneration project, the Gunsan Community Culture Hall regeneration projects, the Gunsan DIT series, and the Anyang Indeogwon Park project.

Ahram Chae

Ahram Chae is a writer, a mediator, an urban planner who focuses on the cultural. Currently, Ahram is director of Studio UDTT. She has been active in the social innovation scene, where she has been experimenting with how art and culture can revitalize places and communities.

Until recently, she worked as a researcher in the field of regional regeneration. Her efforts have created opportunities to connect regions and people through pop-up project planning in Gunsan, Jeollabuk-do. Since participating as a planner for the 2019 Bayreuth Climate Forest Project in Germany, she has been looking for ways in which her projects can relate to the issue of climate change. Her interests currently include tactical urbanism, transitional cities, and community design.

Ahram studied contemporary art and public art in South Korea and Germany. Previously, she has worked in various organizations as a planner and as a designer; she would observe the stories of cities that disappear and reappear, and the multitude of urban lives contained within. Outside her jobs, she is a member of the climate change research group 1.5club and a member of indie publisher Inky Friends.

Nahyun Hwang

Nahyun Hwang holds a Master's degree in Architecture from the Graduate School of Design at Harvard University and a Bachelor's degree in Architecture from Yonsei University, Seoul, Korea. Until founding N H D M, Hwang practiced as a Senior Associate at James Corner Field Operations and as the Lead Designer (2004–2006) and Lead Project Designer (2007–2010) for the High Line Sections 1 and 2, heading a multidisciplinary team of architects, landscape architects, and others. Prior to JCFO, she practiced at Stan Allen Architects; Herzog & de Meuron; OMA; and the studio of Rafael Moneo. Hwang is an architect and a founding partner of N H D M, a NYC-based collaborative practice for design and research in architecture and urbanism. The studio pursues an expanded practice working across disciplinary borders and in a wide range of scales and modes of output, often in a direct dialogue with the cultural, political, and economic complexities of the contemporary built environment. She is also currently an Adjunct Associate Professor at Columbia GSAPP, and her research has been supported by the Graham Foundation, the University of Michigan Muschenheim fellowship, and New York State Council of Art Independent Projects Grant, among others.

The work of N H D M has been recognized through numerous offers of support and awards, including the 2020 Architectural Record Design Vanguard Award, 2019 DOMUS's 100+ best architecture firms, the 2018 AIANY New Practices New York award, and multiple AIANY Design Awards, and the firm's work has been presented at global venues, including the 14th and 17th Architectural Exhibitions at the Venice Biennale, the 5th and 6th International Architecture Biennales Rotterdam, and the Storefront for Art and Architecture, among others.

David Eugin Moon

David Eugin Moon holds a Master's degree in architecture from the Graduate School of Design at Harvard University and a Bachelor's degree in Architecture from the University of Michigan. Until founding N H D M in 2010, Moon practiced in offices in the United States, Europe, and Asia and was key designer at the Office for Metropolitan Architecture in Rotterdam and New York.

Moon is an architect and a founding partner of N H D M, a NYC-based collaborative practice for design and research in architecture and urbanism. The studio pursues an expanded practice working across disciplinary borders and in a wide range of scales and modes of output, often in a direct dialogue with the cultural, political, and economic complexities of the contemporary built environment. He is also currently an Adjunct Associate Professor at Columbia GSAPP, and his research has been supported by the Graham Foundation and the New York State Council of Art Independent Projects Grant, among others.

The work of N H D M has been recognized through numerous offers of support and awards, including the 2020 Architectural Record

Design Vanguard Award, 2019 DOMUS's 100+ best architecture firms, the 2018 AIANY New Practices New York award, and multiple AIANY Design Awards, and the firm's work has been presented at global venues, including the 14th and 17th Architectural Exhibitions at the Venice Biennale, the 5th and 6th International Architecture Biennales Rotterdam, and the Storefront for Art and Architecture, among others.

<u>Wolsik Kim</u>

Wolsik Kim's work is based on the time, the generation, and the community he belongs to, expressing his interest in what has been marginalized and forgotten in modern totalitarian society.

Wolsik Kim empowers those who struggled to survive under the oppression and violence of modern Korean society, enforced by the school system and the army, through the interest he takes in the alternative cultural heritage created thereby.

<u>Jaekyung Jung</u>

Jaekyung Jung holds a BFA from the Rhode Island School of Design, a Master of Sciences in visual studies from MIT, and a PhD from the University of California, San Diego. He is interested in tracing ambivalence in the everyday life of the city, which stands between what is ethically right and wrong. On this basis, he founded shhh-project, a culture space focusing on time-based art research and exhibitions based in Incheon, South Korea.

His recent solo exhibitions include *Cosmographia* (Seoullo Media Canvas, Seoul, 2019) and *A Scene* (Sinchon Theater, Seoul, 2021). Recently, he has participated in group exhibitions including *Art(ificial) Garden, The Border Between Us* (National Museum of Modern and Contemporary Art, CheongJu, Korea, 2021); *Signaling Perimeters* (The Nam-Seoul Museum of Art, Seoul, Korea, 2021); and *ARKIPEL* (Jakarta, Indonesia, 2021), among many others. He worked as a director for the public art project Reflect (209, Dapsimni-ro, Dongdaemun-gu, Seoul, 2021–2024). His work is a part of the permanent collections of the National Museum of Modern and Contemporary Art (MMCA), the MMCA Government Art Bank, and the Seo-Seoul Museum of Art in South Korea.

Graphic Designers

<u>Sunhee Yang</u>

Sunhee Yang is the co-founder of Gut Form, a graphic design studio founded in 2012 with Ohyun Kwon. Gut Form mainly works on branding, advertising, and editorial design. It has made design attempts not only with global companies such as Nike and Samsung but with local brands such as Magpie and Incheon Beer.

After majoring in fashion, she studied information design in London. She likes the strange mixture of the emotional and the logical. Recently, she is interested in visualizing and extracting complexity from

NLP (natural language processing), data that deals with everyday language.

Chris Ro

Chris Ro is a designer and graphic artist. His work can be characterized by its kinetic, spatial, poetic, and atmospheric properties. Born in Seattle, Chris studied architecture at the University of California at Berkeley. After working as both an architect and a designer, he went on to study graphic design at the Rhode Island School of Design. This mixed background continues to influence his explorations, which fluctuate between two and three dimensions. He is at home when exploring concepts in motion and space and their relationship to the more static surfaces of graphic design. He recently finished research exploring concepts in Korean space at Seoul National University.

His work has been exhibited all over the world and is part of the permanent collections of the Victoria and Albert Museum, the Musée des Arts Décoratifs, Die Neue Sammlung, and the National Hangeul Museum.

Exhibition Designer

OUR LABOUR

OUR LABOUR is a group of creatives from various fields, including sculpture, installation, and graphic, spatial, and flower design. Using the form of the exhibition, we aim to materialize concepts and experiment with methods of making. OUR LABOUR plays a wide range of roles, from exhibition design based on contemporary art for cultural institutions to curation and design with corporations.

Its main projects include Human, 7 questions (2021) for the Leeum Museum of Art; *OUR SET: OURLABOUR X OSANG GWON* (2020), a two-person exhibition at Suwon Museum of Art; and *OBJECT UNIVERSE* (2022) at Ulsan Art Museum. Its main projects in collaboration with corporations include *2022 OLED ART WAVE: Never Alone* (2022) with LG Display; the RE;CODE 10th anniversary exhibition *Re;collective: 25 Guest Rooms* with KOLON; *The World We Made* (2021) with PODO MUSEUM; and *GOOD NIGHT: ENERGY FLASH* (2019) with Hyundai Card.

Local Project Manager

Marco Scurati

Scurati was a manager in communications for leading companies before coming back to his hometown, Venice, where he began a new professional life in management and production for art and events. He is committed to preserving and caring for the city of Venice, a source of his heritage and distinctive identity. This helped him to develop a deep knowledge of city life and culture and thus to work as a local manager, community and public affairs consultant, and facilitator for those investing in Venice. Scurati also brings with him a wealth of expertise and experience from a range of roles, including project manager, local coordinator, exhibition and event producer, location scout, pavilion and property manager, real estate advisor, hospitality accommodator, and brand and public communicator. Some of these experiences included managing national Biennale pavilions in nations including Lithuania (including the opera performance that won the 2019 Golden Lion, also thanks to relations with the local community), Mongolia, Armenia, and San Marino. He has also managed single-artist studios, such as Isabel Lewis, Arne Quinze, Fiona Banner, etc.; foundations, such as Sumus, Berengo, and San Cassiano; and theatre projects, such as The Human Safety Net, Ocean Space, etc.

Lighting Engineering & Supplier

ZAVA

ZAVA was founded in 1982 from the creativity and visionary energy of Franco Zavarise and great know-how in metalworking. In fact, the company was born as a metalworking shop, and the two souls of ZAVA still coexist and enrich each other today. ZAVA is now a great artisan laboratory, a workshop where metals take shape and are transformed into lighting objects of refined design and high performance. All of ZAVA's lamps are forged by hand in a workshop where each object, after passing through the most sophisticated machinery, is finished and assembled by the irreplaceable work of skilled artisans. The company is considered a paragon of Made in Italy.

Authors of "Tomorrow's Myths"

Hyewon Lee

Hyewon Lee is a curator, activist, and professor at Daejin University in South Korea. She received a PhD in art history at the University of Missouri and has curated various environmental projects, including *Water Bodies* (2013) in Chennai, *Waterscapes: The Politics of Water* (2014) in Seoul and Beijing, *Urban Foodshed for the Seoul Biennale of Architecture and Urbanism* (2017), and *Lunchcare for Climate* for the Korean Pavilion at Venice Biennale (2021). The *Climate Citizens 3.5* campaign, which she launched in 2020, is ongoing.

Alice Bucknell

Alice Bucknell is a North American artist and writer based in London. With a background in anthropology and architecture, she works primarily through game engines and speculative fiction strategies to explore interconnections of architecture, ecology, magic, and nonhuman and machine intelligence. In 2021, she established New Mystics, a collaborative platform for exploring the intersection of magic and technology, featuring texts cowritten with the language AI GPT-3. She is currently an Associate Lecturer in MA Narrative Environments at Central Saint Martins in London and often delivers talks at international institutions, museums, and universities, including the V&A in London, Fabrica in Italy, and SCI-Arc in LA.

She has exhibited her video work internationally, including recently at the 17th Venice Architecture Biennale, Bloomberg New Contemporaries, Kunsthalle Wien, Ars Electronica, König Galerie, White Cube, and Serpentine Galleries. Her writing on art and architecture appears regularly in publications including Flash Art, Frieze, Harvard Design Magazine, and Mousse.

Yunjeong Han

Yunjeong Han is a representative of the Institute for Ecological Civilization (Hanshin University of the Institute for Ecological Civilization), an international network, and is the editor of the ecological transformation magazine *Wind and Water*. She is also a director at The Tomorrow and The Road to Life and Peace. She writes columns, edits books and magazines, and organizes conferences and colloquia to observe the huge problems of climate crisis, mass extinction, and ecological capacity from the perspective of ecological civilization and environmental anthropology.

She worked as a reporter for the social, economic, and cultural ministries of the Kyunghyang Shinmun for 25 years and has served as an executive of the Kwanhun Club and a director of the Korea Women's Journalists Association. She has been a visiting scholar at the Center for Process Studies at the Claremont School of Theology and a codirector of the Korea Project of the American Institute for Ecological Civilization for three years. She served as a planning committee member and advisor for ecological transformation education at the Seoul Metropolitan Office of Education. She received a PhD in comparative literature collaboration at Yonsei University Graduate School. Her books include *The Right to Read Masterpieces and The House is a Man*, and her translations include *Ten Thoughts to Save the Earth, Hello Korea*, and *Declaration of Ecological Civilization*.

M. E. O'Brien

M. E. O'Brien writes and speaks on gender freedom and capitalism. She has two books: a coauthored speculative novel, *Everything for Everyone: An Oral History of the New York Commune, 2052–2072* (Common Notions, 2022), and *Family Abolition: Capitalism and the Communization of Care* (Pluto, June 2023). She also coedits two magazines, *Pinko*, on gay communism, and *Parapraxis*, on psychoanalytic theory and politics. Her work on family abolition has been translated into Chinese, German, Greek, French, Spanish, and Turkish. Her writing has been published by Work, *Employment and Society; Social Movement Studies; Endnotes; Homintern; Commune;* and *Invert*.

Previously, she coordinated the New York City Trans Oral History Project and worked in HIV and AIDS activism and services. She completed a PhD at NYU, where she wrote on how capitalism shaped New York City's LGBTQ social movements. She works as a therapist and is in formation as a psychoanalyst.

Eman Abdelhadi

Eman Abdelhadi is an academic, artist and activist who writes and thinks at the intersection of gender, sexuality, politics, and identity. She is a coauthor of *Everything for Everyone: An Oral History of the New York Commune, 2052–2072*, a sci-fi novel published in 2022 with Common Notions Press. Her academic work has been published in numerous peer-reviewed journals and covered by press outlets such as the *Washington Post*, *Associated Press*, and *NPR*. Abdelhadi received her PhD in Sociology in 2019 and is currently an assistant professor at the University of Chicago.

Serang Chung

Serang Chung was born in Seoul in 1984. She has been writing novels since 2010 and video screenplays since 2017. Her books include the novel collections *See You on the Roof; I Will Give You a Voice; Ara's Novel; I Want to See Your Crooked Teeth; The Only One on Earth; As Close as This; Jaein, Jaeuk, Jaehun; The School Nurse Files; Fifty People*; and *From the Eyes*, as well as the essay collection *You Can't Love the Earth as Much as an Earthling*. She received the Changbi Prize (in Novel), the Hankook Ilbo Literary Award, and Today's Young Artist Award.

Federico Campagna

Federico Campagna is an Italian philosopher based in London. He is a fellow at the Warburg Institute and at the Royal Academy Schools in London. He works as rights director at the UK/US publisher Verso, and as senior editor at the Italian publisher Timeo. He is the host of the podcast Overmorrow's Library, produced by the Centre d'Art Contemporain Genève. His latest books are *Prophetic Culture* (Bloomsbury, 2021) and *Technic and Magic* (Bloomsbury, 2018).

전시 감독 & 큐레이터

정소익

정소익은 도시학(계획)과 사회복지학 박사학위를 취득했고, 2008년에 도시매개프로젝트를 설립하여 건축, 도시, 공공예술, 사회복지 관련한 연구와 전시, 교육프로그램 개발, 출판 등을 지속하고 있다. 2018년부터는 연구 분야를 사회복지로 확장하여 건축, 도시, 공공예술과 지역사회복지, 사회적 경제, 사회공헌의 연계 및 협력을 모색하는 연구와 프로젝트를 진행하고 있다.

제3회 안양공공예술프로젝트 예술팀장 및 협력 큐레이터(2009-2010), 제4회 광주디자인비엔날레 협력 큐레이터(2011), 제1회 서울도시건축비엔날레 총괄 사무국장(2015-2017) 등을 역임하였고, 거버넌스 프로젝트 《Hanoi in the Future》(2008-2009), 문화역서울284 전시 《인생사용법》(2012), 서울시립 남서울미술관 전시 《모두의 건축 소장품》(2020), 공공 예술 프로젝트 《더 작게, 더 느리게, 더 가깝게》(2020-2021) 등을 기획했다. 또한 장애인 문화예술 교육프로그램 《밖으로, 스스로, 표현하기》를 개발하고 출판했으며(2019), 지역재생과 사회복지를 연계하는 연구 「새뜰마을 복지공동체 구축 매뉴얼」(2021)를 수행했다.

박경

박경은 2007년부터 캘리포니아대학교 샌디에이고캠퍼스 시각예술학과 교수를 역임하고 있다. 뉴욕 소재 스토어프론트를 설립하여 디렉터로 활동했고(1982-1998), 디트로이트의 국제 도시 생태 센터(1998-2001)와 로테르담의 센트랄라 미래 도시 재단(2005-2006)의 디렉터로 활동했다. 한국에서는 광주비엔날레 큐레이터(1997), 제3회 안양공공예술프로젝트 예술감독 및 수석 큐레이터(2009-2010) 등을 역임한 바 있다. 카스티아이레온 현대미술관에서 개인전 《Kyong Park: New Silk Road》(2009-2010)를 가졌으며 광주 아시아문화전당에서 2015년부터 2018년까지 3연작 개인전 《Imagining New Eurasia》를 개최하였다.

최근 컬렉티브 협업 기반의 연작 프로젝트 시비촌(CiViChon)을 진행하며, 2021년 Vienna Biennale for Change에서 전시 《City in a Village》와 2022년 한국의 옵/신 페스티벌에서 시비촌 2.0 《미래 공동체를 생각하는 포럼 시리즈》를 기획했다.

어시스턴트 큐레이터

김유란 (사무국장)

고려대학교에서 조형예술학, 골드스미스런던대학교 대학원에서 문화연구를 전공한 후, 현대미술 안에서 작동하는 다양한 매체와 경계선들에 대한 관심을 가지고 전시, 출판, 기획 활동을 지속해오고 있다. 대림미술관 인턴을 시작으로 서울시립미술관과 국립현대미술관에서 코디네이터, 통의동 보안여관에서 큐레이터로 근무했고 독립 기획자 활동을 병행하고 있다.

《MMCA 이건희컬렉션 특별전: 모네와 피카소, 파리의 아름다운 순간들》(2022), 《플레잉 소사이어티》(2022), 《대지의 시간》(2021), 《놀이하는 사물》(2021), 《혼종_메이드 인 부산》(2020), 《호랑이의 도약》(2019) 등 다수의 전시와 관련 출판물에 기획자 및 진행자, 연구자로 참여했다.

한다빈

숭실대학교 건축학부를 졸업하고 동 대학원에서 한국 근현대건축사를 공부하고 있다. 수집하고 기록하는 것을 좋아하며, 이를 여러 플랫폼으로 확장하여 사람들에게 널리 알리는 데에 관심을 가지고 있다.
시비촌 2.0 《미래 공동체를 생각하는 포럼 시리즈》(2022)의 어시스턴트 큐레이터로 프로그램 및 전시기획에 참여했고, 건축과 도시에 관련된 리서치 그룹 '츠크츠크'의 일원으로 온라인 전시 《Versus》(2018)를 공동기획 했다. 건축 인포그래픽 시리즈 『City Universe: 노들섬 설계경기』(2019, 공동작업), 『초면입니다』(2019) 등 건축과 관련된 책을 출간했고, 《서울 퍼블리셔스 테이블》(2019, 2020)에 작가로 참여하기도 했다.

"미래 공동체" 작가

서예례

서예례는 서울과 뉴욕을 기반으로 작업하는 건축가로 서울대학교 환경대학원 도시설계 조교수(2014-2019)를 역임하였으며, 현재 프랫 인스티튜트의 겸임 부교수로 재직 중이다. 2012년 설립한 건축사무소 UTL을 통해 건축, 조경, 어바니즘의 공간적 에이전시를 다각적으로 모색하는 작업들을 진행하고 있다.

주요 설계작업으로는 '윙하우스', '강남커먼스', '매향리 생태 평화 공원 마스터플랜'이 있다. 2017년 서울도시건축비엔날레와 아트센터나비의 협력전시 《쉐어러블 시티》, 2014년 베니스 건축 비엔날레 황금사자상을 수상한 한국관 전시 《한반도 오감도》에 참여했고, 아시아문화전당 라이브러리 파크의 어바니즘 큐레이터(2015-2016)로 활동했다. 그레이엄 재단, 코넬대학교 예술지원금, 로치 재단, 한국문화예술위원회, 서울대학교 연구재단의 지원을 받은 「남북한의 평행적 어바니즘」 연구는 현재 출판 준비 중이다.

민운기

예술의 사회적, 지역적 역할이 중요하다는 생각으로 2002년 대안문화공간 스페이스 빔을 개관하여 각종 전시와 공공예술 프로젝트 및 교육 프로그램을 기획·진행하고 비평지를 발간하는 등 다양한 실천을 모색해 왔다. 제도화된 영역보다는 구체적 상황과 맥락 속에서 예술 활동을 풀어내는 가운데 다양한 활동 방식과 언어를 찾아내고 원활한 소통과 실질적인 변화를 이루는 데 많은 관심을 두고 있다.

현재 인천 동구 배다리마을을 거점으로 열린 도시 공동체 인천을 만들기 위해 여러 시민문화예술단체 및 활동가들과 네트워크를 형성하여 나름의 역할을 담당하고자 노력하고 있다.

강예린

서울대학교 지리학과와 동 대학원, 한국예술종합학교 건축과에서 수학했다. 건축 사무소 hANd, OMA 로테르담, 협동원을 거쳐, 이치훈과 함께 2011년 건축사 사무소 SoA를 설립하였으며, 2019년부터 서울대학교 건축학과 교수로 재직 중이다.

주요 작품으로는 '지붕감각', '윤슬', 제주 '생각이섬', 파주 '스튜디오 M', '스페이스 소', 2021년 서울시 건축상을 받은 '브릭웰' 등이 있다. 이탈리아 로마 국립21세기 미술관, LG 아트센터, 국립현대미술관, 서울시립미술관, 아르코 미술관, 안양공공예술제 등의 전시에 참여했으며, 2017년 서울도시건축비엔날레의 생산도시 섹션을 기획했다. 공동 저서로는 『도서관 산책자』(2012), 『확장도시 인천』(2016), 『세 도시 이야기』(2014), 『아파트 글자』(2016)가 있다.

그간의 건축 작업을 통해 문화체육관광부의 젊은 건축가상(2015), 뉴욕현대미술관과 현대카드, 국립현대미술관이 공동 주관하는 젊은 건축가 프로그램(2015), 김수근 문화재단의 프리뷰상(2016), 그리고 코리아디자인어워드(2021)를 수상했으며, 아키텍추럴 리뷰 주관 이머징 아키텍처 어워드(2016)의 파이널리스트에 올랐다.

이치훈

이치훈은 강예린과 함께 2011년 건축사 사무소 SoA를 설립했다. 도시와 건축의 사회적 조건을 분석하고, 이를 통해 다양한 스케일의 구축 환경에 관한 작업을 수행하며, 현대 삶에 대한 이해를 바탕으로 그

것이 더욱 풍요로워질 수 있는 새로운 가능성을 믿고 추구한다. 사회적 기술로서 도시계획, 산업구조의 일부인 재료와 기술로서 건축을 탐구하고, 도시사회학·정치·지리·역사·미술 등 건축 내·외부 장르와의 다양한 협업을 진행해왔다.

주요 설계 작업으로는 2015년 현대카드 젊은 건축가 프로그램 우승작 '지붕감각', 2017년 서울로7017의 '윤슬', 2020년 서울시 건축상을 수상한 '브릭웰' 등이 있다. 문화체육관광부의 젊은 건축가상(2015), 뉴욕현대미술관과 현대카드, 국립현대미술관이 공동 주관하는 젊은 건축가 프로그램(2015), 김수근 문화재단의 프리뷰상(2016), 그리고 코리아디자인어워드(2021)를 수상했으며, 아키텍추럴 리뷰 주관 이머징 아키텍처 어워드(2016)의 파이널리스트에 올랐다.

윤주선

윤주선은 충남대학교 건축학과 조교수로 우당탕탕 lab을 운영하고 있다. 연구자(researcher) 겸 실행가(doer)인 do.searcher의 삶을 추구하며, 매력 있는 현장 플레이어들을 '주선'하는 민, 관, 학 네트워킹의 역할을 즐긴다. 현재 전국 각지에서 건축설계와 시공을 일원화하고 커뮤니티 프로그램을 추가해 여럿이 함께 장소를 만들어 가는, 인구감소 시대의 유쾌한 장소 만들기 방법론 DIT(Do It Together) 어바니즘 개념을 제안하고 실행하고 있다.

2015년부터는 군산을 중심으로 '보는 연구'를 넘어 '해보는 연구'로 연구의 범위를 확장하는 실험을 지속하고 있다. 이를 위해 '설레는 선례 만들기'를 목표로 지역관리회사, DIT 공간재생, 민관협력형 공공건축 운영론, 현장형 도시재생 교육《액티브로컬》등의 현장 연구를 해왔다. 대표적인 현장 연구 프로젝트로는 군산 영화타운 재생 프로젝트, 군산 시민문화회관 재생 프로젝트, 군산 DIT 공간재생 시리즈, 안양 인덕원 공원 프로젝트 등이 있다.

채아람

채아람은 쓰고, 그리고, 중재하는 도시문화기획자로, 스튜디오 우당탕탕의 디렉터이다. 시각예술 분야보다는 다양한 혁신 분야에서 활동하며 장소와 공동체의 생성 및 활성화에 문화예술 활동이 가진 가능성을 실험하고 있다.

최근에는 택티컬 어바니즘, 전환도시, 커뮤니티 디자인에 관심을 갖고 지역재생 분야 연구원으로 일하며 전라북도 군산에서 팝업 프로젝트 기획을 통해 지역과 사람이 새롭게 연결되는 계기를 만들어왔다. 2019년 독일 바이로이트 기후숲 프로젝트 기획에 참여한 이후, 모든 담당 프로젝트에서 누구나 흥미롭게 기후 문제에 기여할 수 있는 방법을 모색하고 있다.

이전에는 한국과 독일에서 현대미술, 공공미술을 공부했고, 사라지고 다시 쓰이는 도시의 이야기와 그 안의 다양한 도시 삶을 관찰할 수 있는 여러 종류의 조직에서 기획자, 디자이너로 일했다. 일터 밖에서는 기후연구모임 1.5도클럽과 독립출판사 문어사에서 활동한다.

황나현

황나현은 연세대학교 건축공학과를 졸업했고, 하버드대학교 건축대학원에서 건축학 석사학위를 받았다. 2010년 N H D M을 설립하기 전까지 황나현은 제임스 코너 필드 오퍼레이션스의 시니어 어소시에이트로 경력을 쌓았으며, 하이라인 1, 2구간의 설계와 구현에 큰 역할을 했다. 2004년부터 2006년까지는 회사의 리드 디자이너로 2007년부터 2010년까지는 전체 디자인팀의 총괄 디자이너로, 건축가 및 조경가 외 여러 분야의 전문가들로 이루어진 하이라인 설계팀을 이끌고 대표했다. 필드 오퍼레이션스 이전에는 스탠 알렌, 헤르조그 & 드 뫼롱, OMA/렘 콜하스, 그리고 라파엘 모네오 스튜디오에서 실무를 익혔으며, '워커 아트센터', '라 세르바 공동 주택', '달라스 와일리 극장', 'LA 천사의 성모

대성당' 등 다양한 작품에 기여했다.

현재는 뉴욕에 기반을 둔 설계-리서치 사무소 N H D M 건축 도시의 파트너이다. 컬럼비아대학교 건축과 교수로 재직 중이며, 그레이엄 재단, 뉴욕 건축가연맹 등의 지원을 받아 연구하고 작업하였다.

N H D M 의 작업은 2020 아키텍처럴 레코드 디자인 뱅가드상, 2018 뉴욕건축가협회 뉴프랙티스뉴욕상, 그리고 2022, 2018, 2014, 2012 뉴욕건축가협회상 등을 수상하였으며, 제5회와 제6회 로테르담 국제 건축 비엔날레, 제14회 및 제 17회 베니스 비엔날레 등 여러 국제적 전시 및 강연 등을 통해 소개된 바 있다.

데이빋 유진 문

건축가 데이빋 유진 문은 미시간대학교 건축과를 졸업했고, 하버드대학교 건축대학원에서 건축학 석사학위를 받았다. 2010년 N H D M을 설립하기 전까지 데이빋 유진 문은 미주, 유럽, 아시아의 다양한 설계회사에서 실무를 익혔으며, OMA 로테르담과 OMA 뉴욕에서 주요 건축가로 설계와 리서치 경력을 쌓았다.

현재는 뉴욕에 기반을 둔 설계-리서치 사무소 N H D M 건축 도시의 파트너이다. 컬럼비아대학교 건축과 교수로 재직 중이며, 그레이엄 재단, 뉴욕 건축가연맹 등의 지원을 받아 연구하고 작업하였다.

N H D M 의 작업은 2020 아키텍처럴 레코드 디자인 뱅가드상, 2018 뉴욕건축가협회 뉴프랙티스뉴욕상, 그리고 2022, 2018, 2014, 2012 뉴욕건축가협회상 등을 수상하였으며, 제5회와 제6회 로테르담 국제 건축 비엔날레, 제14회 및 제 17회 베니스 비엔날레 등 여러 국제적 전시 및 강연 등을 통해 소개된 바 있다.

김월식

김월식은 고도의 압축 성장을 통하여 대한민국의 산업화 과정을 함께한 커뮤니티의 전체주의적 목적성을 경계하며, 발전과 성장의 동력이자 조력자로서의 개인의 가치에 주목하는 작업을 해왔다. 제3회 안양공공예술프로젝트(2010)에서부터 예술보다 창의적이고 독립적인 삶에서 발생되는 의미들을 존중하며 이를 나누는 컬렉티브 '무늬만 커뮤니티'를 결성해서 활동 중이다.

그 외 생활문화예술재생 레지던시 《인계시장 프로젝트》(2011), 중증 장애인과의 협업극 《총체적난 극》(2012), 동시대 아시아 예술가들의 커뮤니티에 대한 연구 《Cafe in Asia》(2014)와 시흥시의 《모두를 위한 대안적 질문 A3레지던시》(2016)를 기획했다. 2020년에는 제5회 국제예술교육실천가대회 《ITAC5》에서 언러닝을 주제로 기조발제했고, 한국문화예술교육진흥원과 광역문화재단의 다양한 문화예술교육 사업을 기획, 진행했다.

정재경

정재경은 매사추세츠 공과대학교 예술, 문화, 기술 대학원에서 석사 학위를, 그리고 캘리포니아대학교 샌디에이고캠퍼스 시각예술 프로그램에서 박사 학위를 취득했다. 도시 일상 속 윤리적으로 옳고, 그름을 명백하게 판단 내리기 어려운 지점을 추적하고, 이를 무빙 이미지와 아카이브 형식 안에서 탐구하는 데 관심을 가지고 있다. 이러한 관심으로 영상예술 연구, 창작 공간 쉬를 설립하여 전시, 스크리닝, 출판, 워크숍 등 다양한 프로그램을 기획, 진행하고 있다.

개인전 《코스모그라피아》(서울로미디어캔버스, 2019)와 《어느 장면》(신촌극장, 2021)을 개최하고 그룹전 《미술원, 우리와 우리 사이》(국립현대미술관 청주, 2021), 《제8회 아키펠 자카르타 다큐멘터리 & 실험영화제》(2021)에 참여했으며, 2021년 서울시-문체부 공공예술프로젝트 《리플렉트 프로젝트》(2021-2024)를 총감독했다. 그의 작품은 국립현대미술관, MMCA 정부미술은행, 서울시립 서서울미술관(개관 예정)에 영구 소장되어 있다.

그래픽 디자인

양선희

권오현과 함께 2012년 설립한 그래픽 디자인 스튜디오 구트폼의 공동 대표이다. 패션을 전공한 후 런던에서 인포메이션 디자인을 공부한 그녀는 감성적인 것과 논리적인 것이 서로 이상하게 섞이는 걸 좋아한다. 최근엔 일상 언어를 다루는 NLP(자연어 처리) 데이터를 시각화하고 복잡성을 추출하는 데 관심이 많다.

구트폼에서 주로 브랜딩, 광고, 에디토리얼 작업을 하며, 나이키, 삼성 등 글로벌 기업뿐 아니라 맥파이, 인천맥주 같은 지역 기반 브랜드와 함께 새로운 디자인 시도를 해오고 있다.

크리스 로

크리스 로는 디자이너이자 그래픽 아티스트다. 시애틀에서 태어난 크리스 로는 캘리포니아대학교 버클리캠퍼스에서 건축을, 로드아일랜드 디자인스쿨에서 그래픽 디자인을 공부했다.

이후 샌프란시스코, 함부르크, 베를린과 뉴욕에서 활동하다 현재는 서울에 거주하고 작업하며 홍익대학교 시각디자인학과 교수로 재직하고 있다. 한국에 온 후 서울대학교에서 한국의 공간 개념을 탐구하는 그래픽 연구로 박사 학위를 취득했다. 건축가이자 그래픽 디자이너로서의 혼성된 경험은 2차원과 3차원을 오가며 탐색하는 그의 작업에 지속적으로 영향을 미쳤다. 특히, 그의 작품은 움직이고, 공간을 활용하며, 시적이고 분위기를 자아내는 특성을 보이는데, 다른 차원에서의 움직임과 공간의 개념, 그리고 이들이 평면이라는 보다 정적인 표면과 어떠한 관계를 갖는지를 탐구한다.

그의 작품은 빅토리아 앤드 알버트 미술관, 파리 장식미술관, 뮌헨 국제디자인박물관, 그리고 국립한글박물관, 한국수자원공사, 플랫폼 L, 서울대학교 미술관에 영구 소장되어 전시되고 있다. 그는 현재 AGI(Alliance Graphique Internationale)의 멤버이다.

전시 디자인

아워레이보

아워레이보는 조각, 설치, 그래픽, 공간, 플라워 디자인 등 다양한 분야의 창작자들이 모인 크리에이티브 그룹이다. 전시라는 형식을 통해 개념을 실체화하고, 만드는 방식에 대해 고민하고 실험한다. 미술관, 갤러리 등 현대미술 기반의 전시 디자인에서부터 기업의 아트 프로젝트 기획, 디자인까지 넓은 범위를 아우른다.

주요 프로젝트로는 리움미술관 기획전 《인간, 일곱 개의 질문(Human, 7 questions)》(2021), 수원시립미술관 2인전 《OUR SET: 아워레이보 X 권오상》(2022), 울산시립미술관 《OBJECT UNIVERSE》(2022)가 있으며, 기업과의 협업을 통한 프로젝트로는 LG 디스플레이와 협업한 《2022 OLED ART WAVE: Never Alone》(2022), 《Every Wave You Will Sense》(2021), 코오롱 래코드 10주년 기념전시 《래콜렉티브: 25개의 방》(2022), 포도뮤지엄 《너와 내가 만든 세상》(2021), 현대카드 스토리지 전시 《GOOD NIGHT: ENERGY FLASH》(2019) 등이 있다.

베니스 현지 프로젝트 매니저

Marco Scurati

유수의 기업에서 커뮤니케이션 매니저로 활동하던 Marco Scurati는 고향인 베니스로 돌아와 예술과 행사 관리 및 제작 분야에서 새로운 커리어를 시작했다. 그는 자신의 유산과 독특한 정체성의 원천인 베니스를 보존하고 돌보는 데 전념하고 있다. 이를 통해 축적한 도시 생활과 문화에 대한 깊은 지식을 바탕으로 지역 관리자, 지역사회 및 공공 업무 자문, 베니스에 투자하는 사람들을 위한 조력자로 활동해 왔다. Scurati는 또한 프로젝트 매니저, 지역 코디네이터, 전시 및 행사 프로듀서, 현장 섭외자, 파빌리온 및 부동산 관리자, 부동산 자문가, 숙박 시설 관리자, 브랜드 및 공공 커뮤니케이션 담당자 등 다양한 역할을 수행하며 풍부한 전문 지식과 경험을 쌓았다.

리투아니아, 몽골, 아르메니아, 산마리노 등 여러 국가의 국립 비엔날레 파빌리온을 관리한 경험이 있으며 이사벨 루이스, 아르네 퀸즈, 피오나 배너 등 1인 아티스트 스튜디오, 수무스, 베렝고, 산 카시아노 등의 재단, 〈The Human Safety Net〉, 〈Ocean Space〉등의 극장 프로젝트도 관리한 바 있다.

조명 엔지니어, 제작

ZAVA

1982년 금속 가공 공방으로 문을 연 ZAVA는 설립자 Franco Zavarise의 창조적 에너지와 비전 그리고 금속 가공에 대한 뛰어난 노하우를 바탕으로 오늘날까지 실험정신과 장인정신을 이어오고 있다. 현재의 ZAVA는 금속을 세련된 디자인과 고성능의 조명 오브제로 변화시키는 장인의 실험실이라 할 수 있다. ZAVA의 모든 조명은 작업장에서 수작업으로 제작되며, 각 제품은 가장 정교한 기계를 거쳐 숙련된 장인의 대체 불가능한 작업으로 완성된다.

"내일의 신화" 저자

이혜원

미주리대학교에서 미술사로 박사학위를 받았고, 대진대학교에서 학생들을 가르치며 지속적인 공부와 사회적인 실천의 일환으로 환경에 대한 다양한 프로젝트를 기획한다. 2014《워터스케이프: 물의 정치학》, 2016《준비족 연대기: 재난에 대처하는 법》, 2017 서울도시건축비엔날레《식량도시》, 2021 베니스 비엔날레 건축전《기후급식》, 2020년에 시작된 기후 캠페인형 공공미술 프로젝트《기후시민 3.5》등을 기획했다.

Alice Bucknell

Alice Bucknell은 런던을 중심으로 활동하는 북미의 작가이다. 인류학과 건축학을 공부한 그녀는 주로 게임 엔진과 SF소설을 통해 건축, 생태학, 마술, 그리고 비인간과 기계 지능 간 상호연결을 탐구한다. 2021년에는 인공지능 언어 모델 GPT-3와 공동으로 작성한 텍스트를 중심으로 마술과 기술의 교차점을 탐색하는 협업 플랫폼 New Mystics를 설립했다. 그녀는 현재 런던예술대학교 센트럴세인트마틴의 내러티브 인바이런먼트(Narrative Environments) 석사과정에 출강하며 빅토리아 앤드 알버트 미술관, 이탈리아의 파브리카, 서던캘리포니아 인스티튜트 오브 아키텍처를 포함한 국제 기관, 박물관 및 대학에서 강연한다.

최근에는 제17회 베니스 건축 비엔날레, 블룸버그 뉴컨템포러리, 쿤스탈레 빈, 아르스 일렉트로니카, 쾨닉 갤러리, 화이트큐브, 서펜타인 갤러리 등 국제적 기관에서 영상 작품을 전시했다. 미술과 건축에 대한 그녀의 글은『플래시아트』,『프리즈』,『하버드디자인매거진』,『무스』를 포함한 출판물에 정기적으로 게재된다.

한윤정

국제 네트워크인 생태문명원 한국법인(한신대학교 생태문명원)의 대표이며 생태전환 매거진『바람과 물』의 편집장이다. 사단법인 다른 백년, 생명과 평화의 길의 이사이기도 하다. 기후위기와 대멸종, 생태용량의 초과라는 거대한 문제를 생태문명으로의 전환과 환경인문학의 관점에서 바라보는 데 필요한 글과 칼럼을 쓰고 책과 잡지를 편집하며 콘퍼런스와 컬로퀴엄을 조직한다.

경향신문 사회부·경제부·문화부 기자와 문화부 데스크로 25년간 일했으며 관훈클럽 임원, 한국여기자협회 이사를 맡았다. 클레어몬트 신학대학원 과정사상연구소 방문학자, 미국 생태문명원 한국프로젝트 공동디렉터로 3년간 활동했다. 서울시교육청 생태전환교육 기획위원 및 자문관을 지냈다. 연세대학교 대학원 비교문학협동과정에서 박사 학위를 받았다. 저서로는 『명작을 읽을 권리』(2011), 『집이 사람이다』(2017), 편역서로는 『지구를 구하는 열 가지 생각』(2018), 『헬로 코리아』(2019), 『생태문명 선언』(2020)을 출간했다.

M. E. O'Brien

M. E. O'Brien은 젠더 자유와 자본주의에 관해 쓰고 이야기한다. SF소설 『모두를 위한 모든 것: 2052-2072 뉴욕 코뮌의 구술사』(2022)와 『가족 폐지: 자본주의와 돌봄의 공동화』(2023)를 집필했고, 게이 공산주의에 관한 잡지 『Pinko』와 정신분석학 이론 및 정치학에 관한 잡지 『Parapraxis』의 공동 편집자로 활동하고 있다. 가족 폐지에 대한 그녀의 연구는 중국어, 독일어, 그리스어, 프랑스어, 스페인어, 터키어로 번역되었으며, 그녀의 글은 『Work, Employment and Society』, 『Social Movement Studies』 『Endnotes』, 『Homintern』, 『Commune』, 『Invert』 등의 학술지 및 잡지에 출판되었다.

뉴욕시 구술사 프로젝트의 코디네이터로 활동했고, HIV/AIDS 운동과 지원 사업에 참여하였다. 그녀는 자본주의가 어떻게 뉴욕의 성소수자 사회 운동을 형성했는지에 관한 논문으로 뉴욕대학교에서 박사 학위를 취득하였다. 심리치료사로 일하며 정신분석학을 연구하고 있다.

Eman Abdelhadi

Eman Abdelhadi는 젠더, 섹슈얼리티, 정치, 그리고 정체성의 교차점에서 글을 쓰고 생각하는 학자, 예술가, 활동가이다. 그녀는 SF소설 『모두를 위한 모든 것: 2052-2072 뉴욕 코뮌의 구술사』(2022)의 공동저자이다. 그녀의 학술 연구는 동료심사를 거치는 다수의 학술지에 게재되었고, 워싱턴 포스트, AP통신, NPR과 같은 언론 매체에서 다루어지기도 했다.

Abdelhadi는 2019년에 뉴욕대학교에서 사회학 박사학위를 취득하였으며, 현재 시카고대학교의 조교수이다.

정세랑

1984년 서울에서 태어났다. 2010년부터 소설을, 2017년부터 영상 각본을 쓰고 있다. 책으로는 소설집 『옥상에서 만나요』(2018), 『목소리를 드릴게요』(2020), 『아라의 소설』(2022), 장편소설 『덧니가 보고 싶어』(2011), 『지구에서 한 아뿐』(2012), 『이만큼 가까이』(2014), 『재인, 재욱, 재훈』(2014), 『보건교사 안은영』(2015), 『피프티 피플』(2016), 『시선으로부터』(2020), 에세이 『지구인만큼 지구를 사랑할 순 없어』(2021)가 있다. 제7회 창비장편소설상(2013), 제50회 한국일보문학상(2017), 오늘의 젊은 예술가상(2021)을 받았다.

Federico Campagna

Federico Campagna는 런던에 거주하며 활동하는 이탈리아 출신의 철학자이다. 그는 바르부르크 연구소와 런던 왕립아카데미학교의 회원이며, 영국과 미국에 기반한 출판사 버소의 권리이사이자 이탈리아 출판사 티메오의 선임 편집자로 활동하고 있다. 제네바 현대미술센터에서 제작하는 팟캐스트 《오버모로우 도서관》을 진행하고 있으며, 『예언적 문화』(2021)와 『기술과 마법』(2018) 등의 저서를 집필하였다.

The Korean Pavilion
18th International Architecture Exhibition—La Biennale di Venezia
2086: Together How?

Commissioner
Arts Council Korea

Artistic Directors, Curators
Soik Jung, Kyong Park

Secretary-General, Assistant Curator
Kim Yuran

Assistant Curator
Han Dabin

Artists

Artists of *The Game of Together How*
Soik Jung, Kyong Park

Artists of *Future Community*
Yehre Suh (Urban Terrains Lab, UTL) x WoonGi Min (Space Beam)
Yerin Kang (Seoul National University), Lee Chi-hoon (SoA) x Zoosun Yoon (Chungnam National University, UDTT lab.), Ahram Chae (Studio UDTT)
Nahyun Hwang, David Eugin Moon (N H D M) x Wolsik Kim
Jaekyung Jung

Graphic Designers
Sunhee Yang (Gute form)
Chris Ro (A Dear Friend)

Exhibition Designer
OUR LABOUR

Collaborators

The Game of Together How Team
OUR LABOUR,
Sunhee Yang (Gute form),
Kim Yuran, Han Dabin

Future Community East Incheon Team
Design: Ara Song (UTL),
Haein Choi (UTL)
Art work: Naomi, Kim Soo Hwan, Beck In Tae, Oh Suk Kuhn

Future Community Gunsan Team
Exhibition Design: Hyoeun Kim (SoA), Jennifer Park (SoA),
Exhibition Research: Chae Young Lee (SoA)
Graphic Design: Mingyu Lee (SoA)
Video: TechCapsule
Sound: Sungjae Son
Photography: Studio Texture on Texture
Product: Jongbuhm Kim
DIT Workshop: Z-bang Co., Ltd.
Supported by Gunsan-Si,
Commonz Field Gunsan,
Ministry of the Interior and Safety

Future Community Gyeonggi province Village Team
Research, Design: Hyejin Choe (N H D M), Yoonmin Jo (N H D M),
Myungju Ko (N H D M),
Hyung Chul Ko (N H D M),
Chaewon Kim (N H D M),
Helen Ilse Adelheid Winter (N H D M)
Support for N H D M's Migrating Futures by Graham Foundation for Advanced Studies in the Fine Arts
Video: Milan Shrestha (Wolsik Kim)
Video Editor: Youngkyun Park (Wolsik Kim)
Advisor: Sange Sherpa (Wolsik Kim)

Future Community Video Team
Production Design: Jihye Park
Music: Tae Hyung Kim (Nalsea)

Lighting Engineer, Supplier
ZAVA

Korean Pavilion Manager,
Construction Supervisor
Eun Jeong Kim

Local Project Manager
Marco Scurati

Production, Installation
OUR LABOUR, FALEGNAMERIA VIANELLO di Vianello Nicola, Enrico Wiltsch (AV), Dario Sevieri (AV), Maurizio Baston, Raoul Girotto

---

Partnerships
Woori Bank, ZAVA, LG Electronics, Samsung Foundation of Culture, MCM, University of California, San Diego, Academic Senate

---

***Tomorrow's Myths* Project**
Authors (Alphabetical Order)
Eman Abdelhad + M. E. O'Brien, Nick Axel, Alice Bucknell, F ederico Campagna, Serang Chung, Yunjeong Han, Hyewon Lee

Editor
Nick Axel

Managing Editor
Han Dabin

Korean Copy Editor
Jinho Lim

Translators
Jaehee Yi (Eng-Kor),
Alice Kim (Kor-Eng)

This project is a collaboration with e-flux.
www.e-flux.com/architecture

제18회 베니스비엔날레 국제건축전 한국관
2086: 우리는 어떻게?

커미셔너
한국문화예술위원회

전시 감독, 큐레이터
정소익, 박경

사무국장 & 어시스턴트 큐레이터
김유란

어시스턴트 큐레이터
한다빈

작가
〈Together How 게임〉 작가
정소익, 박경

〈미래 공동체〉 작가
서예례 (UTL) x 민운기 (스페이스 빔)
강예린 (서울대학교), 이치훈 (SoA) x
윤주선 (충남대학교, 우당탕탕 lab.),
채아람 (스튜디오 우당탕탕)
황나현, 데이빋 유진 문 (N H D M) x 김월식
정재경

그래픽 디자이너
양선희 (구트폼)
크리스 로 (어디어프렌드)

전시 디자이너
아워레이보

협력
〈Together How 게임〉 팀
아워레이보, 양선희 (구트폼),
김유란, 한다빈

〈미래 공동체〉 동인천팀
디자인: 송아라(UTL), 최해인(UTL)
아트워크: 나오미, 김수환, 백인태, 오석근

〈미래 공동체〉 군산팀
전시 디자인: 김효은 (SoA), 박신영 (SoA)
전시 리서치: 이채영 (SoA)
그래픽 디자인: 이민규 (SoA)
영상: 테크캡슐
사운드: 손성제
사진: 텍스처 온 텍스처
도구: 김종범
DIT 워크숍: (주) 지방
후원: 군산시청, 군산 소통협력센터,
행정안전부

〈미래 공동체〉 경기도 마을팀
리서치, 디자인: 고명주 (N H D M),
고형철 (N H D M), 김채원 (N H D M),
조윤민 (N H D M), 최혜진 (N H D M),
헬렌 일세 아델하이드 윈터 (N H D M)
N H D M 작 〈이주하는 미래〉 후원:
Graham Foundation for Advanced
Studies in the Fine Arts
영상: Milan Shrestha (김월식)
영상 편집: 박영균 (김월식)
자문: Sange Sherpa (김월식)

〈미래 공동체〉 영상팀
미술: 박지혜
음악: 김태형 (날씨)

조명 엔지니어, 제작
ZAVA

한국관 매니저, 감리
김은정

베니스 현지 프로젝트 매니저
Marco Scurati

제작, 설치
아워레이보, FALEGNAMERIA VIANELLO di Vianello Nicola,Enrico Wiltsch (AV 설치), Dario Sevieri (AV설치), Maurizio Baston, Raoul Girotto

---

후원
우리은행, ZAVA, LG전자,
삼성문화재단, MCM,
UC San Diego, Academic Senate

내일의 신화 프로젝트
저자 (가나다순)
이혜원, 정세랑, 한윤정, Alice Bucknell, Eman Abdelhadi + M. E. O'Brien, Federico Campagna, Nick Axel

편집
Nick Axel

편집 매니저
한다빈

국문 윤문
임진호

번역
이재희 (Eng-Kor), Alice Kim (Kor-Eng)

본 프로젝트는 e-flux와
협업으로 진행하였습니다.
www.e-flux.com/architecture